D0374543

THE
VICTORIAN
REVOLUTION

THE VICTORIAN REVOLUTION

edited and with an introduction

1973   *New Viewpoints*

GOVERNMENT *and*

SOCIETY *in*

VICTORIA'S BRITAIN

by PETER STANSKY

A Division of Franklin Watts, Inc., New York

Library of Congress Cataloging in Publication Data

Stansky, Peter, comp.
    The Victorian revolution.

    Includes bibliographical references.
    CONTENTS: MacDonagh, O. The nineteenth-century
revolution in government: a reappraisal.—Parris, H.
The nineteenth-century revolution in government: a
reappraisal reappraised.—Clark, G. K. Statesmen in
disguise: reflexions on the history of the neutrality
of the Civil Service. [etc.]
    1. Great Britain—Politics and government—1837–1901
—Addresses, essays, lectures. 2. Great Britain—
Social policy—Addresses, essays, lectures. I. Title.
JN216.S7   320.9'42'081   73-2740

    ISBN 0-531-06482-4 (pbk)

Cover design by Nicholas Krenitsky

Book design by Diana Hrisinko

Contents

Preface   *vii*

(v)

Contents

Preface

How DOES ONE recover the past? Presumably there is something there which did happen, and the historian wishes to be able to describe an approximation of what it was, and to explain it. On the whole, he accepts the limitations and imperfections of his task. A complete reconstruction is never possible; indeed it would not be desirable as it would be too monumental to be comprehensible. The material that survives is a fraction of what there once was, and in fact much information which would be extremely useful—a total description of people and places for instance—was never available. No historian, or group of historians, could ever achieve a full awareness of the ideas and motives of the participants in past events.

Quite rightly, historians do not allow themselves to be discouraged—their object is to try to explain the past as best they can. As I conceive of this collection of essays its purpose is twofold: to show present-day historians going about their tasks, and to suggest some of the problems which, according to these scholars, Britain faced in the nineteenth century. I have decided to select only articles rather than to make excerpts—or to use the derogatory term, snippets—from books, valuable as the latter might be, since I feel that it is more rewarding to view an argument in its entirety and not just a particular segment somewhat arbitrarily selected. In the pages that follow are some of what I consider the most important articles to have appeared over the past fifteen years: they will indicate something of the direction which Victorian studies have taken and may suggest new areas to be investigated. It is one of the classic generalizations of the study of British history that considerable changes became manifest in British society towards the end of the eighteenth century. Historians are given to the defining of periods, and then to arguing over the definitions, or to creating titles for periods, and then disputing the dates selected, even the very validity of the title. Little would be gained by entering into such a debate here, but it can be very roughly and crudely stated that there was something which might be called an Industrial Revolution, that there probably was something which might be called an Agricultural Revolution, and that there certainly was an American Revolution and a French Revolution. One can also safely say that these events had important effects on British society. Of course as soon as one attempts to assess the nature and significance of these effects, historians cease to agree and the fight is on. This has been particularly true over the whole question, within the discussion of the Industrial Revolution, of the standard of living in relation to industrialization: Were workers worse or better off at particular times in the late eighteenth and early nineteenth centuries than they had been in the past? (This debate, incidentally, also suggests the obvious point that historians are rarely removed from present-day concerns: values which individual historians hold about their contemporary world influence their judgments of the past. And the further obvious point can be made that certain historical events may have immediate contemporary relevance. Interest in how new nations become industrialized, for example, focuses attention on how the first industrial nation coped with that problem, and at what price, or to what benefit, for its inhabitants.)

From the time of the American Revolution on, life in Britain certainly grew increasingly complex and the problems of government in all its manifestations—the tasks of the king, Parliament, civil servants, and indeed the role of the governed—vastly increased. The country was mobilized to an extent which had never happened before, and in certain ways never would happen again. (Land was cultivated during the war with France that would not be cultivated even during the Second World War.) The forces of change within the country and from without were truly monumental and could justly be so represented in scholarly articles on almost any aspect of it—the articles on the standard-of-living discussion alone would probably fill several volumes. The Napoleonic War ended in 1815 and Britain attempted, as nations so frequently do after wars, to return to "normalcy." But there was hardly any consensus over what "normalcy" might be—and even if that could have been agreed on, how could it have been achieved? In fact, the economic and ideological pressures upon society were probably greater after the war than before: a further volume might be filled with the debates of historians over the intentions and accomplishments of those who were active in government and opposition, both inside and outside of Parliament, in the years from 1815 to 1832.

Particular events are convenient punctuation marks. They provide a means for historians to talk about the past through their assertions, demonstrations, arguments, about what *were* particular events and what they meant. This has been noticeably true of two events of the early 1830s, the Reform Act of 1832 and the Poor Law of 1834. In these cases the immediate question of what they were can be easily stated: they were acts passed by Parliament. The first modified the electoral structure of the country, in terms both of where representatives would come from and of who could vote for them. The other was officially an adaptation of the old Elizabethan Poor Law: how were those who could not earn a livelihood to be dealt with or cared for? But what the two laws meant, and what the politicians who favored them and those who opposed them thought they meant, as well as what those who were outside the immediate parliamentary circle thought of them—that is a matter of vast historical dispute. No historian would claim that there would be but one answer to any of these questions. Change and the making of decisions are basic concerns for historians, and the past will be fatally misunderstood if the historian too readily moves his own preconceptions backwards. At the same time, distance allows him to see a pattern in the past which helps to make sense of what happened, even if the participants themselves would not have fully sensed such a pattern. Whether the Reform Act and the New Poor Law were forward- or backward-looking—or to what degree were they which?—may remain in dispute, but it would not be too controversial to state that they were significant and can be taken to mark a new sort of development. One could easily assemble a book of readings—indeed it has been done—on each of these Acts, either of primary material, scholarly comment, or a combination of both. But I did not wish to limit this collection to the problems of one set issue.

Indeed I wished to move beyond those important events of the first half of the 1830s. Despite the degree of conservative impetus behind them, they can be taken to inaugurate a whole new sequence. One does not wish to fall into the Whig heresy that British history has been marked by the development of democracy, broadening out from precedent to precedent; yet the *effect* of the Reform Act—which did result in a small but significant expansion of the electorate—was to be the first step towards the broadening of the franchise in 1867, 1884, and 1918. The effect of the New Poor Law, whether a matter of policy or the result of events, was to strengthen the role of central government. As is frequently the case in Britain, neither of these results was desired, certainly not by the majority of those who could be seen as in control. Instead, they were backed into, with a pious wish to preserve as much of the past as possible and to operate within the British tradition of private and public endeavor, to continue spheres of local activity and initiative. But within reason it is legitimate, I believe, to regard the two acts as a significant, if slow-working, shifting of perspective, and as setting the stage for the rest of the century. It is the period *after* these events which I have made the focus of this collection of essays.

Victoria came to the throne in 1837, after the reigns of two of her "wicked uncles," George IV and William IV. It took some time for the new monarch—although it happened within her lifetime—to give her name to the period. Technically, the Victorian age lasted from 1837 until the nineteenth century was over in January 1901, when the Queen died, although some have argued, with justification, that 1914 would be a better terminal date. The period could easily be divided into fourths. The first fourteen years of her reign, until 1851, were marked by the emergence of a politics dominated by the intelligent conservatism of Sir Robert Peel, even though she lost his guidance in 1846 when he fell from power (he was abandoned by his own party after his successful attempt to repeal the Corn Laws). In broader terms, the country was adapting and absorbing the difficulties of industrialization until, as the conventional dating has it, the Crystal Palace exhibition of 1851, with its extraordinary display of British goods, marked Britain's triumph as the most important country in the world. The Crimean War of a few years later illustrated not only her international position and its weaknesses, but also her domestic failures. Gradually the political picture organized itself into the working of some sort of two-party system, marked by the contrasting and alternating ministries of the Liberal Gladstone and the Tory Disraeli from 1868 until 1886. That year the split over Home Rule divided the Liberal Party. Until 1906 the Tories dominated a society aggressively self-assertive as its world position became increasingly shaky. John Roach, in the article which concludes this collection, suggests some of the doubts, in the context of what major Victorian intellectuals thought of their society, and of its attempts to "police" itself, which in some sense are the burden of the previous articles. I do not wish to make a snap summation of the century; any good textbook will provide the reader with that picture, and in a brief bibliographical note, I mention a number of them that might be consulted.

The purpose of this collection is, rather, to try to indicate some of the abiding problems of the century. I have chosen to concentrate on the domestic picture, and in a somewhat limited way—largely, the world of government. Problems of imperialism have quite rightly demanded much attention recently, and are obviously closely related to what happens in the "heart of the Empire" itself. The scholarly debate on this issue has shared some of the characteristics that one sees in the articles that follow. Was what happened in the Empire—formal or informal—the result of deliberate policy on the part of the government, or a haphazard or deliberate response of the man on the spot to particular problems? And was the government primarily concerned with strategy or economic exploitation of the Empire? Indeed, what did the men who were actually running the Empire think they were doing and what did their society think they were up to? The same sort of questions are even more vivid, perhaps, in the domestic sphere.

Any area of British society would reveal some of the same pressures, and any institution closely studied might add significantly to the picture of Victorian Britain, but I have not wished to make the range of subjects too diffuse. In these articles, concentrating to a considerable degree on the role of government, some central themes begin to emerge. Innovation under traditional guises, with or without the aid of philosophical underpinnings, seems to be an abiding characteristic in Britain: adaptations tend to allow the nature of British society to change with a minimum of haste. The powers that be are rarely so rigid that they will snap rather than bend; they attempt to preserve the old by accepting the new on their own terms.

Here are investigations of the problems of civil servants, political thought, parliamentary issues, education, party developments, and intellectual responses to a world of far greater complexity than what had come before. Perhaps the emphasis has been too much on "official" Britain. But the expanding role of the government was easily one of the most important characteristics of the time, and it can too easily be underrated in a traditional political narrative. It is the complexity of that operation which I have tried to emphasize through the selections included here. I hope that new dimensions have been suggested of crucial aspects of British life.

I should like to thank George Behlmer, Peter Cline, Leslie Friedman, Gloria Guth, F. M. Leventhal, Michael MacDonald, Patricia Otto, and Robert Thorne for their indulgence in giving me of their time to discuss the contents of this collection.

THE
VICTORIAN
REVOLUTION

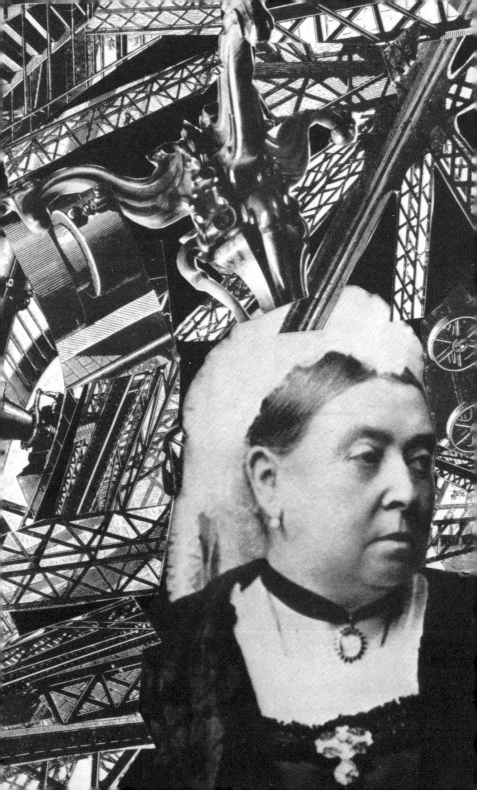

It is appropriate to begin this collection with a famous article, somewhat theoretical in approach, which has been central in stating the terms of debate on how government—most particularly civil servants—acted in the nineteenth century. MacDonagh considers the relative importance of both theory and practice. He takes the position that it is through civil servants responding to particular problems—rather than setting out a plan to be implemented—that change takes place. That Benthamism could be used either as a support for state action or as an argument against it was pointed out in an important article by J. B. Brebner, "Laissez faire—State Intervention in Nineteenth-Century Britain," Journal of Economic History Supplement, VIII *(1948). But Mac-Donagh's argument undercuts the importance of Benthamism— ideology—as a major reason that change took place, and he raises concerns crucial for any consideration of the dynamics of change and the making of policy in nineteenth-century England. He has investigated his "model" through example in his study, A* Pattern of Government Growth, 1800–1860: The Passenger Acts and their Enforcement (*London, 1961*). *Professor MacDonagh teaches at the University of Cork. This article was originally published in the* Historical Journal I *(1958), 52–67, and is reprinted by permission of the publishers, Cambridge University Press.*

OLIVER MACDONAGH

The Nineteenth-Century Revolution
in Government: A
Reappraisal

I

PART, AT LEAST, of the historian's work consists of the formulation of general notions and the subsequent refinement of these generalities. One advance is made when a notion like romanticism is conceived, another when that notion is broken down and divided, both in terms of time and region and by the clarifications of logic, and fresh categories can be stated. This paper is concerned with proposing and distinguishing a generalization of this type, an administrative or governmental revolution in the United Kingdom in the nineteenth century. It must be granted at once that this revolution has not the standing of its industrial and agrarian cousins. It can neither match them in "scale" nor present such tangible or arresting phenomena. The very words have scarcely yet entered the historian's vocabulary, except perhaps to the accompaniment of deprecatory inverted commas. And even if the fact of its occurrence be allowed, it is clearly neither the first of its race nor indisputably the foremost. Mr. Elton has staked a high claim for the corresponding Tudor change,[1] and it is no doubt possible to point to really critical shifts in governmental behavior in almost every succeeding age.

Not only have these points to be admitted: they must be made. For the more highly articulate, the more firmly established, an historical concept, the more are historians conscious of its inadequacy. To recognize this, we need only think of the reservations which instantly spring to mind, not merely with the specialist economic historian, but also with every general practitioner when he confronts such tried ideas as "the manorial system" or "a dependent economy" or "mercantilism." The converse is also true. Historical abstractions "operate" or influence the historian, not in the degree to which they are precisely named, but in inverse ratio. Willy-nilly, every corner of the subject is inhabited by concepts; and the less the historian is aware of their presence in his mind, the less he forces them into the open, gives them names and thereby prepares for their redefinition, the more powerful are they likely to be, at any rate, in leading him astray.

II

Clearly, our administrative or governmental revolution belongs to the second category. Most historians take it for granted that the function and structure of executive government changed profoundly in the course of the nineteenth century. They would probably agree, moreover, that this change was revolutionary in a sense in which the changes of the seventeenth and eighteenth centuries, or even that of the first half of the twentieth century, were not; and also that it was revolutionary both in kind and "quantity." Yet, it seems fair to say, these important assumptions are made casually, without thought of their bearing upon other fields, and without consideration of administration as anything more than a passive end- or by-product of the "dynamic" forces, social, political, and economic. If my hypothetical (but, I trust, existent) historians were asked why they believed the nineteenth-century change to be revolutionary, they would very likely think of the terminal conditions—the *ancien régime* of the early nineteenth century and the current paraphernalia of the collectivist state—and truly observe that so extraordinary a contrast implies a revolution in the middle. But if they were pressed to explain its cause or nature, they might well find that the answers sleeping in their minds were uncoordinated and interminable. A common list might run as follows: the Northcote–Trevelyan inquiries and recommendations; the Crimean scandals; the doctrine of utilitarianism; the sentiment of humanitarianism; the new economic relationships and the living and working conditions born of wages contracts, urbanization, and industrialized environments; and the implications for executive government of the process of political change initiated by "economical reform" or 1832 or what one will.

Each of these is clearly relevant to the question, but equally clearly their sum total even with the addition of as many similar factors as may be found does not provide a satisfactory answer. This is so for three reasons. First, the factors are very different in kind and in historical operation. Second, without a prior analysis and time-scale, the relative weight and place of the particular factors cannot be decided. Finally, and not least important, without a clear recognition that a genuine historical process was at work, molding men and ideas just as it was molded by them, the causal function of the factors is bound to be misunderstood. We can easily see how this last is true in the sense in which all administration tends towards bureaucracy. "The forms acquire an independent life of their own, and the original purpose of meaning is forgotten; the Thibetans are not the only people to employ praying wheels." [2] But it is also true in a less obvious and more important sense. In some circumstances—in the peculiar circumstances of the nineteenth century, at any rate—administration may be, so to speak, creative and self-generating. It may be independent, not in the sense of congealing into forms, but in the sense of growing and breaking out in character and scope. It may gather its own momentum; it may turn unexpectedly in new directions; it may reach beyond the control or comprehension of anyone in particular. No doubt such a process is always both initiated by external forces and continuously affected by them. But it is a grave error to treat it altogether as their creature. [3]

III

An attempt at reconstruction may perhaps best be begun by noting and examining the main elements of explanation. These are, in my view, what men thought, and what men felt, contemporary practices should be (doctrines and sentiments, if one wishes); what external or overt events directed the current of affairs decisively, or made men fully conscious of the tendencies of their time; what the underlying social and economic pressures and the medical, engineering and mechanical potentialities consisted in; and what was actually taking place within executive government itself.

Clearly, these elements belong to different orders of explanation and each has peculiar snares. The first two are explanations in terms of other abstractions, either of an ideological kind such as Benthamism, or of the *Zeitgeist* kind such as humanitarianism. There is an obvious danger of *post hoc propter hoc* in, say, establishing the relationship of the doctrine of utilitarianism to many, if not indeed most "rational" or "useful" reforms. And there is an equivalent, if less obvious, danger of forgetting the concealed hen-and-egg problem when a *Zeitgeist* like humanitarianism is said to have produced various pieces of merciful legislation. As Dicey wisely observed, law itself is the creator of law-making opinion. Next, there is the element of explanation which elucidates a concrete event or series of events relevant to governmental change but stops short of considering the operation of the connections. Thus, a political historian, investigating the waning of the influence of the crown, may discover some pertinent change in the function or distribution of patronage, or in the relationship of the House of Commons to executive government, without concerning himself whether public servants were much the same sort of persons, or adopted the same sort of procedures, or did the same sort of things, before and after. This is, of course, no criticism. The political historian is not making it his business to look for or explain possible changes in administration. But, for our present purpose, it is important to draw attention to his omission to do so.[4] Fourthly, there is the element of explanation which looks to the preconditions of change, moving back into the vast social and economic hinterland to estimate the problems calling for solution. It may be argued that this is the master factor; that once one has discovered the revolution in the forms of society, one has also discovered the inevitable corresponding revolution in government; that, in the long run, social problems of the nineteenth-century kind will force out the same type of administrative answers, come what may. Up to a point, this is true enough, and much of my later argument is built upon these impulses towards administrative action inherent in particular situations. But it cannot be too strongly emphasized that it is neither a complete answer nor an automatic operation. The correlation between social problem and administrative remedy is seldom exact. The impulse is always prone to be distorted by accidents of personality or ideology or politics, of finance or the state of expert opinion, at the moment when the remedy is debated. Moreover, the mere timing of the particular reforms may have important and even permanent effects upon the whole course of subsequent administration. Just as industries which have developed "too far too early" find themselves heavily committed to yesterday's processes of production, and vice versa, so there is a very significant element of investment in setting up new government or in consolidating legislation. Finally, there is the silent metamorphosis taking place within such long-established arms of government as the Colonial or Home Offices or the Board of Trade,[5] as new areas of administration were placed under or; we might even say, grew into their jurisdiction. It is enough to remark at this point that a really satisfactory explanation of the governmental revolution must take these unobserved departmental developments into account.

The second fact which emerges from a consideration of these

elements of explanation is that our original question, insofar as it has been asked and answered up to the present time, has been asked and answered almost exclusively in terms of the first three. This is so, I think, because Dicey's *Law and Public Opinion*,[6] first in the field, has dominated it ever since. *Law and Public Opinion* is a great book. Other merits apart, it virtually uncovered and stated for the first time the developments which it attempted to explain. But it is the work of a lawyer and a student of political ideas, not that of an historian; and whatever else we find there, we shall not find a *history* of the change in the nature of the state. No public servant is mentioned from beginning to end, unless he were also a political economist or "thinker." No reference is made to the cumulative effects of parliamentary investigations or departmental inquiries or reports. The extent to which legislation was actually enforced and the development of the experimental sciences are alike ignored; and a few generalized paragraphs provide the only description of the changes in the size and distribution of the population, and in the domestic and occupational conditions of life. It is political doctrine, trends in articulate opinion, specific statutes marking changes in principle, and the corresponding decisions of the law courts which hold the stage. Dicey does make it clear that the conflict or process was not a conscious one, that despite a plethora of anti-collectivists, there were no pro-collectivists *partout*. Nonetheless, he is absorbed with the abstract and the overt. If he avoids a Whig interpretation, if there are no human heroes or villains in his story but simply the unrecognized *Zeitgeist* of collectivism, he nonetheless (from the historian's standpoint) falls into an equal error, that of intellectualizing the problem altogether.

Many have worked in this field, of course, since Dicey first wrote in 1905. Preeminent amongst them is, perhaps, Professor S. E. Finer. Now it is certainly true that his *Chadwick* [7] involves all the elements of explanation which I have outlined. The ideology of utilitarianism; the palpable demonstrations of departures in principle (such as in the Factory Act of 1833); the exact state of things in the new towns and in the relevant experimental sciences; and Chadwick's relations with the politicians, the Poor Law Board's interpretations of the statute, and the conduct of the assistant commissioners in the field, are all interwoven in his narrative. But there are, for our present purposes, two vital omissions. The subject of the inquiry is never administrative change as such, but always a particular person, doctrine, episode, or branch of government; and, secondly, however much we may learn about the momentum of administration from his own researches, Professor Finer himself never discusses or draws attention to it. These points apply equally to Mr. Lewis's study of Chadwick,[8] and *a fortiori* to the great majority of the other works in this field.[9] By and large, the governmental revolution has not been treated as presenting a distinct and individual problem to nineteenth-century historians, or as involving a distinct and individual process of its own; that is to say, from the standpoint of this present paper, it has not been treated at all. There have been valuable studies of particular departments of state, particular measures, public servants, and philanthropists, and some penetrating surveys of the growth of the modern state. But the former are, almost without exception, self-enclosed; and the latter, where they are not merely ideational in bias, interpret growth in an arithmetical and accumulative rather than an organic sense. The truth is that Dicey's is the sole effort to offer on a really considerable scale an explanation of the change as such,[10] and that, although the materials for an answer to the original question have increased prodigiously since 1905, no serious, sustained attempt has been made to formulate an alternative to Dicey's thesis.

A well-grounded alternative must await much more laborious research. But even at the present stage it may be useful to set up new hypotheses in the light of some of the discoveries of the past half-century. Even if only in the course of modifying or rejecting these hypotheses, the problem may be redefined and fresh methods of approach suggested. In particular, some advances may be made by concentrating attention upon the last and more neglected factors, the pressures working within society and the "spontaneous" developments in administration. This emphasis will not, of course, preclude consideration of the other factors. Indeed, it is hoped that their part and place in the general process will become clearer in the source of the reappraisal.

IV

In very general terms, the change with which we are concerned is the transformation, scarcely glimpsed till it was well secured, of the operations and functions of the state within society, which destroyed belief in the possibility that society did or should consist, essentially or for the most part, of a mere accumulation of contractual relationships between persons, albeit enforced so far as need be by the sovereign power. Now our first proposition is that very powerful impulses towards such a change were generated by a peculiar concatenation of circumstances in the nineteenth century. Again in very general terms, these circumstances were as follows: the unprecedented scale and intensity and the other novelties of the social problems arising from steam-powered industrialization, and from the vast increase, and the new concentrations and mobility, of population; the simultaneous generation of potential solutions, or partial solutions, to these problems by the developments in mass production and cheap and rapid transport, by the new possibilities of assembling great bodies of labor, skills, and capital, and by the progress of the technical and scientific discovery associated with this economic growth; the widespread and ever-growing influence of humanitarian sentiment and of stricter views of sexual morality and "decency"; the increasing sensitivity of politics to public pressures, and the extraordinary growth in both the volume of legislation and the degree to which its introduction became the responsibility of governments, with the corollaries of changes in parliamentary practice and of the rapid development of Parliament's investigatory instruments.

The legislative-cum-administrative process which this concatenation of circumstances set in motion may perhaps best be described by constructing a "model" of its operation. Very simply, the most common origin of this sort of process was the exposure of a social evil. Sometimes, the exposure was sudden and catastrophic, the consequence of an epidemic, a mine explosion, a railway calamity; sometimes, dramatic in another sense, the revelation of a private philanthropist or of an altogether fortuitous observer. On the whole, exposures were, so to speak, exogenous. Rarely were they, in this first instance, the fruit of the practice of administration or regular inquiry. Nor was sensationalism unimportant, for exposures were effective insofar as they directed public or parliamentary attention to particular dangers, suffering, sexual immorality or injustice. Once this was done sufficiently, the ensuing demand for remedy at any price set an irresistible engine of change in motion. Once it was publicized sufficiently that, say, women on their hands and knees dragged trucks of coal through subterranean tunnels, or that emigrants had starved to death at sea, or that children had been mutilated by unfenced machinery, these evils became "intolerable"; and throughout and even before the Victorian years "intolerability" was the master card. No wall of either doctrine or interest could permanently withstand that single trumpet cry, all the more so as governments grew ever more responsive to public sentiment, and public sentiment ever more humane. The demand for remedies was also, in the contemporary context, a demand for prohibitory enactments. Men's instinctive reaction was to legislate the evil out of existence. But at this point the reaction was usually itself resisted. As the threat to legislate took shape, the endangered interests, whatever they might be, brought their political influence into action, and the various forces of inertia, material and immaterial, came into play.

Almost invariably, there was compromise. Both in the course of the drafting of the bill, when trade interests often "made representations" or were consulted, and in the committee stage in parliament, the restrictive clauses of the proposed legislation were relaxed, the penalties for their defiance whittled down and the machinery for their enforcement weakened. Nonetheless the measure, however emasculated, became law. A precedent was established, a responsibility assumed: the first stage of the process was complete.

The second stage began when it was disclosed, sooner or later, gradually or catastrophically, that the prohibitory legislation had left the original evils largely or perhaps even altogether untouched. For, generally speaking, first statutes tended to be ineffective even beyond the concessions yielded to trade and theory in the course of their drafting and passage. This was so because the draftsmen and the politicians (preliminary parliamentary inquiry in some cases notwithstanding) knew little or nothing of the real conditions which they were attempting to regulate, and paid little or no attention to the actual *enforcement* of penalties and achievement of objects. In consequence, the first act was commonly but an amateur expression of good intentions. Of what value was it, for example, to offer remote (and, incidentally, irrelevant and insufficient) remedies at common law to very poor and often illiterate men? As James Stephen, with characteristic fatalism, observed of one such case, "These [men] are not the first, nor will they be the last to make the discovery that a man may starve and yet have the best right of action that a special pleader could wish for." [11] Simply, the answer was to provide summary processes at law and the like, and special officers to see that they were carried into action; and sooner or later, in one form or other, this was done where mere statute making of the older sort was seen to have been insufficient.

Like the original legislation, the appointment of executive officers was a step of immense, if unforeseen, consequence.[12] Indeed we might almost say that it was this which brought the process into life. There was now for the first time a body of persons, however few, professionally charged with carrying the statute into effect. As a rule, this meant some measure of regulation where before there had been none. It also meant a much fuller and more concrete revelation, through hard experience and manifold failures, of the very grave deficiencies in both the restrictive and executive clauses of the statute; and this quickly led to demands for legislative amendments in a large number of particulars. These demands were made moreover with a new and ultimately irresistible authority. For (once again for the first time) incontrovertible first-hand evidence of the extent and nature of the evils was accumulating in the officers' occasional and regular reports; and there was both a large measure of unanimity in their common-sense recommendations for improvements, and complete unanimity in their insistence upon the urgency of the problems. Finally, side by side with the imperative demand for further legislation, there came an equivalent demand for centralization. This, too, arose as a matter of obvious necessity from the practical day-to-day difficulties of their office. For, without a clearly defined superior authority, the executive officers tended towards exorbitance or timid inactivity or an erratic veering between the two. Usually the original appointment had left their powers and discretions undefined, and usually the original statute was both imprecise and framed before an executive was contemplated. In consequence, the officers' efforts to secure "substantial justice" often led to miserable wrangling, partiality, "despotism," and bad relations with the parties with whose conduct they were concerned. On occasion it even led to counterprosecution. Thus the officers themselves soon came to recognize the need for an authoritative superior both for the definition of law and status and for protection and support against the anarchic "public." Moreover, centralization was quickly seen to be required for two other purposes, the systematic collection and collation of evidence and proposals for reform, and the establishment of an intermediary or link between Parliament and the executive in the field. Sooner or later, the pressures born of experience succeeded in securing both fresh legislation and a superintending central body. The point at which they did may be taken as the culmination of our third phase.

The fourth stage in the process consisted of a change of attitude on the part of the administrators. Gradually it was borne in upon the executive officers, and through them upon the central authority, that even the new amending, and perhaps consolidating, legislation did not provide a fully satisfactory solution. Doubtless, it embodied many or most of their recommendations and effected substantial improvements in the field concerned. But experience soon showed that it was possible, endlessly possible, to devise means of evading some at least of the new requirements, and equally that the practical effects and judicial interpretations of statutory restrictions could not be always or altogether foreseen. Experience also showed, though less rapidly and clearly, that the original concept of the field of regulation—we might almost say the very concept that there were definite boundaries to such a field at all—was much too narrow. Finally, the appetite for regulation (not in the pejorative sense of regulation for regulation's sake but in the sense of a deepening understanding of what might and should be done) tended to grow with every partial success. All this subtly wrought a *volte face* in the outlook of the administrators. Gradually they ceased to regard their problems as resolvable once for all by some grand piece of legislation or by the multiplication of their own number. Instead, they began to see improvement as a slow, uncertain process of closing loopholes and tightening the screw ring by ring, in the light of continuing experience and experiment. In short, the fourth stage of the process witnessed the substitution of a dynamic for a static concept of administration and the gradual crystallization of an expertise or notion of the principles of government of the field in question.

In the fifth and final stage, this new and more or less conscious Fabianism worked itself out into modes of government which seem to us peculiarly modern. The executive officers and their superiors now demanded, and to some extent secured, legislation which awarded them discretions not merely in the application of its clauses but even in imposing penalties and framing regulations. They began to undertake more systematic and truly statistical and experimental investigations. They strove to get and to keep in touch with the inventions, new techniques, and foreign practices relevant to their field. Later, they even called directly upon medicine and engineering, and the infant professions of research chemistry and biology, to find answers to intractable difficulties in composing and enforcing particular preventive measures; and once, say, ventilation mechanisms or azimuth compasses for ocean-going vessels, or safety devices for mines or railways, or the presence of arsenic in certain foods or drinks, had been clearly proved, the corresponding regulations passed effortlessly into law, and, unperceived, the ripples of government circled ever wider. In the course of these latest pressures towards autonomy and delegated legislation, towards fluidity and experimentation in regulations, towards a division and a specialization of administrative labor, and towards a dynamic role for government within society, a new sort of state was being born. It was modern in a much fuller and truer sense than even Edwin Chadwick's bureaucracy.[13]

V

Let us repeat that the development outlined above is but a "model," and a "model" moreover which, with a few important exceptions such as slavery reform, applies peculiarly to the half-century 1825–1875. It does not necessarily correspond in detail with any specific departmental growth. Even in the fields of social reform where it was most likely to operate "purely," it was not always present. In an exact form, in an unbroken adherence to the pattern, it was perhaps rarely present. Nor are the stages into which the process has been divided to be regarded as sacrosanct or necessarily equal in duration or indeed anything more than the most logical and usual type of development; and it is true, of course, that minor variants and elements have been omitted from the structure for purposes of simplification. To sum up, what has been attempted in the preceding section is simply a description, in convenient general terms, of a very powerful impulse or tendency, always immanent in the middle quarters of the nineteenth century, and extraordinarily often, though by no means invariably, realized in substance.

To guard further against exorbitance, it may be useful to try to say why this momentum was but relatively effective in its operation. In the first place, the sort of pressures which set the process in motion obviously varied in intensity from field to field. "Evils" in, for example, the postal service or education might not in the nature of things appear so "intolerable" or urgent as their counterparts in affairs where great mortality, physical suffering, or moral degradation were involved; although *mutatis mutandis*, and less dramatically, the same patterns can fairly be traced even in many of the former subjects. Secondly, we must recollect the point made earlier in this essay, that the manifold accidents of publicization and personality, of politics and parties, of the state of the exchequer or the character of the chancellor or the volume of government business already on the boards, might have far-reaching consequences both *per se* and in the all-important timing of reform. Thirdly, a large number of forces positively and more or less effectively resisted the process. High among these forces, perhaps highest of all, was the contemporary passion to hold down and even to reduce if possible the level of public expenditure, and with it the size of the public service. Two traits of the nineteenth-century judiciary, a contractualist view of society and a professional hostility to statute, also provided a formidable opposition. Similarly, interested groups possessing political influence, the general parliamentary acquiescence in commercial norms and ethics, and the master ideologies of the day, political and economic atomism, had all to be overcome or circumvented, if aroused. Finally, despite a certain ambivalence in the matter, it seems fair to say that the closer a subject engaged the attention of public opinion, the politicians or civil servants with both power and *idées fixes*, the more was the process likely to be diverted or frustrated. True, the process was itself dependent on public and "Parliamentary" opinion in that a certain measure of humanitarianism and of receptivity to the findings of experts and of first-hand experience was a precondition of all such change. But, on balance and unless assailed by powerful contrary forces, this opinion tended towards an uncritical acceptance of the status quo in law or an uncritical acceptance of the current shibboleths on the corruption, extravagance, and inefficiency of government's conduct of any business, and on the proper limits to the state's area of "interference." One corollary of this is that, to observe the process in action, it is often best to look to the subjects which were furthest removed from public notice, passion, and commitments. Hence, for example, the great significance of Ireland in a multitude of extrapolitical questions: it formed, as Professor W. L. Burn observes, "a social laboratory. . . . The most conventional of Englishmen were willing to experiment in Ireland on lines which they were not prepared to contemplate or tolerate at home." [14]

Assuming now the validity of the "model," subject to these cautions as to its application, what of its usefulness to historians? In general terms, this, it is hoped, is twofold. First, it provides an explanation, or rather a vital part of the explanation, of the catastrophic and very general collapse of political individualism in the last quarter of the nineteenth century. "We are all socialists now" meant not, of course, that the majority or even any significant proportion of the traditionally ruling classes favored collectivism in any form, but that they were, at last, confronted with the brute *facts* that collectivism was already partially in being and that their society was doomed to move ever further in that direction. To a considerable extent, these brute facts were the product of the governmental momentum which we have described. Although diverted, confined, and unrecognized at many points—indeed *because* its nature, extent, and tendency towards self-multiplication were unrecognized—the process had spread like a contagion out of sight; and though the collapse of the old idea, or the revelation of its untruth, was naturally a sudden thing, piecemeal contradictions had been accumulating, and the corrosion working steadily for many decades. Dicey's comment on one aspect of this change is profound.

> That law creates opinion is plain enough as regards statutes which obviously give effect even though it may be imperfectly, to some wide principle, but holds at least equally true of laws passed to meet in the readiest and often most offhand manner some pressing want or popular demand. People often, indeed, fancy that such random legislation, because it is called "practical," is not based on any principle, and therefore does not affect legislative opinion. But this is a delusion.[15]

It is hoped that our "model" of governmental change has shown that this great truth applies to a very much wider and more complex group of happenings than acts of Parliament and the deliverances of courts of appeal.

The second respect in which the "model" may be useful is in answering the questions posed in the early paragraphs of this essay, namely, the cause and nature of the nineteenth-century change in government. For, in the first place, the very construction of the "model" indicates that a genuine historical process was involved; and this, it is argued, is a vital change in perspective and a necessary step in understanding the "revolution." Secondly, the "model" provides a center in relation to which the particular factors can be grouped and the particular developments evaluated. The story becomes at last coherent if we regard it as the norm, and its modification, expulsion, or acceleration by exterior forces (however frequent) as a deviation. The relationship of the main factors to the process needs no elaboration now. It will be clear from the course of the preceding argument why, for example, humanitarianism is to be looked on as an indispensable precondition of the process, yet in itself both passive and secondary. But the use of the new concept in evaluating particular phenomena and movements in relation to the "governmental revolution" as a whole may need further explanation; and in an attempt to provide it, we shall try to measure the Northcote–Trevelyan type of reform and Benthamism against our yardstick. For even still it is sometimes assumed that these two between them virtually created the modern form of government.

Now the administrative reform movement of the 1850s derived essentially from that amalgam of Peelism and middle-class radicalism [16] which was to form the hard core of the later liberal creed. In the first place, it was a logical follow-through of the Reform Act of 1832; as Gladstone himself put the point, "This is *my* contribution to parliamentary reform." [17] For high among the objects of many of Trevelyan's supporters were the further loosening of the aristocratic hold on government, and the eradication of those forms of political corruption which had either survived or been generated by 1832. Second, it was "economical reform" as contemporary businessmen understood the term. A major purpose was the cheapening of government, the simple saving of pounds and pence by the dismissal of superfluous clerks, by getting value for money from the survivors and by those improved "methods of production" which might be expected to follow from the management of intelligent and conscientious men. Finally, it was impregnated with the radical ethics of self-help and competition. If the fit were to survive, the unfit were to perish: open competition, probation, and the single criterion of merit were to establish a species of free trade in public servants. Neither the strange connections of administrative and educational reform,[18] nor the intertwining of Treasury control and open recruitment, should be allowed to obscure the plain fact that the prime objectives were political and economic. As to the significance of this, from the standpoint of the present paper, it is almost enough to point to the omnipresence of Gladstone, who was in command at the Exchequer or as Prime Minister when each of the major advances along this line of change took place.[19] That is to say, there was a total absence of either bureaucratic or collectivist intention. No increase in public expenditure, no enlargement of the state's field of action, no multiplication of departmental activities was envisaged—quite the contrary. Nor were any alterations in administrative method, other than those implicit in political radicalism and the hoped-for centralization of audit and decision, so much as dreamt of; while the notion that state spending might in any circumstances hasten and not retard the economic growth would have seemed an outrageous foolery. In short, the Northcote–Trevelyan concept of administration was at many points contradictory to ours; and if (and it is still far from proved) open competition and Treasury control contributed significantly to the development of the latter, such an outcome was unintentional and would certainly have been anathema to the reformers.

Benthamism is, of course, a very different matter. In its concern with the regulatory aspects of law and the problems of legal enforcement, in its administrative ingenuity and inventiveness, in its downright rejection of prescription, in its professionalism and its faith in "statistical" inquiry, it worked altogether with the grain of our "revolution." Wherever it was the operative force in these respects, it may be said to have displaced or rendered superfluous the administrative momentum. But we must be very circumspect indeed in deciding that Benthamism was the operative force in any particular instance. Broadly speaking, so far as the administrative matters with which we are concerned go, Benthamism had no influence upon opinion at large or, for that matter, upon the overwhelming majority of public servants. It is to a small group of individuals, it is to the actions of a handful of doctrinaires who were placed in positions of high and decisive power, it is to men like Chadwick and Fitzjames Stephen,[20] that we must look almost exclusively for a genuinely Benthamic contribution. In general, nothing is more mistaken than a "blanket" prima facie assumption that "useful," "rational," or centralizing changes in the nineteenth century were Benthamic in origin. On the contrary, the *onus probandi* should rest on Benthamism. The great body of such changes were natural answers to concrete day-to-day problems, pressed eventually to the surface by the sheer exigencies of the case. Indeed, even so apparently idiosyncratic an element as the Panopticon was substantially repeated when, in the late 1840s, the executive officers of both the United Kingdom and New York State emigration commissions (men who had very likely not so much as heard the name of Bentham) independently proposed vast central supervisory offices as the only satisfactory solution to all the difficulties of regulating which bore upon them.[21]

There are moreover other qualifications to be made upon the Benthamic contribution. In the first place, Benthamism in its later form was heavily entangled with two great anti-collectivist influences, political individualism and the notion of the natural harmony of economic interests; and although a few of those who spoke of themselves as utilitarians preserved Benthamism's hard administrative core through thick and thin, this is by no means true of the majority. More important still, even "administrative" Benthamism had, by the yardstick of our norm, a large measure of eccentricity and irrelevance, mainly through its "empiricism" and "science." As to the first, we can say generally with Professor Oakeshott that "to understand politics as a purely empirical activity is to misunderstand it, because empiricism by itself is not a concrete manner of activity at all, and can become a concrete manner of activity only when it is joined to something else." [22] As to the second, even on its own showing Benthamism was scientific only in the sense in which its inquiries were to be conducted in a disinterested and rational manner. What was to be done was classification of data rather than experiment, yet what was to emerge from the inquiry was to be not hypothesis, but dogma. Moreover, the actual investigations made by individual Benthamites were rarely what they pretended to be. They were not exhaustive, but fragmentary; not detached, but heated; not Olympian, but doctrinaire. In short, Benthamism was in certain respects none the less *a priori*, generalized and abstract for believing itself to be nothing of the kind. As to the consequences of this illusion for our subject, the abstract atomistic notion of political man led on to the assumptions that a felicific calculus embraced all that the administrator-legislator needed to know, that his law would encounter no unforeseeable or novel obstacle, and that the essence of his work consisted in an initial adjustment of social unbalance and, subsequently, but a maintenance of the equilibrium; while the universalism of the doctrine led on to a fatal disregard of social and political patterns of behavior, as was apparent, for example, in Chadwick's ill-fated independent Poor Law Board where, in effect, French bureaucracy was torn away from its native context of a division of powers. Thus, generally we can say, first, that the genuine contribution of Benthamism to modern government must be measured in terms of the particular actions of particular individuals; secondly, that Benthamism, insofar as it took color from other contemporary ideologies, was an obstacle, after their fashion, to the development of modern government; and thirdly, that "administrative" Benthamism, where it was effective, also made a peculiar, idiosyncratic contribution to nineteenth-century administration, and one which was extraneous and at points antagonistic to the main line of growth.

All these points, and the equivalent observations on North-cote–Trevelyan reform, are no doubt obvious enough once the matter is regarded from a proper point of judgment. But this, a proper point of judgment for the whole course of the nineteenth-century change in government, is precisely what, in the writer's view, has hitherto been lacking. And if the present attempt to formulate a general notion for this neglected field and to construct an ancillary, explanatory "model" helps to provide the necessary perspectives—still more if it stimulates further refinements of the notion and further understanding of the independent historical process in operation—this paper will have succeeded in its objects.

Henry Parris has argued powerfully against the previous article in the piece that follows. The student could undertake an investigation of his own in order to attempt to discover which approach would be most valuable. It would probably emerge that both provide insights into the past and that together they assist one's understanding of many of the developments of the nineteenth century, particularly those which were a matter of government action. But more indirectly the articles discuss the nature of the articulate part of nineteenth-century society. The present collection could have exclusively concerned itself with this debate: further examples of the two approaches would undoubtedly include Jennifer Hart's vigorously polemical, and powerful, article, "Nineteenth Century Social Reform," Past and Present 31 (1965), attacking MacDonagh and others whom she considers as part of a "Tory" view.

Henry Parris has written at greater length on the nineteenth century in Government and the Railways in Nineteenth-Century Britain *(London, 1967) and in* Constitutional Bureaucracy: The Development of British Central Administration since the Eighteenth Century *(London, 1969). He is director of studies in public administration at the Civil Service College in England. This article was originally published in the* Historical Journal III *(1960), 17–37, and is reprinted by permission of the publisher, Cambridge University Press.*

HENRY PARRIS

The Nineteenth-Century Revolution
in Government: A
Reappraisal Reappraised

B Y HIS "ATTEMPT to formulate a general notion" of the nineteenth-century revolution in government, and "to construct an ancillary, explanatory 'model' " of its operation, Dr. MacDonagh has initiated a discussion of great importance.[1] For general notions are what we lack in the field of administrative history since 1832:

> No doubt the most obvious way to begin the charting of so great an area is to tackle institutions piece-meal, to fill the learned journals with close studies of every governmental agency, and thus to provide a mass of evidence from which a pattern of narrative and motive will in time emerge. But to accept this method exclusively would postpone for any indefinite time any study of the machinery of administration as a whole and of the general influences at work in shaping it.[2]

As he himself recognizes, however, his paper does more to stimulate further thought on the subject than to offer final solutions to all the problems raised. It is the purpose of this article to put forward some of the "further refinements" of the notion for which Dr. MacDonagh calls,[3] partly in continuation of his line of thought and partly in criticism of it.

I

Any discussion of the nineteenth-century revolution in government must, as Dr. MacDonagh recognizes, base itself on Dicey's *Law and Opinion* which was, he says, "first in the field, [and] has dominated it ever since. It is a great book." [4] His appreciation is widely shared. Professor Smellie considered it "the best introduction to the interplay between thought and political action" in the period since 1832.[5] Professor Wheare has said that it contains "the classic exposition of individualism and collectivism." [6] Most impressive of all, the London School of Economics arranged a series of seventeen public lectures in the academic year 1957–1958 to mark the sixtieth anniversary of the first delivery of Dicey's lectures. Given by scholars of high distinction under the general title *Law and Opinion in the Twentieth Century*, they were "at once a continuation of [Dicey's] work . . . and a widening of it." They have since been published.[7]

Yet *Law and Opinion* is a highly misleading book, and if we are misled about the nineteenth-century revolution in government, it is largely because Dicey has misled us. It is curious that in the quarter of a century since Sir Ivor Jennings first published his devastating examination of Dicey's *Law of the Constitution*,[8] no similar reappraisal of *Law and Opinion* has appeared; and a matter for regret that Dr. MacDonagh does not make good this omission. He criticizes Dicey for not having taken account of such factors as the growth of science, and movements of population. To these charges, Dicey could have fairly replied that he did not set out to write that sort of book. As for the book he did write, Dr. MacDonagh is singularly uncritical. He follows Dicey in asserting that "there were no pro-collectivists" and that collectivism was an "unrecognized *Zeitgeist*" rather than a system of thought. Yet Dicey himself ultimately revealed the untenability of that position of equating collectivism with "the authoritative side of Benthamite liberalism." [9] Dr. MacDonagh even believes that Dicey "avoids a Whig interpretation." In fact, Sir Ivor Jennings's comment on *Law of the Constitution,* that "just as Macaulay saw the history of the eighteenth century through Whig spectacles, so Dicey saw the constitution of 1885 through Whig spectacles," [10] applies equally, *mutatis mutandis,* to *Law and Opinion.* Dicey's career as a political partisan is of the greatest relevance to an understanding of his thought. An orthodox Liberal until 1885, he broke with his party over Home Rule, and devoted much time and effort thenceforth as a speaker and pamphleteer to combating the doctrines and measures of his former associates. *Law and Opinion* is, of course, much more than a political pamphlet. Yet to read it solely as a work of scholarship is to miss much of its significance. Dicey's purpose was not only to describe the consequences of radical Liberalism, but also, as a Whiggish exponent of the true Liberal faith, to denounce them.

The main respects in which Dicey's work stands in need of reexamination are as follows:

1 His summary of Benthamism.
2 His summary of legislation in the middle decades of the nineteenth century.
3 His division of the nineteenth century into periods.

Dicey's Summary of Benthamism

It must be emphasized in the first place that Dicey does not offer a summary of Bentham's ideas. "My objects . . . are," he says, ". . . to sketch in the merest outline the ideas of Benthamism or individualism, *insofar as when applied by practical statesmen they have affected the growth of English law.*" And in a footnote he goes on to explain that the principles he is about to outline "are not so much the dogmas to be found in Bentham's works as ideas due in the main to Bentham, which were ultimately, though often in a very modified form, accepted by the reformers or legislators who practically applied utilitarian conceptions to the amendment of the law of England." [11]

What Dicey himself understood by Benthamism in this special sense is summed up in three words from the passage quoted above: "Benthamism or individualism." Variations on this theme recur throughout the book, as these examples show: "that faith in *laissez-faire* which is of the very essence of legislative Benthamism." "[Benthamites] looked with disfavour on State intervention. . . . Legislative utilitarianism is nothing else than systematised individualism." [12]

It is obvious that this is a mere travesty of Benthamism. If proof is required, it is supplied by a close examination of Dicey's own argument.

> It is a curious question [he says], how far Bentham's own beliefs were directly or logically opposed to the doctrines of sane collectivism. He placed absolute faith in his celebrated "Principle of Utility." He held that, at any rate in his time, this principle dictated the adoption of a policy, both at home and abroad, of *laissez-faire*. But it is not clear that Bentham might not in different circumstances have recommended or acquiesced in legislation which an ardent preacher of *laissez-faire* would condemn. It may be suggested that John Mill's leaning towards Socialistic ideals, traceable in some expressions used by him in his later life, was justified to himself by the perception that such ideals were not necessarily inconsistent with the Benthamite creed.[13]

He is aware that Herbert Spencer's argument, that "the *laissez-faire* doctrine or something very like it, and not the dogma of the 'greatest happiness for the greatest number,' is the fundamental doctrine of sound legislation," is directed against Bentham.[14]

But the most astounding proof of Dicey's ambivalent attitude towards Bentham's thought is contained in his ninth lecture, which he calls "The Debt of Collectivism to Benthamism." He points out that Bentham himself admitted that the principle of utility was dangerous to an unjust society, and "as in any State the poor and the needy always constitute the majority of the nation, the favourite dogma of Benthamism pointed to the conclusion . . . that the whole aim of legislation should be to promote the happiness, not of the nobility or the gentry, or even of shopkeepers, but of artisans and other wage-earners." [15] He goes on to note that the consequences of a "legislative tendency . . . [towards] the constant extension and improvement of the mechanism of government . . . and the increasing application of a new system of centralisation, the invention of Bentham himself, were favoured by Benthamites and promoted utilitarian reforms; but they . . . in fact limited the area of individual freedom." [16] He points out that "Benthamites . . . differed among themselves . . . as to the relative importance of the principle of utility and the principle of non-interference with each man's freedom. Nominally, indeed, every utilitarian regarded utility as the standard by which to test the character or expediency of any course . . . [and some], e.g. Chadwick, were practically prepared to curtail individual freedom for the sake of attaining any object of immediate and obvious usefulness, e.g. good sanitary administration." [17]

The lecture concludes with the following remarkable passage:

> The Liberals then of 1830 were themselves zealots for individual freedom, but they entertained beliefs which, though the men who held them knew it not, might well, under altered social conditions, foster the despotic authority of a democratic State. . . . Somewhere between 1868 and 1900 three changes took place which brought into prominence the authoritative side of Benthamite liberalism. Faith in *laissez-faire* suffered an eclipse; hence the principle of utility became an argument in favour, not of individual freedom, but of the absolutism of the State.

Parliament under the progress of democracy became the representative, not of the middle classes, but of the whole body of householders; parliamentary sovereignty, therefore, came to mean, in the last resort, the unrestricted power of the wage-earners. English administrative mechanism was reformed and strengthened. The machinery was thus provided for the practical extension of the activity of the State. . . . Benthamites, it was then seen, had forged the arms most needed by socialists.[18]

Dicey does not argue, then, that laissez-faire was the basic principle of Benthamism. Indeed, he admits that "this dogma of *laissez-faire* is not from a logical point of view an essential article of the utilitarian creed." [19] What he does argue is that "though *laissez-faire* is not an essential part of utilitarianism it was practically the most vital part of Bentham's legislative doctrine, and in England gave to the movement for the reform of the law, both its power and its character." [20] The validity of this thesis can be tested only by an examination of the legislation of the period when, according to Dicey, Benthamism was the dominant opinion.

His Summary of Legislation in the Middle Decades of the Nineteenth Century

Dicey has no difficulty, of course, in producing a number of examples to show that Benthamism influenced the trend of legislation in the period 1830–1870 in the direction of individualism and laissez-faire. It is not necessary here to say more about such events as the repeal of the Corn Laws than that their significance is recognized. What is important is to examine Dicey's treatment of those events which do not fit into his general thesis; for example, factory inspection, exchequer grants for education, the New Poor Law, and other similar measures.

Dicey is under no illusions about the importance of factory legislation for the validity of his thesis: it was here, he tells us, that "Benthamite liberalism suffered its earliest and severest defeat." [21] He attempts to explain it (or explain it away) by two lines of argument. First, he attributes it to a current of opinion hostile to Benthamism: "the factory movement gave rise to a parliamentary conflict between individualism and collectivism." But he does not seriously argue that such men as Oastler, Sadler, and Shaftesbury were exponents of a coherent philosophy of society, comparable with Benthamism. Indeed, he has already told us that collectivism "cannot, in England at any rate, be connected with the name of any one man, or even . . . any one definite school." [22] Secondly, he attributes it to a force which he labels "Tory philanthropy." The Factory Movement "from the first came under the guidance of Tories. With this movement will be for ever identified the names of Southey, Oastler, Sadler and above all of Lord Shaftesbury." [23] No one will dispute this statement in its application to the men named as individuals, but the attempt to stick a party label on the movement soon fails. Dicey himself quotes Shaftesbury on the hostility of three leaders of his party—Peel, Graham, and Gladstone—to the Ten Hours Bill, while admitting "Nor was there anything in the early factory movement which was opposed either to Benthamism or to the doctrines of the most rigid political economy." In illustration of this admission, he points to the support of McCulloch (1833), Cobden (1836), and Macaulay (1846).[24]

In discussing the assumption by the State of a share of the responsibility for elementary education, Dicey adopts a different line of argument. He points out that this departure in policy dates from 1833. He is quite clear, too, about its relevance to his theme: "our present system [of elementary education] is a monument to the increasing predominance of collectivism." [25] What, then, were the currents of opinion which led to the foundation of this monument? None worth discussing, it seems; Dicey chooses the first exchequer grant for education as his example of the way in which "a principle carelessly introduced into an Act of Parliament intended to have a limited effect may gradually so affect legislative opinion that it comes to pervade a whole field of law." [26] It is true, of course, that the historic vote of 17 August 1833 was passed by a very small House; but to suggest that there was anything casual about the interest which such men as Hume and Roebuck were taking in education at the time is to ignore the vital role played by education in the whole system of Benthamite thought. But Dicey was scarcely capable of understanding the part of such a man as Hume; for him, "no politician was a more typical representative of his time than Joseph Hume. He was a utilitarian of a narrow type; he devoted the whole of his energy to the keeping down or paring down of public expenditure." [27] Yet Hume criticized the 1833 grant, not because it was too big, but because it was too small.

The 1833 grant was a very small seed; but by 1869 it had grown into a considerable plant. In the latter year there was accommodation in schools under government inspection for more than 1,200,000 children.[28] It is generally agreed that the main obstacle to greater progress had been sectarian tensions. Dicey however, has another explanation; although the first grant had been made in 1833 to elementary education, "the assumption of this duty was delayed by the distrust of State intervention which characterised the Benthamite era." [29]

With all his ingenuity, Dicey found himself in some difficulty when he came to fit the new Poor Law into his chosen categories: "it may appear to be a straining of terms if we bring under the head of freedom in dealing with property the most celebrated piece of legislation which can be attributed to the philosophic Radicals. The Poor Law in 1834 does not, on the face of it, aim at securing freedom of any kind; in popular imagination its chief result was the erection of workhouses, which, as prisons for the poor, were nicknamed Bastilles." [30] He recognizes that the effect of the 1834 Act was to increase the power of the State: "the new Poor Law . . . placed poor relief under the supervision of the State." [31] And again "the rigorous and scientific administration of the Poor Law (1834) under the control of the central government . . . [was a measure which] limited the area of individual freedom." [32]

A curious footnote is worth a mention also. It occurs apropos of an assertion that "confidence in the beneficent effects of State control . . . is utterly foreign to the liberalism of 1832," and runs as follows: "if anyone doubts this statement let him consider one fact, and ask himself one question. In 1834 the Whigs and Radicals who reformed the poor law expected the speedy abolition of out-door relief; they hoped for and desired the abolition of the poor law itself." [33] No doubt it is true that there were doctrinaires who hoped for the abolition of the entire Poor Law; but to suggest that such a hope was general or typical is surely quite erroneous. To echo Dicey, if anyone doubts this statement let him consider one fact and ask himself one question. All over the country are to be found large solid buildings put up in the late 1830s as Union workhouses; many are still in use today. If those who built them expected the Poor Law to wither away, why were they so prodigal of the taxpayers' money? It is fitting to correct a misrepresentation of Benthamism by an argument which Bentham himself might have styled "a simple idea in architecture."

In conclusion, a minor example of Dicey's mode of argument may be cited. "Between 1835 and 1844," he tells us, "agricultural training schools and model farms were established in Ireland" but they were much restricted by Peel and Cardwell. "This illustrated both the *laissez-faire* of the day and the attitude of Peel and the Peelites." What then does their establishment illustrate? [34]

*Dicey's Division of the Nineteenth Century
into Three Periods in the Relation Between
Law and Public Opinion*

It may seem merely pedantic solemnly to consider whether Dicey was right in discerning three periods into which his subject could be divided. What can it matter, one may ask, whether there were three periods or only two—or for that matter, four? The question is of importance, however, because most of the distortions of his argument are closely bound up with his determination to demonstrate distinct trends in opinion and legislation before and after 1870. His three periods are as follows: [35] (1) Legislative Quiescence, 1800–1830; (2) Period of Benthamism or Individualism, 1825–1870; (3) Period of Collectivism, 1865–1900.

Dicey himself was in considerable difficulties about his second turning-point. Speaking of the "characteristics of law-making opinion in England" he lays down a general proposition that "the opinion which affects the development of the law has, in modern England at least, often originated with some single thinker or group of thinkers. No doubt it is at times allowable to talk of a prevalent belief or opinion as 'being in the air,' by which expression is meant that a particular way of looking at things has become the common possession of all the world. But though a belief, when it prevails, may at last be adopted by the whole of a generation, it rarely happens that a widespread conviction has grown up spontaneously among the multitude." [36]

This has an obvious application to the role played by Bentham and his school in the transition from the first to the second period. But when Dicey comes to the next point of transition he cannot point to anyone who played a similar part: "hence a curious contrast between the mode in which an inquirer must deal with the legislative influence on the one hand of Benthamism, and on the other hand of collectivism. He can explain changes in

English law by referring them to definite and known tenets or ideas of Benthamite liberalism; he can, on the other hand, prove the existence of collectivist ideas in the main only by showing the socialistic character or tendencies of certain parliamentary enactments." [37]

Nor is Dicey any more successful in pointing to the date when the period of individualism gave place to the period of collectivism. Since all division of the past into periods is artificial, it would be reasonable to say that these periods shade so insensibly into one another, that no precise turning-point can be fixed. But Dicey does not do that. "The difference," he tells us, "between the legislation characteristic of the era of individualism and the legislation characteristic of the era of collectivism is, we perceive, essential and fundamental. The reason is that this dissimilarity (which every student must recognise, even when he cannot analyse it) rests upon and gives expression to different, if not absolutely inconsistent, ways of regarding the relation between man and the State." [38] So profound a change should be capable of being precisely dated, and in fact when the period of collectivism is first introduced we learn that it began in 1865.[39]

Unfortunately, at other points in the argument a number of other dates are mentioned. Let us review them in receding order of time. "Socialistic ideas were, it is submitted, in no way a part of dominant legislative opinion earlier than 1865, and their influence on legislation did not become perceptible till some years later, say till 1868 or 1870, or dominant till say 1880." [40] "At this point [i.e. the Limited Liability legislation of 1856–1862] individualistic and collectivist currents of opinion blend together . . . [since] the transference of business from individuals to corporate bodies favours the growth of collectivism." [41] "In 1854 the opponents of Benthamism were slowly gaining the ear of the public." [42] Collectivist influence is to be seen in housing legislation, dating from 1851; in municipal trading, from 1850 onwards; and in public health legislation, from 1848 onwards.[43] "At the time when the repeal of the corn laws gave . . . what seemed to be a crowning victory to individualism, . . . the success of the Factory Acts gave authority . . . to beliefs which, if not exactly socialistic, yet certainly tended towards socialism or collectivism." [44] "Between 1830 and 1840 the issue between individualists and collectivists was fairly joined." [45] Elementary education "is a monument to the increasing predominance of collectivism." It dates from 1833.[46]

Hence, on Dicey's own showing, the era of collectivism began in 1833, only three years after the end of the period of legislative quiescence.

But how, it will be asked, could a man of Dicey's undoubted ability, learning, and wisdom be wrong? That he could, on occasion, be wrong, not in small details, but in questions of great moment closely related to his special field of study, we know from his treatment of *droit administratif* in France and the alleged absence of administrative law in England.[47] In *Law and Opinion* he was working in a field not entirely his own: "An author who tried to explain the relation between law and opinion during the nineteenth century undertook to a certain extent the work of an historian." And he recognizes that there are limits to the degree to which "an English lawyer ought . . . to trespass . . . upon the province of historians, moralists, or philosophers." [48] He was aware, moreover, of the peculiar difficulty attendant on his inquiry: "few indeed have been the men who have been able to seize with clearness the causes or the tendencies of events passing around them." Even those who have come nearest to success have usually missed something of first-rate importance; and he instances Bagehot's lack of reference to the importance of political parties.[49] In addition to all this, Dicey candidly admits that he approached his subject in an uncritical frame of mind; his book, he says, "cannot claim to be a work of research; it is rather a work of inference or reflection. It is written with the object, not of discovering new facts, but of drawing from some of the best

known facts of political, social, and legal history certain connections which, though many of them obvious enough, are often
overlooked." [50]

Dicey, then, writing his lectures at the end of the nineteenth
century, made no attempt to go beyond the accepted accounts of
what took place two generations before, either in regard to what
men were thinking or to what men were doing. He believed
that, since he was "writing of a time not long past, [he] was almost delivered from the difficulty with which an historian of
eras removed by the lapse of many years from his own time often
struggles in vain, the difficulty, namely, of understanding the
social and intellectual atmosphere of bygone ages." [51] But he was
born in 1835, and on his own admission, his memory of public
affairs went back only to 1848.[52] It may be said that of all periods
of history, the quarter-century preceding a man's twenty-first
birthday are likely to be those of which he has least understanding, unless he makes a conscious effort to understand them. Too
remote from his adult mind for him to know of his own knowledge, they are too near to form part of history, as it is generally
taught and learnt. How much understanding of the 1930s do
we find today in those born in 1930? What would be our expecta-
tions of a book about, say, the General Strike by an author born
in 1911, who told us at the outset that he has undertaken no original research but has contented himself with "drawing from some
of the best known facts . . . certain connections which . . . are
often overlookeed"?

Halévy has described the intellectual atmosphere in which the
young Dicey grew up:

> Thus was developed in England, twenty years after Bentham's
> death, a new and simplified form of the Utilitarian philosophy.
> Disciples of Adam Smith much more than of Bentham, the
> Utilitarians did not now include in their doctrine the principle
> of the artificial identification of interests, that is, the govern-

mental or administrative idea; the idea of free-trade and of the spontaneous identification of interests summed up the social conceptions of these new doctrinaires, who were hostile to any kind of regulation and law: . . . While Darwin was extending Malthus' law to all living species, Buckle reduced the whole philosophy of history to the principles of Adam Smith's political economy. In his *Social Statics*, Herbert Spencer expressly assimilated the natural laws of the economists with the natural law of the jurists. . . . He regarded with the same scorn both the meddling Conservatism of Lord Shaftesbury and the meddling Radicalism of Edwin Chadwick: both demanded the intervention of governmental authority in social relations, and this was enough to make them both stand condemned.[53]

These trends in thought were paralleled in the world of administration. Chadwick finally left the field of Poor Law in 1847. By the Act of 1844, the factory inspectors lost their power to make regulations and act as magistrates, and until 1878, the number of inspectors failed to keep pace with the number of factories liable to inspection.[54] The abandonment of the Railway Regulation Bill in 1847 marked the turning-point in the trend towards greater public regulation of railways, which was not resumed for another two decades. With Kay-Shuttleworth's departure from the Education Department in 1849, his policy of central control of voluntary grant-aided schools was tacitly abandoned; and, following the adoption of "payment by results" in 1862, explicitly reversed.

This, however, was the climate of opinion in which Dicey's ideas were formed. He wrongly supposed that it had existed since about 1830. His erroneous beliefs, very closely interwoven with profound perceptions and great wisdom in *Law and Opinion*, have helped to perpetuate a myth about nineteenth-century government—the myth that between 1830 and 1870 or thereabouts, central control in Great Britain was stationary, if not actually diminishing. We all know, as Dicey did, of facts (e.g. the setting up of the Poor Law Commissioners) which contradict this hypothesis. But, for lack of a conceptual framework into which these facts would fit, they have been treated as mere isolated facts, apparent exceptions to an assumed general rule. The importance of Dr. MacDonagh's paper is that in it he offers such a framework; it is a criticism of Dicey, in that it is based on assumptions which are inconsistent with the basic ideas of *Law and Opinion*.

II

If anything of a structure survives a bombardment, it is likely to be the foundations. So it is in this case. The criticism advanced above has left untouched three of Dicey's most important arguments: that there is a close connection between law and opinion in general; that that connection was particularly close in the case of Benthamism; and that the practical influence of Benthamism dates from the period 1825–1830. Although Dr. MacDonagh does not explicitly criticize Dicey's views on any of these points, his own argument implies a rejection of them.

He offers a model of administrative change in five stages. In the first, the exposure of a social evil leads to prohibitory legislation. But such legislation was generally ineffective, and the second stage was reached when special officers were appointed to enforce it. Once appointed, the officers pressed for further legislation and for a superintending central body; the point at which they succeeded was the culmination of stage three. The fourth stage saw a dynamic concept of administration take the place of a static one, in which administrators ceased to regard their problems as soluble once for all by legislation and increases in their own number. The main characteristic of the fifth stage was that the ambit of administrative discretion became wider. Administrators could not only enforce the law, but also impose penalties and frame regulations—regulations which often reflected statistical inquiries, experimental investigations, and up-to-date knowledge of advances in science and technology.

His model allows for public opinion in the ordinary sense of the term; that is, the sort of popular sentiments and attitudes to particular questions of the day that are today assessed by the Gallup poll. But it has no place for opinion, as Dicey understood the term, either in general or in the particular case of Benthamism. "Broadly speaking, so far as the administrative matters with which we are concerned go, Benthamism had no influence upon opinion at large or, for that matter, upon the overwhelming majority of public servants. . . . In general, nothing is more mistaken than a 'blanket' prima facie assumption that 'useful,' 'rational,' or centralizing changes in the nineteenth century were Benthamic in origin." [55] A similar note is struck elsewhere in Dr. MacDonagh's work. The regulation of the emigrant traffic developed, he tells us, "without the faintest spur from Benthamism or any other a priori influence." [56] The corps of emigration officers "did not originate in . . . Benthamic . . . inquiry." [57] Within this field, "the plain truth is that political persuasion or ideas counted for little and operated only occasionally." [58]

The ideal way to answer these assertions would be to do for Great Britain (or Ireland) what Professor Stokes has so admirably done for India.[59] Within the limits of a short article, however, a more restricted form of argument must be employed. Dr. MacDonagh concedes that, in some cases, Benthamism was important, insisting only that "the genuine contribution of Benthamism to modern government must be measured in terms of the particular actions of particular individuals." [60] This is either a truism, a glimpse of the obvious, since the historian should seek to assess the contribution of any idea to any historical process in the way described, or it is a counsel of perfection, since the historian does not and cannot know enough about the majority of individuals to evaluate their actions in the light of particular ideas. If it is wrong to assume that men were influenced by Bentham's ideas, it is equally wrong to assume, as Dr. MacDonagh does, that they were not. The one contention, like the other, needs to be supported by evidence, and this he does not supply.[61] His omission is scarcely surprising, since it is almost always more difficult to prove, historically, a negative than a positive; it nonetheless weakens his argument. Moreover, public administration is a field where all men are very definitely not equal. It is quite true that the contribution of the obscure and the anonymous should not be overlooked; [62] but one Chadwick (whose Benthamism Dr. Mac-Donagh admits) counted for more than many hundreds of rank and file public servants.

In any case, Dr. MacDonagh makes no allowance for the unconscious influence of ideas on men's minds:

> Indeed, even so apparently idiosyncratic an element as the Panopticon was substantially repeated when, in the late 1840s, the executive officers of both the United Kingdom and New York State emigration commissions (*men who had very likely not so much as heard the name of Bentham*) independently proposed vast central supervisory offices as the only satisfactory solution to all the difficulties of regulating which bore upon them.[63]

It is a mere assumption that these men were not consciously following Bentham's precepts. The resemblance between their proposals and the Panopticon could be used with equal effect to support the hypothesis that they were Benthamites. However, it is far more likely that, without having heard of him, they were unconsciously influenced by Bentham's thought, which had by the period in question become very widely diffused. If Dr. Mac-Donagh seriously contends that a man's ideas can affect the course of events only through those who have heard his name (and presumably have some knowledge of his beliefs), few indeed would be the thinkers who could be shown to have had any practical influence at all. The influence of Freud and Keynes, for example, would be factors barely worth the notice of the contemporary historian.[64]

Since Dr. MacDonagh does not deny that in certain cases administrative changes were linked with Bentham's ideas, and since the neo-Diceyan need not dispute the validity of his findings about emigrant regulation, the sole question is, which process was the more typical? Has he in fact provided a "description, in convenient general terms, of a very powerful impulse or tendency, always immanent *in the middle quarters of the nineteenth century*, and extraordinarily often, though by no means invariably, realized in substance?"[65] To decide the answer, the model must be tested in operation. He makes a number of qualifications,[66] which, while testifying to his intellectual modesty, have the drawback of making it difficult to do so. But two points stand out:

1 The model is valid, with certain exceptions, only for the middle quarters of the nineteenth century—that is, a period closely corresponding to Dicey's period of Benthamite dominance. There is nothing in the model itself to show why this should be so, but Dr. MacDonagh attributes it elsewhere to "a peculiar concatenation of circumstances in the nineteenth century," for example, social and economic changes, scientific and technical discoveries.[67] When men became aware of an evil arising from such circumstances, their "instinctive reaction was to legislate the evil out of existence,"[68] and the result was an Act of Parliament.

2 The stages of the model follow one another logically, as well as chronologically. This is particularly important at the point where the second stage succeeds the first. The appointment of enforcement officers "was a step of immense, if unforeseen, consequence. Indeed we might almost say it

was this which brought the process into life." [69] It was taken when "mere statute making of the older sort was seen to have been insufficient." [70]

The regulation of emigrant traffic, which Dr. MacDonagh's researches have done so much to illuminate, may very largely be explained in these terms. There was "a peculiar concatenation of circumstances in the nineteenth century," since it was essentially a new problem. It can to a great extent be expressed in terms of arithmetic: "the annual average had risen from some 25,000 in the years between 1815 and 1820 to over 70,000 in the early thirties"; and "from an annual average of 75,000 during 1835–1845 to one of more than 250,000 in the succeeding decade." [71] Stage one of the model culminated in the passing of the Passenger Act of 1828. This proved ineffective through want of enforcement, and stage two was reached with the appointment of the first emigration officer in 1833. Thus stage two resulted from stage one within the limits of the period specified, namely, "the middle quarters of the nineteenth century."

An attempt must now be made to apply the model to other fields, where events took place which seem to correspond to stage two of the model. Four such events, which must figure prominently in any account of the nineteenth-century revolution in government, may be cited; namely, the creation of the Metropolitan Police in 1829, the appointment of the first factory inspectors in 1833, the setting up of the Poor Law Commissioners in 1834, and the beginning of prison inspection in 1835. In each of these fields the model breaks down. The social evils complained of were in no case new. "Peculiar concatenations of circumstances" in the eighteenth century had led to legislation to deal with three of them. In 1802, the first Factory Act attempted to deal with the fourth. Moreover, it was widely realized that the existing legislation was ineffective. But this realization led, not to the appointment of enforcement officers, but to further legislation. Stage two did eventually follow stage one in time; but there was no logical connection between them. The model explains neither why the transition occurred when it did, nor why it had not done so long before. An essential component is missing. By considering each of these developments separately, it will be shown that that component is Benthamism.

The "peculiar concatenation of circumstances" in London which required a police force to maintain order was already in existence in the middle of the eighteenth century. Minor changes in the existing arrangements were in fact made, but periodic upheavals, such as the Wilkes riots from 1763 onwards, the Gordon riots of 1780, and the Corn Law riots of 1815, demonstrated their inadequacy. A number of parliamentary inquiries either failed to recommend the setting up of a police force, or did so, only to see their recommendations not implemented. Unlike most of these inquiries, that of 1828, which led to the creation of the Metropolitan Police Force in the following year, was not the result of any particular outbreak of disorder. The problem is to explain in terms of the model why the transition from stage one to stage two was so long delayed. Nor does it help to think in terms of a narrow and exclusive ruling class resisting a popular demand for reform. For this reform might be expected to increase the security of the ruling class, whereas it was unpopular with the masses.

In Diceyan terms, on the other hand, the chain of events is easily explicable. In the eighteenth and early nineteenth centuries, men believed that a police force under the control of the central government would be destructive of the liberties of the Englishman. Hence the thought of an efficient police was even more intolerable than periodical anarchy. Certain thinkers sought to change men's opinion, however, the most important being Bentham himself, his associate, Colquhoun, and his disciple, Chadwick. The case for police was argued not only on its own merits, but also on the ground that it was a necessary part of the reform of the criminal law. Certainty of detection would be a more efficient deterrent than severity of punishment. They showed that the problem which had so long resisted "the mere pressure of new circumstances in a new environment . . . the mere existence of unprecedented problems, arising from an unprecedented increase and dislocation of population" [72] was soluble after all. Particularly illuminating is the fact that the statesman who took up the measure and carried it through was Peel.[73] It suggests that the role even of the Whigs' advent to power in 1830, and of the reform of Parliament, were secondary, though still of course extremely important. It seems likely that had the Tories remained in power after 1830, the nineteenth-century revolution in government would have proceeded nevertheless, though no doubt with differences in detail and speed.

Is Dr. MacDonagh's model any more successful in explaining the appointment of the first factory inspectors? Stage one runs smoothly, culminating in Sir Robert Peel the elder's first Factory Act of 1802. But "first statutes tended to be ineffective. . . . Simply, the answer was to provide summary processes at law and the like, and special officers to see that they were carried into action." [74] The 1802 Act was soon found ineffective; the question is why was the simple answer delayed until 1833? It is not the case that nothing was done at all; on the contrary, further Acts were passed in 1810, 1820, 1825, and 1831, but they were little, if at all, more effective than the first. Is the 1833 Act to be attributed to "the increasing sensitivity of politics to public pressures"? [75] No doubt parliamentary reform had increased to some extent the pressure from those who demanded some such measure: but it had undoubtedly increased still more the power of the mill-owners who opposed it. In any case, if the measure had passed in its original form, as drawn up by its promoters, there is no reason to suppose that it would have been any more effective than its predecessors. Those provisions which make it a landmark in administrative history—the appointment of inspectors and the delegation to them of extensive powers—were the work, not of Shaftesbury or any of the leaders of the agitation, but of the Benthamite, Chadwick.[76]

The influence of Benthamism on the New Poor Law is so well known that even Dr. MacDonagh seems prepared to recognize it.[77] The situation in 1832, with the Poor Rate standing at over £7 million, was indeed intolerable. But it had been even higher in 1818, and the ineffectiveness of the existing legislation was recognized long before that. The appointment of the Poor Law Commissioners cannot, therefore, be explained as a merely spontaneous reaction to a set of social problems. No doubt something would have been done; but what was in fact done was the work of the Benthamites.[78]

Similarly with the appointment of the inspectors of prisons, and the assertion of central control over local penal institutions. The evils of the existing system had been recognized since the days of John Howard. Moreover "half a century of experience had proved beyond doubt that it was futile to pass elaborate Acts of Parliament, if there was no official machinery for ensuring that these Acts should be obeyed by the multitude of local prison authorities." [79] Nor was the 1835 Act merely an automatic response to the challenge inherent in the situation, for "the Whig ministry, in all its projects of reform, was dominated by two leading assumptions, both of them derived at second hand from Bentham, and untiringly pressed on them by Nassau Senior and Chadwick, namely, the value of uniformity of administration throughout the country and the impossibility of attaining this uniformity without a large increase in the activity of the central government. The prison was a sphere in which these principles were specially applicable." [80]

The administrative changes considered so far all originated before "the middle quarters of the nineteenth century." It might be supposed that the model would work more smoothly in the case of those which originated after 1825, so that it would operate solely within the period where it is said peculiarly to apply; but this is not so. A "peculiar concatenation of circumstances" led to initial legislation during this period in a number of important fields, of which five examples may be cited: regulation of railways (1840), inspection of mines (1842) and steamships (1846), public health (1848), and the administration of exchequer grants to local police forces (1856). In all these cases, the first statutes provided also for the appointment of officers to administer them. The model requires that officers should be appointed because men had learnt from experience Before 1825, men acquired the experience but did not learn from it; after 1835, they gave themselves no time to learn from experience, but appointed enforcement officers at once. Dr. MacDonagh seems to anticipate this criticism when he says that "the stages into which the process has been divided [are not] to be regarded as sacrosanct . . . or indeed anything more than the most logical and usual type of development." [81] But this will not do. He also insists, with complete justification though uncharacteristic diffidence, that "we might almost say that it was [the appointment of executive officers] which brought the process into life." [82] If, therefore, this "step of immense . . . consequence" [83] was not taken as the result of experience, some other explanation must be found.

It is not far to seek. After about 1835 a demonstration effect came into existence between different branches of the central administration. The example of the first enforcement officers had set the pattern, and it became normal to appoint them simultaneously with the first incursion into a new field. The Education Committee of the Privy Council, for example, with its inspectors, was organized by Kay-Shuttleworth, who had transferred to the new department in 1839 from service under the Poor Law Commissioners. It was natural that he should be influenced by the methods he had learnt in his old department in setting up the new.[84] Dr. MacDonagh's model could easily be adapted to allow for this demonstration effect, if it could be shown that emigration regulation influenced other branches of administration. But, on his own showing, there is no reason whatever to suppose it did. It was "an obscure . . . branch of the administration . . .

which had not even a distinctive name . . . no considerable attention was ever drawn upon its officers. Indeed, by and large, the British public was unaffected by, and probably ignorant of, its existence." [85] When other services came to be set up, they were modeled on such well-publicized exemplars as the Metropolitan Police, factory inspection, and the New Poor Law, and thus came under the indirect influence of Benthamism.

To sum up: Dr. MacDonagh's model fits well enough the facts of emigrant regulation. Indeed, it would be strange if it did not, for that appears to be the sole branch of administration from which it derives. But in considering the development of ten other branches of administration, not one has been found where there is even a reasonable degree of fit between model and reality.

III

Why should anyone seek to eliminate Benthamism as a factor of importance in nineteenth-century history? A possible answer is that it is one way of resolving an apparent contradiction which has puzzled many students of the subject. Some have discerned contradiction within the theory itself. Halévy, for example, contrasted the principle of artificial identification of interests, on which Bentham founded his theory of politics and law, with the principle of natural identity of interests, which appeared fundamental to his view of economics.[86] Sir Cecil Carr has remarked, "How the Benthamites could reconcile [their theory of law] with their natural addiction to the doctrines of *laissez faire* is one of the puzzles of political science." [87] Others have perceived contradictions between theory on the one hand, and the course of events, on the other. Professor Prouty, for example, has written:

> Laissez faire in early nineteenth-century Britain was never a
> system. . . . While . . . as a general principle or as an argu-

ment against a particular measure [it] might continue to receive wide publicity, it was persistently defeated in practice. . . . The most determined liberal could not consistently argue for laissez faire; he sooner or later found himself advocating a measure which involved the Government in the regulation of some part of industry. State intervention may not have been the policy but it was the growing reality.[88]

Dr. MacDonagh is similarly puzzled; he begins one of his valuable papers by saying that it "is concerned with the extraordinary contrast between this appearance of a 'free society' and the realities of the situation"; and ends, "We have seen how a 'despotic' form of administrative discretion came into being almost casually in the very hey-day of liberal individualism and *laissez-faire*." [89]

An extreme solution to this problem was propounded by the late Professor Brebner.[90] His attitude to Dicey resembles that of Marx towards Hegel. Dissatisfied with his argument, he sought to correct it by turning it the other way up. Dicey had assumed that the consequences of Benthamism were limited, in practice, to the promotion of laissez-faire. Brebner suggests, on the other hand, that "laissez faire was a political and economic myth in the sense formulated by Georges Sorel." But "although laissez faire never prevailed in Great Britain or in any other modern state, many men today have been led to believe that it did. In this matter . . . Dicey . . . seems to have been the principal maintainer of the myth for others." *Law and Opinion* "amounted to an argument against increasing collectivism. The lectures were so passionately motivated as to be a sincere, despairing, and warped reassertion of the myth in terms of legal and constitutional history. . . . In using Bentham as the archetype of British individualism he was conveying the exact opposite of the truth. Jeremy Bentham was the archetype of British collectivism." Developments of laissez-faire did of course take place; but these Brebner attributes to a separate current of opinion, deriving ultimately from Adam Smith, and though often working in alliance with Benthamism, never assimilated to it.

Valuable as a corrective to Dicey, Brebner's argument is too violent a reaction against it. The twin themes of his paper— laissez-faire and state intervention—were equally characteristic developments of the middle quarters of the nineteenth century, and it is not necessary to assume that they were in contradiction to one another. Professor Robbins has shown how they were reconciled in the field of economic theory.[91] He denies Halévy's argument that there was a contradiction between the assumptions underlying Bentham's theory of law, on the one hand, and classical economics, on the other. The latter was not based on an assumed identity of interests. "If [the classical economists] assumed anywhere a harmony, it was never a harmony arising in a vacuum but always very definitely within a framework of law . . . they regarded the appropriate legal framework and the system of economic freedom as two aspects of one and the same social process." They advocated free enterprise as the general rule in economic affairs on the grounds that it was the system most likely to benefit the consumer. But they recognized no natural right of free enterprise. Like any other claim to freedom, it had to be justified by the principle of utility. As a rule, it was so justified; but there were many situations (e.g. where producers enjoyed a monopoly) where the State should intervene.

Following this lead, it is possible to suggest a model which avoids the difficulties inherent in those discussed above, while taking into account all the facts enumerated. Its stages are as follows:

(1) The nineteenth-century revolution in government, though a response to social and economic change, cannot be understood without allowing for the part played in it by contemporary thought about political and social organization; to adopt Dicey's

terminology, there was a close connection between law and opinion.

(2) In the relationship between law and opinion, the nineteenth century falls into two periods only, with the dividing line about 1830.

(3) Throughout the second of these periods, the dominant current of opinion was Utilitarianism.

(4) The main principle of Utilitarianism was what its supporters themselves believed and asserted—the principle of utility. The application of this principle led to considerable extensions both of laissez-faire and of State intervention simultaneously.

(5) Once special officers had been appointed to administer the law, they themselves played a leading role in legislation, including the development of their own powers.

It is unnecessary to add much in elaboration of what has already been said. The first stage (as also the last) incorporates factors which Dicey ignored, and to which Dr. MacDonagh rightly calls attention. But there is nothing inevitable about the process by which institutions respond to changes in the society around them. The nineteenth-century revolution in government was one example of such a response; the French Revolution, and the Hitler regime, were others. One essential factor differentiating the three situations is the nature and quality of current thought about society, its problems, and their solution. It would be absurd to argue that Bentham revolutionized the British system of government by power of abstract thought alone. His ideas were influential because they derived from the processes of change going on around him. He was working with the grain. But it does not follow that the same solutions would have been reached had he never lived.

The second point does not deny that there was a change in

the tone of legislation after about 1870. But it resulted from such factors as the Great Depression, the extension of the franchise, and pressure from the administration itself, rather than from the adoption of a hypothetical philosophy of collectivism. Utilitarianism was at work throughout—"that current of thought which arises in Bentham at the beginning of the century and flows into Fabianism at its end." [92]

The fourth point may appear something of a paradox. Yet at the time, there were those who believed in both principles simultaneously. Nassau Senior, for example, believed in laissez-faire, but not in the "nightwatchman" conception of the State:

> many political writers . . . have declared that the business of government is simply to afford protection, to repel, or to punish, internal or external violence or fraud, and that to do more is usurpation. This proposition I cannot admit. The only rational foundation of government . . . is expediency—the general benefit of a community. It is the duty of a government to do whatever is conducive to the welfare of the governed.[93]

So celebrated an advocate of State intervention as Chadwick still allocated a large, though limited, area to private enterprise:

> He had great faith in self-interest. He commended it as the spring of individual vigour and efficiency; and it figures prominently in his thought as the most persistent and calculable element in human character. But he saw no evidence at all that social benefits resulted of necessity from its pursuit, and much which persuaded him that without the barriers erected by the law its undirected energies might disrupt society. He put his trust, therefore, not in the rule of some "invisible hand" blending the interests of the individual and society in a mystic reconciliation, but in the secular authority of the State which, abandoning the superstitions of *laissez-faire*, should intervene to guide the activities of individuals towards the desirable goals of communal welfare.[94]

When, therefore, existing institutions were subjected to the test of utility the result might be either more free enterprise or less. When it was asked "Do the Corn Laws tend to the greatest happiness of the greatest number?" the answer (in 1846) was "No." When it was asked "Since free competition does not work in the field of railway enterprise, would public regulation tend to the greatest happiness of the greatest number?" the answer (in 1840) was "Yes." The question was then, as indeed it is today, not laissez-faire or state intervention, but where, in the light of constantly changing circumstances, the line between them should be drawn.

Dr. MacDonagh has done well to draw the attention of administrative historians to the importance of factors which Dicey did not take into account. Some of these were external, such as economic and technical change; others were internal, for example, the influence of the administrators on legislation. Few would deny the importance of these factors, although little has been done so far to work out their implications in detail. In this respect, his studies of the regulation of emigrant traffic are important pioneer work.[95] He has shown that it is possible to account for the development of one minor branch of central administration without considering the influence of Benthamism. But he has not shown that other branches developed in a similar way, as would be necessary to sustain his thesis that Benthamism was a factor of, at most, very minor importance. The accepted view holds the field; namely, that the nineteenth-century revolution in government, though not attributable to Benthamism as sole cause, cannot be understood without allotting a major part to the operation of that doctrine.

Civil servants were a central force for coping with the problems of the nineteenth-century state, and their position is brilliantly discussed in this article by George Kitson Clark. Kitson Clark himself has played an influential role in the reevaluation of events and forces in the nineteenth century, as testified to in his own work in articles and books, most notably in The Making of Victorian England *(London, 1962), and in his position as a teacher at Cambridge University. Three of his students are represented in this collection, Oliver MacDonagh, D. C. Moore, and James Cornford. They and others have contributed important articles on nineteenth-century Britain in Robert Robson, ed.,* Ideas and Institutions of Victorian Britain *(London, 1967). The present article first appeared in the* Historical Journal, II *(1959), 19–39, and is republished by permission of the Cambridge University Press.*

G. KITSON CLARK

"Statesmen in Disguise": Reflections on the History of the Neutrality of the Civil Service

ITHOUT QUESTION CONSTITUTIONAL and democratic principles demand that the permanent officials of this country, even the most important and intelligent of them, must be content to deserve the proud title of servant. The ministers of the Crown who are responsible to Parliament and enjoy their places because they have been chosen by the electorate, must, while they retain power, have an absolute control of the whole machinery of state, and that includes the unstinted service of the experts who alone can work that machinery. Of course a loyal servant has no need to be servile, nor in the right context dumb. The civil servant must give his counsel freely, and his criticism boldly; but the policy he must put into effect must obviously be that of the ruling political party and not his own. He must give order and practicability to the program to which ministers are pledged, if that is at all possible. If he is in a position in the service for his opinions to affect his work then his opinions must be unknown to the public, and he must avoid public controversy and eschew party politics. Discreet, anonymous, and uncommitted he must be free to serve equally effectively any party, to carry into action any policy, which the sovereign people in its wisdom has favored at the polls.

In recent years the rules which safeguard this position have been the subject of inquiry, discussion, and codification;[1] but the principles involved had been established by an older tradition and a very strong one. They seem to secure their purpose. It is indeed significant that two carefully considered tributes to the impartial service which permanent officials give to ministers have recently been published by very experienced statesmen,[2] one by Lord Attlee and the other by Mr. Herbert Morrison; but perhaps more significant still is the absence in recent years of serious complaint on this particular head. There have indeed been complaints about the power of the anonymous civil servant, but these have been concerned with the extent of discretionary power apparently committed to him at the expense of the private rights of the ordinary members of the public, not with anything that infringed on the prerogatives of the ministers of the Crown. They have in fact been rather directed at the nature of modern government in general than inspired by any clear knowledge of the part actively played in it by civil servants personally. If civil servants had offended against ministers we should presumably have heard about it, for politicians are not as a class apt to be inarticulate about their grievances.

Nevertheless the position is a remarkable one. It entails the control of the expert by the inexpert, the subordination, in the last resort, of the man who has grown gray in the skilled handling of certain problems to the man who may not have given a thought to them six months before, and whose sole claim to authority is that he has been sponsored by a public which has never, in all probability, thought of them at all. Perhaps, therefore, it is worth while to spend a short time considering the history of this position to try to see some of the principles which it may embody, some of the preexisting conditions which it may require.

Indeed it may be more worth while to do this since the way in which this history is generally regarded seems normally to be obscured by the fact that this result is too comprehensively attributed to the proposals made in the report of Sir Stafford Northcote and Sir Charles Trevelyan in 1854—as for instance when Lord Attlee, speaking of the impartiality of the civil servant in this country, talks of "the very special position of the British civil service, a position which has developed during the last hundred years as the result of the Trevelyan–Northcote reforms." [8] This is, at best, an oversimplified account of a very complicated matter. To say this is not to deny the importance of the recommendations of the Northcote–Trevelyan report; to do that would be very foolish. Indeed the report is so important that it has become something of a trap for historians who have been tempted to refer everything to it, to use it as something like a magic formula, a name of power which caused, and can therefore account for, any change for the better in the practice and organization of the civil service in the nineteenth century. Obviously this leaves much out of account, and as obviously some of the phrases which are often used in this context call rather urgently for further analysis.

For instance whether it is true to say, as is often said, that the Northcote–Trevelyan proposals pointed to the means by which the civil service was "withdrawn from party politics" must depend on what this "withdrawal from party politics" means. It could in fact mean one of two things. It might mean that civil servants are no longer to play with party politics, are not to use their position to impose their own policies on the country—that is that the civil service has been neutralized. Or it might mean that party politicians are no longer to play with the civil service, they are no longer for instance to use patronage in the civil service to secure political support, or the votes of civil servants to win elections—that is that the method of recruitment to the civil service has been purified, and its integrity guaranteed.

The two processes may be connected, but they need not be. A man may have been recruited in the most irreproachable manner by statesmen whose sole desire was to serve the best interests of the country, and yet he may attempt to use his position in the civil service to advance his own personal policies, which may be very enlightened but are possibly not those approved by his political masters. Or conversely, a man may have come into the service through the most ordinary political jobbery, he may have been given a place simply because a minister, who had no interest in his capacity to do the work, desired to gratify some supporter, and yet he may be prepared to maintain the traditions of his office and to serve the state impartially without reference to the political interest of whoever it was who originally nominated him. Indeed the history of much of the civil service before the days of entry by open competitive examination suggests that a man appointed by ordinary political nomination would give such impartial service that three conditions were fulfilled; he must have been appointed at the beginning of his adult life, he must enjoy reasonable security of tenure, and promotion must not be by political favor. It was this last condition which that very experienced and conscientious administrator Sir James Graham thought to be all important. In what follows he is speaking of dockyard appointments in 1853 and he takes the old view of the government's use of patronage, that it is impossible to conduct a government without giving a fair preference to the friends and supporters of the government; but, said he, provided that there was a strict examination before acceptance and a probationary period, "I care not from whom the nominations emanate; but it is of vital importance when once you admit persons within the yards, that promotion should proceed on the ground of merit, and of merit only." [4] It is true that experience showed that none of these conditions secured that a civil servant should be either intelligent or industrious—but that is a different story.

It was with the question of the purification of the methods of recruitment that nineteenth-century reformers primarily concerned themselves—and no wonder. Political jobbery had been a source of gross political abuse in the eighteenth century. As the demand for political reform became urgent this universal political jobbery, which seemed to exploit all the posts in Church and State and was extended by a monstrous welter of sinecures, pen-

sions, and grotesque medieval survivals, appeared to angry reformers as the worst obstacle in their path. It was the means by
which the aristocracy had both riveted their power on the country and also exploited its resources. Since about 1780 the old
system had in fact been slowly dying, but it took an unconscion-
able time to die. In the 1850s political nomination was still the
normal way into the civil service. In 1853 and 1854 its results were
under criticism, and while men's minds were on the matter there
came from the frozen mud of the Crimea the ugliest stories of
callous official incompetence. If the facts of those very dreadful
administrative failures are carefully analyzed it will be realized
that appointment by political jobbery and the influence of the
aristocracy were probably not the main causes for what went
wrong. But political jobbery had possibly played its part, and
certainly the evil effects of aristocratic influence could be seen
in the bad administration of those noblemen who had purchased
for themselves high posts in the army, and in the outrageous attempt of the Horse Guards to stifle the critics. If these things
were so why look further? The mood of frustration and anger
which that situation produced, and the diagnosis of the evil which
that mood naturally suggested, can be studied in Dickens's introduction to *Little Dorrit* and the famous Chapter x of that book
on the Tite Barnacle family and the Circumlocution Office, which
contains some of the most brilliant political satire in the language.
It is very bitter, but considering what grotesque and dreadful
things had happened and could still happen it is only justifiably
so.[5] Nevertheless it is not necessarily a satisfactory diagnosis of
the whole situation.

It was against these evils that the reforms that derived from
the Northcote–Trevelyan report were aimed.[6] The system of
open competitive examination would close forever the doors
to the Tite Barnacles. That for Dickens and for others like him
was the most important, the all important, point at issue. Abolish
political jobbery, get rid of aristocratic influence, and the iniqui-

tous system that protected them, and you could easily reorganize the system of government and—at least Dickens if not all the reformers cared about this—get to work on urgently needed social reform. The view has been widely inherited and it is no doubt for this reason that many writers have not been able to see further than the Northcote–Trevelyan report. But in fact there were other sources of trouble with which political jobbery had nothing to do, as, for instance, either the devastating results of savage official economy itself, often the result of ignorant but powerful parliamentary or public criticism, or the results of the general clumsiness and disjointed character of much of the British machine of government. Indeed there were some issues which the Northcote–Trevelyan report did not even intend to touch at all—and one of them was the neutralization of the civil service, if that means the prevention of civil servants from taking action which is likely to land them in party controversy.

If anything the report went the other way. It was hoped that entry by examination would attract a better class of candidate and that the service could be so rearranged that men in certain grades in it would not be overwhelmed with drudgery but work more reflectively and intelligently. But insofar as a man becomes more reflective and intelligent the more likely is he to have his own views about things and the less content will he be to be a docile servant and no more. If this is so it is possible that he will be more likely to take on his own initiative action which may come into the sphere of party politics. As soon as the Northcote–Trevelyan report was produced this point was grasped by Sir James Stephen, then a professor at Cambridge but for a long time permanent head of the Colonial Office. Sir James made the point that an examination such as was proposed was designed to select candidates with qualities which were not needed by a civil servant, if you took into account the kind of functions he had to perform and the restrictions of the position he had to fill. "You stand in need," said he, "not of statesmen in disguise, but of intelligent, steady, methodical men of business." It is significant that a note of bitterness creeps into his language when he talks of the frustrations natural to the position of the civil servant, and the abuse he may have to receive without being able to answer. It is probable that in all this he was calling to mind his own uncomfortable experiences; however, it is unlikely that anything that he said much troubled that confident man Sir Charles Trevelyan, even though he too was a permanent official.[7]

This does not of course mean that a contingent result of the Northcote–Trevelyan reforms, when they were put into effect, may not have been an increase in the anonymity and neutrality of the civil service. Professor S. E. Finer, in an article on the responsibility of ministers, has claimed that the abolition of recruitment by patronage after 1870 did much to render the civil servant anonymous, since it severed personal allegiances between ministers and civil servants.[8] That may very well be so, certainly tradition and practice in this matter were in the period before 1870, for a variety of reasons, unsettled and insecure, but as certainly the principle upon which the anonymity and neutrality of the civil servant is based was well known long before 1870.

For instance in July 1859 Mr. Gladstone, who had just become Chancellor of the Exchequer in Lord Palmerston's government, was criticized in the House of Commons on a point connected with the income tax by Sir Stafford Northcote, who had been Financial Secretary to the Treasury in Lord Derby's government which had just retired. The point can never have been of much, and is now of no imaginable, interest; but in his argument Sir Stafford contrasted the assurance which the Chancellor of the Exchequer claimed to have received from the "heads of the revenue department" that a certain course was practicable with the contrary advice they had given when the matter was discussed a few months before, and Mr. Gladstone endeavored to prevent Sir Stafford proceeding with his argument "by a prolonged shaking of his head." It should be explained that Sir Stafford had originally been introduced into both administration and politics by Mr. Gladstone, and, though they were now on different sides of the house, it is clear that Sir Stafford still deeply respected his old master and probably still went to him for personal advice, therefore this head shaking was rather tutorial and admonitory than polemical and partisan. Indeed Mr. Gladstone explained it to Sir Stafford afterwards; it was not, he said, meant for a denial of fact, but "was intended to intimate that references from the opposition bench to opinions of the permanent officers of the government, in contradiction to the Minister who is responsible in the matter at issue, were contrary to rule and to convenience." [9] Now the significant point about this incident is not the fact that by a queer chance it involves at least two of the men who were most closely concerned with the report, Mr. Gladstone and Sir Stafford Northcote; it is rather the nature of the message which Mr. Gladstone believed that he could convey to his pupil by merely shaking his head. He must have felt that his principle was in some form commonly known and commonly accepted, otherwise he could not have hoped to have been understood however long he went on.

Of course for a principle to be commonly known and commonly accepted does not mean that it will be commonly observed, and Mr. Gladstone's principle only covers part of the field; it is, after the manner of Mr. Gladstone, carefully guarded. Nevertheless it draws attention to the basic principle on which the necessity for the neutrality and anonymity of the civil servant is grounded—the sole responsibility of the minister. For if the minister is to be responsible for what happens then neither the opinions nor the actions nor the words of civil servants who are not responsible must embarrass him, or force his decisions.

This principle can be traced back into the nineteenth century without reference to the Trevelyan–Northcote reforms, or to their authors. For instance in 1864 the 3rd Earl Grey is explicit on the point in the second edition of his book on *Parliamentary*

Government. He says: "It is no arbitrary rule which requires that all holders of permanent offices must be subordinate to some Minister responsible to Parliament since it is obvious that without it the first principle of our system of government—the control of all branches of the administration by Parliament—would be abandoned"; [10] and he fully recognized the consequences of this doctrine, he believed that civil servants must not engage in public controversy, or write for the newspapers, an action of which he seems to have noted one or two examples recently.[11] But he had not gained his opinions from Gladstone, Northcote, or Trevelyan; in fact it is clear that he disliked the views of their report; he devotes a certain amount of space in his book to the usual arguments against selection by competitive examination,[12] and he takes, as did Sir James Graham, the old view of patronage. "The power," says he, "which the Ministry of the day possesses of conciliating its Parliamentary supporters by favours conferred upon them, either directly, or indirectly, through their friends and constituents, is one of the principal means by which the necessary authority of the Government in both Houses of Parliament is supported." [13] In this instance therefore, the case for the neutralization of the civil service is absolutely divided from any belief that it would be desirable, or right, to remove it from the sphere of political jobbery.

There is, however, no need to stop in 1864, it is possible to step back two decades further, and in fact into the office of which Sir James Stephen was at one time permanent head. Sir Henry Taylor, the poet, entered the Colonial Office in 1824 and in 1836 he published his well-known book *The Statesman.* In it there is a description of a government department which closely resembles a modern government department in embryo. There is the minister and one or more political and parliamentary subordinates, and in the office an official of similar rank to them who holds his office on a more permanent tenure without reference to changes of ministry. In order to satisfy the claims of the constitution the minister who is dependent for his place upon a majority in the House of Commons must be responsible for everything, though in fact much that is done in the office will not be likely to come into party politics; of this the minister's knowledge will not be great, and for this his responsibility will be nominal.[14] In fact Taylor realizes the essential doctrine of the concentration of responsibility upon the minister, if he also realizes how it must work—in those days and presumably now. But he realized something else that was going to be important. He foresaw the need for a legislative and administrative policy which should be based upon knowledge gained through official experience, and he desired to see an increase in the number of civil servants who could handle it. Some of them he believed might even be given leisure to reflect on it. What he wanted was in fact an increase to four or six under-secretaries, who could become in his picturesque phrase "efficient closet statesmen" and provide "a wise and constant instrumentality at work upon administrative measures (distinguished as they might be from the measures of political parties)." [15]

The suggestion is pregnant, but it is also dangerous. Party politicians may very well not accept the distinction between the measures which they propose and debate and the measures which are purely administrative, and men have an inexpugnable dislike to being governed by "closet statesmen" however wise and reflective they may be; they do not know how they got into the closet, what they are doing in the closet, or who is going to be responsible or even to know what is happening there. There was a man, as has been suggested, very close to Taylor who could have told him all this. *The Statesman* is in fact dedicated to that very able, rather gloomy, highly conscientious permanent official James Stephen who was to talk about "statesmen in disguise." Taylor calls him "the man within the author's memory in whom the active and the contemplative most often meet"; and no man knew better than Stephen how unfortunate it may be for an official to be suspected of possessing those dangerous qualities. During the struggle for the emancipation of the slaves he was abused by the West Indian interest, and after that to roast the other side he was abused by the Colonial reformers. He was "King Stephen," "Mr. Over-Secretary Stephen," he was "Mr. Mother Country"; indeed Charles Buller's account of him as "Mr. Mother Country" must stand for ever as the classical account of the habitual triumph of the all-pervasive self-deprecatory power of the permanent official over the inexperience of his successive political masters.[16] It is very brilliant, whether it is just or not is another question. What is certain is that Stephen had no desire to stand for that portrait. He knew that he was a subordinate limited by the fact that he was not responsible, and would have much liked to have been anonymous.

Professor Hughes has published two rather moving letters written by him to the 3rd Earl Grey on two occasions. The second letter was written in 1845, its occasion being the harsh attacks which the New Zealand Company had made on Stephen's integrity. In 1844 Stephen had turned to the Colonial Secretary, Lord Stanley, for protection. But Stanley though he deplored these attacks felt that neither Stephen nor he could answer an apparently peculiarly offensive one that had appeared in a magazine. Stephen could not do so for he, Stanley, not Stephen was responsible for the actions of the Colonial Office, and he could not do so because he was responsible not to the press, but to Parliament and the Queen. The best that he could think of doing was to supply Stephen with a letter expressing an absolute belief in his integrity which he could show to anyone. This letter Stephen showed in self-protection to Earl Grey as chairman of the New Zealand committee. On the first occasion, in 1833, Stephen begged Earl Grey, then Lord Howick, not to associate his name in honor with the bill for the abolition of slavery, which owed in fact a great deal to him, because his unpopularity would only prejudice the measure and also because he could not claim credit for it since his political masters not he must carry the responsibility. This is twenty years before the Northcote-Trevelyan report.[17]

It is difficult to carry the history of the exclusive responsibility of ministers and the irresponsibility of civil service behind 1830, because before that date conditions tend to be very different. Of course a doctrine of ministerial responsibility existed and that carried with it, as it must, the corollary that a minister was responsible for his assistantts. As Wilberforce said in the debate in the House of Commons on the case of Lord Melville, there would be no security remaining for the faithful discharge of any public trust if the House was once to suffer a minister to say that he had connived at a breach of law by his deputy, and that the superior was to pass uncensored, because no personal corruption had been proved against himself.[18] This, however, is a case of precise legal responsibility about to be tested by impeachment; the problem of what might be called political responsibility would, at least in the eighteenth century, present a more complicated problem, nor is it always easy in the eighteenth century to be sure who ought to be identified with the leading permanent civil servants of today. There exists a kind of intermediate class of under-secretaries, secretaries to the Admiralty and Treasury and such like. These men seem by nature and functioń and length of tenure closely to resemble the permanent heads of government departments today and they are in some ways below the political level, yet they occupy seats in the House of Commons, indeed the posts which they hold are expressly excluded from the operation of the act of 1742 (15 George II, cap. 22) which prevents "assistants" from sitting in the House of Commons.[19]

It is possible that matters were being sorted a little in the period between 1780 and 1830, partly owing to political developments but largely because of the administrative reform which was going forward.[20] There may have been a tendency to appoint "stationary" under-secretaries; as was proposed for the Treasury in 1786,[21] or for those secretaries and under-secretaries who were in Parliament to become definitely political. But the whole period is one of transition and it is necessary to move very warily and not to generalize.[22] It is not to be taken for granted that, even perhaps after 1800, a subordinate who sat in the House of Commons was held to be a politician. J. W. Croker was Secretary to the Admiralty between 1807 and 1830; he held a seat in the House of Commons all the time and was without question or concealment a politician; but he believed that he was the first politician to hold that post, in spite of the fact that his predecessors had also been members of the House, and when he resigned with the Duke of Wellington in 1830 he wrote specially to Sir James Graham, the incoming First Lord, because as he said: "There never has been an instance of the Secretary of the Admiralty being removed on a change of ministry." [23] Nor is it to be taken for granted that a subordinate who did not sit in Parliament and had no close political relations with the ministry occupied a permanent position.[24]

By 1830 the elements of the situation—the responsible political minister and the nonpolitical permanent civil servant—seem to have been established, but the immediate past was probably too confusing and too different from conditions after 1830 to have left any very clear conventions as to how permanent civil servants should be treated or should behave. Nor was the machinery of government which had been inherited likely to make the working of any doctrine of political responsibility at all easy. Much of the machine of the state had been created as need from time to time demanded and then heaped together without much thought of ministerial control. At the center were indeed the great officers of state, but surrounding them was a confused pile of administrative bric-à-brac, each piece fashioned separately for some particular purpose, known or forgotten, and with no connecting links. There were autonomous bodies of commissioners appointed, often with power to make regulations, to put some act or group of acts into force like those bodies engaged in the collection of revenue, whose number Blackstone views with such apprehension.[25] There were statutory autonomous bodies with local powers, like improvement act commissioners. There were departments of government which had been developed to fulfill a particular function for one service with no very clear connection with other departments who were performing other functions for the same service. For instance at the end of the Napoleonic wars there are said to have been "no less than thirteen distinct offices concerned with some aspect of army administration," while "in March 1854 at the outbreak of the Crimean War there still remained six important authorities each of which claimed independent powers." [26]

Such diverse and dislocated arrangements might well render the actual attribution of responsibility, to say the least of it, difficult, and when after 1830 men started to erect a new state to deal with the problems that were crowding upon them they started in the old spirit of hugger-mugger. The Corps of Emigration Officers called into existence in 1833 had at first no clearly designated superior. It was not clear at first whether the inspectors who were appointed in the same year to enforce the factory acts were under the Board of Trade or the Home Office.[27] Most important of all, the new Poor Law of 1834, that act which for good or ill is the starting-point of so much administrative history, was to be put into effect by a body of independent commissioners with power to make regulations, but with no one to speak for them in the House of Commons. Something of the same model was followed two years later with the Ecclesiastical Commissioners.

If this confusion had continued and extended itself, then probably no intelligible system of ministerial responsibility would have developed. The principle might have been there, but the practice would have been impossible. But as far as central gov-

ernment was concerned, mid-nineteenth-century conditions prevented this confusion from continuing. In his very important
article on what he calls "The Nineteenth Century Revolution in
Government," Dr. MacDonagh describes the various stages by
which public services were built up, and how in due course if a
service was to be effective its officers had to be integrated into
some existing department, as the factory inspectors became integrated into the work of the Home Office.[28] As these new demands developed the departments affected had to be rationalized
to meet them.[29] Of course there were those who refused to
sacrifice the venerable confusion hallowed by the habits of their
lifetime; in particular the Horse Guards and other army departments put up a gallant and stubborn fight against rationalization.
It was his partial failure to deal with this recalcitrance to the
dissatisfaction of the holy demon Florence Nightingale that deep-
ened the tragedy of the early death of Sidney Herbert.[30]

But it was not only the needs of the service that demanded
this integration, it was also the demands of Parliament. The great
example here is that of the Poor Law Commissioners. They
worked hard and conscientiously and contrived to become the
most hated men in England. Naturally the House of Commons
would not leave them alone, but they had no one to speak for
them in the House of Commons. The situation became impossible, so that in due course their pride had to be brought low and
they were turned into a board under a minister in 1847. Bagehot
read a moral in this for all departments of state without ministerial
cover, and he was quite right.[31] The unlucky Board of Health
set up in 1848, in which an official and voluntary member could
outvote a minister, was reduced to ministerial discipline in 1854,
and this road was followed by that part of the Ecclesiastical Commission whose work really interested Parliament, that part which
dealt with the holding of land.[32]

The change was made gradually, tentatively, very much in
the English fashion, hesitating over words but transmuting things.

Committees that had never met for years, Boards that were created with no intention that they should ever meet, turned slowly but inevitably into ordinary departments of state under a political minister, and then in the shameless twentieth century men began openly to create ministries, and the decent pretense was over.[33] Even as late as 1864 the system was still sufficiently confused to cause trouble in the working of the chain of political responsibility in certain departments.[34] But the process by which the central government of Great Britain was departmentalized went steadily forward, and so was erected that continuous barrier of ministerial responsibility behind which the modern civil servant works in anonymous seclusion. There is, however, a formative period between 1830 and about 1880, and in that period there are some of the most formidable divergencies in the behavior of eminent officials from anything that could be called neutral or anonymous. The fact is of the greatest importance in British administrative history.

It is certainly significant that one of the most notable offenders was Sir Charles Trevelyan himself. In 1843, the year of O'Connell's last agitation, Trevelyan, then assistant Secretary to the Treasury, visited Ireland. When he returned he seems to have reported to the Prime Minister, Sir Robert Peel, and the Home Secretary, Sir James Graham, but in October when the government were very anxious about the results of O'Connell's arrest he also thought fit to describe his experiences in the *Morning Chronicle* under the pseudonym "Philalethes," in an open letter in two portions to be published successively, and apparently to boast of his action to Sir Thomas Freemantle, the political Secretary of the Treasury, after the first portion came out. Trevelyan wrote to Sir James Graham, the Home Secretary, to say that perhaps he might have made a mistake in publishing at all, but that, since the first portion had been published, the second, which he enclosed, might perhaps as well be published also. Graham would not read the second portion, or advise about publication, but, not unreasonably, wrote to Trevelyan with some severity. "In a critical state of affairs you have erred in judgment," he told him, "on a point of great delicacy and importance." Peel agreed with Graham. "How a man," he wrote to Graham, "after his confidential interview—with us—could think it consistent with common decency to reveal to the Editor of the *Morning Chronicle* and to the world—all he told us—is passing strange. He must be a consummate fool." [35] Since the matter had been left to Trevelyan's discretion the second portion duly appeared in the *Morning Chronicle*.

Sir Charles Trevelyan was not on any calculation a "consummate fool"; but he was "Sir Gregory Hardlines," a very able, determined man who normally knew he was right and was by no means reluctant to use the newspapers to further his views, whatever position he occupied. When the famous Northcote-Trevelyan report was to come out a copy reached *The Times'* newspaper office some time before publication. This was objected to, and it may be held that the disclaimer in the last paragraph of the reply made by Trevelyan and Northcote to Sir Charles Arbuthnot does not exclude the possibility that *The Times* had in fact been primed in favor of the report and in support of the savage criticisms it promulgated against the rest of the civil service. The abuse which the report received was considerable, but Macaulay, Trevelyan's brother-in-law, noticed that Trevelyan was not disturbed, not nearly as disturbed as was Macaulay.[36] Indeed he went on his way with self-assurance and in March 1860 came to momentary disaster because a minute which recorded his views as Governor of Madras and those of his council, adverse to the policy of the government of India, became generally known and found its way to the press on his responsibility.

He was not, however, unique in his recourse to the newspapers. Perhaps the most interesting public servant in the second quarter of the nineteenth century was that passionate north countryman Sir Edwin Chadwick. For a brief period Alexander Bain, the Scots philosopher, served as assistant Secretary to the Metropolitan Sanitary Commission, having been appointed on Chadwick's recommendation largely, as far as one can see, because he could write for the press. Bain says in his autobiography: "In supporting Chadwick's various schemes we had frequent recourse to the newspapers which it was his custom all through his career to inspire on topics that he was pushing forward. I had to take a considerable part in this work, and to write leaders on such papers as we had access to, chiefly the *Globe* evening paper and the *Observer* weekly." [37] Nor were the newspapers the only allies which Chadwick invoked. He would cause independent members of Parliament to raise matters on his behalf,[38] he would collaborate with them when they attacked his enemies in the public service.[39] He would use the reports of Royal Commissions, which he had tuned to his purpose, reports on inquiries that he had conducted as a government servant, reports of government bodies on which he sat, to promote his ideas, or, as in 1854, to attack his enemies.

Moreover the schemes in question were his schemes and known to be so, warmly praised or bitterly attacked as the work of his hands. Neutrality would have been meaningless for him, anonymity was impossible. His name was associated with the new Poor Law, it was associated with public health. He might be criticized in public by the ministers he purported to be serving,[40] he might covertly oppose bills they were likely to promote.[41] He recognized some principles as a civil servant. He refused, as a civil servant, to join the Health of Towns Association, though in fact he seems to have inspired its findings.[42] He felt that, as a civil servant, he could not directly reply to his assailants, and therefore it was or should be contrary to rule to attack him; it was, he said, like hitting a woman.[43] This, however, was a rule which no one observed in his case, and since he was patently the author of so much that people heartily disliked it was not likely that they would do so.

Chadwick was a man of fiery genius, and his career is unlike anything else in British history, but his use of members of Parliament, as of the press, has its parallels elsewhere. Sir Rowland Hill, the originator of the penny postage, and for some time permanent head of the Post Office, was clearly a calmer man, but he was prepared to do things which go far beyond the official proprieties of today. When he returned, after a season of exile, to the Post Office in 1846 he found himself joint secretary with Colonel Maberly, a man who had been longer in the service than he had, but who impeded his efforts. It was Hill's view that Maberly ought to be retired on an adequate pension or be suitably promoted out of the office. In order to secure this he approached various members of the House of Commons, not members of the government, to get them to put pressure on the Chancellor of the Exchequer to make him do what was wanted. He too had some conscience as an official. When he consulted Cobden about his troubles at the Post Office he declined to go, as Cobden suggested, to *all* members of Parliament who might be interested as he felt that would be a breach of faith, but in the end he went to a very fair number. He also used to get his friends in the House to make motions that would be useful for his policy, and he too had confidential relations with *The Times*.[44] His work also could not be anonymous. The policy of the penny post was his invention and was necessarily associated with his name. He was also personally and publicly attacked for his organization of Sunday services.

Between about 1839 and about 1847 possibly the most sharp controversy in the country was over free trade and protection, particularly over the protection of corn which was assailed with very great violence by the Anti-Corn Law League. The two joint secretaries of the Board of Trade—supposedly nonpolitical civil servants—were J. Macgregor, appointed in 1840, and G. R. Porter, who was appointed in 1841, having been in the statistical department since 1834. Both were known free traders. Each assisted in organizing the Parliamentary Committee on Import Duties in 1840 which was intended finally to win the cause of free trade and to demonstrate the commercial and moral damage that derived from protection, a committee against whose recklessly partisan methods of proceeding protectionists, and members who were not protectionist, made what seem to be very justifiable complaints. Both were on intimate terms with leaders of the Anti-Corn Law movement, much too intimate, considering that that body was conducting a violent and very vituperative campaign against those who became by the ordinary processes of the constitution the governors of the country in 1841. In 1841, also, Macgregor published an anonymous tract called *The Protective Interest, or the Miscalled Protective Duties shewn to be Public Oppression addressed to all parties and classes.* Its standpoint can be judged from its title, it is not that of a neutral: nor did Macgregor see any reason why he should not give public utterance to his opinions. Apparently about the time that Trevelyan was sending his letter to the *Morning Chronicle* Macgregor had been delivering himself of his views on commercial and financial policy to the merchants of Glasgow and manufacturers of Manchester. The behavior of neither commended itself to Sir Robert Peel. "It is really difficult," he wrote to Graham about them both, "in these times to place confidence anywhere, the love of talking and the desire for notoriety make people forget their duty." [45]

Probably the real difficulty at that moment was that there were no rules or conventions to define at all clearly what a civil servant's duty was, that though in the years that followed the Reform Bill, men realized that some rules ought to govern the behavior of officials, there was no clearly defined generally accepted code to restrain the civil servant and protect his minister. When ministers complain they often make a personal matter of it, not a matter of principle, and when civil servants seem to acknowledge a principle it is difficult to see that they follow one consistently—no, not even Sir James Stephen. But, as has been suggested, this is not surprising. The situation had changed, and was changing. Before 1830 the line between a political minister and a permanent official was much less clearly defined than afterwards, and if anything lay in a different place. Even a most obviously political minister would tend to think of himself as rather a servant of the Crown than the agent of a party, and many office-holders who had seats in the House of Commons were nearer to being permanent civil servants than anything else.[46] These conditions would not provide the precedents to govern the initiative and self-expression of public servants who were much more than clerks and yet could not enter the House of Commons at all.

But this was what was needed. Even before 1830 the number of important public servants who had no seats in the House of Commons was probably increasing, because the "assistants" who could hold seats in the House of Commons remained limited by the Place Acts, particularly the Act of 1742.[47] The number excluded was no doubt greatly increased when after 1830 it would seem that all seats in the House of Commons were occupied by politicians. After this, if responsibility to Parliament was to mean anything, rules should have developed to secure that officials outside Parliament should remain neutral and anonymous while the initiative lay with the minister in Parliament. But those rules did not become clear immediately, partly no doubt because of the confusions which still existed in the organization of government, but partly also because in the ten years that followed the Reform Bill a number of men were appointed to official positions who were accustomed to express themselves freely, and likely to take the initiative into their own hands, that is men not in their first youth and already established experts and journalists. All those who have been mentioned were over thirty years of age when appointed, while Hill, Macgregor, and Porter were over forty. All, except possibly Trevelyan, were well known to the public for the views which they had expressed before appointment on the subjects they were going to handle as officials.

Such men were not likely to build up a tradition of anonymity, neutrality, and docility towards responsible, but possibly incompetent, ministers. And here, perhaps, the introduction of the reforms envisaged by the Northcote–Trevelyan report may have been important. Young men caught up into the service by open competitive examination, with their milk teeth hardly shed and the ink hardly dry on their last university papers, are more likely to accept, and develop, traditions of service and discipline than veteran publicists and controversialists. The same thing is, however, true of those recruited in their youth by the wicked ways of patronage. Young Anthony Trollope, or young Edmund Yates, or the Three Clerks of Trollope's imagination, do not seem to have entered the service with any presuppositions about the work they were going to do, except that some of them did not want to do any work very much. Nor, as far as one can see, were their actions affected by whatever political interest it was that had nominated them.[48] These and many others like them could be, and in fact were, molded into the civil service tradition as it developed. If in fact there was a delay in developing tradition and aberrations from what we might think they ought to be, it was probably not so much due to the survival of jobbery as to the appointment at a critical moment, when the tradition was unsettled but the needs of government expanding, of known and mature, and often obstreperous, experts to the official positions.[49]

However, if that phase delayed the formation of an important tradition and was an aberration in constitutional development, it was a desirable delay, a necessary aberration. To realize this it is necessary to reflect upon the new tasks government had to learn to perform in the half-century that followed the Reform Bill. By 1830 Britain had become a miserable, overcrowded, undergoverned country, confronted by the new problems of an expanding, mass-producing industry yet pressed towards higher standards of humanity by the fitful blasts of an extremely articulate public opinion. Unless disease and degradation were to range unrebuked and unchecked the vast new towns must at least be scavenged, drained, and provided with water. It was at least desirable that the country should be properly policed, which in the first half of the century was by no means the case. Humanity demanded that children in mill and mine should be protected, and even that they should be educated.

Where it existed the old machinery of government was most often useless for these purposes, indeed it was often an impediment. New institutions had to be developed, and also new knowledge had to be acquired and put to use. Sometimes, as in public education, the experience of other countries could be of some assistance. Often, as in public health or factory legislation, what had to be done could only be worked out by experiment, or by the systematic analysis of the situation based upon the accumulation of accurately observed facts and statistics. Now, as it happened, at that moment there were in Britain an unusually large number of people whose habits of mind fitted them for this task, men who could be trusted to apply to any problem careful systematic observation and self-confident and rigorous argument, working from relatively simple and superficial first principles and not confused by too profound or intrusive a philosophy. The followers of Jeremy Bentham were such men, but to call all such men Benthamites is certainly to narrow too much to one group a much more generalized contemporary cast of mind. For instance there were also the men who had received a medical training. Early nineteenth-century clinical medicine may not have had much to offer to the sick, except brutal and dirty surgery and some violent and very dubious remedies, but it did contrive to train a number of systematic observers whose importance in the formation of public feeling cannot be exaggerated. But there were also the Civil Engineers, and, a slightly different group, the officers of the Royal Engineers. Horner, the factory inspector, was a geologist; that of course had nothing to do with his work as an administrator, but the discipline and system which geology had now developed were typical of his age, and perhaps significant in him.

In fact Britain was at that moment peculiarly well supplied with men who might become scientific administrators, and in fact many men of this sort did become public servants, and very remarkable was the service they gave. In public health, to the name of Chadwick must be added that of Sir John Simon, whose personal efforts brought victory from defeat in a marvelous fashion after he had been appointed to a post with no administrative resources at that black moment in 1854 when Chadwick had been hounded out of public life and the forces of dirt and decentralization raged horribly in the House of Commons.[50] There was Kay-Shuttleworth, whose services to public education have probably never been properly valued. There were the factory inspectors, particularly perhaps Horner and Saunders. But indeed the list of such pioneer public servants is too long to rehearse here.

They all, however, suffered from the same disability. They were civil servants, not ministers; they were not the kind of men who could become ministers and it was very seldom that they had the force of a ministry behind them. The party politics of the day were largely unconcerned with these issues, they did not produce governments with a coherent policy upon them, they were liable to produce irrelevant crises at inconvenient moments. Indispensable and invaluable political co-operation could very often be obtained from the odd interested minister or member of Parliament, but such a man might well find his opponents on the same side of the House of Commons as himself, or even in the same government. And to make matters worse in the middle of the century was that unsatisfactory period, "the golden age of the private member"; the party system had broken down so that the House of Commons often lacked any consistency of purpose and was at the mercy of sectional interests or irresponsible dialectics.

It was possible to appeal from all this to public opinion. As Dr. MacDonagh has pointed out, the revelation of "intolerable conditions" in the press or by public agitation and inquiry was the motive power behind much social reform in the nineteenth century. But it was a wayward power, a wind which could blow up the gale force, and, when still desperately needed, drop off or give place to cross or contrary breezes. But all the time the natural resistances to any extension of government power remained pretty constant, the opposition of those who disliked any extension of the powers of government as a matter of theory, the opposition of those who disliked particular extensions as a matter of practice because they might interfere with their properties, or what they had an interest to do or were anxious to neglect. The strength of resistances can be judged by the violence of the storms of Chadwick's career, or in the early troubles, borne with exemplary patience, of the metropolitan police.

In such circumstances all effective progress in social policy might at any moment come to a full stop, or even be reversed in such a way as to sacrifice all previous gains. To prevent this, opinion had to be continually informed, willing politicians effectively instructed, and the necessary knowledge and the necessary initiative for this purpose could only come from the civil servant. He alone had done the necessary systematic research into the subject, he alone could accumulate the necessary experience.

Now there were ways in which the personal knowledge of the civil servant could legitimately be brought before the public: there was, for instance, the official report, or there was the evidence he might give before a Parliamentary Committee or Royal Commission. Even these might place him in an equivocal position from a constitutional point of view. The official report might give to the published opinion of a civil servant, possibly a junior civil servant, a status which might create a very awkward relationship with his official superior, or his political chief. It was this difficulty which seems to have been responsible for some of the very ugly squabbles about the reports of the Assistant Poor Law Commissioners in the 1840s, and was the initial cause of Robert Lowe's very undeserved troubles in 1864.[51] Evidence before a committee or a commission also gave prominence to the personal opinions of civil servants, particularly perhaps when the civil servant had in fact vigorously manipulated the inquiry from behind the scenes to make sure that it came to the right conclusions.

But the trouble was that these legitimate methods, even when stretched to a point at which they were hardly legitimate, did not suffice to meet the need. To make sure that necessary information reached the right quarters the press had to be privately informed, members of Parliament, not members of the administration, confidentially instructed, organized opinion covertly guided. But even these measures did not suffice. Where the government showed a tendency to act wrongly opposition had to be organized, where it was likely to be negligent or recalcitrant it was necessary for the civil servant to see that the initiative was taken up from outside.

Here then, indeed, you have most patently closet statesmen, statesmen in disguise, or at least statesmen in the civil service, for Chadwick's aims were not disguised, though some of his methods were covert and the methods of other discreeter men such as Simon were still more so. Certainly very many of these actions are incompatible with the doctrine that the initiative should rest with the minister who is responsible to Parliament, or at the least that nothing should be done behind his back or against his wishes. What however do the technicalities of political responsibility matter, if the people perish? If some of these men had not acted as they did, not only would some of the most valuable develop-

(*86*)

ments in the science of government have never taken place, but life might very well have become intolerable in these islands. We do well to be thankful to some of these men for their improprieties. This is the heroic age of the civil servant who was also a social reformer.

However, one important point about heroic ages is that by the grace of God and the force of circumstance they do come to an end, and their manners and methods are not suited to any other kind of age. Necessity is a perilous plea; probably we could not justify by the plea of necessity all that was done by Porter and Macgregor, or even perhaps by the great Sir Charles Trevelyan, and unless we are to give up all show of parliamentary government and to allow ourselves to be ruled even more than we are by "closet statemen" we must not permit civil servants to behave nowadays as did Sir Edwin Chadwick, Sir Rowland Hill, or Sir John Simon. But they are not likely to do so. By now the tradition is too strong, and, also, they have not the same need. The basic essentials of government that those men had to fight for are now assured in the work of a government department today. The work of a government department nowadays has the same proportions as an iceberg, one-third of it, if so much, is above water in the daylight world of party politics and public controversy, two-thirds of it, if not more, is below in the dark important technical world which the public cannot see. Over what happens in that world, probably public and parliamentary controversy would be about as useful as public and parliamentary controversy over the technical details of nuclear physics. But there need be no controversy over much that is done because it is part of the common practice of the office carried over from government to government, and made possible by the discretionary powers granted by a mass of previous legislation. In many cases it was the nineteenth-century administrators who started to deposit this common factor. They left for their successors what they did not themselves possess, a secure field of labor in which civil servants can work in all political circumstances, and use their discretion, without breaking the rules.[52]

So we reach our present happy position. The ancient doctrine of the sole responsibility of the minister is fully accepted, and our government machinery allows it to operate satisfactorily. As a result of the work of the nineteenth and early twentieth century the work of government has been so developed, its methods are so well accepted that it goes forward whatever ministry is in office, and the expert in the office in Whitehall is not in danger of finding all his life's work vitiated because a new man occupies a minister's room. The process is safely over. Or is it so? Is any historical process ever safely over? Will it always be possible for new technical knowledge, the results of systematic research, to find its application in the work of government without being impeded by the irrelevances of public controversy? Or conversely are the discretions now available to the expert so wide that in fact we are ruled by "closet statesmen" or "statesmen in disguise" to an extent which makes nonsense of our political philosophy, either of parliamentary government or of personal freedom? These, however, are large questions which it is not the intention of this article to discuss.

William O. Aydelotte, professor of English history at the University of Iowa, discusses in the article reprinted here the difficult problem of the degree to which political parties were divided in the 1840s. His article has implications for the nature of party at any period, but it also suggests the ways in which the complexity of issues Parliament had to face affected opinions and added confusions to the interplay of party and opinion. Aydelotte is the most prominent practitioner of quantification in nineteenth-century British studies and has written important further articles on the problems treated here. As he points out in his first footnote here, his article in Comparative Studies in Society and History *(also reprinted in D. K. Rowney and J. Q. Graham, eds.,* Quantitative History, Homewood, Ill., 1969) *is a more extensive discussion of the quantitative aspects. Readers would also be interested in his "The Conservative and Radical Interpretations of Early Victorian Social Legislation,"* Victorian Studies xi *(1967), "The Country Gentlemen and the Repeal of the Corn Laws,"* English Historical Review lxxxii *(1967), as well as other articles listed in his excellent* Quantification in History *(Reading, Mass., 1971). The present article is reprinted, by permission of the publisher, from* The Journal of British Studies v *(1966), 93–114.*

WILLIAM O. AYDELOTTE

Parties and Issues in Early
Victorian England[1]

I T HAS NEVER been established how far, in the early Victorian House of Commons, voting on issues followed
party lines. It might in general seem plausible to assume
—what political oratory generally contrives to suggest—that there
are ideological [2] disagreements between parties and that it makes
a difference which of two major opposing parties is in control
of the government. This is, indeed, the line taken by some students of politics. A number of historians and political observers
have, however, inclined to the contrary opinion and have, for
various reasons, tended to play down the role of issues in party
disputes. Much of what has been written on political history and,
in particular, on the history of Parliament has had a distinct
anti-ideological flavor.

One line of argument is that issues on which disagreement
exists are not always party questions. Robert Trelford McKenzie
begins his study of British parties by pointing out that Parliament
just before 1830 was "divided on a great issue of principle, namely
Catholic emancipation," and just after 1830, on another, parliamentary reform. He continues: "But on neither issue was there a
clear division along strict party lines." [3] The distinguished administration of Sir Robert Peel in the 1840s was based, according to
Norman Gash, on a party "deeply divided both on policy and
personalities." [4] The other side of the House at that time is usually
thought to have been even more disunited. It has even been sug-

gested that, in the confused politics of the mid-nineteenth century, the words *conservative* and *radical* each meant so many different things that they cannot be defined in terms of programs and objectives and that these polarities may more usefully be considered in terms of tempers and approaches.[5]

A second, rather different argument is that both parties in any smoothly running two-party system pursue identical or closely similar objectives. By this view either parties do not differ on the issues of the day, or at the most their disagreement is so trivial as to amount for practical purposes to no disagreement at all. Small differences of opinion may, of course, be exaggerated for factional purposes, since party leaders are generally looking for issues which they can use, with some appearance of plausibility, to attack the other side. Nevertheless, party disputes are contained within a general framework of consensus on fundamentals: they deal with details rather than principles, and with means rather than ends. The area of consensus between the opposing sides is far larger than the area of controversy. Hence, by this argument the two principal parties, in their respective programs and objectives, are really equivalent, like Tweedledum and Tweedledee, and do not present the electorate with significant alternatives.

This interpretation of British party history has been summarized in a famous passage by A. J. Balfour:

> Our alternating Cabinets, though belonging to different Parties, have never differed about the foundations of society. And it is evident that our whole political machinery presupposes a people so fundamentally at one that they can safely afford to bicker; and so sure of their own moderation that they are not dangerously disturbed by the never-ending din of political conflict.[6]

Harold J. Laski, writing in 1938, ascribed the success of the British parliamentary system up to that time to the fact that "since 1689, we have had, for all effective purposes, a single party in

control of the state." Though this single party had two wings
which went by various names, such as Liberal and Conservative,
both wings were, in Balfour's phrase which Laski is said to have
quoted again and again, "fundamentally at one." Laski went on
to argue that in his own day this state of affairs had terminated
and that, with the rise of the Labour Party to front rank and
with its conversion to socialism, the ideological gulf between the
two major parties had now become great enough to raise seriously
the question whether parliamentary politics could still be carried
on in the traditional fashion.[7]

Other writers, while not disputing Laski's diagnosis of the
nineteenth century, have disagreed with his proposition that the
age of consensus had come to an end in his own lifetime, and
have insisted that his generalizations about the earlier period apply
with equal force to the twentieth century as well. McKenzie
argues that Laski overestimated both the revolutionary ambitions
of the Labour Party and the resistance of the property holders
to innovation, that the centralization of authority during the
Second World War facilitated the coming of nationalization, and
that, for these and perhaps for other reasons, the two major parties have still remained close in their objectives.[8] Sir Ivor Jennings
in his three-volume survey of British party politics puts the case
even more strongly: "Conflicts of principle are, however, the
exception. Much of the Parliamentary programme is not con-
tentious. . . . It follows that much of the Parliamentary battle
is shadow-boxing." Jennings concludes his final volume by saying: "In respect of internal politics, therefore, the Conservative
and the Labour parties tend to have similar policies; and very
largely the choice before the electors is one of persons." [9]

It is interesting that there appears to have been a similar revalu-
ation in American historiography. In many American presidential
campaigns, writes Richard Hofstadter, "the area of agreement was
so large and the area of disagreement so small that significant
issues could never be found! Above and beyond temporary and

local conflicts there has been a common ground, a unity of cultural and political tradition, upon which American civilization has stood." [10] John Higham has described several American historians, including Hofstadter, Louis Hartz, and Daniel Boorstin, as "carrying out a massive grading operation to smooth over America's social convulsions" which is "dissolving the persistent dualisms . . . and substituting a monistic pattern. Instead of two traditions or sections or classes deployed against one another all along the line of national development, we are told that America in the largest sense has had one unified culture." "Liberals and conservatives no longer seemed clearly distinguishable" and "the ideological gap between them appeared to shrink." [11] C. Vann Woodward identifies, as one of the principal recent developments in American historical writing, "an inclination to minimize or neglect the conflicts, contrasts, polarities, or antitheses in American history and to emphasize basic similarities, continuities and syntheses." Although disagreements existed, he says, "we are often reminded that such tensions were always contained within a tacitly assumed consensus." [12]

The interpretation of British politics in these terms is no novelty of the twentieth century. Expressions of the same opinion can be found through the middle decades of the nineteenth century. Anthony Trollope in *Phineas Redux* (1873), in the chapter on the opposing party leaders, wrote:

When some small measure of reform has thoroughly recommended itself to the country,—so thoroughly that all men know that the country will have it,—then the question arises whether its details shall be arranged by the political party which calls itself Liberal,—or by that which is termed Conservative. The men are so near to each other in all their convictions and theories of life that nothing is left to them but personal competition for the doing of the thing that is to be done.[13]

Walter Bagehot in 1867 attributed the success of the British parliamentary system in part to the moderation of men on both sides of the House and explained, in a brilliant rhetorical passage, how the mechanics of the system led to a close approximation of aims between the government and the opposition.[14] A similar theme appears in an article published by William Ewart Gladstone in 1856, in a passage that foreshadows one of Bagehot's arguments.[15] Even in the mid-1840s, before the disorganization of party following the events of 1846, Charles Greville wrote (August 21, 1845):

> nobody cares about parties for there is no party distinguished by any particular badge of principle, with a distinct colour, and standing in open and defined antagonism to any other; none which has any great object to advance—constitutional, political, or commercial—in opposition to another party ranged against it. All is confusion, intermingling of principles and opinions, political rivalry and personal antipathy.[16]

About 1830 the Duke of Wellington, in a comment that anticipates strikingly what Jennings has to say on the same subject today, stated that "there is very little difference of principle among public men in general. The opposition is, generally speaking, *personal*." [17]

It has been argued, furthermore, that a consensus of this kind is essential for the successful operation of a parliamentary system: that the issues dividing parties "must not involve vital matters, such as life or confiscation"; [18] that "a party system cannot be built in a society of irreconcilable sects, each of which proposes to install its own brand of political system"; that "those bent on mortal combat cannot practice a party politics"; [19] and that a modern system of parliamentary opposition with peaceful changes of government could not "become the norm before agreement on fundamentals made resort to revolution unnecessary." [20]

Such opinions, expressed by men well qualified to judge, raise the question whether much can be gained by studying parties in terms of their programs and objectives. Some writers appear to suggest that, on the contrary, this may be the least profitable of any of the several approaches to party history. D. W. Brogan condemns "the simple and erroneous assumption that parties are and must be primarily doctrinal bodies." The doctrinal unity of a party, he says, "may be only one of the factors that accounts for its existence and efficacy" and may also be "largely fictitious and accidental." He quotes with approval Robert de Jouvenel's epigram that "there is more in common between two deputies, one of whom is a revolutionary, than between two revolutionaries, one of whom is a deputy." [21] Sir Lewis Namier, in a rather sweeping generalization, states: "parties at all times rest on types and on connexions, rather than on intellectual tenets." [22] Perhaps it might be argued that the notion that parties compete over substantial issues, that they are in some important sense vehicles of ideas, is an exploded fallacy from which the more sophisticated students of party history have over the last generation begun to emancipate themselves, and that the great step forward in this field of study has been the diversion of attention from party programs to party composition and support, the mechanics of party organization, and the techniques of parliamentary maneuver.

Yet the notion of political consensus, despite its current popularity, is too indefinite to serve as a satisfactory tool of analysis. "There is . . . no self-evident line to mark off those things that are revolutionary or fundamental." [23] It is not easy to distinguish between general principles, on which there is supposed to be agreement, and the details of their application, as to which opinions may differ. Issues cannot be simply divided into ends and means, principles and applications, and distinctions of this kind are matters of degree. Furthermore, the existence of a consensus on the basic rules of politics does not necessarily preclude party disagreements on matters of some import. Substantial differences in objectives may conceivably exist even when the realization of these objectives is not likely to precipitate a revolution by violence. Nor does it seem reasonable to assume that the extent of consensus between opposing parties must always be the same; it may vary from one time to another.

It may be more helpful, then, instead of speaking in general and dogmatic terms about a "consensus" on "fundamentals," to study party votes on issues and to find out what the facts were.[24] This has not yet, to any great extent, been attempted. Though some interesting and suggestive opinions have been offered, some of them based on an extensive knowledge of political history, not much detailed research has been done to show how far, in the nineteenth-century House of Commons, voting on issues corresponded to party boundaries. Since, however, this is a subject on which the facts can be ascertained, and since they have not been ascertained, the debate has a certain unreality. The proper way to resolve the question whether parties differed on issues is not to introduce a quotation from Balfour, nor even one from Bagehot, but to inspect the division lists and learn what actually happened. An attempt will be made here to do this for a single Parliament, that of 1841–1847, the second of Queen Victoria's reign.

Before the evidence is considered, one other point must be clarified. There may be some question whether, for the 1840s, such terms as "party program" or "party policy" have any meaning. To Sir Robert Peel, the statesman who dominated the politics of the decade, the notion that his party should possess a clearly defined political program would doubtless have been unwelcome. Peel, according to Gash, thought it no part of the duty of a political party to supply a program, and he regarded the country gentlemen who supported him as not qualified to formulate a policy. Further, "his cast of mind . . . was administrative rather than legislative," and "the notion of a programme . . . which implied a pledge to action in advance of the circumstances in which the action was to be carried out, was clearly intolerable to him."

Though he occasionally "defined his attitude towards current problems, . . . he did so with caution and always tried to reserve for himself the maximum freedom of action." [25] Peel's position does not, however, seem to exclude the discussion of a party policy in the sense considered here: a set of attitudes and objectives revealed by the votes of party members in the divisions. Peel's objections were to pressure upon the administration from the backbenchers and to pledges in advance. He would scarcely have denied the possibility that a consistent policy might be framed as the events occurred to which the policy was addressed. If, therefore, attention is directed not to campaign pledges but to votes in the House of Commons, not to what men promised but to what they did, it seems possible to speak of a party program or a set of party attitudes in a sense not inconsistent with Peel's views.

It has also been disputed whether in the 1840s parties in anything like the modern sense existed at all. It is true that the reform legislation of 1832 did stimulate and accelerate the development of party organization, as Gash has described in interesting detail. Nevertheless, parties of the mid-nineteenth century, as compared to those of the mid-twentieth, were parliamentary groupings rather than national organizations, and even in Parliament they were rudimentary in structure, undisciplined, loosely organized and controlled, and frequently unable to provide the support needed for a firm government. Such remarks are most commonly made about the Liberal side of the house, but Gash has described the Conservative Party of the 1840s in very similar terms.[26] Other writers have questioned the existence or, at least, the importance of parties in this period. "Nineteenth-century parliamentary historians," writes Namier, "now seem agreed in deferring the full emergence of the modern party till after the Second Reform Bill: what preceded it were intermediary forms which should not be treated anachronistically in terms of a later age." [27] Derek Beales states: "The history of party should probably be regarded as of minor importance in British history, at least before the late nineteenth century." [28]

It is doubtless necessary to avoid attributing to the parties of the 1840s the rigidity and formal structure of the present-day organizations that go by similar names. Nevertheless, it seems possible to speak of party affiliations in the 1840s at least in the elementary sense of the political labels attached to members of Parliament. These can be clearly determined: defensible ascriptions of party can be made for each of the 815 men who sat in the House of Commons between the general elections of 1841 and 1847.[29] It may be useful to consider the problem in these simpler and more literal terms: to examine whether the men who went by these party labels did actually differ in the objectives they pursued. How far either of the two main party groups in the 1840s or any of the sub-groups within them constituted a political party in the modern sense is a question that may be left open for the present.

Among the 658 men who may be described as the original members of this Parliament,[30] after the general election of 1841, the Conservatives possessed a majority of 80, 369 to 289, or 56 per cent to 44 per cent. This majority had slightly increased by the dissolution in 1847 to 90, 373 to 283, or 57 per cent to 43 per cent. (The final figures add to two less because of the disfranchisement of Sudbury in 1844.) The other side of the House was composed of a number of splinter groups. At the general election of 1841 there were returned: 73 Whigs, 80 Liberals, 69 Reformers, 25 Radical Reformers, 18 Repealers, and 24 men who belonged to this side of the House but are not clearly denominated in Dod's *Parliamentary Companion* or other contemporary sources by any of these specific labels. Figures for the original members, for those sitting at the dissolution, and for all the 815 men who sat in this Parliament are presented in Table I.

TABLE I

	Original members of the Parlia- ment 1841–1847	Sitting at time of dissolution in 1847	Total number who sat in Parliament at any time between general elections of 1841 and 1847
Conservatives:	369	373	469
"Liberal" Side of House:			
Whigs	73	67	82
Liberals	80	88	101
Reformers	69	56	74
Radical Reformers	25	24	30
Repealers	18	24	29
Others on "Liberal" side of House but not clearly denomi- nated by any of above labels	24	24	30
Total "Liberals"	289	283	346
Grand Total	658	656	815

In view of the diversity of political nomenclature on the Left, it seems simplest to begin by casting these various groups into a single entity which may be arbitrarily referred to here as the "Liberals." A division of the House into two party categories is consistent with contemporary practice: the London *Times*, for example, in reporting the elections of 1841, posted the results in two columns, one headed "Conservatives" and the other headed "Whig Radicals" or "Whigs." [31] Possibly, in view of the language used in the *Times*, it would be better to refer to the nonconservative side of the House as the "Whigs." However, the term "Whig" has some special connotations, not all of them political,[32] and for the whole group the description "Liberal" may be less confusing. The terminology is in any case merely intended as a shortcut, a brief way of referring to the members of the House who were not Conservatives. The tiny group of Repealers, though a separate entity, has been included, since they almost invariably voted with the Left, and if the House is to be divided into two parts, they clearly belong here rather than on the other side. The voting of the separate sub-groups on the Left will be considered later.

Party attitudes on issues in the 1840s are not easy to describe in any simple fashion. This is not because of lack of information; on the contrary, there were many divisions in the Parliament of 1841–1847 on a variety of questions, and the documentation is abundant. The difficulty is, rather, that the picture is complex and, at first sight, confused. Some questions were voted on according to party lines; some split one party or the other; some split both. It is not at once apparent whether it is possible to make sense out of all this: whether these varied types of behavior can be subsumed into any larger pattern. However, a technical device that has proved of considerable assistance in attacking this problem has become available relatively recently: the method of scalogram analysis developed by Louis Guttman just before and during the Second World War.[33] Though Guttman scaling was originally devised for the analysis of responses to questionnaires, it has also proved effective for the study of votes in legislative bodies. In particular, votes in the House of Commons in the 1840s have turned out to be highly amenable to this kind of analysis. It is possible to arrange a substantial number of divisions in Parliament in this decade in a rank order in which they form a cumulative scale of the Guttman type. A simple illustration of such a scale is given in Table II, which compares the votes in five divisions and shows how far those voting positive or negative in each voted positive or negative in each of the others. It will be observed that the five divisions form a clearly marked progression in the sense that those voting positive in any division also voted positive in all divisions lower in the scale, while those voting negative in any division also voted negative in all divisions higher in the scale. Perfect scales are seldom met with in practice, and this scale is quite a good one as these things go. In each of the ten paired comparisons the number of "irregular" cases—men positive on the higher item and negative on the lower—is shown in the upper right-hand cell. It will be observed that this figure is, in each instance, very small: always under 4 per cent of the total in the four cells and, in eight of the ten fourfold tables, under 2 per cent. Table II presents only a small part of the findings. Many other divisions also fit this scale and could have been either substituted for one of the items shown or inserted between two of them without impairing the pattern. Some of these additional divisions have been included in Table III.

TABLE II

	Corn Laws, 1843		Income Tax, 1842		Corn Laws, 1846		Health of Towns, 1847		Totals	
	+	−	+	−	+	−	+	−		
Chartist petition,	37	2	43	2	40	0	19	2	51	+
May 3, 1842	26	224	48	195	117	111	72	25	289	−
Repeal of Corn			93	4	111	0	60	2	127	+
Laws, May 15, 1843			31	247	119	194	70	34	383	−
Opposition to					146	8	84	1	190	+
Income Tax Bill,										
April 18, 1842					87	138	44	27	287	−
Repeal of Corn							137	7	349	+
Laws, May 15, 1846							32	45	251	−
Health of Towns									193	+
Bill, June 18, 1847									52	−

The final vertical column of totals gives the positive and negative votes in each of the five divisions in the first vertical column. The figures in between, when read horizontally, show how those positive or negative on each of these questions divided on the issues listed subsequently in the table. The figures do not, in any case, add to the total since, in each pair of divisions, some of those voting in the first division failed to vote in the second and, to save space, absences have not been included.

An advantage of a Guttman scale is that it is a summarizing device: it incorporates into a single pattern a large amount of information that, without such a scheme, would be unmanageable —too complex to be readily understood. Beyond this, a scale can serve as a kind of ideological measuring stick which divides a group of men not just into two categories, as would happen if only one division were used, but into a series of graduated steps which are defined in the concrete terms of the votes men cast for or against various proposals. It thus provides an instrument for measuring party attitudes which is both comprehensive in the amount of information it includes and refined in the number of gradations or nuances it reveals.

Even with the aid of scales it is not always possible to make comparisons between different parties on the basis of their votes on a given set of issues. In certain modern legislative bodies that have been studied by this method, it turned out that members of the two principal parties ranked the issues in different ways. As a result, scales could be constructed only for each party by itself and not for the legislature as a whole, and hence the parties could not be compared in terms of their positions on a single scale. Fortunately this difficulty does not arise for the House of Commons in the 1840s since, so far as the division lists show, almost all members of Parliament including those belonging to both the main party groups put the items in this scale in the same order, so far as they voted on them. Members of the House, though they disagreed on individual questions, agreed surprisingly well on the order in which these questions stood in relation to one another.[34] For this period, then, a single scale can be used to test attitudes on both sides of the House, and a comparison of the two parties by this means is feasible.

Table III presents the votes of "Liberals" and Conservatives in the divisions listed in Table II and, to give a more complete picture, in a number of other divisions that also fit this scale. Party votes in these eighteen divisions suggest two conclusions:

TABLE III

(Percentages only)

	"Liberals"		Conservatives	
	+	−	+	−
Opposition to Russell's Education Proposals, April 22, 1847	24	76	1	99
Chartist petition, May 3, 1842	43	57	0	100
Abolition of parliamentary oaths, March 30, 1843	56	44	0	100
Repeal of Corn Laws, May 15, 1843	71	29	0	100
Ballot, June 21, 1842	83	17	0	100
Repeal of Corn Laws, June 10, 1845	89	11	0	100
Opposition to Income Tax, April 18, 1842	96	4	1	99
Reduction of sugar duties, June 3, 1842	99	1	1	99
Cobden's motion on agricultural distress, March 13, 1845	98	2	2	98
University Reform, April 10, 1845	98	2	0	100
Motion for committee on state of Ireland, February 23, 1844	99	1	0	100
Motion for committee on temporalities of Church of Ireland, June 12, 1844	99	1	1	99
Roman Catholic Relief Bill, February 24, 1847	100	0	12	88
Repeal of Corn Laws, May 15, 1846	96	4	32	68
Motion for select committee on Navigation Laws, February 9, 1847	100	0	38	62
Health of Towns Bill, June 18, 1847	98	2	57	43
Jewish Disabilities Bill, July 17, 1845	100	0	77	23
Drainage of Lands Bill, March 31, 1843	100	0	89	11

(1) In the first place, each of the two main party groups was internally divided on a substantial number of questions. The existence of extensive disagreements within each party, which was already notorious at the time, is abundantly confirmed by

this evidence. Indeed, the cleavages in each party were more numerous than Table III indicates, for it presents only part of the total findings and many other divisions could have been included which fit this scale and which divided one party or the other. The Liberal side of the House disagreed on, among other things, public education, the Chartist petition, reduction of the national debt, legacy and probate duties on real property, the franchise, the ballot, and (in 1843–1845) the repeal of the Corn Laws. Conservatives disagreed not only on the Corn Law question in 1846 but also on prison reform, the Masters and Servants Bill of 1844, the Navigation Laws, public health, and Jewish disabilities. On only a few questions, those appearing in the middle of the scale, was there a straight party vote with a dissidence of 10 per cent or less on each side. These included most of the income tax divisions, a few free trade divisions, and two important divisions in 1844 relating to Ireland. Since the number of straight party questions was limited, the evidence, far from showing the unanimity of parties in this period, confirms the view that both parties were disunited and internally divided in regard to major questions of policy.

Furthermore—a point of some interest—these various questions divided the parties in different ways. The evidence will not support the theory that the Liberal group can be clearly separated into a moderate section and a radical tail, each of which by itself voted with a fair degree of consistency. On the contrary, breaks occur at a number of different places: the section of the Liberal group that took the "radical" line ranged, in the divisions shown, from 24 per cent to 89 per cent of the members of the "party" voting. A similar state of affairs prevailed among the Conservatives: the proportion of them who voted positive increased, in the last six divisions in the table, from 12 per cent to 89 per cent. In both parties the breaks were not concentrated at a single point but appear along a wide front, and each party was divided by its opinions not into two groups but into several.

(2) These disagreements within each party might at first seem

to suggest that the party conflict of the 1840s was not an ideological one, except perhaps in regard to the relatively small number of issues on which there was a straight party vote. If, apart from these, neither party as a whole stood for anything, it would seem difficult to argue that the two parties stood for different things. There is, however, a second feature of the evidence which indicates another conclusion.

This is that each party occupied or was principally concentrated in a different section of the ideological spectrum defined by the scale. Almost all the "Liberals" fall into the upper part of this spectrum, and almost all the Conservatives into the lower part. This can be readily observed from Table III. The eighteen divisions selected for illustration in this table fall into three groups of six each. In the first six divisions Liberals disagreed: a certain proportion of them joined the Conservatives in casting negative votes. Conservatives voted, on these first six questions, almost uniformly in the negative. On the six items in the middle of the scale, each party group was almost unanimous, Liberals voting positive and Conservatives voting negative. These were straight party questions. The last six items divided the Conservatives: on each, a certain proportion of the Conservatives joined the Liberals in voting positive. Liberals were almost unanimously positive on these last six items.[35]

It will be observed that each party was almost unanimous in twelve of the eighteen divisions listed: Liberals in the last twelve and Conservatives in the first twelve. It follows from this that it is possible, from a man's party affiliation, to infer his vote on certain questions, though not on all questions. If it is known that a man was a Liberal, it can be asserted with a relatively high degree of assurance that he voted positive, if he voted at all, on the last twelve items in Table III. If a man is known to have been a Conservative, it can be asserted with even more assurance that he cast a negative vote, if he voted, on each of the first twelve items in the table. Furthermore, not only can votes on certain questions be inferred from party, but also, by the same token, party can be inferred from votes. If a man voted positive on one or more of the first twelve divisions in Table III, he was very probably a Liberal, while a man who voted negative on one or more of the last twelve divisions in the table was almost certainly a Conservative.

Thus, though neither party was unanimous on all questions, it would be incorrect to say that, for this reason, party had no relation to vote whatsoever. On the contrary, a pattern of party voting emerges strong and clear: a graduated progression or cumulative scale, in which Liberals appear almost exclusively in the upper register and Conservatives almost exclusively in the lower. The break between parties comes at a clearly defined point on the scale, with relatively few Liberals below it and relatively few Conservatives above it. Though there were some exceptions to the pattern, the proportion of these, as can be seen from the table, is extremely small, almost insignificant.

These findings appear to provide a clear answer to the question raised at the outset of this paper: whether parties differed on issues. In terms of the scale that has been described, and the great nexus of issues that fits into it and constitutes it, the two main party groups, despite their internal disagreements, did differ substantially from each other in the range of causes that their members supported. The view that each party represented a hodge-podge of opinions and objectives not clearly distinguishable from those of the other party—that the party conflict was a sham battle unrelated to questions of policy—seems altogether excluded by this evidence. On the contrary, party lines corresponded to differences of opinion on substantive issues, and the principal lines of political cleavage were closely related to significant ideological cleavages. It appears, then, that party conflict in this period did have an ideological content to a considerably larger extent than has always been appreciated. The proof, though a little complicated, is a neat one, and it is hard to see how it can well be disputed.

Not all issues were party questions in this sense. Votes on a number of other subjects do not fit this scale and, further, show almost no statistical relation to party affiliation. Divisions on factory regulation, for example, form a separate little scale by themselves, a different ideological dimension quite unrelated to the other scale. On factory reform party voting was irregular, and neither party as a whole took a clearly defined position. Several other issues do not fit this scale and do not divide parties in the manner described. The divisions that do fit the scale, however, and were, in this sense, related to party include the majority of those analyzed, and include also the questions that appear to have been regarded by Parliament as most important, so far as their importance may be inferred from the amount of time allocated to them in debate and from the size of the divisions.

The votes of the various sub-groups on the Left in the House of Commons do not show so clear a pattern. Those arbitrarily listed as "Liberals" in Table III include, as has been explained, not only those so designated in Dod's *Parliamentary Companion* but also those described by other names such as Whig, Reformer, Radical Reformer, and Repealer, as well as a number who clearly belonged to this side of the House but to whom Dod does not assign a party label. Table IV shows how far this difference in terminology was reflected in votes. It presents the votes of all those who can unmistakably be assigned to one of these five sub-groups on each of the first six divisions in Table III. It was not necessary to show their votes in the remaining twelve divisions since, on these, the Liberal wing of Parliament was virtually united.

Table IV reveals some differentiation among these five groups, particularly on items at or near the top of the scale; on lower items, near the party break, the distinction becomes so small that it is scarcely noticeable. The five groups form a rough progression, the Whigs being the most conservative and the Radical Reformers and the Repealers, on the whole, the furthest to the

Left. The Repealers, though in organization not a part of the Whig-Liberal group, voted with it and, furthermore, with respect to the issues in this scale, generally constituted the most radical segment of it. Despite these interesting differences, however, these small sub-groups do not fall into so sharply defined a pattern as do the two larger groups. Though the ideological line separating all Liberals from all Conservatives can be drawn with great distinctness, the lines separating the various constituent groups of the Liberal wing in Parliament are less clear. By the test of votes the Liberal Party as a whole, inchoate and disorganized though it may have been, can be much more clearly delineated than can any of the sub-groups within it. This contemporary nomenclature appears to have had only limited meaning in terms of program, and the deep cleavages of opinion on the Liberal side did not correspond very closely to these labels.[36]

TABLE IV
(Percentages only)

	Repealers		Radical Reformers		Reformers		Liberals		Whigs	
	+	−	+	−	+	−	+	−	+	−
Opposition to Russell's education proposals, April 22, 1847	57	43	43	57	41	59	18	82	10	90
Chartist petition, May 3, 1842	100	0	88	12	48	52	36	64	12	88
Abolition of parliamentary oaths, March 30, 1843	0	0	71	29	50	50	55	45	50	50
Repeal of Corn Laws, May 15, 1843	68	32	96	4	79	21	64	36	61	39
Ballot, June 21, 1842	100	0	100	0	89	11	82	18	73	27
Repeal of Corn Laws, June 10, 1845	100	0	100	0	93	7	91	9	77	23

It seems scarcely possible to deny, in view of these findings, that there existed between the two main party groups in the Parliament of 1841–1847, substantial ideological differences. It might be objected, however, that these differences were, for practical purposes, not important: that the admittedly considerable range of opinion throughout the whole of Parliament did not greatly signify since the leaders on both sides, and the official party policies which they formulated and executed, tended to be moderate rather than extremist. Peel and Sir James Graham and the others who led the Conservatives stood to the left of the majority of the members of their party, while men who led the other side like Lord Palmerston and Lord John Russell were generally near the right of the Liberal group. It has been pointed out that the party leaders on each side were converted to free trade in corn at about the same time.[37] The extremists, those at the top and bottom of the scale, could be described as the intransigent backbenchers who were not in a position to determine policy. Hence, it might be argued, the objectives actually pursued by the two parties were much closer than the range of the scale indicates, and the Tweedledum-Tweedledee thesis gives a more accurate representation of what was really happening.

The best answer to this objection is that, if it is desired to offer a generalization that applies to the whole of Parliament, the rank and file as well as the party leaders, account must be taken of the full measure of difference revealed by the scale. The point is not a trivial one. A hazard in political history, which thoughtful historians have identified more than once, is that of concentrating on a few prominent individuals and disregarding or overlooking those who were less conspicuous. Further, the division lists, the principal source for this article, are particularly useful just in this respect, since they yield information not for a few men only but for almost the whole of Parliament. As a description of the whole Parliament, however, the Tweedledum-Tweedledee thesis is manifestly inadequate. Even if the leaders on each side generally held positions near the center of the ideological spectrum, this is still only part of the story. The other part is that the gamuts of opinion in each party radiated away from this central point toward opposite ends of the scale. What might be called the ideological centers of gravity in the two party-groups were some distance apart, and the majorities on each side, so far as their wishes were considered, would presumably have exerted pulls upon the leaders in opposite directions. To say that the parties touched at one point in the scale is not to say that they touched at all, and the failure to make this distinction is the misconception upon which the Tweedledum-Tweedledee thesis is based.

In conclusion, some further attention might be given to the argument summarized near the beginning of this paper that these disagreements between parties, even if their existence must be conceded, were not "important" since both parties agreed on "fundamentals" and the grounds of dispute between them were never so far-reaching as to produce a political or social revolution if one party succeeded the other in office. This claim cannot be countered by a resort to the figures, for it is an opinion or judgment and not amenable to verification. All that was attempted in the formal analysis, and all that could be attempted, was to show how parties differed on issues and what these issues were. Yet—speaking now merely in terms of opinion—it seems scarcely persuasive to argue that the party differences of the 1840s, even if they were not likely to precipitate a revolution by violence, were for that reason altogether insignificant. Even measures that appear limited in some respects may prove to have consequences that go further than was originally intended. Norman Gash has shrewdly suggested that the movement for political reform which culminated in the legislation of 1832 was more revolutionary in its implications than the details of the bill and the arguments made for it would suggest, and that the ultimate results of this legislation were more correctly appraised by the Tories who opposed it than by the Whigs who supported it.[38] More generally, the objectives represented by the issues in the scale constituted an attack on the old scheme of things which did, in the course of years, succeed in changing the class basis of politics and in profoundly altering the political structure of modern England.

Furthermore, when one considers what these issues were, the claim that they were merely trivial appears to push the argument beyond what the terms will bear upon a common-sense interpretation. Party disputes of this period, even if they did not strike at the foundations of the political order, still involved questions of some substance. Some men wanted free trade; others protection. Some wanted to extend the franchise and to adopt the secret ballot; others opposed these objectives. Some wanted to curtail the privileges of the established church; others sought to maintain them. Some attacked the special privileges of landowners; others defended them. It is not plausible to dismiss these matters as inconsequential or as factional bickering over exaggerated trifles. The fact that party disputes were related to these issues suggests that the party battle of the 1840s revolved around some of the principal political and social tensions of the age.

In this article D. C. Moore puts forward a new view of the reasons behind the repeal of the Corn Laws in 1846. One reason this discussion has been included here is to point out the variety of factors present as British society and government attempted to adapt to the new pressures of the nineteenth century. In a brilliant, and controversial, series of articles Moore has called attention to the many "conservative" elements in events which too frequently historians have viewed as automatic triumphs for new elements in society. Moore puts forward a compelling picture of nineteenth-century England in "The Other Face of Reform" Victorian Studies v *(1961); "Social Structure, Political Structure, and Public Opinion in Mid-Victorian England," in R. Robson, ed.,* Ideas and Institutions *(London, 1967); "The Sociological Premises of the First Reform Act,"* Historical Journal ix *(1966); "Political Morality in Mid-Nineteenth Century England: Concepts, Norms, Violations,"* Victorian Studies xiii *(1969), as well as in a discussion of the First Reform Act of 1832 between him and E. P. Hennock in* Victorian Studies xiv *(1971).*

D. C. Moore teaches English history at the University of California at Los Angeles. The article published here, which has had one slight revision, was originally published in The Economic History Review *2nd ser., xviii (1965), 544–560, and is republished by permission of the author and the editors of the journal.*

D. C. MOORE

The Corn Laws and High Farming

IN POLEMICAL TERMS the repeal of the Corn Laws was by far the most important element in that legislative package which Sir Robert Peel presented to the House of Commons on the evening of 27 January 1846. But if the other elements in the package are ignored—in effect, if polemical importance is allowed to become the sole measure of significance—the meaning of repeal to the men who drafted the Corn Importation Bill tends to be distorted. It becomes confused with the meaning of repeal to those other men who did so much to project the Corn Laws to the forefront of British politics. Almost inevitably, such a procedure obscures the variety of factors which made it essential that a solution to the Corn Law question be found. Almost inevitably, it also obscures the fundamental distinction between those factors on the one hand which made a solution essential and those on the other which, by making a solution possible, defined its nature.

In large part the need to do something about the Corn Laws derived from their growing polemical importance. In the context of such new types of social movement as Chartism, which focused attention on class unity and the lines of division between classes, the Corn Laws served to reinforce the status of the existing elites of both town and countryside by reemphasizing the notion that the prosperity of the various classes which composed the same interest group was primarily affected not by one another but by a rival interest group. However, the Corn Laws only served to strengthen the traditional units of British society up to that point at which the dangers inherent in interest group rivalry did not exceed the benefits inherent in interest group cohesion. By 1846 many men believed such a point had been reached. As a rule, however, they accepted at face value the arguments which have served so well to enhance the cohesion of the urban and rural interest groups. In consequence they helped to create the impression that the nature of Corn Law repeal is to be explained in terms of the major reason it became essential—that the Corn Laws were repealed not only to prevent interest group rivalry from degenerating into violence but also to register the victory of the urban interest group over the rural.[1] In effect, they assumed that the Corn Laws were really that boon to the landed interest which interest group polemics required them to be. By the forties, however, the economic value of the Corn Laws to the landed interest was no longer so clear.

The Corn Laws were predicated on the notion that rural prosperity could be had only on the basis of high arable prices. It was this which lay behind the Act of 1815 which forbade the importation of foreign grain until the domestic price reached a fairly high level. As attempts to support prices, however, both the Act of 1815 and the subsequent sliding-scale measures of 1828 and 1842 were dismal failures. In spite of the fact that importations remained marginal, prices rarely touched the levels these measures projected. The impact of protection was fairly well canceled out by deflation and rising production. In both town and countryside, however, many people continued to assume either that the Corn Laws really had the effects upon price which their authors intended, or at least that they served in significant fashion to prevent further reductions of price. While every Corn Law polemicist considered the relations between price and supply, the Corn Laws themselves tended to provide their arguments with an international focus. Thus only a few of them considered the question whether those domestic producers who complained of low prices and who looked to the Corn Laws as their major defense were really being threatened by the foreign producers whose costs were consistently lower or by other domestic producers whose efficiencies were increasingly higher. Instead, they confined themselves to the question whether the Corn Laws were justified.

In the countryside the answer to this question was generally "yes." In the towns it was generally "no." Because, like Adam Smith and David Ricardo, protectionist and free trader assumed that townsmen and countrymen could not both be prosperous at the same time—that the one could only be prosperous at the expense of the other—it was a matter of common doctrine that agricultural protection was a means of enhancing rural prosperity at the expense of the urban consumer. By the same token the repeal of the Corn Laws was looked to as a means of reducing the prices paid by the urban consumer at the expense of the landed interest. Especially in the towns where industrialization was progressing rapidly and population growing apace the Corn Laws were increasingly regarded as a device by which the "anti-progressive" elements in British society—in polemical terms the landed interest —still managed to inhibit the growth and exploit the wealth of the "progressive" elements—in polemical terms the urban interest.

Aware of the accelerating industrial development which followed Corn Law repeal, most historians have been repeating this argument ever since. In consequence, Corn Law repeal is still considered a case of political surrender on the part of the landed interest to the pressures of their urban rivals. It was this meaning which repeal acquired from such men as George Wilson and Archibald Prentice on the one hand, from the Duke of Buckingham and Lord George Bentinck on the other.

One way of restoring the meaning which repeal had for the men who drafted the Corn Importation Bill is to restore the proposal itself to its legislative context. If this be done, Corn Law repeal ceases to be that symbol of political surrender which has always made its association with Peel somewhat anomalous. Instead, it becomes a symbol of social and economic adaptation. In the same speech in which Peel outlined his plans for Corn Law repeal he also outlined his plans for the drainage loan and for a number of other measures designed to encourage those agriculturists who had not done so to refocus their hopes of prosperity upon high production instead of high prices.

Peel's speech reflects two concerns, only one of which has been adequately noted. While trying to remove a point of violent social contention he was also trying to convince a large group of British agriculturists that their own economic as well as political interests would best be served if they were to emulate those of their neighbors who were managing to make comfortable profits while they themselves were crying depression. In effect, while the Anti-Corn Law League helped to make repeal essential by raising the tensions between the urban and landed interests to a point of imminent explosion it was the progress of agricultural technology which made repeal possible. But to a large extent this progress also contributed to the need for repeal. With their hopes still focused on high prices, many agriculturists were doing little or nothing to adapt themselves to the low prices of which they complained and which in large measure are attributable to their neighbors' increasing efficiencies.

Simple inertia was an element in these men's behavior. But other elements having to do with the structure of rural society were more important. In effect, the crucial aspect of the Corn Law crisis—that which lent cogency to the polemical arguments on both sides—had to do with the problems of adapting rural society to the exigencies of high farming.

II

High farming was a development of the post-Napoleonic period when the collapse of agricultural prices created serious rural problems. To this price collapse there were two major types of re-action. Occasionally both types are evident in the behavior of the same individual. But for analytical purposes they should be care-fully distinguished. The one was primarily political. The other was primarily economic.

Asserting that agricultural depression was national in scope and legislative in origin many farmers and landowners demanded one or another national solution which only Parliament could provide. Some of these men sought to restore rural prosperity by restoring prices to wartime levels. As a rule their panacea was cur-rency reform. Others sought to achieve the same goal by re-ducing the fiscal burdens of the landed interest. As a rule their panacea was malt tax repeal. But there were other agriculturists who, while sometimes joining in these political activities, espe-cially in the initial postwar period, took far more effective action by draining their estates of surface water and by stimulating their productivity with larger and larger doses of fertilizer. Coinci-dentally perhaps, but no less fortunately, in their attempts to in-crease their supplies of fertilizer many of these latter enlarged their flocks and herds, thus adapting themselves to the shift in demand from arable to pastoral and dairy products.

During the wars when high prices, high rents, and inflation had helped to pay the cost many agriculturists had been happy to in-vest in land purchase, land enclosure, and even land improvement. Writing in 1826, Sir James Graham estimated that 90 per cent of British landowners had increased their debts during the wars either by mortgaging one estate to buy another or by mortgaging an estate to raise money for land improvement.[2] With the end of the wars and the restoration of the metallic currency which spelled deflation, the flow of capital into land improvement de-creased sharply. Thereafter, for more than a decade, the public image of the landed interest was drawn from those men who ceased to invest and cried depression. But not all landowners and farmers had given up trying to get more out of the land by put-ting more into it.

That little was heard of these others in the twenties was probably due as much to their lack of organization in England as to the strength of the residual hope—in which of course they shared —that cash flow in the countryside might be restored to wartime levels. Somewhat paradoxically, their emergence in the thirties was an indirect consequence of the organization of the Central Agricultural Association, a body whose members were committed to the proposition that they did not exist. But in trying to prove their case these men did just the opposite. They encouraged the government to appoint the select Committee on Agriculture of 1836 at which many high farmers explained how they themselves were prosperous while many of their neighbors were not.

The ideological position of the Central Association is indicated by the resolution adopted by all but unanimous vote, that rural prosperity could only be restored "[by] some measure which will either raise the price of produce to the level of the burdens imposed, or bring down the burdens to the level of the present prices." [3] Many of the witnesses who appeared before the committee argued from this position. Others, however, especially from Scotland, took the opportunity to explain in detail that there were no real problems in the countryside except on the undrained clays and among those men who still farmed as their fathers and grandfathers had farmed. These men made out the case, later reiterated by Charles Shaw Lefevre in his pamphlet, *Remarks on the Present State of Agriculture*,[4] that whatever depression existed in the countryside was due to the lack of capital invested in the land and the lack of skill of the farmer. Lefevre was chairman of the committee. His pamphlet consists of the draft report which he submitted to the committee but on which they could not agree. In the end their decision not to adopt a report but merely to report their evidence was probably due far less to the difficulties of distilling a single conclusion from the conflicting evidence than to the high farmers' reluctance to pour salt into their neighbors' various wounds.[5]

III

Obviously, some agriculturists had little to complain of. By means of drainage, fertilizers, and new rotations they were so increasing their yields and reducing their costs that they could still make a profit at prices far below those which drove their neighbors to despair.[6] Indeed, because the postwar depression in agriculture was a price depression, and one which mainly affected arable prices, their own increased yields tended to prevent that rise of arable prices to which many other agriculturists looked as the only source of renewed prosperity. However, their prosperity raised a number of complex sociological, ideological, and legal problems. It suggested a means of restoring the general prosperity of landlord and farmer without the tensions between the urban and landed interests inherent in the Corn Laws. But since these tensions had much to do with the cohesion of the various interest groups—and thus with the status of their spokesmen—prospects of reducing them were not always enthusiastically received. Furthermore, their prosperity was usually predicated upon radical and expensive innovations which, for reasons having to do with the traditional structure of rural society and with the land laws, many of their neighbors could ill afford.

In these circumstances a number of agricultural politicians tried to explain the high farmers' prosperity in other terms.[7] In 1838 the high farmers faced considerable opposition when they met to form the English Agricultural Society (later the Royal Agricultural Society of England) as a nonpolitical body patterned after the Highland and Agricultural Society of Scotland. The English Society was precluded by its constitution from discussing any question which might arise in Parliament. It was conceived solely as a means of improving agricultural technology and of propagating the attitude reflected in its motto, "Practice with Science." In consequence, it incurred the deep suspicions of many agricultural politicians, especially those associated with the Central Association. A number of the prestigious members of the Central Association joined the English Society. But the orientations of the two groups were diametrically opposed. This was clearly indicated at the inaugural meeting of the English Society when several men identified with the Central Association moved that such a nonpolitical body was "delusive in principle." When their motion was ruled out of order the secretary of the Central Association together with a number of his associates got up and walked out.[8]

Four years later, in vastly more dramatic circumstances and with vastly greater clarity, the issues implicitly raised at this meeting were raised again when Peel proposed to reduce the levels of agricultural protection and, at the same time, urged domestic agriculturists to increase their production.[9] The following autumn, at the meetings of several local agricultural societies, various men who, like Peel, were high farmers and politicians both, faced up to the issue squarely. At Yeovil the incoming chairman of the local agricultural society declared that now, with reduced protection, agriculturists should "look to that which could not slip through their hands, to the increased productiveness of the soil, which was only to be effected by improved husbandry, by calling in the aid of chemistry, and by using the most portable, best, and cheapest manure." [10] Free traders exulted in such remarks. But the defenders of traditional rural society were aghast. With the functional relationship thus clarified between the Corn Laws and high farming they dug in for what proved to be their last stand. Their two major polemical weapons were appropriate to the position they hoped to defend, first, that high farming could never be a substitute for high prices, and second, that high farming could not be widely adopted except by subverting the traditional structure of rural society.

On one level the former argument provided a reasonable way of coming to grips with the relationship between costs and prices.

More importantly, however, it provided an ideological refuge for the many men who had contempt for novelties of every sort. Meeting in 1834 under the chairmanship of the Duke of Buckingham—his son the Marquis of Chandos, the so-called Farmer's Friend, had been present—the members of the Royal Buckinghamshire Agricultural Association had loudly applauded a passage in a song which proclaimed,

> New fangled nonsense an't the thing
> To gull the British farmer.[11]

Relative simplicity was almost all that distinguished such a statement from those made by Robert Baker, the man generally credited with organizing the Central Agricultural Protection Association, often called the Anti-League, in 1844. At a meeting also in 1844 Baker implictly rejected the notion that high farming might be a source of agricultural prosperity when he declared that such prosperity could only be restored by reforming the currency or by reducing the taxes which bore on the landed interest.[12] Indeed, while high farmers argued that they could still make profits at prices far below those then obtaining, Baker and his associates were committed to the proposition that high prices were the essential prerequisite to high farming. In February 1845, at the first anniversary dinner of the Anti-League—the "Farmer's Friend," now Duke of Buckingham, vice-president—a speaker declared, "The cry on the one side is 'Cultivate, cultivate.' My answer, in the name of the tenant farmers of England is, 'Remunerate, remunerate.'" His statement was greeted with "immense cheers." [13]

But the latter argument went to the heart of the matter. In 1843 Earl Stanhope described as an "error" the point of view he associated with the Royal Agricultural Society, that drainage and high farming would restore the prosperity of the countryside. But the "error" he had in mind had nothing to do with technology. It had to do with the social implications of the question how the necessary capital could be made available. In trying to refute the high farmers' contention Stanhope merely asked, where could the money be found? [14] The previous year James Johnston, the author of a number of high-farming manuals, had dealt with the same question somewhat more fully in *Blackwood's Edinburgh Magazine*. He estimated that with proper drainage the production of wheat on some 20 million acres might be increased by as much as a quarter. He granted that such increased production would create a large exportable surplus. But, he added, the social costs of mobilizing the necessary capital would be too great to bear. He looked to the gradual spread of high farming. At the same time he urged that those pressures be held in check which might accelerate the process. Otherwise, he explained, thousands of landowners would be forced to sell or mortgage parts of their estates to pay for improvements to the remainders.[15] As he clearly implied, the principal question at issue had to do with the efforts of many landowners to build up and perpetuate estates which were in the nature of small kingdoms. In terms of the increasing amounts of working capital per acre which the high farmers were declaring to be necessary, many of these estates were already much too large. Furthermore, many of them were administered not as commercial entities but as sources and agencies of individual and family status.

According to the high farmers the restoration of rural prosperity depended upon the common willingness of landlord and tenant to adopt new procedures and to invest capital in the soil. But with prices depressed one of the primary sources of capital as well as motives for investment was lacking which had been so effective during the war years. Furthermore, in a great many cases the investments recommended by the high farmers not only implied a complete reversal of the traditional attitudes towards land; they were also effectively precluded by the customs of rural society and the laws by which these customs were reinforced.

The capital which high farming required of the landlord was potentially available from any of three sources, his personal property, the current income of the estate, or a mortgage of the estate. However, with prices depressed many rent rolls declined sharply. Furthermore, what with the widespread skepticism as to the economic value of land improvement, such prices tended to deter many landowners from allowing whatever personal wealth they possessed to tarnish on the land. Then again, on settled estates, improvement mortgages were effectively prohibited until the value of land improvement was recognized. To those who denied the value of such improvement such mortgages were simply means of weakening the economic basis of the family by burdening the estate for no good reason. Since the primary function of the land law was to protect the reversioner against the possibility that his estate would be wasted by tenants for life or tenants in tail, strong legal impediments remained against the negotiation of improvement mortgages until the question was settled that high farming was worth the cost. An owner in fee might mortgage as he wished. In 1847, however, it was estimated that two-thirds of English land was controlled by testamentary settlements.[16] On these estates the tenant for life had no powers to negotiate an improvement mortgage unless such powers were specifically granted in the settlement under which he held—and this was evidently rare—or unless he obtained such powers by private Act of Parliament or, after 1833, from the Court of Chancery.[17] While proceedings in Chancery were somewhat less expensive than proceedings by private Act their expense remained a major impediment to the spread of high farming.

Nor was it easy to start the flow of capital which high farming required of the agricultural tenant. Few existing farmers had the necessary capital or the necessary experimental orientation. In the light of this Lord Kinnaird later suggested that they be replaced by men from the towns who were endowed with capital and who were not afraid to use it, "knowing," as he explained, "that thus alone can their land be made productive." [18] James Caird's cure was not quite as drastic as Kinnaird's. But his diagnosis was similar, and the end result would have been the same. When he emphasized the therapeutic value of high rents—farmers with low rents lacked adequate incentive [19]—he too was urging a revolution in rural society. It was this which W. E. Aytoun, writing in *Blackwood's Edinburgh Magazine*, held against them both.[20]

IV

The crux of the rural problem lay in the dialectical opposition between those customs and policies on the one hand which served to reinforce the hierarchical structure of rural society and the cohesion of the rural interest group, and, on the other hand, the exigencies of agricultural prosperity in an era of high farming. Throughout much of the century the English land system was regarded by many as a social and political good. Yet in a period of increasingly rapid capital accumulation, when agricultural prosperity was coming to depend upon expensive land improvement, this land system came to have serious disadvantages for those on whose behalf it had evolved. As long as capital accumulation progressed relatively slowly the land system tended to prevent the dilution of landed capital while encouraging the purchase of land by would-be *arrivistes*. But as capital accumulation became increasingly rapid, and as more *nouveaux riches* sought to obscure their origins through the purchase of landed property, the customs and privileges associated with landownership became a brake upon the ability of the older landed classes to retain their preeminence.

Because of the intimate association between the land system and the political powers of the landed classes, many Radicals hoped to abolish the peculiar legal privileges which served to reinforce the customs of rural society. For analogous reasons many landowners were violently opposed to any tamperings at all with the land laws. Yet there were other landowners—especially those whose appetites had been whetted by the high farmers' menu—who were, if anything, even more interested in land law reform than the Radicals. Their motives, however, were far different. While the Radicals sought to destroy the elevated position of the landed classes in society and State, the others sought to perpetuate it. Towards this end they sought to transform agriculture into a capitalistic activity—at least as it concerned the landowner's ability to borrow money for purposes of land improvement. By and large, however, they were opposed to any similar commercialization of the status of the agricultural tenant. Obviously—the point is crucial—they believed it possible to increase the productivity of the countryside without disturbing the hierarchical structure of rural society, and without affecting the role of the landed classes within the State. Their efforts at land law reform were clearly premised on the assumption that the landed classes could only retain their preeminence in British society if they were willing and able to exploit the new agricultural techniques.

In 1845 the close relationship between high farming and land law reform was reflected in the proceedings and report of the so-called Richmond Committee, the Select Committee of the House of Lords appointed to inquire into the expediency of a legislative enactment being introduced to enable possessors of entailed estates to charge such estates with a sum, to be limited, for the purpose of draining and otherwise improving the same." The star witness before the committee, perhaps even its guiding light, was Josiah Parkes, a man who combined the roles of private drainage contractor, consulting engineer for the Royal Agricultural Society, surveyor for the West of England and South Wales Land Drainage Company, and adviser to several of the other witnesses.[21] Parkes's testimony, and that of most of the other witnesses, was focused on two main points: the profits which landowners might anticipate from high farming, and the impossibility of limited owners ever enjoying these profits unless they could mortgage their estates for productive purposes. However, the ramifications of the latter point went beyond the problems of the prospective borrower to those of the prospective lender. Chartered both to lend money for land drainage and to perform drainage work itself, the West of England and South Wales Land Drainage Company had found it could neither raise the money for the one function nor perform the other because of the "want of power on the part of proprietors of entailed estates to give security on the estates for the money advanced and laid out in draining and other permanent improvements." [22] Unfortunately for the Company many of the men who wished to improve their estates held under settlements which did not allow them to mortgage their estates for that purpose.

No one appeared before the Committee who was not on Parkes's side. Yet much of the testimony was directed at points they might have raised, that high farming was particularly foolish with the prospect of further price reductions, that it was far better to invest in land purchase than land improvement. The possibility of Corn Law repeal and a subsequent drop in the domestic price level was obviously in Parkes's mind when he explained, ". . . If rents have a tendency to fall the drainage of an estate which is water-logged may keep them up to what they are now, and even increase them." [23] Applying Parkes's logic to the problem of the status of the landed classes the Committee reported, ". . . The operation of draining, properly conducted, not only tends by its immediate effect to increase the produce of the soil and to facilitate its cultivation, but also permanently enhances the value of the inheritance to all future proprietors." [24] But many men denied this completely. Some years later Aytoun declared in *Blackwood's*, ". . . If high farming could be shown to be productive, high farming would be the rule and not the exception." [25] According to these men, if limited owners were gulled by extravagant hopes, and if they were allowed to burden their estates for purposes of land improvement, their families might be wiped out. But the Committee were not totally blind to such possibilities. They did not wish to free the limited owners from all restraint. It was important, they insisted, "for the security of property, that much caution . . . be exercised in the application of any powers which may be given for placing a charge upon the inheritance at the instance of persons having only a limited interest in the estate. . . ." [26] They merely recommended that steps be taken to make it cheaper and easier for limited owners to obtain such powers where they were already available, in Chancery.

V

Peel's "general scheme"—such he described it [27]—should be considered within the context of these problems. Himself a charter member of the English Agricultural Society, he obviously realized that while many agriculturists were still complaining of depressed prices others were not only exulting in their high yields but proclaiming to the world that because of their heavy investments, especially in drainage and fertilizer, because of their emphasis upon pastoral and dairy farming, and because of their new rotations, they could sell wheat at a profit at almost half the going price. In proposing to repeal the Corn Laws, Peel was trying to spike the guns of the Anti-Corn Law League. At the same time he was trying to encourage the adoption of high farming techniques by those agriculturists who either still resisted the blandishments of science or could not afford to hear them. In his appeal to these men Peel used both the carrot and the stick. Yet because the stick was the same shape as the bludgeon with which the Leaguers hoped to beat their rural opponents, the existence of the carrots has been almost totally ignored and the purpose of the stick seriously distorted.

In his "general scheme" Peel made a clear distinction between the repeal of the Corn Laws, which was not to take effect entirely for three years, and those other provisions which were to come into effect immediately. These included an immediate and sharp reduction in the duties on grass and clover seeds. As he explained to the House, since clover seed was produced in only a very few British counties, and since it was required "where agriculture is most advanced," the reduction in these duties should not be considered a "removal of protection, but a benefit to agriculture." [28] Then, maize and buckwheat, which were coming into wide use as fatteners for cattle, were to be admitted at a nominal duty immediately. Again drawing upon his knowledge of high farming he reminded his listeners, ". . . There is nothing more important than the fattening of cattle to an improved system of agriculture because no other fertilizer is as good as manure." [29] The same reasoning lay behind his proposal that the duties on linseed cake and rape cake be reduced at once.[30] He also proposed several ways by which the burden of rates might be reduced, particularly in the countryside. One of these involved reforms of the highway administration.[31] Another, more important, involved reforms of the Poor Law administration. He proposed to amend the law of settlement so that men born in the countryside but employed in a town could not be returned so easily to their parishes of birth when depression hit the towns.[32] The purpose here was to prevent the Poor Law authorities in the towns from throwing the economic burden of urban unemployment upon the taxpayers in the countryside. But most important of all was the drainage loan.[33]

The drainage loan was not calculated to provide the total capital necessary for land drainage. The amount of the loan was far too small for that. While Peel mentioned no figure in January, the initial sum later set aside under the Public Money Drainage Act, introduced in May and finally passed in August, was a mere two million pounds. During the previous few years the costs of land drainage had been radically reduced.[34] But even at the reduced costs two million pounds would only have drained a small fraction of the land which the high farmers said required it. In effect the loan was primarily a psychological measure designed to popularize high farming by facilitating the prerequisite land drainage on exactly those estates on which, as the Richmond Committee had reported the previous year, there was a "natural reluctance of proprietors to expend capital upon the permanent improvement of land." [35] These were the settled estates.

Since the existing inhibitions to land improvement on these estates were partly legal the loan contained an *ad hoc* reform of the land laws. As Peel explained, two of the major purposes of the loan were to obviate the expense and remove the uncertainty of procedures in Chancery, where, under existing requirements, tenants for life of settled estates usually had to appeal for the powers necessary to charge their estates with the costs of improvement. He proposed that unless an objection were filed by someone who had an interest in the estate the tenant for life should be able to obtain the powers necessary to borrow from these funds and to make the repayment a prior charge upon the estate by simple administrative means. Authority to approve applications for funds and to make the repayment a prior charge upon the land was to be given to the recently established Enclosure Commissioners. As far as concerned a loan from the public funds recourse to Chancery would only be necessary in the event of an objection.[36]

The essential relationship which Peel conceived between Corn Law repeal and the drainage loan is apparent from two of his observations. First, he expected that only a few objections would be made to charging an entailed estate with the costs of its own improvement. As he explained, even though repayment of the loan would be the first charge upon the estate—this priority being required by the need to obviate any loss to the Treasury—and even without protection, the improvement of the estate would be a guarantee of all other charges.[37] Secondly, while he looked to the loan itself for many improvements, he also anticipated that the spirit of improvement would be strengthened when the effects of these initial improvements were seen.[38] Juxtaposed with Corn Law repeal the drainage loan was an obvious attempt to rouse a large portion of the agricultural community from their fears and lethargy. Clearly Peel was addressing the many men who, either directly or indirectly, still stood out against high farming when he acknowledged the widespread fears of foreign competition and added that with "the application of capital, skill, and industry" this competition could be beaten.[39] Implicitly, Lord George Bentinck acknowledged the same relationship between the two measures when he appeared at the last effective meeting of the Anti-League in May. Beaten politically the previous week when he led the protectionists' last stand in the House of Commons, he now acknowledged the economic and ideological corollary of that defeat: he explained that the only salvation for English agriculture lay in the application of capital and science.[40]

VI

Recently, Mr. O. R. McGregor and Professor David Spring have each called attention to Peel's drainage loan. But neither has recognized the true nature of either the loan or the relationship between the loan and the repeal of the Corn Laws. In part this may be due to the fact that neither Mr. McGregor nor Professor Spring seems to realize that the loan was outlined in the same speech in which Peel outlined his plans for repeal. In part it may be due to the fact that neither seems to be aware of the intensity of opposition to high farming. Professor Spring's assertion is somewhat misleading, that "The Public Money Drainage Act first came before the House of Commons at the end of May, 1846 . . . ," especially since he follows this assertion with the observation that "the immediate background of the Act remains obscure," and since he fails to note that the main provisions of the loan had already been sketched in January.[41] In his discussion of the Enclosure Commissioners, Professor Spring has redeemed the loan from the obscurity into which it had been allowed to fall by previous historians who focused their attention solely on the Corn Laws. But he has followed them in refusing to recognize any essential relationship between the two measures. "The improvement party," he explains, "of which Peel was a notable member, had for some years been moving towards a scheme such as that embodied in the [Public Money Drainage] Act." Repeal merely provided a "welcome opportunity for the improvement party to fashion legislation on a subject which had deeply interested them for some time." [42]

The problems of chronology and of the opposition to high farming are also apparent in Mr. McGregor's description of the loan as "a *quid pro quo* for the landed interest after the repeal of the Corn Laws." [43] While he comes closer to the truth of the matter because he recognizes the close relationship between the loan and repeal he tends to distort the nature of this relationship and to beg the question of the costs of land drainage. The size of the loan suggests it was scarcely a *quid pro quo*. Furthermore, such a description makes to allowance for the crucial fact that many English landowners still required considerable time to reorient themselves to the exigencies of high farming. In all probability the three years Peel offered them would scarcely have been enough. The earliest applications for funds under the drainage loan came largely from Scotland where the assumptions of high farming were already well established.[44] Only gradually did English landowners learn the ways of their northern neighbors. By the middle fifties, however, when the funds provided by a second public loan, similar to the first, had been exhausted, a number of private companies were chartered to provide additional funds to meet the then mounting English demand.

Like the drainage loan, the Acts chartering these companies contained *ad hoc* reforms of the land law. Furthermore, all but one of them assigned to the Enclosure Commissioners the same two functions of approving the loan and making the repayment a prior charge upon the estate which had been assigned to them under the Drainage Acts. Because the rent charges the Commissioners imposed took precedence over all existing charges even when the need to guarantee the Treasury against loss did not provide the rationale for such an arrangement, the Commissioners' services were often appealed to by owners in fee whose estates were already mortgaged but who wished to obtain additional funds for land improvement. The money on loans the Commissioners approved was available at a far lower rate than it would have been otherwise. That the owners of previous rent charges did not as a rule object to this procedure was a measure of the growing confidence in high farming. One of the Commissioners used the same argument Peel had used earlier when he explained that before approving a loan the Commissioners always assured themselves "that the land [would] be improved to an extent exceeding the amount of the charge created." [45] Thus, he continued, a landowner could "get money very much cheaper [by dealing through them than he could otherwise], even assuming he could borrow at all, which of course a tenant for life could not. . . ." [46]

VII

In practical terms it was the agricultural tenant who paid the immediate costs of land improvement. Improving the land "to an extent exceeding the amount of the charge created" simply meant raising the rent by an amount exceeding the sum of interest and principal. As the agent of one of the lending companies explained, in most cases the increase in the rental value of an estate was almost double the amount of the rent charge which his company received in respect of the interest and principal on its loan. [47]

Initially, many farmers were obviously willing to shoulder the economic burden. As the same agent explained, "If one man objected at all to the charge for the improvement, other competitors would appear, and the highest bidder would take the lands and pay the interest for proper improvements." [48] But as time went on the point was finally reached at which many farmers were no longer willing to pay for these improvements without greater compensation. The point was also reached at which many farmers were no longer willing to increase their capital commitments in the exploitation of their farms without a positive guarantee that the ownership of this capital would remain in their own hands. In effect, it proved to be impossible to do what the men who drafted the Corn Importation Bill and the drainage loan tried to do, commercialize the status of the landlord without also commercializing the status of the tenant.

From the present perspective it is obvious that the drainage loan was a step in each of three complementary processes, two of which culminated in the Settled Land Act of 1882, the third of which culminated in the Agricultural Holdings Act of 1883. By the measure of 1882 the individual tenant for life of a settled estate became an almost totally free agent for the purposes of administering his estate while the estate itself was redefined from a unit of land to a unit of value. The tenant for life was empowered on his own authority to sell off portions of the land either to pay for improvements to the remainder or to obtain the capital which he might invest in certain specified securities. Settlement was finally shifted "from the land to the purchase money." [49] According to the Agricultural Holdings Act of the following year the agricultural tenant could no longer contract himself out of the right of ownership which he had acquired to his farm. Thereafter, in most instances, his landlord was legally obligated to compensate him for his improvements at such time as he quitted his farm.

But the men who passed the Drainage Acts or administered them had not tried to create a landless landed gentry [50] or a class of agricultural tenants with legally defined rights in their farms. They were not interested in Joseph Hume's suggestion, in 1847, that instead of voting additional public funds which landowners might borrow for land improvement Parliament should allow these landowners to sell off portions of their estates to raise the money necessary for improving the remainders.[51] They were mainly concerned to obviate the need for such sales in Britain if not in Ireland. Indeed, in the middle fifties the possibility that debts might be incurred which ultimately would force the breakup of British estates prompted one of the Enclosure Commissioners to criticize the provisions of one drainage company's charter according to which a man with a limited interest in an estate could, under certain circumstances, mortgage the estate without the Commissioners' approval, "and in fact without any control at all." [52] While the Commissioner may have been speaking as a jealous bureaucrat the question of his bureaucratic authority was only raised in the context of his concern for the reversioner's interest.

As to the creation of a class of agricultural tenants with legally defined rights in their farms, many of the men who voted for the drainage loan voted against tenant right when the question was first broached in the forties. The emergence of the question is important for what it reveals of both the social implications of high farming and the tensions in the countryside which high farming stimulated. Based on the long-recognized right of the agricultural tenant to harvest the crop he had planted, tenant-right agreements were means of bypassing the law according to which any investment a tenant made in his farm automatically became his landlord's property. In law this rule was not breached at all until 1850 and not basically altered until 1875. Much earlier, however, in certain areas of the kingdom, tenant capital had been mobilized for high farming by means of private agreements by which landlords promised to compensate their tenants for the unexhausted value of their improvements at such times as they quitted their farms. To those who believed in high farming the value of such agreements was obvious. Until fairly late in the century, however, certain legal difficulties surrounded them: no such agreement negotiated by a tenant for life was considered legally binding upon the tenant in tail which was not supported by local custom.[53] To alter the law or enlarge the scope of custom were both difficult because they diminished the landlord's rights of owernship of his property, and because they were a means of placing landlord and tenant upon a basis of contractual equality. In these circumstances, the Bills introduced by Lord Potman and Philip Pusey—it is significant that both men were prominent members of the Royal Agricultural Society, both devoted to the job of encouraging agricultural improvement—were voted down by Peel and many of the others who voted for the drainage loans. Evidently, Portman and Pusey understood the social implications of high farming in a way the others did not. These kept repeating the argument that tenant right would destroy the "happy relationship" between landlord and tenant—in effect, that it would destroy the cohesion of the rural interest group. While they hoped to secure the economic well-being of the landed classes they failed to recognize the impossibility of commercializing the status of the landlord without also commercializing the status of the tenant. Some even claimed that Portman's and Pusey's Bills, because they required the landlord to give his written consent to his tenant's improvements, would put an end to land improvement on the part of the tenant. Almost inevitably, where a compensation agreement obtained, it was necessary to call in a referee to determine the value of the unexhausted improvements which the tenant had made on his farm. The importance of the structural problem is reflected in the statement that no landlord would agree in writing to compensate his tenant if by doing so he were to place himself in a position in which his relations with his tenant became a matter which others might judge.[54]

VIII

Ever since the Corn Laws were repealed men have cited their repeal as evidence of the increasing susceptibility of Parliament to

the pressures of extraparliamentary organizations. Recently, however, Dr. McCord cast some doubt on the validity of this procedure.[55] Miss Kemp cast even more by emphasizing how repeal
was "the work of Parliament, not of the people" and by citing
Peel's decision to resign rather than dissolve Parliament following
his defeat on the Irish Coercion Bill. As she explains, "Peel was determined that the decision [to repeal the Corn Laws] should be a
parliamentary one. Parliament, he believed, was sovereign and
should decide this as all other questions of policy that arose; the
people's function, at general elections, was to choose a House of
Commons, not to decide on policy nor to designate a Government." [56] But while demonstrating the unwonted longevity of pre-
Reform concepts of political management—Peel's view of the
functions of Parliament and the functions of the people is, she
notes, "usually labelled a pre-1832 view" [57]—she perpetuates the
notion that in social terms Corn Law repeal was a clear victory
for the urban interest over their landed rivals.[58]

Such an interpretation of repeal is consistent with the main
body of nineteenth- and twentieth-century social theory according to which major legislative enactments tend to be considered
primarily within the context of the declared needs of new social
classes. Whether this theory is a useful device for the study of
long-term movements is not here at issue. What is at issue is the
usefulness of this theory for the understanding of a specific political phenomenon. In all probability it was this theory which obscured the complexities of Peel's "general scheme." As a rule,
Corn Law repeal has been considered in terms of the Ricardian
arguments that urban prosperity could only be had at the cost of
declining rent and subsequent landlord depression. But these arguments have no relevance to Peel's "general scheme." As Peel
conceived it, Corn Law repeal was not a means of solving the economic problems of the towns by reducing food prices. He sought
to extricate the kingdom from the social dilemmas reflected in
Malthusian and Ricardian economies by implementing a policy

based on the concept of growth. Corn Law repeal was not a means of redistributing a limited fund of wealth along the lines which the Corn Law repealers had been demanding. It was a means of increasing this fund by removing the psychological and legal impediments to productive investment.

By dwelling on the polemical arguments of the period, and by ignoring the legislative context of repeal, historians have implied that Corn Law repeal was a conscious step in that long process by which the rural aristocracy and gentry were finally displaced by the "rising middle classes." To account for the anomalous role which such an interpretation assigns to Peel they have generally stressed the threat of revolution or the growing importance of the industrial sectors of the Britis economy *vis-à-vis* the rural. They have implied either that Peel was finally convinced by the Leaguers' arguments or frightened by their organization. However, from the evidence of his "general scheme" it is clear that if the timing of repeal was affected by the threat which the League represented, the manner of repeal was not at all affected by their arguments. The Corn Laws were not repealed as a means of replacing one social group by another. Rather, they were repealed as a means of perpetuating the status of the landed classes in new technological conditions.

In the first half of the nineteenth century, Parliament had to face problems arising from industrialization. It has been commonly assumed that Conservatives were willing to cope with social abuses as part of their political philosophy. The industrialists in turn, it had been thought, were attacking the agricultural interests of landed class. In his article David Roberts demonstrates that this assumed quid pro quo *is too simple a picture; political attitudes in fact were more complex particularly on the Tory side, and were more closely tied to traditions of local government. He has further explored the workings of government in his important book,* The Victorian Origins of the British Welfare State *(New Haven, 1960). The present article was originally published in* The American Historical Review LXIII *(1958), 323–337, and is reprinted by permission of the author. David Roberts teaches modern British history at Dartmouth College.*

DAVID ROBERTS

Tory Paternalism and Social Reform in Early Victorian England

UCH HAS BEEN written about the theories and principles of Tory paternalism in England, but little has been said about its practice. Samuel Taylor Coleridge in his later writings gave eloquent and profound expression to its principles; Robert Southey in his *Colloquies on the Progress of Society* espoused them with warmth and imagination. In 1838 William Gladstone, still a very earnest Tory, reaffirmed the ecclasiastical ideals of Coleridge in his famous discussion of *The State in Its Relations with the Church*. Twelve years later Thomas Carlyle declared war against liberalism by writing his *Latter Day Pamphlets*, in which he fulminated against those who worship mammon. Benjamin Disraeli in his novels *Sybil* and *Coningsby* dressed Tory paternalism in a gallant and chivalrous costume and taught more than one generation to admire its lofty sentiments.

The ideas of these writers, varied and complex as they are, have caught the imagination of a distinguished array of historians and political philosophers. Alfred Cobban, Crane Brinton, and R. J. White have written brilliantly, and at times sympathetically, about them. But it has remained for the new conservatives of our age to write about them in a spirit of hallowed veneration. Anxious to construct a political philosophy to clothe the present conservative temper of America, they have looked back to the humanitarian, Christian, and romantic philosophy of Coleridge and Southey. Clinton Rossiter in *Conservatism in America* expresses his admiration for Coleridge and Disraeli. Peter Viereck in *Conservatism Revisited* praises that English conservatism which "tends to put social justice ahead of laissez faire." Neither of them, however, gives such praise to Tory paternalism as does Russell Kirk. In *The Conservative Mind*, Kirk draws once again the classic picture of Tory paternalism pitted against an unsentimental liberalism, a picture familiar to all who have read Monypenny and Buckle's *Life of Benjamin Disraeli*, or Wingfield-Stratford's *History of British Civilization*, or even Keith Feiling's recent *History of England*. In redrawing this picture Kirk has added color; it now has its heroes and its villains, contesting for the souls of men and struggling to control the destinies of the new industrial society. The backdrop to this drama is a scene of grim factory towns with overworked children, squalid slums, and unsightly mills. The dramatis personae include the Benthamites, unfeeling and rational, the Whig aristocracy, jaunty and indifferent, and the hard and pious Manchester Liberals. All of them argue for an atomized society built on self-interest, laissez-faire, and that utilitarianism which Kirk calls "the surly apology of a hideous and rapacious industrialism." Contending against these Benthamites, Whigs, and Liberals are the Tories, alarmed at the cruelty of life in factory towns, "these fungeous excrescences on the body politic," as Southey said. Not only do the Tories see the evil, they are also possessed of a vision of an organic, benevolent society, which will remove cruelty and ugliness and neglect. To the fashioning of this society in England they are solemnly dedicated.

But in all this discussion, few writers have asked whether the Tories did translate these ideals into practice, whether they did contribute to the well-being of the working class. The answer to this question comes up immediately against an imposing difficulty. The principles of Tory paternalism do not lend themselves to effective legislation or improved administration. Coleridge, the most profound and influential of these theorists, looked to the moral regeneration of the individual, not to the reforming state, and he envisaged the Church of England as the head of a paternalistic society. He despised what he called "act of Parliament reforms," and he exalted the Church as much as he feared the state. In a complex industrial society, nearly one-third of whose churchgoers were Nonconformists, this scorn of legislation and this loyalty to a single church bode ill for effective reforms. Carlyle's fierce sermons and Disraeli's literary dreams were no easier to translate into legislation. They offered little practical guidance to successive Parliaments facing hard and intractable social problems. They offered no alternative to the old Poor Law, which had pauperized and demoralized the agricultural laborer; they offered no means to prevent the exploitation of children in textile mills; they did not say how slums were to be removed, slums in which an illiterate proletariat lived in misery, disease, and vice, unrelieved by any serious attempt at education and sanitation. Coleridge and Southey may have placed their faith in charitable endowments and church schools, but these voluntary efforts were powerless to stop the rising tide of distress and ignorance. The workers themselves preferred to place their faith in gin, crime, and chartism. "Civilization is threatened," said Thomas Macaulay, "by the barbarism it has engendered."

The existence of these problems furnished the Tories both in and out of Parliament an undoubted opportunity to translate whatever humanitarian ideas they cherished into effective reforms. As members of Parliament, as justices of the peace, as members of voluntary societies, and as agitators for factory reform, they could mitigate the harsher evils of the new industrial society. Their activities were in fact diverse and widespread. The Tory party was no homogeneous unit, no few men in Parliament. It included, though many a Tory wished it did not, the Yorkshire Tory Radicals, the Oastlers, Sadlers, Stephens, and Ferrands, men who carried Tory paternalism into the short-time committees and anti-Poor Law associations. That these men cared genuinely for the well-being of the factory workers and the poor and fought zealously for shorter working hours and generous poor relief has been ably demonstrated in Cecil Driver's biography of Richard Oastler and in R. H. Hill's *Toryism and the People, 1833–1846.* But other than Ferrand, none of these Tory Radicals sat in Parliament after 1833, and Ferrand himself was viewed with suspicion. The Yorkshire Tory Radicals were never accepted by the bulk of respectable Tories. They were too violent in speech and too ardent for popular causes to join what Disraeli called the "smartest club in town." Yet it was to that club that England's Conservatives returned their favorites, and it was in its halls that the Tories, diverse as they were, had the best opportunity to make their humanitarianism effective. And though the debates and votes of the Parliamentary Tories do not tell the whole story of Tory paternalism, they certainly form a solid enough test to merit close examination. Of what avail Oastler's unflagging zeal for the ten-hour day if Parliamentary Tories refused to support it.

The greatest of Tory social reformers, Lord Ashley, realized this fact when he proposed a bill to end the exploitation of children and adults in the cotton mills of England. His bill would have excluded from textile mills all children below nine and restricted all other workers to a ten-hour day. It was the bill which the workers wanted, one for which two Tory Radicals, Richard Oastler and Michael Sadler had aroused the North. But it did not win the support of the leaders of the Conservative party nor of the bulk of the 150 Conservatives who sat in the Commons. The most vocal in urging its passage were not Conservatives at all but were either Radicals like John Fielden, Joseph Brotherton, and John Hardy, or Liberals like Thomas Attwood and Colonel Torrens. These men did not represent the squirearchy; they represented Oldham, Salford, Bradford, Bolton, and Birmingham. No one party supported Lord Ashley's fight for the ten-hour bill, and no one party supported the bill which passed in its stead.[1] This bill, drawn up by two Benthamites, Edwin Chadwick and Southwood Smith, excluded all children below nine from the mills, limited the hours of labor to eight for children between nine and thirteen, and employed central inspectors to enforce the act. The principle of inspection, which alone would make the legislation effective, was repellent to Oastler and Sadler; [2] it was a principle drawn from Bentham's *Constitutional Code*, it meant centralization, and it was un-English. The first and most significant measure for industrial regulation thus came from many traditions: Tory evangelicals gave it impetus, the utilitarians defined its form, and the Whigs, masters at compromise, passed it through Parliament. It was not, as Peter Viereck would like to believe, a Tory measure.

Neither can the new Poor Law of 1834, with its harsh workhouse test for relief, be blamed on the Whigs alone, though that is what the Tories did at the hustings in 1837 and 1841.[3] Tory support of this measure is unmistakable. Not one of their leaders spoke against it, and on the second division only two representatives of the county squirearchy, the stronghold of the Tories, opposed it.[4] On the third division only eleven of the 150 Tories in the Commons were part of the fifty M.P.s who voted against it. More Liberals than Tories entered the opposition lobby. Even the Radicals, far fewer than the Tories in the Commons, mustered a dozen members against it. Furthermore, it was also the Radicals from the northern boroughs, the Brothertons and Fieldens, and not the Tories, who spoke most frequently and ardently for the rights of the poor [5] and opposed most consistently the measure which Disraeli in 1837 called "a moral crime and a political blunder." The harshness of the measure came in its insistence that all relief to able-bodied paupers be given in workhouses. Yet on the amendment to allow local authorities to give outdoor instead of workhouse relief, the Tories counted only nine of the thirty who supported it. The workhouse test, which the Tories' *Quarterly Review* had supported in 1832, seemed no more objectionable to the House of Lords than to the Commons, and the measure passed the upper house easily.[6] Tory peers, like Tory squires, knew that poor rates, now totaling seven million pounds, imposed the heaviest direct tax levied in the country and that if these oppressive rates were to be lowered reform had to come, and effective reform at that, centralized and strict. They reaffirmed their desire for a strict Poor Law in 1841 and 1842 when the Conservative party, victorious at the polls, renewed the new Poor Law. That belligerent Radical, Thomas Duncombe, much distressed at this action, complained that the renewed bill "evinced as much despotic Toryism as philosophical Whiggism"; Thomas Wakley, also a Radical, observed that those Tories who opposed the Poor Law during the elections were now as "mute as mice." Wakley and Duncombe in 1841 could muster only twenty-two votes in a Tory house for an amendment to give local authorities power to give outdoor relief. The Conservative ministry marshaled 216 votes to defeat the amendment. In the debates on the renewal of this measure, Disraeli remained silent, though in 1837 he called it a "moral crime and political blunder." [7]

Disraeli had spoken out more vigorously when the Privy Council in 1839 decided that £30,000 was not too much to spend on the education of England's poor. He condemned it outright. So did the Conservative party and press, which with one accord denounced the Whig measure. They found its proposals for the inspection of schools unconstitutional, despotic, and a threat to right religion. The Conservatives, of course, recognized the great need for education and admitted what the secretary of the British and Foreign School Society called "the utter and hopeless ignorance of the labouring class." [8] No man was more appalled at that ignorance than Coledrige, who looked to education for England's salvation; but he favored parish schools managed by a "national clerisy," not an assortment of church schools inspected and aided by the state. [9] Tories such as Gladstone, Ashley, and Southey's disciple Sir Robert Inglis felt the same way, [10] but their convictions that the Church of England alone should educate the poor, though earnest and noble, were quite impractical. England's powerful Nonconformists would not tolerate state grants to Church of

England schools alone; but the Church without such grants had failed, and failed decisively, to educate the poor.[11] Despite these realities, the Tories clung to their conviction that the Church of England alone, and not state-aided schools, should educate the poor—a conviction that prevented any real answer to the wide-spread ignorance of England's lower classes. Only state aid to all voluntary schools could extend education, but the Tories would not tolerate state intervention in a sphere reserved for the Church. In a grandiloquent speech to the Commons, Disraeli played deftly on this deep jealousy of the state. He raised the specter of a centralized despotism comparable to those which oppressed China, Persia, and Austria, and somberly warned that the grant would force a return "to the system of a barbarous age, the system of a paternal government." The Whigs and Radicals did not share Disraeli's fears, and by a majority of two, with all the Conservatives against them, voted the £30,000 to the Committee in Council on Education and thus took the first step toward the construction of a national system of public education.[12]

The slim margin of victory on the education grant betokened the growing weakness of the Whigs in the Commons. In the election of 1841 they lost control of the House completely, and Sir Robert Peel, with a rejuvenated party behind him, formed a Tory government. The Tories now had a chance to practice what many of them had long professed. At Tamworth in 1835, Peel had set the tone of the new conservatism. He accepted the Reform Act of 1832 and promised his electors "to redress all real grievances." [13] Disraeli in 1841 was even more ardently humanitarian. He told the electors: "There is no subject on which I have taken a deeper interest than the condition of the working class." [14] Gladstone, still inspired by the ideals of Coleridge, urged at Newark in 1841 that a greater concern be shown for the aged, the sick, and the widowed and that greater freedom be given to local Poor Law authorities.[15] Ostensibly free from those mercantile interests that tied down the Whigs, the Conservatives boasted a greater sensitivity to the sufferings of the working class. With a majority of ninety-one in the Commons and sure control of the Lords, they now had the opportunity to make Tory paternalism a genuine answer to the condition of England question.

Lord Ashley for one wished to exploit this opportunity. In 1841 he had discovered that the worst hardships of the over-worked factory hands could not compare to the miseries and dangers suffered by the miners. In 1842 he told the Commons of these evils, of boys and girls pulling sacks of coal through narrow seams, of six- and seven-year olds sitting alone in dark recesses opening and closing ventilation traps for hours at a time, of half-naked women worked as beasts of burden, of foul air, dangerous explosions, long hours, fatigue, indecencies, and immoralities. It was a depressing story, and it left little grounds for opposition. The Commons quickly passed a bill to prohibit women, boys under the age of thirteen, and all apprentice labor from working in the mines. The peers, on the other hand, were not so deeply moved. Led by Lord Londonderry, the great Tory mineowner, they reduced the age of exclusion for boys to ten, and secured an amendment permitting the use of apprentice labor. Lord Wharncliffe, the government's leader in the Lords, did nothing to prevent these concessions. By the time the amended bill had been returned to the Commons, the coal interests had grown bolder and the government more timid. As a result, the amendments were accepted. The bill had never been a government bill but was the result of Ashley's private endeavors. The most it won from the ministry was a quiet assent. Peel spoke only once, and then to urge the acceptance of the Lords' amendments. Gladstone voted against the bill and Disraeli was absent.[16] All this the embittered Ashley recorded in his diary.

In 1844 Ashley suffered further disappointments. In that year his Conservative colleagues prevented the passage of his ten-hour bill for factory labor.[17] Both Sir Robert Peel, the Prime Minister, and Sir James Graham, the Home Secretary, denounced the ten-hour restriction as an invasion of the rights of property, and they mustered their Conservative colleagues to defeat Lord Ashley's ten-hour amendment by three votes.[18] *The Economist,* ever scrupulous about property rights, decried the fact that so large a portion of the Liberals and Whigs supported Ashley and added that in the future the manufacturers should look to the Conservatives to defend their interests.[19] Deserted by most of his party, Ashley lost another battle in his fight to extend the protection of the government to the laboring man. The ten-hour day had to await the return of the Whigs, who in 1847, with the help of rural Tories now free of Peel's whips, carried it through Parliament.[20] Despite ministerial indifference and Disraeli's silence, Ashley himself never wearied in his efforts to promote social reform, forcing through Parliament in these years bills for government inspection of insane asylums and for the regulation of print works. The House of Lords often discouraged him. In 1840 the Lords talked of defeating his bill to protect chimney sweeps. "The Conservative peers," Ashley sadly noted in his diary, "threatened opposition and the Radical Ministers warmly support the Bill." [21]

Ashley desired a strong, benevolent government which would protect the weak and the downtrodden, but the most prominent of the Conservatives, Peel, Gladstone, and Disraeli, did not share his convictions. Evidence of their paternalistic activities is not abundant. From 1841 to 1846 they failed to make substantial advances in public education, to bring order to the chaos of railway construction, to end notorious evils in the merchant marine, or to promote urgently needed sanitary reforms. Their efforts to create factory schools floundered on the rocks of Nonconformist indignation: twenty-four thousand petitions with four million signatures condemned a bill which insisted that all teachers and a majority of school trustees (even in Nonconformist towns) be Churchmen.[22] Their railway bill, which contained a clause limiting profits to 10 per cent, ended up, after negotiations with the railway companies, with another clause guaranteeing 10 per cent profits should the rates ever be regulated. *The Economist* thought the clause a joke and unworkable and the bill itself the natural result of putting an ingenious metaphysician on the Board of Trade. The Conservatives not only evaded any effective limits on profits but failed to take effective steps to end the anarchy of private bill legislation, the corruption of railway financing, and the chaos of hasty and ill-advised railway construction, all of which fostered the railway panic of 1845.[23] The ministry also did nothing to end abuses in the merchant marine, and its antipathy to centralization prevented a comprehensive health measure. Peel as Prime Minister and Gladstone at the Board of Trade shied away from such reforms. Said Peel, in opposing government regulation of railways: "It was precisely by the vigorous, judicious, and steady pursuit of self interest that individuals and companies ultimately benefitted the public at large." [24] And Gladstone, in religious matters a believer in a strong ecclesiastical state, was on economic matters a believer in a weak central government. An opponent of Ashley's mining inspection act and ten-hour factory act, he showed himself at the Board of Trade more sensitive to the interests of the proprietors of mines, factories, and railways than to the pleas of millhands and miners. His background, like Peel's, was mercantile, and he believed as strongly as did the political economists in a laissez-faire economy.

Disraeli, on the other hand, represented the landed aristocracy and the new ideals of Young England. He spoke for that faction of the Conservative party, the agriculturists, who distrusted Peel, feared his talk of lower tariffs, and resented his connections with the manufacturing interests. Disraeli, the leader of the dissidents, the apostle of rural Toryism, and the opponent of the Poor Law, now had his chance to push social reforms. But in this era of Conservative majorities he was busier writing of these ideals in his novels than translating them into reforms. He showed little practical interest in the construction of a benevolent state. He gave a silent vote for the ten-hour act of 1844 and that alone constitutes his record of support of Lord Ashley's reforms. The practical reality of Tory paternalism during Peel's ministry rests, upon closer examination, almost solely on the greatness of Lord Ashley, certainly a firmer foundation than the sentiments of *Sybil* and *Coningsby*.

In 1846 the Whigs and Liberals returned to power, and from that year until 1854 they enacted substantial social reforms. They expanded public aid to church schools of all denominations, passed the Ten Hour Act of 1847, the Public Health Act of 1848, and the Mining and Merchant Marine Acts of 1850, all of which increased the paternalistic role of the central government. The attitudes of the Conservatives to these measures were mixed. Their former leader, Peel, opposed the Ten Hour Act, and their new chief, Disraeli, was, as usual, silent. The Tory protectionists, led by Disraeli, showed little enthusiasm for the Health of Towns Bill of 1847 and the Public Health Act of 1848. To be sure, they desired sanitary reform. Had not Disraeli become a member of the Health of Towns Association in 1847? No Liberal more cordially detested the muddy streets of London than did the Conservative M.P. or felt more uneasy about the diseased slums of Manchester, the general want of drainage in most towns, and the lack of an adequate supply of pure water. But the Conservatives wanted no central board of health with its meddling inspectors, no interference with their rights as local magistrates and town councilors, and no sudden increase in rates for fancy sewer projects. The Health of Towns Bill, said Lord Lincoln in 1847, gave too much power to Whitehall, and in 1848, when the Conservative press denounced the Public Health Act for its centralization, Disraeli and a few intransigent Tories voted against it, though they were not numerous enough to kill it.[25] Disraeli's defeat was only temporary. In 1854 when local interests fought against a Board of Health arrogant enough to insist on pure water and good drainage, Disraeli and his friends were able to kill a bill which would have given a new lease of life to the General Board of Health.

Thus did they testify to their interest in a healthier England. Palmerston, who understood the value of the Board of Health, dubbed the Tories "the party of dirt" and called this vote the foulest in his Parliamentary experience.[26]

The Whigs' mining and merchant marine reforms passed through Parliament without difficulty in 1850. Conditions in the merchant marine were so wretched and mining explosions so frequent that few dared oppose the measures. It was in fact Joseph Hume, a strong believer in the "dismal science," who championed the mining measure. Two Young Englanders, Lord John Manners and Benjamin Disraeli, led the minority in opposition. Lord John pleaded the cause of the shipowners and Disraeli that of the mineowners. Disraeli protested that the bill to reduce accidents by closer inspection was an "interposition between labour and capital." [27] The voting record of the author of *Sybil* was hardly distinguished by a compassion for the working class. He voted against the Education Order of 1839, against cheap bread in 1846, against the Public Health Act of 1848, against the Mining Act of 1850, and against the General Board of Health Act in 1854. On factory legislation his record was, in D. C. Somervell's words, "dubious and meagre." [28] His single speech for the ten-hour factory bill was the only time he spoke for any reform designed to better the condition of the working classes.

The above survey of the Tory party's record on social reform raises disturbing questions about the nature of early nineteenth-century English conservatism. Was it as paternalistic as Russell Kirk would have it, or as humanitarian as Clinton Rossiter believes it to have been? Were these conservatives, as Peter Viereck argues, dedicated more to social justice than to laissez-faire? Of the sincerity of Coleridge's and Southey's responses to the coarseness, misery, and selfishness of the new industrial society there can be no doubt; nor is there need to be cynical about Gladstone's earnest convictions and Peel's desire to remedy real grievances. And even the sentiments of *Sybil* and *Coningsby*, medieval and fanciful as they are, ring true. Yet these ideals were not translated into practice. What is the explanation of this failure?

The question is fundamental to an understanding of early Victorian conservatism, yet it admits of no simple answer. The ideals of conservatism, for one thing, were hopelessly varied. How different were the passionate pronouncements of Coleridge from the elaborate reflections of Burke, how unlike the sentiments of Disraeli were the calculations of Peel. Another reason that no simple answer explains their failure is the complexity of the problems faced. Neither the knotty complications of the new Poor Law nor the religious jealousies involved in the question of education were amenable to simple paternalistic solutions. Yet the reasons for the failure must be sought, and in that search two frequently forgotten characteristics of early Victorian conservatism must be considered—its deep attachments to local interests, the basis of the laissez-faire of the eighteenth century, and its high regard for the rights of property, the basis of the laissez-faire of the nineteenth century.

Coleridge above all others appealed to the Englishmen's deep attachments to local interests. He expressed their suspicion of Whitehall and of "act of Parliament reform," and he looked to the local clergy, the squire, the magistracy, and the ordinary citizen to promote the Christian society. "Let us become better people," said Coleridge, "let every man measure his effort by his power in his sphere of action . . . let him act personally and in detail wherever it is practical." [29] Disraeli fully shared this belief that the regenerated individual, working in local spheres, could create the ideal society. Among the squirearchy it was a deeply felt prejudice expressed rather bluntly in its journal, *John Bull*. The journal proudly asserted in arguing against the Public Health Act that England needed local corporations, not central bureaus.[30] The Tories were possessed of a deep loyalty to their corporations, whether they were quarter sessions or borough councils, parishes or endowed hospitals. When the rights of these corporations were threatened by the central government, the Tories cried out against the evils of centralization. Disraeli invoked the fear of centralization in his war against police, education, and sanitary reforms.[31] *The Times*, in its most Tory phase, raised this specter to condemn all government commissions.[32] And Conservatives as diverse as David Urquhart, Lord Lonsdale, and the railway king, George Hudson, opposed the Public Health Act for the same reason.[33] A young Tory barrister, Joshua Toulmin Smith, who attributed the growth of the powers of the central government to the false humanitarianism of the Whigs, wrote pamphlet upon pamphlet against centralization.[34] "Centralization" was an evil word. It evoked the deepest of Tory prejudices and touched the most sacred of Tory interests. "Centralization," said that staunch English patriot, Mr. Podsnap, "No, Never with my consent. Not English!" [35] The Tories guarded their local privileges vigilantly and defended with equal regard the right of the clergy to educate the poor, the right of the borough to run its prisons, and the right of the parish to repair its roads. In 1839 the Tory localists, among them Benjamin Disraeli, thwarted the Whig plan for a centrally supervised county police and for the central inspection of highways; and so there continued the unregulated system of parish highway surveyors and constables, unpaid, annually appointed, and ineffective.[36] The many blue books of the period show that the localism of the eighteenth century did not answer the problems of the nineteenth century; streets remained undrained and unpoliced, prisons mismanaged, schools unsupported, asylums and charities inefficient.[37] Few countries have known such an administrative laissez-faire.

The Conservative's attachment to local government arose from many sources; from traditionalism, from vested interests in local power and patronage, from a loyalty to the Church, and from a fear of higher rates. The last motive was of no small magnitude. It persuaded them to accept in 1834 the most centralizing of all measures and one against which all their sentiments rebelled—the new Poor Law; but it persuaded many of them in 1848 and 1854 to oppose a further measure of centralization, the Public Health Act. Landlords, such as the Marquis of Salisbury in Hertford and Lord Lonsdale in Gateshead, attacked the measure for its encroachments on local rights.[38] Whatever the motives, whether self-interest or traditionalism, or loyalty to the Church, the Tories generally opposed those very paternalistic reforms which an industrial society demanded. That this localism was another form of laissez-faire is evident in the pronouncements of David Urquhart, Colonel Sibthorp, and George Buck, all staunch, albeit eccentric, Tories and all vehement in their attacks on centralization. Sibthorp told the Commons in 1847 that he "detested the rapid strides of government power," and George Buck told them in 1848 that "he was opposed to every kind of Commission." [39] Urquhart asserted in Dodd's *Parliamentary Companion* (1847) that he had one rule, "to vote for any measure which is to abrogate an old statute, and against every measure which is to introduce a new one."

These Tories detested "act of Parliament reforms," and their suspicion of the government ran deeper than that of Adam Smith, deeper even than that of the Benthamites. The situation was paradoxical. The Tories, many of whom abhorred the principles of laissez-faire, defended its practical application, while the Benthamites and Whigs, avowed disciples of Smith and Ricardo, promoted those social reforms which brought a strong paternalistic state.

Not all Conservatives, of course, opposed the doctrines of the economists. William Pitt the younger greatly admired the teachings of Adam Smith, and it was Edmund Burke who first introduced political economy into conservative orthodoxy.[40] Under Pitt, George Canning, and William Huskisson the Tory party welcomed the lords of the exchange and the lords of the mill and the ideas of Smith and Ricardo. Nearly one-half of those representing business interests who sat in the House of Commons from

1841 to 1847 sat on the Conservative side of the House, according to Professor Aydelotte's statistics.[41] There they heard their leaders defend the rights of property as ardently as the Whigs and Liberals. Gladsone voted against the first mining inspection act and Disraeli against the second.[42] Gladstone's defense arose from a deep conviction (he possessed no other variety) that the laws of political economy were immutable; Disraeli's from an almost medieval loyalty to his Lord and Lady Londonderry. Lord Londonderry, the greatest mineowner in Britain, was the principal opponent of all attempts to send inspectors into the mines. Most Conservatives owned property, and not all of it was agricultural. Lord Lonsdale, for example, owned not only broad acres of farm land but mines as well, and he was the ground landlord of the Gateshead slums. The Marquis of Salisbury drew much of his income from rents on the tenements of Hertford. Both lords opposed the application of the Public Health Act to their property. For the inhabitants of Gateshead this meant a failure to improve the sanitation of the town and consequent serious losses from the cholera epidemic of 1854.[43] Another leading Conservative, George Hudson, opposed not only the Public Health Act but any effective regulation of railways. He was joined in this opposition by Sir Robert Peel himself. Men of property could, as *The Economist* said in 1844, trust Peel. He argued ably against any regulation of the hours of adult labor and against any interference with the rights of capital. He feared the torpid hand of the government and had a firm belief, as did Burke, in the doctrines of the economists.

Peel was indeed the bearer of the tradition of Burke, just as Disraeli was the bearer of the tradition of Coleridge. As a result Peel won the praises of *The Economist* for his allegiance to commercial principles while Disraeli earned the applause of the squirearchy for his defense of local liberties. Each represented different groups in the Tory party and each stood for opposing social philosophies. Peel was the architect of the new conservatism ready to make its peace with the nineteenth century, attempting, as

Burke preached, to blend cautious reforms with old traditions. Disraeli on the other hand was, like Coleridge, a prophet declaiming against the evils of a materialistic, commercial age and extolling men to be charitable to the poor. Peel believed in sound finance, efficient administration, and responsible laws, and he spoke for the business interests. Disraeli had faith in a hierarchical society governed by a humane aristocracy, and he spoke for the great landed interests.

The two factions and the two outlooks fitted very ill together after 1842, the year Peel failed to end the malt tax and talked of tariff reform. The conflicts between them, and the struggle over the Corn Laws which broke Peel's party, were hardly encouraging to measures of social reform. Of the two factions, it was rural Toryism that most vociferously condemned the abuses in factories, and its leaders sympathized most openly with the plight of the working classes. In the realm of social ideas Disraeli stands out as the true Tory humanitarian. He urged Parliament in 1839 to consider the chartists' petition and their grievances; in *Coningsby* he reprimanded landlords for mistreating their tenants; in *Sybil* he showed a real understanding of the grievances of industrial workers. Yet he gave little support to practical legislation to end these grievances. His fear of a strong central bureaucracy and his alliance with local corporate interests and a propertied aristocracy persuaded him to express his paternalism in appeals for rejuvenation of national character and not in mining inspectors and boards of health. His allies among the rural Tories hated such central commissions. The Peelites, closer to administrative realities, knew the use of such commissions. They accepted the Poor Law Commission in 1841 and the Board of Health in 1848. But on questions of industrial regulation they spoke for that half of the business interests who sat on the Conservative side of the House, for the Hudsons, Cardwills, and Barings; and they argued for an untrammeled capitalism and a free labor market. Thus, though greatly dissimilar in outlook, the corporate localism of Disraeli's Protectionists and the political economy of the Peelites both encouraged a practical policy of laissez-faire.

The failure of most of the Tories to support reform does not tell the whole story of nineteenth-century conservatism. It does not tell of the later Disraeli, quite altered by the responsibility of office and the need to win the votes of the workingmen. It leaves out the humanitarian work of the Yorkshire Tory Radicals. It does not do justice to Lord Ashley, whose monumental social reforms (though supported more often by Radicals and Whigs than Tories) offered some foundation for the humanitarian reputation of the Tory party.

There may be no reason to discredit the ideals of Tory paternalism, but one may question how much these were ever put into practice. Historians might think twice before accepting Wingfield-Stratford's view of the young Disraeli flinging himself "heart and soul into questions of social reform" or Keith Feiling's generous praise of Disraeli's social conscience. Political philosophers might raise an eyebrow when they hear from Peter Viereck that the Tories tended "to prefer social justice to laissez faire." Even historians of American history, such as Louis Hartz in his *The Liberal Tradition in America*, may have fallen into the error of believing that "Southern Feudalism fell short of Disraeli's standard of humanitarianism." The truth is that recent historians and new conservatives alike have romanticized nineteenth-century conservatism. It was not as benevolent, as generous, nor as heroic as they imagine.

This article provides a sense of the larger community, the urban working class in the 1850s and 1860s. The author is concerned with the ways in which the middle class was able to secure working-class cooperation. Trygve R. Tholfsen is a professor of history at Teachers College, Columbia University, and is at present engaged on a study of the working classes and mid-Victorian urban culture. He has recently investigated another aspect of the topic discussed here in his article, "The Intellectual Origins of Mid-Victorian Stability," Political Science Quarterly LXXXVI *(1971). He is also the author of* Historical Thinking *(New York, 1967). The article is reprinted by permission of the author and publisher from the* International Review of Social History VI *(1961), 226–248.*

Several articles which he mentions as footnotes in his essay have now been superseded by books by the same authors: K. S. Inglis, Churches and the Working Classes in Victorian England *(London, 1963), and Royden Harrison,* Before the Socialists: Studies in Labour and Politics 1861–1881 *(London, 1965). Also a full-length study of George Howell has now appeared: F. M. Leventhal,* Respectable Radical *(Cambridge, Mass., 1971).*

TRYGVE R. THOLFSEN

The Transition to Democracy in Victorian England

I

THE ORGANIZATION AND the establishment of democracy in Christendom," de Tocqueville wrote in 1835, "is the great political problem of the time." [1] Nowhere was the problem more urgent than in England, whose industrial towns were soon to be torn by intense class conflict. Yet England resolved the tensions of the 1830s and 1840s, and went on to build a tough and supple political democracy in a massively undemocratic society.

How did England become a democracy? The question has received little explicit attention from historians. Implicit in most narrative accounts of Victorian politics, however, is an answer of this sort: in response to outside pressure Parliament passed the reform bills that gradually democratized a long established system of representative government. Although this interpretive formula is unexceptionable up to a point, it conveys the impression that England became a democracy primarily as a result of statutory changes in the electoral system, whereas in fact the historical process involved was a good deal more complex. This exploratory essay is intended as a preliminary inquiry into the nature of that process.

Extending the franchise to the working classes was the nub of the problem of democracy in England. As Disraeli remarked to Bright in March 1867, "The Working Class Question is the real question, and that is the thing that demands to be settled." [2] The franchise issue was not exclusively political, however, but an expression of a much larger and more complicated problem of class relations. As a result of rapid industrialization, England in the middle third of the nineteenth century had to devise arrangements that would enable the middle and working classes of the industrial towns to live together peacefully on terms they considered just. Hence, in order to understand the transition to democracy in England, it is necessary to treat political developments as an integral part of a wider pattern of settlement and adjustment between the classes. Moreover, "becoming a democracy" required not merely the extension of the franchise, but the creation of new habits and attitudes governing political relations between the working classes and the rest of the community.

If these heuristic suggestions are valid, it becomes necessary to devote considerable attention to the mid-Victorian industrial towns, not only as sources of pressure for parliamentary reform, but also as centers of conflict and accommodation, where the middle and working classes negotiated the terms of their social and political relations. In the towns the contending classes found a modus vivendi that preserved the hegemony of the middle classes while satisfying the immediate aspirations of the workingmen. The working classes came to accept a well-defined social role—co-operating with the bourgeoisie in an effort to achieve their allotted share of progress and improvement within the existing framework of power and status. In politics a parallel pattern of class relations emerged, as workingmen accepted the ideology and the leadership of middle-class Radicals in demanding household suffrage. On these terms the towns found a solution to the franchise issue.

These developments in the mid-Victorian towns influenced the transition to democracy in England in three distinct ways. First, the rapprochement between the middle and working classes removed the chief barrier to a substantial extension of the franchise, the fears and suspicions generated by the Chartist episode. Second, the parliamentary reform agitation in the towns forced the House of Commons to take action on the franchise issue. Third, in the towns there took place those readjustments in habits and attitudes that constituted the essence of the process of "becoming a democracy"; classes divided by a vast social gulf found ways of collaborating politically; in the towns was forged that consensus on fundamentals so necessary to the smooth functioning of a democratic polity. Moreover, the political evolution of the industrial towns in the 1850s and 1860s contributed directly to certain typically conservative features of English democracy in the late Victorian period: the ascendancy of liberal ideology among the working classes, working-class acceptance of middle-class political leadership, and the Lib-Labism of the aristocracy of labor.

This sequence of events did not unfold automatically as a result of the operation of predetermined historical forces. On the contrary, the most important single factor in the process—middle-class Radical espousal of household suffrage—violated the strict logic of mid-Victorian urban culture, which sanctioned at most a limited extension of the franchise to the "intelligent and respectable artisan." Only because the Radicals chose to ignore the inhibitions imposed by their social situation were they able to impart a distinctive form to the emergence of democracy in England—the combination of a fairly large dose of electoral equality with political patterns congenial to an inegalitarian society.

From this perspective I shall sketch two aspects of the transition to democracy in the industrial towns of the 1850s and 1860s: first, the cultural patterns that embodied a solution to the overall problem of class relations; second, the political patterns that emerged in that cultural setting under the auspices of middle-class Radicalism.

II

A deep crisis in class relations engulfed the industrial towns of early Victorian England. An apparently irrepressible conflict between the middle and working classes gave rise to a series of turbulent agitations: the recurring struggle for shorter hours; the outburst of Owenite utopianism; the bitter battle against the new Poor Law; and the Chartist explosion. Toward the end of the 1840s the waning of the trade depression brought a relaxation of tension, but it did not remove the underlying problem of class relations. An uneasy truce prevailed.

The tensions of the 1840s finally disappeared when the bourgeoisie fashioned a way of life that won the allegiance of the working classes. In this enterprise the middle classes showed consummate skill in adapting old forms to new circumstances. To begin with, they were able to utilize attitudes of deference and acquiescence that persisted among the working classes despite the troubles of the Chartist era. In addition, the bourgeoisie could proceed within the framework of a fairly widespread consensus about traditional values: the capitalist ethic; the moral and intellectual values of the Christian and liberal traditions; the growing faith in progress and improvement. Finally, there already existed in early Victorian England the beginnings of a network of institutions devoted to the practical realization of these purposes. Building on these foundations, the middle classes introduced two innovations that made possible the remarkably stable and cohesive culture of the mid-Victorian industrial towns. First of all, they came to put a new and prominent emphasis on extending values to an ever larger segment of the population. In the second place, they sought to bring about the fullest working-class participation in the pursuit of socially approved goals.

Middle-class initiative was essential to the effective functioning of this social system. The bourgeoisie took up the mission of "elevating the masses" with their wonted earnestness. This meant transmitting appropriate traits and habits to the upper strata of the working classes. The capitalist virtues of thrift and diligence—redefined in the gospel of work—were singled out for special attention. Morality and intelligence were to be fostered in a context of deference and respectability. To accomplish these ends existing institutions were expanded and new ones constructed. But workingmen were not to be merely passive recipients of charity. In keeping with the principle of self-help, they were to be admitted to a junior partnership in the joint enterprise of improvement and advancement. Assisted by their superiors, whose superiority they would continue to acknowledge, they would run their own institutions wherever possible.

Thus, mid-Victorian urban culture rested on a tacit agreement among the classes as to values and roles. All groups in the community were devoted to a common purpose: social, moral, and intellectual improvement. Within that framework, however, there would be considerable variation from class to class. The bourgeoisie would assist the working classes to advance themselves, but without in any way disturbing established power and status relations. Workingmen were to be encouraged to strive to achieve bourgeois values, but always in a form appropriate to their station.

The arrangements devised by the bourgeoisie were bound to attract an immediate and enthusiastic response from the aristocracy of labor. Even at the height of the Chartist upheaval the ideal of moral and intellectual improvement, for example, enjoyed an unchallenged prestige among many skilled artisans. William Lovett's National Association for Promoting the Political and Social Improvement of the People declared itself "in favour of establishing *Public Halls* and *Schools* for the people; in which their children may be properly educated and themselves mentally and morally improved." The seventh "object" of the Association anticipated one of the standard social pieties of the mid-Victorian towns: "To promote the education of the rising generation and the political and social improvement of the people by means of *Schools, Lectures, Public Meetings, Discussions, Classes for Mutual Instruction, and Meetings for Rational Amusement* after their hours of toil." [3] Similarly, the Friendly Societies and the new co-operatives of the 1840s testified to the strength of the ideals of thrift and self-help among the artisan classes. With the coming of prosperity at the end of the decade, the middle classes showed a growing disposition to play the part of benevolent patron in helping the working classes to help themselves along these lines.

On countless occasions representatives of the middle classes proclaimed their dedication to the task of elevating the masses. A speaker opened the industrial and art exhibition of a Salford Workingmen's Club with these familiar words: "These exhibitions ought not to be lightly skimmed over, for, if the people were to advance in the appreciation of what was great and good and noble, they must study such collections." The exhibition was designed to set before workingmen "higher types of thought and expression, so as to lead them by degrees to a keener appreciation of the beautiful." He included the usual homily: "Success in this matter, as in all others, required study, thought, reflection, practice, and observation. Thought must be perfected by work, and labour guided by thought." [4] Editorials exhorted the middle classes to play their part: "if the organizations which exist for the instruction of the wealthy can be extended to a different class, a perennial source of moral, industrial, and political improvement will have been opened." [5] Likewise, public baths deserved support, because they would "tend greatly to promote habits of cleanliness among the working classes, which are essential to their health and self-respect." [6] By 1863 one observer could state as a fact the middle-class image of its role. The middle classes, he wrote, would "go to almost any length" to improve the material condition of the working classes. "Every kind of benevolent project finds, and for thirty years has always found, the heartiest sympathy and support." [7]

In elevating the lower orders the bourgeoisie had in mind a particular type of working-class character—reasonable, respectable, deferential—that was to be the end-product of their benevolent activity. This cultural ideal was summed up in an editorial in the *Manchester Guardian* in 1858, in which the writer was expressing satisfaction with the moderation displayed by the working classes. He concluded that education had "made the lower classes more intelligent, more self-reliant, more energetic, has taught them to think more justly of their fellow countrymen, to feel ashamed of their former prejudices, and to acknowledge that it rests with them and not with any Government to ameliorate their social condition." He noted that even in strikes "moderation and order are generally manifested in their proceedings, and there is a better appreciation of the laws that govern the rise and fall of wages." [8] This passage underlines the ideological function of mid-Victorian social values and roles, in preserving and justifying the wealth, power, and prestige of the middle classes. Every step taken to elevate the workingmen was expected to reinforce their acquiescence in the existing order. But the culture demanded that this acquiescence be completely voluntary, and not extorted by coercion. A Norwich minister noted that there had come about "a far better spirit between classes, and a sounder feeling of trust in the men, both as between themselves and as regards employers and the richer orders. As elsewhere there had been far greater personal intercourse between the labouring and higher classes of late years than formerly, which has tended to a more human feeling on both sides." [9] Smoothing class relations was almost a cultural obsession. The task of overcoming the effects of class differences required "delicacy and earnestness," and could be accomplished "only by perfect singleness of purpose and manliness of heart." [10]

The sentimental language was peculiarly characteristic of mid-Victorian social sensibility. Living through the Indian summer of the Evangelical revival, the middle classes found a social outlet for their earnestness and piety. A wholesale transfer of religious emotion to secular objects took place in the middle years of the nineteenth century. Evangelicalism, however much secularized, was responsible for the highly moralistic coloration of prevailing social values. More than most societies the mid-Victorian towns found moral significance in every aspect of the life of the community. Invariably, however, cultural values were circumscribed within uncriticized presuppositions inherent in the social and power structure of the community.

Mid-Victorian social values took for granted the vast disparity in power and status between the working class and the rest of the community. The acceptance of these class relationships, ingrained in the custom and habit of centuries, entered into every facet of the culture. In the bald clarity of the law these social facts found their clearest expression. Employers and employees were not equal before the law. The "servant" who broke a contract with his "master" had committed a crime; the "master" who broke a contract with his "servant," however, could only be sued for damages.[11] Likewise, common law hostility toward trade unions and their activity reflected not only the application of legal principles but also the traditional view of proper relations between masters and men.[12]

The workingmen were an inferior class, clearly set apart from their superiors. Clergymen were reminded that "the broad line of demarcation which on week days separates the workman from his master" did not fade away on Sunday. "The labouring myriads . . . forming to themselves a world apart," would be uncomfortable with "persons of a higher grade." [13] It was virtually impossible for the classes to meet "on the common platform of their humanity." [14] As a result of these unalterable social facts, the middle classes could not avoid a condescending attitude toward "the lower orders." To patronize inferiors was simply one of the many habits instilled by the society into which they had been born.

Likewise, it was habitual for workingmen to accept the claims of their superiors.

By the middle of the nineteenth century one segment of the working class found itself in a good position to play the new role that was expected of it within the traditional social framework— collaborating actively with superiors in the pursuit of approved objectives. During the 1850s and 1860s the skilled artisans established themselves firmly as an aristocracy of labor.[15] The more complex technology of a maturing industrial economy had created new skills. In particular the growth of the metal industries led to "an immense reinforcement of the labour aristocracy." At the same time the handicrafts had held their own. The skilled artisans, intent on setting themselves even farther apart from the laboring masses, were especially responsive to the sort of leadership being provided by the mid-Victorian bourgeoisie. They operated the proliferating institutions devoted to self-improvement and self-help.

Intellectual improvement was the objective of a bewildering array of institutions: Sunday Schools, Ragged and Industrial Schools, National Schools, British Schools, Mechanics' Institutes, Working Men's Colleges, Working Men's Reading Rooms, Mutual Improvement Societies, and libraries.[16] Social roles varied as much as the institutions themselves. In some instances the initiative rested entirely with the middle class, which dispensed charity in the traditional manner; often the classes collaborated; sometimes the workingmen did the job all by themselves. In the Mechanics Institute at Newcastle a member of the middle class "acted as secretary, and was, indeed, the animating spirit of the organization." [17] In contrast, the Working Men's Club at Kendal originated with workingmen and was entirely managed by them. The four hundred members had a newsroom, library, class and lecture rooms, and a chess room.[18] The Workingmen's Institution at Hartshill, Stoke-upon-Trent, possessed "a beautiful building, erected at the sole expense of Colin Minton Campbell, Esq., at the cost of some

£600." [19] All these groups shared a common goal. In the familiar language of mid-Victorian culture, as expressed by an M.P. at the eighth annual soirée of the Accrington Mechanics' Institution, their aim was "the moral and intellectual advancement of the people." [20] The sort of character that these institutions were trying to develop was described in these terms by a workingman who was a Methodist lay preacher: "Who amongst the teeming masses of our artisan and labouring population are marked by staidness of character, forecast, and consequent prudence and thriftiness, and who show the greatest skill in their respective employments? They are the numbers who frequent the class rooms and lecture rooms of our lyceums and mechanics institutions—those who avail themselves of the scanty provisions of our evening schools." [21]

Another cluster of institutions was devoted primarily to encouraging "prudence and thriftiness": the friendly societies and co-operatives.[22] They enabled skilled workers to make some provision for the contingencies ignored by the state, to practice capitalist virtues outside the profit system, and to invest whatever surplus remained after meeting subsistence needs. Poor Law policy, of course, made thrift a necessity as well as a virtue, since improvidence ensured the swift loss of everything the artisan had been striving for. The workhouse stigma put an edge on the sort of homily delivered by an M.P. at the annual meeting of the Bury district of the National Order of Oddfellows in 1866: "He hoped that in the season of prosperity which was dawning upon them [the working classes] they would lay up for a time of adversity. He called upon all young men not connected with such a society to at once join one, and advised young ladies to look shy at any man who did not thus display an inclination to be provident." [23] The artisan did not really need to be reminded that he had to be provident, or else.

The immense apparatus of self-help tended to attach the artisan classes to the established order and contributed to a relaxation of the tensions of the early Victorian period. When a Norwich minister described the "change for the better" that had come about in the town since the days of "distrust of class against class and man against man," he cited the growth of the provident institutions: "The Co-operatives have had a large store, with branches, for eight or nine years, very successfully carried on. . . . The societies of Odd Fellows are very large. Building Societies are successful, but I think mostly among the upper artisans and small shopkeepers, the average of low wages preventing the ordinary workman from using them." He noted also that "the Co-operatives and other clubs are reading far more than formerly, both books and papers." [24] It was characteristic of the interconnectedness of the various segments of mid-Victorian culture that the co-operative stores should not limit themselves to merchandising, but tried to do a great deal more, as in the North, for example: "They [co-operative stores] generally have their own buildings, which include commodious halls for the purposes of public meetings, lectures, concerts, tea-meetings and conversazioni, chiefly promoted by and for the members of the Society and their families." [25]

The trade unions of the skilled artisans held a unique position in the institutional structure of the industrial towns. On the one hand, they were at odds with the prevailing patterns of the society, because they carried the threat of a shift in power relations between the classes and because they interfered with the right of the capitalist to dispose of the factors of production as he saw fit. In this respect, they constituted an important countervailing force in the community, limiting the dominance of the bourgeoisie. On the other hand, the New Model unions accepted the same values and presuppositions that defined the purposes of other institutions in the society.[26] Their lines too came from the same script. The Manchester district division of the Amalgamated Society of Engineers, at its annual festival in 1866, took pride in fact that in the last fifteen years "they had progressed in moral tone, in education, and in the method of conducting their disputes." They were proud that "they no longer relied on physical force, but on their own intelligence, and on the fact that they were recognized as a body having a right to meet and transact their own affairs." Nevertheless, their moderation did not restrain them from denouncing the employers' association "from whom had emanated such documents as their society would be ashamed to issue." [27] Precisely because they accepted in good faith the ideals of the culture, the trade unionists were apt to be shocked when employers' actions violated the code.

The New Model trade unions were preeminently Victorian in their preoccupation with self-help. In return for fairly high dues they provided their members with a wide range of benefits covering sickness, unemployment, and death. Moreover, as representative mid-Victorian institutions, the trade unions did not think of themselves as devoted to exclusively utilitarian objectives. Like the Amalgamated Society of Carpenters and Joiners, they hoped that "by the establishment of libraries and listening to the voice of the lecturer on all subjects connected with our interests, we and our sons shall become respectful and respected, and make rapid progress in the onward march of reform." [28]

Among the varied institutions that touched the life of the industrial towns, church and chapel exerted a most pervasive influence.[29] In one way or another, they reached all classes in the community, even those at the very bottom of the social scale. Town missions were designed for the unskilled laborers. A group of Manchester lurrymen, employed in stables operated by the goods department of a railway, received a good deal of attention. For eighteen months they were visited every Sunday morning by two of the city missionaries. The lurrymen responded in the manner expected of them: "They have been so well pleased with the advice and religious papers—about six thousand in number— which have been given them, that they were anxious to testify their grateful thanks for the persevering labours of those who had thus sought to do them good." At a tea-party celebration in the Methodist Chapel, four of the men "gave short but clear statements of the benefit they themselves had derived as well as that which they had observed in others." A member of the middle classes described the practical value of bringing religion to the masses: "One gentleman from a merchant's warehouse bore the most gratifying testimony to the marked improvement in the language and conduct of the lurrymen in their daily work of delivering and collecting goods." [30] The Manchester Town Mission conducted this sort of missionary work on a large scale. In 1850 it employed fifty-two agents "who read the scriptures from house to house, converse with the inmates upon the truths of the gospel, and urge the importance of all attending places of public worship, and of parents sending their children to school." [31] Significantly, the Mission's report recorded £200 in contributions from workingmen's district associations. The better-off workingmen were thus encouraged to take part in elevating their own social inferiors.

The skilled artisans were being assimilated into the religious community of the mid-Victorian cities on much of the same terms that characterized their position in the society as a whole. They were welcomed into the congregations, chiefly of the Nonconformist denominations, with the understanding that they would continue to play a clearly defined deferential role. Class lines were firmly drawn. Even within a single church or chapel there developed "religious groups of different social levels that seemed incapable of merging. Thus the Bible classes were distinct from the congregations, the frequenters of the Workmen's Mission would not go to the classes." [32] The workingmen had to put up with the sort of thing that irritated a Methodist lay preacher in Salford: "As a member and local preacher in the body, I move and have continual intercourse with my own order—operatives and artizans of intelligence—who complain to be so misrepresented. The fact is, our opinions are unascertained; we are never consulted." [33] He complained that the Wesleyans were dominated by "the Pluto-cracy." In many instances "the indiscriminate poor" did not join a chapel at all, but preferred to attend services in the Church of England, "where they could probably worship with less inhibition than in a large predominantly middle-class chapel." [34] Many work-ingmen, including artisans, remained estranged from religious institutions. For the most part, however, the respectable working-man participated in religious life in the manner deemed appropri-ate to his station.

Religiously significant activity was not considered the exclu-sive province of church and chapel, however. Even so secular a figure as the Registrar of Friendly Societies could be described as "a minister of self-help to the whole of the industrious classes." [35] In justifying this analogy the speaker explained the "true moral unity" that could be discerned in the functions of the Registrar, who handled not only savings banks and benefit clubs, but also scientific and literary institutions devoted to mental improvement. The same "moral unity," reflecting a transfer of religious earnest-ness to interconnected secular values and institutions, was the most distinctive characteristic of mid-Victorian culture.

This unity was formally manifested in a standardized ritual. At tea parties, annual meetings, festivals, Christmas parties, exhibi-tions, and soirées the middle and working classes acted out their roles and affirmed the values of the community. The middle classes were benevolent and condescending, the working classes were grateful and respectful. Speaker after speaker intoned the litany of social, moral, and intellectual improvement. The reassuring rit-ual bespoke a society in equilibrium.

There was one unsettled issue that threatened to disrupt this delicately balanced system, however.

III

The franchise issue could not readily be settled according to the standard formulas of mid-Victorian urban culture, because any substantial extension of the right to vote seemed likely to produce a major shift in the balance of power between the classes. Political equality ran against the grain of a highly stratified society. To the average merchant or manufacturer in 1850 it seemed the height of demagogic irresponsibility to suggest enfranchising a large segment of the ignorant and impoverished masses, since it was only reasonable to assume that such voters would immediately use their new power to hold the rich for ransom. When the *Manchester Guardian* denounced John Bright's "wild and mischievous doctrines" in 1858, it was merely expressing the normal bourgeois fear of household suffrage. Yet workingmen were bound to demand the vote on grounds of principle and expediency. The Chartist crisis had dramatized the predicament that had to be resolved before England could begin to become a political democracy: without strong pressure the propertied classes would not extend the franchise; but the stronger the pressure the more stubbornly they were bound to resist; and middle-class resistance was sure to provoke another explosion of the Chartist type.

England found a way out of this impasse largely as a result of the initiative of middle-class Radicals, whose efforts in behalf of household suffrage facilitated the transition to democracy. Despite the fears generated by Chartism, a vigorous middle-class Radical movement emerged in the industrial towns at a very early date. Throughout the 1850s and 1860s working-class advocates of parliamentary reform knew that they could count on growing middle-class support.

At the height of the last Chartist outburst, an influential group of free traders, led by George Wilson and Richard Cobden, announced the goal that middle-class Radicalism was to pursue for the next generation: "a union of the middle and working classes for the purpose of obtaining an extension of the suffrage, vote by ballot, equal electoral districts, and a reduction of taxation." [36] The House of Commons spokesman for the "New Movement" was Joseph Hume, who called for petitions in support of a household suffrage resolution that he proposed to introduce. The towns responded enthusiastically to the appeal of "Messrs. Cobden, Hume & Co." [37] Early in June *The Times* reported: "The Ultra-Liberals in the West Riding of Yorkshire, as in other parts of the kingdom, are making efforts to get up public meetings and pass resolutions" in favor of Hume's motion.[38] By June 20 the House of Commons was deluged with petitions calling for household suffrage.[39] No action was taken, however, and the agitation ended abruptly.

Although the New Reform Movement disappeared quickly, the attitudes and purposes that it expressed were to give life to middle-class Radicalism throughout the 1850s and 1860s.[40] The major premise of the movement remained unchanged: the middle and working classes shared a common interest in wresting "reform" from the ruling aristocracy and its satellites. On that basis the Radicals were determined to forge an alliance between the classes that had been at odds for so long. Although the middle-class Radicals did not organize a continuous and sustained agitation, on three occasions they conducted large-scale campaigns for household suffrage.

The Parliamentary and Financial Reform Association organized the first of these campaigns between 1849 and 1852. Branch societies were formed in a number of provincial cities, and several national conferences were held.[41] The Association won a strong following among middle-class Radicals in the industrial North and claimed that its delegates included "some of the largest manufacturers and employers of labour in Lancashire and Yorkshire." [42]

Even when the formation of a Tory government in February 1852 seemed to threaten the revival of protectionism, the Association did not neglect household suffrage, but resolved that "this meeting believes radical Parliamentary Reform to be the great practical want of the day." [43] By 1853 the Association was inactive; in 1855 it was formally dissolved.

The next outburst of Radical activity in behalf of household suffrage came in 1858–1859 under the leadership of John Bright. When Bright called for a parliamentary reform agitation in his Birmingham speech in October 1858, the middle-class Radicals responded swiftly and energetically. By the end of the year the *Manchester Guardian* had to console itself with the thought that in Parliament Bright "will find how exceedingly small his party is, in proportion to the clamour it raises throughout the land." [44] The "clamour" continued unabated in January and February. In industrial towns large and small, reform associations sprang up; [45] in Lancashire they joined together in a Lancashire Reformers Union, under the leadership of George Wilson and other former Leaguers; in Yorkshire local associations formed the West Riding Reform Association. [46]

The third and most ambitious of middle-class Radical undertakings preceded the passage of the second Reform Bill. The chief instrument of the movement was the National Reform Union, which presided over an extensive agitation between 1864 and 1867. Although the Union was strongest in Lancashire and Yorkshire, its conferences attracted delegates from all over the country; in May 1865 over 170 towns were represented. [47]

What motives prompted so many able middle-class leaders to violate the normal inclinations of their class by advocating household suffrage? One unifying impulse behind the movement was a deep antipathy to the social and political hegemony of the landed classes. In carrying on what Cobden called "the great struggle against feudalism," the Radicals wanted every possible source of strength. All Radicals shared Cobden's annoyance that "we are the only nation where feudalism with its twin monopolies, landed and ecclesiastical, is still in power." [48] Even in the universities there were men "who incline to democracy not on broad doctrinal grounds, but because they entertain a jealous dislike of a privileged order." [49] The class struggle between manufacturer and squire nourished the reformist impulses of middle-class Radicalism. Nonconformist resentment at Anglican privileges had the same effect. The desire for allies against the ruling Tory–Anglican oligarchy helped persuade many manufacturers and merchants to overcome their natural misgivings about enfranchising working-class householders. Moreover, the ever-growing numbers of "respectable artisans" served to quell theoretical fears about "the masses."

As earnest Victorians many Radicals were also actuated by principle. They urged an extension of the franchise because justice demanded it. To be for reform was to be on the side of truth and morality. Characteristically, however, they also advocated household suffrage for realistic and conservative reasons. Bright argued that "great discontent and turbulence might arise if the workingmen felt that they are distrusted, that they are marked as inferiors, that they are a sort of pariahs [sic]." [50] In a similar vein Cobden pointed out the advantages of middle-class leadership of the masses: "I can tell the manufacturers, capitalists, and men of station in this country, that whether it be time of crisis, or of tranquillity the only safety for them is to be at the head of the great mass of the people, and I therefore rejoice at the proceedings of this day, which have given us so favourable a prospect of that union, in which there is not only strength, but safety." [51]

IV

In the course of the parliamentary reform agitation that unfolded under the leadership of middle-class Radicalism, the industrial towns settled the franchise question, found a mutually acceptable pattern of political relations between the middle and working classes, and completed the critical phase of the transition to democracy in England. By the time that Parliament took up the matter in earnest in 1866 the suffrage issue no longer was a source of social and political conflict as it had been twenty years before. An essential aspect of the process of becoming a democracy—the development of the necessary habits and attitudes on the part of all classes—had taken place before Parliament passed the Reform Act of 1867. Moreover, the political and ideological forms that grew into existence in the 1850s and 1860s, firmly rooted in the structure of mid-Victorian urban culture, contributed significantly to the conservative character of English democracy in the last third of the nineteenth century.

The middle-class Radical campaigns for household suffrage ended the political isolation of the Chartists, accustomed the working classes to the leadership of their social superiors, vastly enhanced the prestige of liberal ideology, and brought the artisan elite into a close relationship with the left wing of the Liberal party. This train of events had been set in motion even before the end of the 1840s by the Parliamentary and Financial Reform Association. On the surface, the Association appeared to have failed, since the militant Chartists remained hostile, the House of Commons refused to act, and the bulk of the middle classes remained aloof. Nevertheless, the movement toward political accommodation between the classes gathered momentum a few years later when the Radicals again took up the question of parliamentary reform.

The turning point in mid-Victorian urban politics came at the end of the 1850s, during the formidable agitation led by John Bright, when workingmen joined forces with the middle-class Radicals. George Wilson noted with satisfaction that "there was no fear of the old game being played; . . . the working classes were thoroughly prepared to accept the leadership of Mr. Bright." [52] Even Ernest Jones, who had led the Chartist opposition to the Parliamentary and Financial Reform Association a few years before, now conceded the need for political co-operation with the middle classes.[53] Typical was the sort of event that took place at Middletown, where former Chartists voted to amalgamate with a middle-class group in order to organize the maximum support for Bright's campaign: "We may add that, considering there were collected on this occasion the most determined Chartists this neighbourhood was so noted for a few years ago, the utmost good temper and most liberal spirit was reciprocated betwixt themselves and that class so much railed against formerly, viz.: the middle class." [54]

Another manifestation of the changed relations between workingmen and middle-class Radicals was the participation of nonelectors' groups in the general election of 1859, usually in behalf of Radical candidates. In various Yorkshire cities, for example, nonelectors were active in the Radical cause.[55] A Bradford group called on like-minded nonelectors to persuade the electors to vote for the Radical candidate: "Urge upon the electors the justice and the necessity of voting for Salt. . . . Tell them, by voting for Harris they politically ignore us as a class, thereby declaring themselves to be our worst and bitterest enemies." [56] In this way workingmen were being assimilated into the local political community even before they were enfranchised.

The middle-class Radical campaign for the leadership of the working classes came to a climax in the 1860s. The Radicals bestowed on the workingmen that full measure of flattery and attention which politicians usually reserve for voters. In their propaganda the National Reform Union and its member associations took pains to play up working-class participation and initiative in the parliamentary reform movement. Although the Union was not actually founded until 1864, the middle-class Radicals proudly traced its origin to a working-class group formed in 1860, the

Leeds Working Men's Parliamentary Reform Association.[57] When a national conference met in Manchester to establish the Union, the organizers did all they could to emphasize the working-class sponsorship of the meeting. In fact, a group of Manchester workingmen was under the impression that they were electing delegates to "a national workingmen's conference." [58] The Union continued to court the working class, and two years later received this rebuke from the *Manchester Guardian:* "The active spirits of the Reform Union have descended into a political alliance which, with all their faults, is unworthy of them, and are taking a leaf out of a book which they once had a right to despise. Since the time when the House of Commons was asked to receive a petition for the People's Charter . . . , the art of political vamping has not been practised on so imposing a scale as in the Radical demonstrations of the present parliamentary recess." [59] Through such "political vamping" the Radicals were bringing the working classes within the pale of the constitution even before the legislation of 1867.

Despite the strictures of the *Manchester Guardian,* many workingmen felt that the Union was being unduly cautious in refusing to go beyond household suffrage. The Reform League, an independent working-class organization devoted to manhood suffrage, was a powerful competitor for popular backing. But the Union managed to overcome even this obstacle. The Radicals were careful to avoid opposing manhood suffrage on principle, but insisted that only household suffrage had any chance of parliamentary acceptance in the near future. The argument was convincing. Eventually the Union even succeeded in achieving a working collaboration with the League. At Manchester in September 1866, for example, the Union went out of its way to cooperate with its competitor. The northern department of the Reform League, a recent outgrowth of the Manchester Manhood Suffrage Association, had arranged an outdoor mass meeting. The Union passed a resolution wishing the League success and calling on its own branches to aid in the meeting. It advertised in the newspapers for men to carry Union banners at the demonstration. The *Manchester Guardian* complained that "a looker-on who was unaware of the real fact might have been led to suppose that the whole meeting emanated from Newall's Buildings." At the principal platform (there were six in all) the leading middle-class Radicals were very much in evidence. The first resolution called for registered residential manhood suffrage. Another expressed "confidence in the honesty and ability of Mr. John Bright to champion the people's cause in Parliament during the coming parliamentary struggle." That evening the League participated in a meeting convened by the Reform Union.[60]

The same pattern appeared in other industrial towns: the outdoor mass meeting, preceded by processions of workingmen carefully organized by marshals; separate platforms for the subdivisions of the main meeting; middle-class Radicals in attendance; then an evening meeting indoors, joined in by the leaders of official Liberalism.[61] Throughout the country, with only minor variations, the middle-class Radicals collaborated with the working classes in a vast campaign for parliamentary reform.[62]

As a result of the initiative of the middle-class Radicals, the artisan classes were able to carry over into politics the role to which they had become so attached: co-operating with superiors in pursuit of objectives deemed appropriate to their station. The relationship between the Liberal workingman and his middle-class leaders was a satisfying one, because it was part and parcel of the way of life of the community as a whole. Lib-Labism, as it was later to be called, fitted neatly into the structure of Victorian urban culture. The Liberal affiliation of the artisan elite, rooted in the political and cultural circumstances of the mid-Victorian towns, was to exert a powerful stabilizing influence on late Victorian democracy.

Another element of stability in English democracy, the prestige of liberal ideology, also was significantly strengthened by the various campaigns for parliamentary reform. The traditional liberal premises—harmony of interests between the classes, the efficacy of reason in politics, and the possibility of progress through rational reform—constituted the sort of optimistic assumptions that were well suited to smoothing the gears of newly democratized constitutional machinery. The parliamentary reform movement helped to impress a liberal form on the political consciousness of the working classes, particularly the aristocracy of labor.

By advocating the enfranchisement of urban householders the Radicals offered convincing proof of their own belief in the harmony of interests between the middle and working classes. Given this fundamental harmony, there was no reason why the classes could not overcome superficial differences and join together in the pursuit of progress. W. E. Forster was articulating a major theme of Radical oratory when he said: "Let us, then, all join together in this great and good work of turning these aliens into citizens; let capitalists and labourers, employers and employed, throw away their jealousies and suspicions and help in this work. I fully believe that, in as far as they perform it, they will find their reward in discovering that even those jealousies and suspicions will melt away and cease to exist." [63] Paradoxically, attacks on the aristocracy enhanced the class harmony theme by creating an image of the middle and working classes united in common devotion to reform in the face of benighted opposition by the landed oligarchy. The Radicals were fond of appealing to "the people" in this fashion: "Once let it be known that capital and labour were united, and the battle would be won peaceably. It would then be impossible that a great people should be over-ridden by an aristocracy too arrogant to be generous and too selfish to be just." [64] This speaker, like Bright, was certainly guilty of "fostering animosities of class." Nevertheless, in fostering a rather harmless and anachronistic animosity between aristocracy and "people," the Radicals were softening a far more dangerous class antagonism between bourgeoisie and proletariat.

Belief in the absence of fundamental conflict between the middle and working classes tended to reinforce the rationalism that constituted a second prominent feature of liberal ideology. Since the classes were not divided by conflicting interests, it was easy to accept the traditional liberal assumption that every problem has a rational solution, which, when discovered, will command the assent of men of reason and good will. In this vein the Radicals extolled the intelligence of the workingmen as evidence of their fitness for enfranchisement. As intelligent men they could be trusted to accept a "sound" policy when it was presented to them. A classic expression of liberal confidence in the role of reason in politics occurs in a manifesto by the workingmen of the Reform League: "When our opponents see us determined, persevering and united, they will no longer refuse our just demands. They are our countrymen, and time and reflexion will lead them to act justly toward us." [65] Attitudes of this sort received powerful confirmation in the soothing reasonableness of the middle-class Radicals' arguments, especially on the ticklish subject of manhood versus household suffrage.

Belief in progress through rational reform constituted a third component of the liberal creed. Every aspect of the campaign for an extension of the franchise drove home the same point; just as the constitution could be reformed by organized persuasion, so other grievances would be removed in the onward march of reform. The Act of 1867 provided forceful proof of the validity of this expectation. The same procedure might be repeated indefinitely with similarly beneficial results.

The parliamentary reform agitation did not impose a factitious ideology of the twentieth-century type; it strengthened and confirmed political beliefs that expressed the deepest values of the culture. In this well-integrated culture there was a close correspondence between political and social values. Belief in progress through rational reform was the political correlative of the faith in individual improvement through intelligence and hard work.

Liberal confidence in class harmony reflected the cultural preoccupation with smoothing class relations. Both in politics and in social life there was the same tendency to describe goals in moral and idealistic terms. In both spheres to be reasonable meant accepting the argument of social superiors. Liberalism was not a narrowly political doctrine, but an expression of the mid-Victorian ethos. As such it was extremely effective in attenuating conflict and fostering cooperation after 1867.

In this context the parliamentary reform meetings appear not merely as political gatherings, but as a crowning ritual of mid-Victorian urban culture, in which the middle and working classes acted out their prescribed roles and confirmed their common faith. The meetings manifested in visible form the class harmony that was acclaimed in oratory. Middle-class Radicals, actuated by reason and good will, demanded justice for the working classes and progress for the nation. Responsible workingmen, dutifully accepting their station in life, welcomed the initiative of their superiors in an enterprise sanctioned by the highest moral and rational principles. Thus the classes gathered together in celebration of a liberal faith that united them morally without disturbing their social separateness. The proceedings corresponded closely to the standardized mid-Victorian ritual of tea parties, soirées, and official dedications. Utilizing familiar ceremonial forms, the reform meetings dramatized the terms on which the middle and working classes of the industrial towns had tacitly agreed to conduct their political relations.

By 1867, then, there had grown into being in the industrial towns political attitudes and habits that enabled England to embark on her experiment in democratic government under conditions conducive to the maximum stability. Working-class acceptance of middle-class leadership and ideology made certain that the newly democratized House of Commons would not have to deal with any really awkward economic and social questions.

England's inchoate democracy was spared the strain that would have been caused by the demands of a less acquiescent working class.

The manner in which the industrial towns dealt with the franchise issue in the 1850s and 1860s also contributed to the profoundly conservative character of English politics in the last third of the nineteenth century. Old habits of deference and subordination, rooted in an inegalitarian society and reinforced by the agitation for parliamentary reform, persisted after 1867. In contrast to the situation in France and Germany, where strong socialist parties emerged at an early date, the English working classes were content with the Liberals and the Conservatives. H. J. Hanham's study has shown the extent to which working-class voters responded to the electoral influence wielded by industrial magnates in behalf of the traditional parties.[66] The majority of employers "simply expected some deference to their wishes because they thought it natural that workingmen should look to their 'betters' for guidance." [67] Such deference continued to be forthcoming for some time.

The most strikingly conservative characteristic of English democracy in the last third of the nineteenth century—the staunch loyalty of the working-class elite to Liberalism and the Liberal Party—also had its origin in the mid-Victorian towns. The basic components of Lib-Labism had been forged in the 1850s and 1860s; their future development was to be determined by Liberal policy. In 1868 the Liberal Whips exploited to the utmost their advantageous position when they made an agreement with George Howell of the Reform League that prevented independent working-class activity in the general election and made the League itself an electoral instrument of the Liberal party.[68] Lib-Labism was even strong enough to survive Gladstone's labor policy, and in the 1870s local workingmen's clubs and associations gravitated into the orbit of the Liberal party.[69] Trade union leaders were solidly

Liberal. In the 1880s and 1890s Lib-Labism put up a strong fight against socialist efforts to establish an independent labor party. Even at the end of the nineteenth century "the great majority of trade-union leaders were members of the Liberal Party, and Gladstonians at that." [70] Only reluctantly, when local Liberal associations insisted on nominating middle-class candidates, did the working-class elite abandon their allegiance to the party of Gladstone and Bright.[71]

Thus, the mid-Victorian towns were of strategic importance in the social and political development of modern England because of their success in solving the difficult problems in class relations inherited from the Chartist era. In politics the middle and working classes found a solution that combined a fairly considerable extension of the franchise with political and ideological forms congenial to an inegalitarian society. On the basis of this settlement in the towns, England moved cautiously in the direction of democracy.

Education can provide an excellent example of the sort of problems which Victorian government and society faced in mid-century. In this article by Richard Johnson one can see the strands of private and public interests, government actions, and particular social aims fuse together in the consideration of the education of the poor.

Richard Johnson teaches in the Faculty of Social Science at the University of Birmingham. This article is reprinted with the permission of the Past and Present Society and the author from Past and Present, A Journal of Historical Studies *49 (November 1970), 96–119. * World Copyright © The Past and Present Society, Corpus Christi College, Oxford.*

RICHARD JOHNSON

Educational Policy and Social
Control in Early Victorian England

*What is the nature and height of the fence
with which the playground is enclosed?*[1]

I

I HAVE FOUND THE hopes of all enlightened men to rest, as
the great hope of staying to some degree this flood of
evil, upon education." So, in 1845, wrote Henry Moseley,
the most perceptive of the first generation of schools inspectors in
England. He added, with a rarer insight, that these hopes were
sometimes less than rational: men took shelter in the education
cry "in despair of any other solution." [2]

It is not difficult to establish the first part of his statement. A
cursory summary of the 1830s and 1840s shows that the education
of the poor was, indeed, one of the strongest of early Victorian
obsessions. In 1839, the Education Department began its cuckoo-
like progess in Charles Greville's Council Office. Earlier in the
decade other government departments with less direct responsibilities in this field, nonetheless looked towards educational remedies. The Prison Inspectorate, founded in 1835, turned, almost
instinctively it seems, to moral and religious education to stem a
rising crime rate, especially among the children of the urban
poor.[3] As in crime so in pauperism, crudely deterrent legal mechanisms were supplemented by attempts at educational rehabilita-
tion—Chadwick's new Poor Law by Dr. Kay's workhouse and
district schools. Similarly, the early Factory Inspectors, following
the Benthamite logic of the Act of 1833, counted education among
their major concerns.[4] The education of the poor figured largely

in many of the social and industrial inquiries of the period, even those appointed under other briefs.[5]

In Parliament, a major part of the Whig party, rather erratically led by Lord John Russell and Henry Brougham and stimulated by the Philosophical Radicals, favored from the late 1830s any practicable measure of official educational action. Tory resistance rested more on distrust of a secular agency than upon opposition to the end itself. Indeed, the most ambitious educational plan of the period came from the office of a Conservative Home Secretary, while the most eager educationalist in the Cabinets of the time was Lord Wharncliffe, Graham's Tory colleague. "Public education" was, of course, a perennial source of very inconclusive debate in both houses of Parliament, many private members making the subject their own.

The growth of interest and of institutions outside government was no less marked. The National Society, educational agency of the established church, reached a peak of fund-raising and project-launching between 1838 and 1843. A similar involvement, notwithstanding deep inner disagreements, may be traced within most branches of old and new dissent. In the late 1840s the Roman Catholic Poor School Committee was founded. The period was marked, too, by the spread of training colleges for elementary schoolteachers and of systems of diocesan organization. The founding of pressure groups like the Central Society for Education (1837–1839), a boom in surveys of educational provision by, for example, the new Statistical Societies, a growth in educational journals, and an enthusiasm for foreign and progressive teaching methods, all testify to the intensity of interest. Piles of educational pamphletry, usually appearing in batches, add *embarras de richesses* for the educational historian.

All this ignores, of course, the real roots of educational enterprise in the voluntary era: the founding and maintenance of schools for the poor in thousands of local communities, the critical subject of an educational history that still largely waits to be written. Omitted too are "educational" enterprises of a less formal sort, to which, as Professor R. K. Webb has shown, orthodox liberal opinion was increasingly addicted.[6] Nor was the orthodox tradition the only one: there were those who sought to teach the people their political rights or move them to co-operation not competition. So it is clear that the condition of the poor came almost to *mean* the condition of their education. As one Birmingham Justice of the Peace put it: "I have no other conception of any other means of forcing civilisation downwards in society, except by education." [7]

Qualifications should, of course, be registered. Concern was not new, for the educators of these decades built upon a well-established tradition of educational philanthropy, while greatly extending its scope and refining its methods. It would be rash too to consider concern universal, even among those with whom this article is concerned, the social "superiors" of the poor. Even in the 1840s, considerable if inarticulate resistance to popular education persisted, especially it was often said among employers of agricultural labor. And a more widespread lack of zest, or a failure of continuing interest, is suggested by the rather general disinclination of the laity adequately to support public philanthropic schools, the favored agencies of orthodox educators. Those who spoke, wrote, and preached so much about education were, no doubt, an articulate minority. The majority voted more silently with their pockets and were forced, at length, to pay by rates.

Even so, recognition of an intensification of interest raises interesting and important questions. What was the nature of this educational enterprise; how is it best understood? How are we to account for it at this particular historical juncture, and how is it to be evaluated? And why was it that despite the intensity of interest rather little was achieved before 1870, at least in terms of a really effective general system?

The aim here is to attempt to answer the first question and the fundamental one. But this is only a necessary prelude to the much bigger problem of explanation for which this article is intended only as a base.

II

There are at least four approaches. The first is to look at the stated intentions and the acknowledged motives of orthodox educators themselves: to see, in other words, what they thought or said they were doing. Although this is the obvious starting point for good pragmatic historians, there are equally obvious pitfalls: in particular the difficulty of penetrating to unacknowledged but possibly powerful motives and, allied to this, the difficulty of distinguishing between rhetoric (albeit significant rhetoric) designed for a particular polemical purpose and the conscious beliefs of the speaker. A bigger question looms too: How far is it sufficient to comprehend in terms of the conscious purposes of contemporaries? Or should we not be concerned with the working out of unconscious function within some wider system of change? An example may illustrate some of these difficulties.

In March 1840, Dr. James Phillips Kay, doyen of orthodox educationalists and the chief educational policy-maker within government in the 1840s, wrote to Sir Thomas Phillips about the need for educational action in the notoriously turbulent region of South Wales.[8] The letter was meant to bully colliery proprietors into promoting education and wielded three distinct sets of arguments. The first centered on the material dangers of "disorganising doctrines" and on the "interests of proprietors who have so much at stake." Educational promotion was represented (was seen?) as analogous to the use of profit to ensure against capital loss. This crudest of appeals to the values of the counting-house was followed by a plea for employees, albeit framed in very moralistic terms. Education would prevent that "self-destruction" attendant upon "high wages" among an "uncivilised" population.

Finally, changing into a top gear of altruism, Kay insisted on the duties of property in succoring a dependent population, a duty akin to that of a parent.[9]

Ambiguities such as these make it difficult to interpret most contemporary statements of intent in a convincing manner. This is especially so, perhaps, of religious educators (the majority) to whom the language of public order came as easily as that of saving souls. On the basis of this sort of evidence the enterprise may be represented as a quasi-coercive and essentially self-protective response or as the genuine outgrowth of humanitarian Christian consciences. And some such division seems to underlie rival interpretations of what we could once call, without any sense of ambiguity, "Social Reform." There is perhaps, more truth, less naïveté in the first than in the second view, but it is doubtful if either, or judicious mixtures of both, can be firmly upheld on this sort of evidence.

This leads to other possible approaches. One of these is to study what was actually taught in schools and, by inference, the sort of results that were expected from such teaching. Another is to examine the social and economic foundations of educational promotion at the level on which it mainly operated, that is the local community. Neither approach has been fully exploited, though it is clear that much can be learned about what was taught in schools from a content-analysis of the most popular school books.[10] Approach via the local community has suffered from the disintegrative effects of historical specialisms. Interesting work on the motives of manufacturers apart,[11] the dynamics of local action remain obscure. What seems to be needed, though the program is an ambitious one, is a combination of educational research, social-structural analysis, and local economic histories in order to examine the functions of schools and the purposes of schools promoters within well-defined communities and regional economies. Since educational research is still too often in rather familiar grooves, proponents of social-structural research still rather in-ward-looking, and economic historians still not as interested as they might be in education, the gaps in our knowledge remain.

The fourth approach, more accessible and more traditional, is the one adopted here: to scrutinize the social assumptions implicit in a particular measure; to study, in a critical way, declarations of intent in conjunction with an item of educational practice. The item of practice chosen is the *Minutes* of 1846; the declarations of intent those of its authors, Dr. Kay and his handful of schools inspectors. Research elsewhere has shown that the *Minutes* did indeed grow directly from their perception of English social conditions, limited though action certainly was by the contingencies of educational politics.

This involves a narrowing of focus: governmental activities, still more those of the Department, form one rather thin thread in the whole complex educational enterprise. But they present an aspect which is unusually well documented and not at all unrepresentative. The makers of the *Minutes,* unusually articulate and committed men, made manifest many contemporary assumptions. The *Minutes* themselves formed the basis of government action in the mid-century and received overwhelming support from a majority of religious educators, extreme High Churchmen and Congregationalists apart. Without some such agreement rooted in a common view of the social purposes of education, government action of this sort would have been impossible.

III

From the educational writings of Dr. Kay (or Kay-Shuttleworth as he became in 1842) and from the reports of his inspectors up to 1846, four recurrent themes emerge: the potential benevolence of economic change, at least in the long run; an indictment of patterns of working-class behavior; an emphasis on the need for some substitute for the abrogated functions of the working-class parent;

an insistent demand for close control over that substitute—the elementary school and the elementary schoolteacher.

The first theme, which might be called a contingent optimism, was strongest in Dr. Kay himself. It is best followed in his Manchester pamphlet of 1832, the real starting point of his educational concern.[12] At first sight it may seem odd to call the pamphlet optimistic for it presented the city as an object-lesson in the disorders of "commercial" society, of a "disease which impairs its energies, if it does not threaten its vitality." [13] As a social diagnostician Kay projected into the future tendencies in Manchester society which he had observed and sometimes measured: the incidence of cholera and typhus, domestic squalor, the collapse of family life, crime, prostitution, drunkenness, irreligion, machine-breaking, pauperism, and Irish immigration (that "colonisation of savage tribes"). He held up to the reader a terrifying but hypothetical picture of "the natural progress of barbarous habits"—an appalling concatenation of evils that would reduce the working population to utter debasement, destroying the very structure of society by the "explosive violence" of "volcanic elements." [14]

Yet his pessimism was not pessimism about industrial society itself—as a system of economic and social organization. These "diseases," he repeatedly emphasized, had a "remote or accidental origin." They were not "necessary results of the commercial system" but stemmed from "foreign and accidental causes." They might "by judicious management" be "entirely" removed. They were temporary embarrassments by which the natural influence of manufacturers was "thwarted." "A system, which promotes the advance of civilization, and diffuses it over the world . . . cannot be inconsistent with the happiness of the *great mass of the people.*" [15]

So optimism was possible if certain conditions were met. These were twofold: environmental and "moral." "Physical" reforms included the control of sanitary and housing conditions, the growth of "civic institutions" (especially an effective police force), and, in a more general sense of environmental, the removal of "arbitrary restrictions and monopolies in trade," including, of course, the Corn Laws.

The people, however, must also be changed to benefit from the system. "Morality is," as Kay put it, "worthy of the attention of the economist." [16] Behavior might be changed through a reform of the Poor Law—"the luckless pseudo-philanthropy of the law," by the discriminating use of charitable endeavor and, above all, by a "general and effective system of education." This should teach the artisan not only occupational skills, but also "the nature of his domestic and social relations . . . his political position in society, and the moral and religious duties appropriate to it." Kay concurred with McCulloch that political economy was an essential element.[17]

There are really two modes of argument in the pamphlet. Sometimes Kay can be read as an environmentalist, disentangling a subtle interaction between conditions that were imposed and patterns of behavior that followed, almost by necessity, from them. He attacked those "prejudiced men" who blamed the poor for all their sufferings. He was acutely aware of the "reflex influence" of conditions upon the "manners." In an analysis of the "moral" effects of the division of labor, he borrowed from Adam Smith and anticipated Marx. He eschewed simple monocausal explanations of evils.

But there is much crude moralism in the pamphlet, too. "It is melancholy to perceive," he wrote, "how many of the evils suffered by the poor flow from their own ignorance and moral errors." [18] He often opposed purely environmental reform, denouncing moves to limit the hours of labor, for instance, as "the nostrums of political quacks." Without education, time "bestowed" would be "wasted" on "misused," spent in "sloth," "dissipation," or "listening in ignorant wonder" to "political demagogues." [19] While making the still-customary exception for handloom weavers, he thought wages generally adequate for a decent comfort, but "their means are consumed by vice and improvidence." He stressed throughout a "contagion of manner," a spread of "barbarous habits," commonly originating among the "degraded" Irish population.

This ambivalence is too deeply rooted in the pamphlet to be resolved by a critical reading. It is a function of the language. Kay was attempting to express the connection between environment, consciousness, and culture in a language of moral censure, of providential causation, and of his native Dissenting religion. The very term "morals" (or "moral") itself, which Kay usually preferred to the kindlier, more neutral eighteenth-century term "manners," was deeply ambiguous. It served at once as a synonym for "culture" (or "cultural") and to impute blame. This significant lack of a verbal differentiation might well be traced through the whole corpus of orthodox early nineteenth-century social comment.

One might speculate on the sources, intellectual or social, of Kay's contingent optimism. Intellectually he was as much a disciple of Thomas Chalmers, to whom the pamphlet was dedicated, as of Professor W. P. Alison, his teacher and his personal hero at Edinburgh University.[20] Alison was a compassionate environmentalist in his analysis of Scottish poverty and public health; Chalmers, building on his experience as a minister in Glasgow, believed in the "supremacy of the moral over the physical." [21] But perhaps Kay's social loyalties were ultimately decisive, for as a young man he identified himself completely with the real makers of Manchester society: not with the landowner, or with the "pure merchant," but with the "enlightened manufacturers" with whom he co-operated so closely in local politics and philanthropy. This distinctive class bias is acknowledged clearly enough in the pamphlet itself.[22] Moreover, there can be no doubt of the functional utility of Kay's diagnosis for the interests, immediate and long term, of this group of men. It promised an expansion of their markets and a pacification of their work forces. Above all, it nearly redistributed guilt away from the makers of a social revolution on to those who suffered most from it, with, it is true, a passing knock at "avaricious speculators" in land.[23] It gave to particular interests the appearance of a universal benevolence.

The young Dr. Kay came to education, the theme that was to dominate his official life, through reflection upon Manchester, the harbinger of an industrial civilization. His inspectors of the 1840s, Joseph Fletcher and Seymour Tremenheere apart perhaps, lacked his close acquaintance with the urban industrial environment or his close personal identification with its leaders. Of the seven full-time English inspectors appointed before 1846, five were Anglican clergymen, sharing a traditional Anglican unease about the industrial town. They were less inclined, therefore, to identify manufactures and some ultimate progress; more prone to regard the whole business as decidedly sinister but regrettably necessary. Moseley's vision of a "great tide of human calamity" (matching Kay's "natural progress af barbarous habits") allowed a less exhalted role to the manufacturer—blind rather than blameless.[24] It was Moseley, indeed, alone of his clerical colleagues, who rivaled Kay in the depth of his analysis. An exceptionally honest and sensitive man, with as acute an interest in science as in theology, he saw deeper than the instinctive or professional moralism of his clerical colleagues. He at least recognized with a humility that was very rare that he and members of his class could not understand what it was like to be a working man. "The fact is," he wrote, "that the inner life of the classes below us in society is never penetrated by us. We are profoundly ignorant of the springs of public opinion, the elements of thought and the principles of action among them—those things which we recognize at once as constituting our own social life, in all the moral features which give to it form and substance." [25]

It is a remarkable passage, yet in the last analysis Moseley himself was unable to bridge the gulf he plainly perceived. His contingent optimism was more muted, but the main contingency was the same: education, the right sort of education, must precede a more concrete emancipation.[26]

IV

The second theme—their denunciation of working-class decadence—was a critical link in the diagnosis of the educational policy-makers. It provided them with their most powerful propagandizing argument within their own class, for as Kay persistently emphasized, beyond "degradation" lay the threat of a spiraling crime rate or even bloody anarchy. An accent on changing the modes of working-class behavior provided, too, a powerful counterargument against those who sought to change industrializing society in more fundamental ways, through, for example, the introduction of manhood suffrage. Above all, perhaps, it eased the conscience of educators, or would-be educators, by giving them a warmer, more sentimental doctrine to preach than obedience to "natural" economic "laws," or the necessity of coercion or punishment to maintain social cohesion. As Kay himself put it, in defending pauper education in 1838: "The attention the [Poor Law] Commissioners have given this subject is likely to prove a means of vindicating their opinions and designs from the imputation of being under the influence of cold blooded economical speculations, without the infusion of a more generous sympathy for the happiness of the poor classes." [27] In short, by blaming the poor for their poverty (and much else besides) the educationalist was *enabled to believe* that his was a humane, an adequate, and an essentially Christian response to potentially removable evils.

The philanthropic indictment of working-class patterns of behavior is, in outline, familiar enough. But the width and the indiscriminate nature of the version which is to be found in the reports of schools inspectors should be stressed. The attack was remarkably comprehensive.

On a relatively trivial level, the sports, the amusements, the language, and the lack of "civility" of working people was severely censured. Inspectors commented on the persistence of "demoralizing sports," which they often associated with sexual immorality or cruelty to animals. One inspector, in Birmingham, found that working people were often sadists: they took "a fiendish exultation in inflicting pain" upon animals. [28] The public house was universally condemned, both for the obvious reason—"the abuse of spirituous and fermented liquors"—and because public houses were recognized to be the local hubs of working-class economic and political organization. They were places of resort "for the pleasure of talking obscenity and scandal, if not sedition, amidst the fumes of gin and the roar of drunken associates." [29] Not only beer, but also, more surprisingly, tobacco and snuff, were regarded as symptoms of domestic irresponsibility.[30] Inspectors waged war too upon "provincial dialect and an indistinct articulation," "coarse provincial accents," and "faults and vulgarities of expression." [31]

In terms of the spectrum of middle-class religion, most of the Inspectors, the resolute churchman Allen apart, perhaps, were men of moderation. They inclined towards a liberal Anglicanism, tolerant of orthodox Protestant Dissent, concerned to stress the general moral precepts of true religion and its power to change ways of life. But they all made the conventional identifications of irreligion and sedition, infidelity, unconcern, and moral iniquity. By their religious tests certainly, the working classes stood condemned, not only for what Horace Mann was later to call an "unconscious" secularism but also for indigenous forms of popular religion and belief. Moseley found the Potteries a district "not less remarkable for the wild forms of religious belief than for the *infidelity* prevalent in it, and the madness of its political combinations." [32] Tremenheere made himself an expert on the superstitions of the "immovable" population of Norfolk: "here a wizard terrifying his neighbours by the power of inflicting injuries by his charms; there supernatural appearances; in another neighbourhood a quack curing all diseases by his knowledge of the stars." [33] In many examples of "gross credulity," inspectors commented on the subterranean paganism of the rural poor, sometimes in anecdotes which were, unintentionally, very funny.[34] The dangers of such "vacuity" were repeatedly stressed: the "legitimate educator" should anticipate the "Socialist." [35]

The political or economic beliefs of more articulate working people were commonly represented simply as "perverted opinion." One doubts whether many inspectors ever talked to a Chartist or an Owenite; only Tremenheere seems to have tried to plumb these depths of mischief. He found, for instance, "much quickness of intellect" among the Norwich weavers, but discovered what one suspects he sought—that "there was hardly a principle of religion, morals, society, trade, commerce, government, which I did not hear perverted by one or the other." [36] More commonly inspectors stressed a blind ignorance of, in Moseley's words, "the simplest and most obvious of those political relations which bind together the frame-work of society." He regretted (in a rather startling comment) that so many children were ignorant of who governed the country: they could not tell him the name of the queen.[37]

Similar attitudes colored inspectoral comments on popular literature: "obscene, exciting and irreligious works." This concern was most sharply expressed in a desire (later to be fulfilled) to control and to control most rigorously the reading matter made available in schools. Books commonly used were of "all kinds": poetry of a "questionable tendency," hymns in "extravagant and presumptuous language," letters addressed to "My Lovely Emma," to "Job Troublesome," or "complaining of the badness of times." [38]

The inspectors believed, of course, that social and economic conflicts were fundamentally a factor of bad faith and misunderstanding, sometimes exploited by the "disaffected." Here and there, they gave hints of a more perceptive analysis, witness Moseley's attempt to comprehend the gulf in class experiences, Bellairs's passing recognition of the social isolation of the rural poor,[39] or the occasional halting admission that some deeper cause was at work in the social system.[40] But the ultimate diagnosis was invariably working-class ignorance; the solution an authoritative direction of sentiment through education.

The most important area of conclusions, however, was the working-class family. Many, perhaps most of the failings which the inspectors perceived seemed to stem from some pathological tendency in "domestic relations." Here again Kay's Manchester pamphlet anticipated later findings. Reading it, it is easy enough to believe that the working-class family had altogether ceased to embody kindlier purposes, or even to perform the most basic of social functions. It did not support the old, for their adult children "cast" them on poor relief. It provided no comfort for its members because resources were squandered even when adequate. It gave neither training nor education for children since "filial and paternal duties" were uncultivated. Even the common care of children and babies was neglected. There is one, just one, more flattering reference to the working-class family in *Manchester*, and that a reference to the families of fine cotton spinners inserted in the second edition in response to criticism.[41]

It is tempting to follow N. J. Smelser and to relate Kay's findings to functional adjustments following the family's traumatic introduction to the factory.[42] Certainly Smelser's analysis allows us to understand some aspects of Kay's rather melodramatic discussion. Yet many of the "diseases" which Kay perceived in Manchester in 1832 were noted too by his inspectors, in many different parts of the country in the 1840s, providing an indictment not less comprehensive than the young doctor's. Their reactions in this sphere seem to have been determined quite as much by their picture of what the family should be (a conception derived no doubt from the bourgeois ideal of that institution) as by the undoubted cultural disruption faced by working people in many different industrial settings.

Thus most inspectors deplored the "imprudent habit of early marriage," tracing many family difficulties to this source.[43] At the same time they were deeply distrustful of unmarried working-men of over twenty-five. Watkins declared that from great experience he "hardly ever knew a middle-aged single man [of the lower class] who was a good character." [44]

Adolescence, however, was regarded as the period of greatest moral peril. From London and the West Riding, from Wales and East Anglia, from the countryside and from the growing cities, inspectors reported on the manifold misdoings of "youths." In Essex and Suffolk, Cook diagnosed a close relationship between adolescent independence and rural incendiarism. He also noted that the local clergy were in "awe and terror" over "the trial to which their best girls will be exposed on contact with rude, sensual and ignorant youths." [45] Watkins, making the adolescent sub-culture of West Riding towns one of his many moral specialisms, pointed to the early financial independence of children, their tendency to take their values from "bigger, rougher and more lawless" boys, and a general failure of parental control. Since children did not honor and obey their parents, they showed no proper deference to their social superiors: "I have often passed with a clergyman through a knot of young people, either of long-haired idling youths, or a flaunting giggling girls, and seen no other notice taken of the minister of religion than an independent nod or a half impudent recognition." [46] But by far the best indication of inspectoral attitudes to the parent is to be found in their early discussion of the problem of attendance—the governing economic and social condition of the education of the "independent poor."

The problem of attendance was in reality a particular symptom, itself more complex than the shorthand term implies, of the demands that an industrializing economy imposed upon the working-class family and through it, upon the child. It arose from the economic necessity (to the family) of extensive child labor, in both town and countryside. Ultimately it stemmed from poverty, mitigated by the growth of some industrial occupations but certainly not removed by them, a poverty that remained deep and endemic in many areas and trades, and cyclical or seasonal in all. Poverty was aggravated by social dislocation attendant upon large-scale migration and the destruction of some previously literate working-class communities. Reports from some urban areas suggest a shifting population even within the towns, a frequent change of dwelling-place disrupting the patterns of schooling. In short, the environments in which most families found themselves in the 1830s and 1840s imposed severe constraints on the use of educational facilities, supposing in the first place that they existed, and in the second that they were wanted.

It would be naïve to suppose that parental attitudes played no part in this situation. No doubt hostility or indifference to education existed, but it is difficult from the available evidence to distinguish between a parental unconcern for education as such, and, a different matter, a distrust (perhaps a rather rational distrust) of the forms of education which philanthropic endeavor offered. The parent who told Watkins "we wants a bit of reading, and writing, and summing, but no'at else" may well have been typical.[47]

The Department was aware of all three dimensions of the problem well before 1846. Inspectors' reports confirmed the findings of the factory inquiries, the Statistical Societies, and the Children's Employment Commission. It was estimated that a sizable proportion of children never attended any school. It was also agreed that those who did attend attended very irregularly, schooling being subject to continuous interruptions, except in the regulated industries where evasion was nonetheless very common. But perhaps the most disturbing aspect of the problem was the very early age withdrawal from school, commonly at the age of ten or eleven. Before 1846 statistical estimates were lacking but the evidence of unsystematic observation was entirely compelling.

Yet explanations of these phenomena were disappointingly superficial. Although in rural areas poverty and the indifference of farmers was sometimes blamed,[48] the main burden of moral guilt was transferred on to the parent. Schools did exist, argued Cook,

and education was cheap, yet "thousands are either too indifferent, or too ignorant, or too vicious, or too little able to command
their children, ever to avail themselves of the opportunity." [49]
Watkins found it strange but "instructive," that parents would "almost starve themselves to give their children bread" but would
make "*no sacrifice whatever* to give them food for their minds." [50]

It followed that before the 1850s (there were significant shifts
of inspectoral thought thereafter) the problem of attendance was
not so much ignored as sublimated. Dr. Kay fully shared his inspectors' views, seeing the problem of attendance as fundamentally
one of conversion. The onus clearly lay with the parent just as
the onus of school provision lay with philanthropic elites. They
were to be offered a greatly improved education for their children
suited to their real needs and status in life, and, in time, like the
sagacious and religious Scots, they would come to appreciate it.[51]
Moseley's belief—that the "whole question resolves itself into that
of the efficiency of schools"—was the typical orientation of the
makers of the *Minutes* of 1846.[52]

This summary may give, then, some idea of the breadth of the
attack. To be fair to them, inspectors did note some significant
differences according to region or occupational group. Tremenheere's examination of the relatively settled and privileged community of the Cornish tin-miners was rather favorable, even decidedly nostalgic.[53] More surprisingly, in view of later philippics
from this region, Allen's early reports from the North Eastern
coalfield were full of cautious praise. ("They are not immoral.
An unmarried man of 25 is scarcely to be found among them.") [54]
Certain aspects of working-class culture too were not condemned
outright, commonly the more folksy, Merrie-England aspects:
Cornish Parish Feasts, some forms of singing, some sports. Yet
even amusements like these were commonly regarded as instruments to be molded to new uses. Singing here was the outstanding
example, witness the efforts of the Department, of John Hullah,
and of Kay himself to capture or to infiltrate a genuinely popular

pursuit. As Kay put it: "the songs of any people may be regarded as an important means of forming an industrious, brave, loyal and religious working class." They might "inspire cheerful views of industry" and "associate amusements . . . with duties." [55]

Yet surveying the evidence as a whole, it is the undiscriminating character of the assault and the highly charged language of censure which leaves the most abiding impressions: "uncivilised," "degraded," "barbarous," "vicious," "supine," and so on. As a guide to the enormous variety of working-class cultures—rural, urban and transitional, serious and anarchic, self-conscious and primitive—inspectoral reports are very inadequate. As an indication of a mood of blanket condemnation they are most revealing.

V

The educationalists' third theme—parental substitution—can again be found in its purest form in Kay's writings. The idea that the school and the teacher could and should take over many of the responsibilities of the parent was a key concept in Kay's educational thought and a guideline of his policies. It provided the link between diagnosis and remedy. Latent in the Manchester pamphlet, it was developed during his service as a very zealous Assistant Poor Law Commissioner in East Anglia and London and strengthened by his experience of Continental educational theory in the late 1830s.

Kay and his colleague and friend, E. C. Tufnell, added a new dimension to Poor Law policy. They argued that the Poor Law should not only sweep away incentives to idleness, but should also provide a positive machinery for rehabilitating the children of paupers. If the pauper child could be taught self-respect and self-reliance, even at the expense of the strict application of less eligibility, the stigma of "hereditary pauperism" and the tendency for pauperism to generate itself might be erased. Pauperism could be seen as a sort of moral contamination transmitted through the parent.[56]

Within the Poor Law then, especially after 1837, Kay's characteristic attitudes to parent, child, and teacher were further developed. Pauper children were either truly orphans or deserted children, or their parents could be held to have signed away their parental rights by a sort of moral abdication. For such children the State was truly *in loco parentis* and the school should provide what a parent could or would not.[57] The Norwood experiment was a complete expression of this view: here Kay attempted to provide a substitute home for orphans, where the "parental" influence might extend even into adolescence.[58] More generally, in his plans for pauper district schools, the doctrine of separation of parent and child was taken to its extreme physical conclusion.[59]

These arguments, still less these devices, could not be applied *tout court* to the education of children of "self-supporting" parents. But very similar ideas and the same basic orientation towards parent, teacher, and child, were certainly imported by Kay into this field. As he put it in 1840: "The influence of the teacher of a day-school over the minds and habits of the children attending his school is too frequently counteracted by the evil example of parent and neighbours, and by the corrupting influence of companions with which the children associate in the street and court in which they live." [60] The problem, therefore, was to equip the elementary school and the elementary schoolteacher with the means of combating these influences.

It followed that the teacher should be equipped to be a "second" or even a "substitute" parent, and the recurrent use of the language of family roles in Kay's descriptions of the ideal school has a more than verbal significance: the school should resemble "the harmony of a well-regulated family"; it should be a sort of extended household; the teacher should perform the "civilizing" role of the idealized parent. As Kay put it in 1841: "The teacher of the peasant's child occupies, as it were, the father's place, in the performance of duties from which the father is separated by his daily toil, and unhappily at present by his want of knowledge and skill. But the schoolmaster ought to be prepared in thought and feeling to do the peasant-father's duty. . . ." [61]

Kay's strong interest in Continental educational theory is best explained, therefore, in terms of a practical concurrence between his perception of English social conditions and the educational beliefs of the followers of Pestalozzi. The Continental reformers stressed the parental analogy in their attempts to comprehend and to exalt the educational process. [62] A personal relationship between teacher and taught, an intimate moral rapport was a necessary condition for success, in contrast to the impersonal regimes of English monitorialism. So at Battersea, his experimental training college, Kay clearly saw himself as the English Vehrli, applying foreign ideas to be sure, and writing in very sentimental and un-English terms about "peasants," but applying these ideas and using this language because they fitted precisely his view of the function of the school in a particular social situation. Simply to regard him as an "educational pioneer," closely in touch with "progressive" teaching methods, misses the significance of this part of the educational diagnosis. [63] The teacher must become a sort of parent for the very good reason that natural parents were held to be disqualified or incapacitated from fulfilling their natural role.

The inspectorate expressed similar ideas in similar language. Drawing his perceptive contrast between the nurture of middle- and working-class children, Moseley noted that whereas education for "our own children" occurred mainly through the "associations of home," "in respect to the child of labouring man, it must be done, if done at all, at school." [64] The pupil–teacher relationship should resemble "a parental confidence and affection." [65] For Fletcher, the school must be an essentially foreign implantation within a commonly barbarized population. It should rest, not on the satisfaction of an indigenous demand, but upon "aggressive movements, on the part of the better elements of society." [66] The essential character of the whole educational project is caught in Fletcher's description of the school as "a little artificial world of virtuous exertion." [67]

The fourth and final theme of the educational diagnosis followed naturally from this vision of the necessary social isolation of the school. Such schools could clearly not be under the control of neighborhood or of parent. On the contrary means had to be found to emancipate them from these ties. Supervision must be entrusted to Fletcher's "better elements."

This theme of control had two related dimensions. The first dimension concerned the schoolteacher himself, the primary agent of "civilisation." Teachers themselves must be emancipated from the local community, made independent of the whims of the parent, more closely linked to local elites (and particularly the clergy), and provided with the financial means of a cultural superiority. They should be raised, but not too far, out of their own class.

It is difficult to comprehend insistence on this imperative without some knowledge of an older generation of teachers, and inspectoral attitudes towards them. Unfortunately we know rather little about this class—if class it was—before the coming of the college-trained, certified teacher. But one thing is clear: the gulf between school and community was often less wide than it was to become and to remain. This seems to have been as true of the more haphazardly organized public philanthropic and older endowed schools as of the private elementary schools which, financed by parents' fees, rested upon a genuinely indigenous demand for some educational provision.

We know least of all about this last and most interesting category of institutions. But both literary evidence and such statistical surveys of local and national school provision as are available suggest that they were genuinely popular, very ephemeral (and hence never accurately counted), rather numerous, and very varied in their ambitions and functions. They ranged from child-minding institutions (a not unimportant function of the much-maligned "Dame School") to sources of, at least, a basic literacy. More significantly perhaps, they, and indeed many public philanthropic schools, seemed to have formed a sort of informal welfare service, providing work and an income for people who were disqualified from common labor—the disabled, the ill, the old, the underemployed, the widows. One suspects, though it is difficult to demonstrate, that teaching sometimes provided a refuge for men who had quarreled with authority. But certainly it is striking how many injured pitmen (commonly Primitive Methodists), ex-soldiers and sailors, ex-domestic servants and artisans, "broken tradesmen," "common labourers" and, in areas of depressed outwork industry, how many underemployed domestic workers, were involved in teaching, often running their own self-financing schools.[68] Inspectors commonly regretted that parents were prepared to pay substantially higher fees to send their children to such people rather than meet the lower costs of public philanthropic schools.

By most of the tests that inspectors were wont to apply, "common schools" and many ill-supervised philanthropic schools were very inefficient. An older generation of teachers were accused of failings ranging from an amateur incompetence to "gross immorality." Anecdotes of the stupidity of "untaught" teachers were a stock-in-trade of reports. Not that inspectors were altogether unaware of the characteristic virtues of the autodidact: as men, if not as instructors of the poor, self-taught teachers were often admired.[69] Generally, however, "common schools" in particular and haphazardly recruited teachers in general, were convicted of failing really to "educate." They might give children a certain competence in elementary subjects, but did not teach them their "duties," or "the habit of self-government," or to be "wise and good men in after life." [70] The older generation of teachers often lacked "the capability of effecting, to any desirable extent, the mental and moral improvement of those under their charge." [71]

This inspectoral distrust of the "common" school and the untrained or unsupervised teacher rested as much upon a social suspicion as upon narrower educational deficiencies. So much is clear from cases in which "independent" teachers were praised for their sincerity and good sense, yet distrusted for the social influence they did or rather did not exercise. Allen's doubts about a Derbyshire lacemaker who was a "nominal schoolmaster," on the ground of the notorious turbulence of his district, was typical of this way of seeing things.[72] Teachers who were socially identified with their clientele might be unreliable.

The debate over the Chester Diocesan Training College in 1845 provides a good illustration of this theme. There great stress was laid upon the teacher as the sympathetic equal of the parent, sharing the cares and preoccupations of his class, this in contrast to most training colleges that sought to "elevate." The Department's attitude to this experiment was ambivalent. The Chester ideal, wrote Moseley, was "not without its perils." To identify the teacher with a lower class would tend to separate him from the class above him—"that class in which all his better and higher impulses will find their chief stay and support." Identified with their own people, teachers might become, by their moral ascendency, "active emissaries for misrule." [73] The Department's ideal was clear: the teacher should stand midway between his patrons and his clients, purveying the values of the clergyman, the training college, the Department, and of authority in general to morally deprived children with the firmness and kindness of a parent. He had to be equipped in his nature, in his skills, and in his economic and social situation for this difficult task.

The second aspect of control concerned the management of the school and the links that bound it to local functions. All the inspectors agreed that a "good" school was a school where there was proper, that is to say socially reliable, supervision. As Allen put it, "schools that are not properly superintended may be a very doubtful good." [74] "There must be constantly at hand the unbought services of some one, either clergyman, esquire, or member of their families, who, keeping the most important ends constantly in view, will be capable, by both education and intelligence, to give that counsel, and infuse that spirit which cannot be looked for from our present race of teachers." [75]

This criterion of proper control informed both inspectors' reports before 1846 and departmental practices. During the early 1840s a procedure developed by which any aided school had first to submit its trust deeds and its management clauses for approval by the Department's lawyer. It is clear that in this, as in other fields, technical advice became the pretext for control. Although management clause policy was not made explicit until 1846, its general tendency can be gauged from the lists of applications published annually by the department. Of the schools aided up to 1846 only four had workingmen on their Boards of Management (three in Scotland, one in England) and in no case did they form a majority. When management policy was spelled out in 1846, the acceptable social composition of committees was specified: clergy, the local gentry, manufacturers, ladies' committees, and, at most, "respectable tradesmen" or "yeomen." [76] As one inspector put it: "We cannot let farmers or labourers, miners or mechanics, be judges of our educational work. It is part of that work to educate them into a sense of what true education is." [77]

The four themes of this contemporary analysis clearly form a whole, providing a justification for a very close social control over educational agencies. Yet this conclusion was not reached without some sacrifice of consistency.

The key lies in that curious mixture of moralist and environmentalist arguments which we have already noted in Kay himself. As moralists, educationalists were enabled to transfer cause and guilt away from a system of social and economic organization which they more or less endorsed, on to the people. The logic of this stress upon a moral responsibility, as also of an ultimate optimism, was to allow to the sufferer some autonomous ability to solve his own problems. If the system was ultimately benevolent, it should presumably allow for this. Yet it was precisely this power which was denied to the working class, and, more specifically, to the working-class family. And it was here that the environmentalist elements in the argument were so important. For the educationalist could also argue, in a much more paternalistic vein, that salvation must come from outside a vicious circle of cause and effect—from above. Kay and his inspectors had, in short, the best of two modes of argument, their conclusion on the necessity of control deriving from a hybrid of a rather optimistic liberalism on the one hand, and a rather self-conscious paternalism on the other. Though their sincerity is not in doubt, the very powerful conservative function of their argument should not be overlooked. One might say that the imperative of control shaped the argument.

VI

Finally, it is necessary to turn briefly from thought to practice. If our analysis of social assumptions is correct, we would expect to see, in the *Minutes* of 1846, an attempt to create powerful systems of control, centering on the teacher as social missionary and the school as a functioning center of sound influences.

This is rather a different approach from that adopted by most educational historians who have discussed the *Minutes*. As Kay has been represented as a precocious forerunner of modern conceptions of teaching, so the *Minutes* have been seen as a sagacious solution to obvious educational problems.[78] They have been seen primarily as an important step in the creation of an elementary schoolteaching profession.

This view certainly embraces a part of the truth, but it may be criticized on two grounds. Firstly, though it is impossible here to establish the point, the educational efficiency and significance of the *Minutes* can easily be exaggerated. As a solution to the salient problems of school attendance and school finance they were rapidly proved to be inadequate. The conception of the profession that informed them was likewise shown to be hopelessly overambitious. They formed, as later administrators came to recognize, a *cul de sac* up which government had to return (a long and painful process) before more comprehensive solutions could be found.[79] Secondly, their full significance lies in some separate educational realm than in their social and political objectives. Educational historians, in short, have tended to miss the political sociology of the measure. And this point may be established by analyzing the *Minutes*, not so much as an educational measure, more as a system of social control.

Under the *Minutes*, control over the teaching profession was achieved by three phases of teacher training and by extended financial support. The trainee teacher and even the qualified professional, so far from being haphazardly recruited as in the past, was subjected to an intricate system of supervision. The agencies of this supervision, however, were not simply departmental: the Department drew into its network of control the essentially voluntary but completely reliable agents of the local clergy, local elites, and denominational training colleges.[80]

Before a child of thirteen could be apprenticed to a teacher in an elementary school, an inspector visited the school itself, reporting very fully on its management, curriculum, finances, and the character and proficiency of the teacher. The teacher's ability to act "as a guide and example in the formation of the character of the apprentice" was particularly examined. Candidates for apprenticeship had to pass a qualifying examination in elementary subjects, and the clergy had to certify, on the basis of personal inquiry, that their moral character and that of their parents was satisfactory. Where a family was deemed unsuitable (for example running a public house), the apprentice was required to board in "some approved household," commonly with the clergyman. On entering upon apprenticeship, the pupil-teacher covenanted to serve his master "faithfully and diligently," and to conduct himself "with honesty, sobriety, and temperance, and not be guilty of any profane or lewd conversation or conduct, or of gambling, or any other immorality." He was, in short, to be a very untypical "youth."

Once apprenticed, the child became, in effect, a paid dependent of the Department, receiving aid to the tune of from £10 in his first year to £20 in his last. The teacher was also paid to instruct him. Progress was tested annually by examination conducted by the Department on a prescribed syllabus with recommended books. Each year three certificates had also to be produced: from teacher, school managers, and the clergy. Each year the school was vetted by an inspector, the teacher receiving a long printed homily full of personal exhortation on the need for diligent self-improvement and the cultivation of "moral sentiments." Scholastic or moral failure on the part of the apprentice, or deficiencies in the school itself, could mean the withdrawal of aid, or, at worst, the blacklisting of the school or the teacher.

The pupil-teacher could enter the second stage of his training by sitting a public competitive examination. Subject to the result and to testimonials he might be awarded a "Queen's Scholarship" tenable at an inspected training college. During his two years there the college itself was subject to the same sort of control as the aided elementary school. Direct grants provided a pretext for increasingly detailed control over the syllabus and regimen.

Supervision extended, however, into the working teacher's career. Once trained he sat an examination for "the Certificate of Merit." Dependent on the result, he qualified for a grant in aid of his salary, graded according to his performance. The receipt of this grant remained conditional upon the state of the school in which he worked and the approval of the managers. One condition of aid was rent-free accommodation, always seen as a guarantee of a healthy independence.

Even secure retirement was, under the *Minutes* themselves, to be dependent upon merit. To acquire a pension, a teacher was to have taught at an inspected school for at least seven years, his character was to be approved and the school efficient.

Taken together, these regulations comprised, on paper at least, a system of control of great rigor. In this sense, over a narrow area, the *Minutes* rivaled any major parliamentary statute dealing with a social matter in the first half of the century. The intensity of control, as an ambition, was all the more striking, since it rested not on statutory sanction but on departmental discretions alone. The apparatus of teacher training, with its conditional offers of stipends, a degree of security, openings in the public service, a modest house and pension, amounted, in effect, to a system of guided, limited social mobility. Not that upward mobility was its governing idea; it crept in as a condition of cultural emancipation. Mission, not mobility was the keynote of Kay's training methods and those adopted by Department and training colleges. Satisfactory recruitment required the offer of substantial benefits, but, as teachers were to find not without chagrin, they were to be social intermediaries, not social aspirants. They were to form, in short, an army of highly trained, highly motivated mercenaries.

VII

The suggestion is that the early Victorian obsession with the education of the poor is best understood as a concern about authority, about power, about the assertion (or the reassertion?) of control. This concern was expressed in an enormously ambitious attempt to determine, through the capture of educational means, the patterns of thought, sentiment, and behavior of the working class. Supervised by its trusty teacher, surrounded by its playground wall, the school was to raise a new race of working people—respectful, cheerful, hard-working, loyal, pacific, and religious.

In itself, of course, this conclusion does not take us very far. But it may provide a fairly stable base from which to launch attempts at explanation and it may suggest too the general forms which explanation might most fruitfully take. For if control was the essence of the phenomenon, explanation should center, not so much upon some objective "educational problem" which wise contemporaries perceived or half-perceived, but rather upon points of contact between class cultures, upon social relations, upon relations of authority, and upon the ways in which these were changing in late eighteenth- and early nineteenth-century England.

*The previous article dealt with problems of lower-class educa-
tion in the earlier part of the period; the present article treats a
somewhat similar problem in the area of the education of the
upper-middle class at a later period. Here again social pressures,
and needs, are reflected in the interplay between private and public actions. Education serves as a convenient example of the complicated response to the challenges of the period.*

*Peter Stansky teaches modern British history at Stanford Uni-
versity. The article was originally published in* Victorian Studies v
(1962), 205–223, and is reprinted by permission of that journal.

PETER STANSKY

Lyttelton and Thring:
A Study in Nineteenth-Century Education

IN NINETEENTH-CENTURY England, education on the primary and secondary levels, and at the universities, was
being made available to more and more of the population.
For most, however, the problem remained one of getting any
education at all. But among the new-rich middle and professional
classes, the desire was not only to educate their sons, but, perhaps more important, to have them endowed with those graces
which would allow them to progress in a society highly conscious of the distinctions of class but still flexible in permitting
the crossing of lines. Such desires were rarely articulated. They
were certainly not the conscious aims of those most intimately
involved in work in education, though some headmasters were
aware of the implications of transforming a Grammar School into
a Public School. By 1874 when the functions of the Endowed
Schools Commissioners were transferred to the Charity Commissioners, the entire picture of education in the Public Schools had
altered; their numbers had been swelled by new and transformed
schools able to give the desired social advantages. Ironically, the
two men who in differing ways had had most to do with the
shape and form that private secondary education was to take—
George William, Lord Lyttelton, Chief Endowed Schools Commissioner, and Edward Thring, Headmaster of Uppingham School
—would, though for different reasons, have been least satisfied
with the results.

Both were concerned with questions of education on the practical and theoretical levels. They had very different ideas, for example, on the role of religion in schools. Although both were devout Anglicans, Lyttelton was a reluctant secularist, and Thring was determined to maintain the role of the established church. But this disagreement, which will not be discussed here, was subordinate to their diametrically opposed concepts of what education should be. Lyttelton was convinced that education was primarily an intellectual pursuit, and should concentrate on scholarship; whereas Thring felt that it was primarily moral, and should emphasize the development of character. This conflict was not resolved then (nor has it been now); it was reflected in the attitudes and careers of the two men, and the work of the Endowed Schools Commission. Eventually Lyttelton and Thring would have an opportunity to express their differences face to face, but the anticlimax of their meeting—and such it was—demonstrates, perhaps as well as anything else, the difficulty of reconciling the two points of view.

I

Lord Lyttelton is a fugitive figure. He considered his career a failure; he did not live up to his early political promise, and he fell a victim to melancholia which "surprised him in January, 1876."[1] In April of that year, he committed suicide by throwing himself over the balustrade of his house. Probably the strain of being Endowed Schools Commissioner and the abuse it brought down upon him aggravated his illness and hastened his end. Recurrent fits of melancholia do not justify calling him mad; still it is hard to agree with Gladstone, his brother-in-law, that the mere daily task of translating Homer would have prevented his death.[2]

Lord Lyttelton, born in 1817, came from an old Worcestershire County family. From 1834 to 1838 he was at Cambridge, and his career there was a brilliant one. The most important event in the formation of his intellectual character was his election to the Apostles, a club made up of men predominantly from Trinity College, which met weekly for reading and discussion. The club allowed an impressive group of young men to try to work out together a set of principles for poetry and metaphysics, and, without demanding agreement, to discuss politics and religion. But for many of them, including Lyttelton, it can be said that the club fostered a form of elitism and an overemphasis on principle; such high standards prevented many of its members from ever allowing themselves to participate fully in the political life of London. It is curious, though hardly significant, how many "Apostolic" careers of brilliant promise were cut short by early death, such as Hallam's and Sterling's, but, more important, how many, like those of Monckton Milnes and Lyttelton himself, never achieved their expected heights. The attitudes of the club prefigure Lyttelton's ideas on education, his belief that it is better to educate and encourage the exceptional few than the mediocre many. He had little sympathy for the view that the ordinary student is especially deserving of attention nor was he interested in the growing desire of the middle class to swell the Public School population. The "Apostolic" concern for self-cultivation in company with a congenial few produced in Lyttelton's logical mind an inability to sympathize either with the emotional strivings of those who wished to educate everybody or with the social ambitions of the middle class. Summing up his lifelong position in 1868, he remarked to the National Association for the Promotion of Social Science, "We consider generally that the best use of Educational Endowments is to bring out and develop the best youthful minds that can be found, in all classes of society, for the service of the state, by giving them facilities and advantages which otherwise they could not have . . . whether remaining within their own class, or rising out of it." [3] This was the intellectual elitism of the Apostles extended to the national scene.

From January to July 1846 he was Under-Secretary of the Colonies in Peel's ministry, but he never again held a position of such prominence in the government itself. In this political sense, his career might be considered a failure; but his important work was in the field of education. He sat on the Clarendon Commission of 1861 and the Taunton Commission of 1864; in 1869 he was appointed Chief Endowed Schools Commissioner. Whereas the Newcastle Commission of 1858 had been concerned with primary education and the Clarendon Commission of 1861 with the nine "great" Public Schools (Eton, Winchester, Westminster, Charterhouse, St. Paul's, Merchant Taylor's, Harrow, Rugby, and Shrewsbury), the Taunton Commission, created by Royal Letters Patent in 1864, was meant to investigate the condition of those schools neglected by the two previous Commissions. Lyttelton had been offered the chairmanship, but, characteristically, declined. Lord Taunton (from whom the Commission took its name),[4] an elderly, moderately distinguished Liberal politician, was persuaded to accept.

The Commission, authorized to investigate education for the middle class, sought to discover how existing educational endowments could be better used. Secondary education meant middle-class education. Even those concerned with working-class education felt that the needs of the middle class must be taken care of first. The Commission reported in twenty-one volumes in 1868, briefly on 2,175 endowed primary schools and at great length on 782 endowed secondary schools.

The first volume contains the report of the Commissioners; the remaining twenty the evidence of the 147 witnesses and the reports of the Assistant Commissioners on particular schools. Of the 782 schools closely examined, only a very few fell into the category of first-grade grammar schools, roughly the seventy-six which had incomes from their endowments of over £500.[5] It was in the area of the richer Endowed Grammar Schools that the Commissioners did their most lasting work. These were the schools—in part, of course, because of their own efforts—that rose out of the mass to become the great Public Schools of the "new creation."

The position of endowed schools had been improved since 1805 when Lord Eldon decided that a grammar school could use only its endowment to pay for the teaching of Latin and Greek. The Acts of 1827 and 1840, and the institution of the Charity Commission in 1853, had made it somewhat easier for the schools to violate their original charters, but still there was a need for drastic change if the educational demands of the middle class were to be met. Lyttelton and his fellow Commissioners felt the necessity to cut loose from the past, away from obsolete and inflexible rules, and the illogical accidents of history:

> Schools have been regarded as the subjects of special trusts of a precisely limited character, not as local contributions to the higher education of the country, which must be freely adjusted to changes as they occurred. . . . Speaking generally, but of course with exceptions, we may say, and say with confidence, that they are not such schools as their founders contemplated. . . . They now exhibit neither the will of the dead for their time nor the will of the living for our time (*Commission Report*, 1, 115).

The Taunton Report advised a system of grading of schools into three ranks, based on the age—18, 16, or 14—at which boys left school. At the same time exhibitions—i.e., scholarships—should be available from a school of a low grade to the next higher, allowing a way for the brightest to rise on the "ladder of education." Therefore, the local demands and conditions that shaped many schools had to be modified and admission policy changed, with, possibly, local boys favored in the award of scholarships to maintain the tie with the locality. The Commissioners were fully conscious of the class implications of the various levels of education, and that education could be a means for advancing from one class to another: "Since the object is to select those who are to make education a means of rising, the best test of all is that the competitors should be pitted against other boys of the very class into which they are to make their way . . . for an open [competition] not only educates those whom it admits, it educates also those whom it rejects" (*Commission Report*, I, 596–598). There was an effort to avoid the awarding of scholarships simply on the basis of intellectual ability, but the definition of other criteria proved extremely difficult. Merit, a word much favored by Lyttelton, seems to have been the catch-all term brought into service. As he remarked in 1873, "Admission to the special advantages of endowment . . . ought to be given solely in respect to merit." [6] But whatever vagueness there may have been about the properties of "merit," at no time was there a belief that scholarship benefits should depend upon the income of the parents—such an invasion of privacy would have been considered intolerable. A free education was, as the later Endowed Schools Commissioners were to point out in 1872, "a reward earned *by the child* and not an incident of the parents' position." [7] It was hoped from the first that poor, ambitious boys would generally win such scholarships, but, without a means test, the probability was that richer boys might be better equipped to carry off the prizes.

The Commission was placing itself in a paradoxical position. Having proposed a regulated system that would offer, on the higher levels, a uniform and probably classical curriculum, it inadvertently recognized the potential social significance of the new education. Parents would prize a certain curriculum not for the "higher" knowledge it might impart, but for the concrete social advantages it would bestow. Although it was not the report's conscious intention, it advocated, in effect, tying the educational system to class distinctions. If education generally was to be a means of rising from class to class, a certain sort of education would necessarily be the mark of admission to a particular class. Although a bright child might have some chance of receiving a better education than the other members of his class, at whatever point he finished school—and was, so to speak, classified—the chances of his rising further were made that much more difficult. The introduction of competitive scholarships raised the standards of the educational system itself and provided a class ladder for the comparatively few who were fortunate enough to benefit by it, but it is doubtful that it was, as some thought,[8] a way of breaking down the barriers between class and class. Rather, it was yet another way of maintaining class distinctions.

The Commissioners recommended incorporating the "ladder" into a comprehensive scheme of secondary education. They wished the powers of the Charity Commissioners to be expanded and simplified so that they might initiate changes rather than wait, as was the case now, on the whim of the trustees of a particular school. They wanted to be absolutely free to reorganize school charters as they thought best and to put what they regarded as outdated charities to the most efficient educational use. Not only would such action improve the quality of middle-class education, but it might even decrease the taxpayer's present responsibilities. The Commissioners' report looked to a national system of supervision of secondary education. There would be both a central and local supervisory board, which would implement a national system of examination and inspection of schools and some sort of certification of teachers. The local board would make certain that funds were distributed fairly within the locality and keep the central board aware of local demands. In fact, the report virtually advocated a comprehensive State system.

Parliament ignored this general plan. The law that it did pass —the Act of 1869—set up for a limited term an Endowed Schools Commission of three which would have the powers the Report had recommended giving to an enlarged and revivified Charity Commission. Although no action was taken towards such organization and inspection as would have made the new Commissioners' work part of a logical and lasting plan, the one recommendation in the report that Parliament did enact was as drastic as could be wished. Sections Nine and Ten of the Act gave the Commissioners powers of astounding range. For example, they were given the power to change the status of a school

> in such manner as may render any educational endowment most conducive to the advancement of the education of boys and girls, or either of them, to alter and add to any existing, and to make new trusts, directions, and provisions in lieu of any existing trusts, directions, and provisions which affect such endowment and the education promoted thereby, including the consolidation of two or more such endowments or the division of one endowment into two or more endowments. Section 10. The Commissioners . . . shall have power to alter the constitution, rights, and powers of any governing body . . . and to establish a new governing body . . . with such powers as they see fit, and to remove a governing body, and in the case of any corporation . . . incorporated solely for the purpose of any endowments dealt with by such a scheme, to dissolve such corporation.[9]

This was short-cutting the courts and the Charity Commission with a startling disregard for vested interests and traditions. When Lyttelton was defending his work in 1874, he could with justice remark, "I am told we have neglected the great principle of compromise. Compromise! Where, I should like to know, in the Act of 1869, is there any indication of compromise? What I find there is not compromise, but thoroughness." [10]

However, the Act was thorough only where it dealt with endowments; otherwise it proved ideal for those who wanted new Public Schools which would not be closely associated with or inspected by the state. The lack of a check meant that some schools, once modernized in administration, would be able to bridge the gap between themselves and the older Public Schools. Section

Fourteen exempted from the Commissioners' jurisdiction those schools founded within the last fifty years. This would allow the so-called proprietory schools, such as Marlborough, Clifton, and Wellington, set up in imitation of the great nine and without trust funds which needed breaking, to proceed unhampered.

Sections Thirty-three through Forty-seven charted the elaborate course a new scheme for a school had to follow before becoming law, a series of complicated steps designed to protect the school and to allow objections to be made. In practice, the system was found to be weak in that once a scheme had been sent by the Commissioners to Parliament, it could not be modified but could only be rejected. The great advantage of this Act over that under which the Charity Commissioners had operated was that now schemes became law unless there was successful objection, while previously schemes had had to be passed by Parliament. From the Charity Commission's inception in 1853 until 1868 it had been able to put only eighteen schemes through Parliament, just nine of which concerned schools. By contrast, the Endowed Schools Commission between 1869 and 1874 was able to have 235 schemes for schools approved, while only ten were rejected.

However, when the Endowed Schools Commissioners touched powerful vested interests, a scheme could be stopped in Parliament. In 1871, for example, although Lyttelton pointed out that the Act almost specifically advocated disregard for wishes of a founder and was meant to be strong, stringent, and sweeping, the Marquis of Salisbury successfully contended in the case of Emmanuel Hospital, Westminster, that money was being transferred from the poor to the middle class, and that the intentions of the founder were being violated.[11]

The Endowed Schools Commission had been set up in 1869, with Lyttelton as Chief Commissioner. Sir Arthur Hobhouse, a barrister and former member of the Charity Commission, was the second Commissioner. The third was Canon H. G. Robinson, a broad churchman who had been active in teacher training in

Yorkshire. Hobhouse had made his attitude abundantly clear: the "dead hand" of a testator should not prevent the most efficient use of an endowment.[12]

Lyttelton, too, was publicly committed to such an attitude:

> I am prepared without scruple to give adhesion to the principle . . . that the supposed obligation on posterity for all time to give unvarying effect, not to the letter, but even to the real intention of Endowments and Wills, for public purposes, ought not to be recognized as necessarily binding; nor do I mean only when such strict obligation has become difficult or nearly impossible, and according to Chancery doctrine of *cy prés*, but when it conflicts with, or falls materially short of, the best public use to which the property might be put ("Address," pp. 65–66).

Lyttelton believed the guiding principle should be what was best for the needs of the present, and that "the competent authority should be allowed, after a given time, to set aside the will of the founder" (*Select Committee Report*, Q. 1364). The Duke of Richmond had expressed objection to Lyttelton and Hobhouse as Commissioners, for he felt that their reforming zeal would be excessive. Hobhouse's defense was that, no matter what his private views, he was capable of administering a law as it stood.[13] But Lyttelton, who in 1868 confessed he feared that the Clarendon and Taunton Commissions had exposed him to so much information about secondary education that he was now almost in a state of mental chaos ("Address," pp. 41, 44) agreed that it was questionable wisdom to intrust the work to men of such decided views. In a letter to Gladstone, he wished to decline serving on the Commission both because he had been a member of the Taunton Commission and because his views were well known. He felt that the new Commission should be allowed to go its way "unfettered and free from all previous conclusions." [14] Moreover, he was anxious to get away from London. But either his brother-in-law's persuasions or his own sense of duty led him, to the detriment of his health and peace of mind, to accept Gladstone's request that he serve.

A particular difficulty for him was the need to effect some compromise between his own intellectual view of what the curriculum should be, and the popular demand for its modification. A Cambridge classicist of the old school, he felt that classics and mathematics constituted *the* education. Yet it was necessary to allow those first-grade schools which had introduced modern subjects to maintain their connections with the universities, and, as Chief Commissioner, he was forced to lead the unsuccessful fight against the continued requirement of Greek for admission to Oxford, Cambridge, and London. Lyttelton's official career was putting him at odds with his own predilections.

Paradoxically, though, it was not winning him the support of the first-grade endowed schools who regarded the very existence of the Commissioners as a threat, seeing in them the possibility of state control. These schools had managed to separate themselves from the mass of grammar schools and approach in status the "mighty nine." Now, in the Taunton Report, they were being officially separated from the nine, and, in treatment and proposed legislation, were to be identified again with the large group of inferior though endowed schools. H. D. Harper, Headmaster of Sherborne, pointed out that

> There is a special injustice done to a class of schools which has the very best right to look for the most considerate treatment. I mean the few Classical Schools of First Grade, which are of the same character as the [nine] Schools . . . and which are struggling into the position of Public Schools of the Country. . . . But . . . it is *not* intended to apply these permanent enactments to *all* Schools (for I miss the element of moral courage in the Bill which would venture to press such an unwelcome clause upon the Schools which are represented by so many *alumni* in the Houses of Parliament). . . . All we ask for is

fair play . . . do not make it now a misfortune to us that we have spent the best parts of our lives and earnings upon our schools; do not let us be so burdened, so unfairly handicapped, that . . . a fixed impassable barrier shall be placed between us and . . . the "Public Schools." [15]

II

Opposition from the first-grade endowed schools took the form of the Headmasters' Conference, whose first meeting was held in 1869. (At the present time, the working definition of a Public School is a school that belongs to the Headmasters' Conference.) The dominant figure in the formation and development of the Conference was Edward Thring, Headmaster of Uppingham School. Thring, like Lyttelton, devoted his life to trying to cope with the increasing demand for boarding-school education. Divergent in their philosophies—Lyttelton concerned with the exceptional, Thring with the average student—the two men represent major forces. The "new" Public Schools evolved in the latter half of the nineteenth century in large part reflect their influence, but they were not accurate reflections of their aims. Neither man was primarily concerned with the wishes and hopes of ambitious parents anxious to make gentlemen of their sons.

Edward Thring was born in 1821; his father was a country squire and clergyman in Somersetshire. Thring went to Eton, first as an Oppidan, then as a King's Scholar, and in 1841 automatically went up to King's College, Cambridge, as a scholar on the foundation. At Cambridge, members of King's still did not take University examinations so that he took no formal test of ability. After three years he succeeded to a fellowship, also automatic, and, during this period, took orders. In all, he spent six years at Cambridge.

Between the time of his departure from Cambridge in 1846

and his becoming Headmaster of Uppingham in 1853—he had earlier turned down a mastership at Eton—the most important experience for the formation of his thought was his service as a priest in a railway-and-dock parish in Gloucester. There, one of his duties was teaching in the church school. His attempt to educate every poor child, no matter how limited his intelligence, taught him that any child has the ability to learn, if given personal attention. He felt that he could ignore such trends of the time as examinations, and go his own way: "the hard fact remains that Socrates, as a Teacher, would starve in modern England, and be plucked himself in a competitive examination." Increasing attention to general examinations such as the Oxford and Cambridge Local Examinations, although stimulating to educational activity, frequently meant that teachers concentrated on their best students in order to send them up to be examined, do well, and reflect credit on the school. Thring was aware of this danger and was determined not to fall a victim to it. "So the school failures are turned out, and great authority quoted to support the practice; and all the energy of the place is expended on the strong and active, who will distinguish themselves in the knowledge scramble." [16]

When Thring became Headmaster of Uppingham in Rutland the school consisted of a few buildings and fewer than sixty students, supported by an income of £1000 from its sixteenth-century foundation. At his death in 1887, it was generally regarded as one of the great Public Schools of England. Thring was a firm believer in a classical education and made no startling changes in the basic subjects taught. But he had a radical new concept of what teaching should be—in his own view his important contribution—and he did revolutionize the physical "plant" of the Public School. In this latter respect, he was second as an influence only to Dr. Arnold. Aware of the importance of the "almighty wall," he recognized how large a part physical surroundings played in a boarding-school education. He did not believe in inadequate quarters sanctioned by tradition but felt, rather, that each boy should have a study of his own and should live in a small dormitory; that classes, in order to ensure attention to all, should be no more than twenty-five; that Houses, a considerable source of income to masters, should only have twenty-five to thirty boys; and that the school itself should have an enrollment of no more than 300, the most the Headmaster himself could know. He felt that education was a delicate and difficult process and that the physical situation should aid rather than, as at most Public Schools, hinder it: "There should be no unnecessary wear and tear of the living material, boys or masters, which a mason and carpenter can prevent. Mortar is cheaper than blood." [17] Because the foundation yielded hardly enough to pay for all he wished to do, he had to put himself under constant financial strain, using his own money and borrowing. He first introduced innovations that soon became necessities for any self-respecting Public School: among others, the first gymnasium, and the first Public School Mission in London. But the innovation to which he attached the most importance was his belief in the thorough teaching of every student: "a dull boy's mind is a wise man's problem" (*Theory*, p. 157). As at the church school in Gloucester, his attempt at Uppingham was to see to it that the individual boy should develop his powers as far as he was able. By 1861, only eight years after becoming Headmaster, he felt he had achieved his aim and wrote to Gladstone, "I believe I am correct in saying that no great school in England has any system or machinery established for dealing with each individual according to his powers excepting that which exists here." [18] Thring was to gain such a reputation for taking care of the average boy that H. W. Eve, the Inspector for the Taunton Commissioners, wrote in his report, "It has been suggested to me that at Uppingham there are signs of a tendency to sacrifice the cleverer boys to those of average ability; but nothing came under my notice to indicate that this is the case; that full justice is done to the latter seems to be generally admitted. . . . The school may almost be said to have suffered from the reputation it has gained for bringing on dull and idle boys" (*Commission Report*, XVI, 133).

To establish a great Public School and to become an influence on a national scale were not Thring's main objectives, nor did he merely wish to raise Uppingham to a competitive position with Eton. His methods were designed to create a school that would be different from and better than other Public Schools, and for a time, at least, he succeeded.

In 1869 Thring came to London, albeit reluctantly, to attend a meeting of Headmasters to protest, as he recorded in his diary, against "the great injustice of" the Endowed Schools Commissioners' "putting the leading endowed schools on so servile a footing, while they exempt so many, and those the greatest" (Parkin, I, 200). Thring, who had gone his way serenely indifferent to other schools, now joined forces with them, because, as he put it, of Uppingham's "position as the leading school under this bill" (Parkin, I, 202). At the London meeting, he suggested that later in the year the headmasters of the threatened schools as well as of the established Public Schools should meet at Uppingham. In December 1869, out of sixty schools invited, twelve gathered with Thring for the first Headmasters' Conference. The second took place the following year at Sherborne and thirty-four schools attended. From the make-up of the Committee on the admission of new members—Winchester, Eton, Harrow, Repton, Cheltenham, Clifton, Uppingham, City of London School, and Sherborne—it is evident that, under the stimulus of attack, most of the old and the new Public Schools joined together to defend themselves. Although the dangers of state interference arising from the Commissioners' proposals disturbed Thring even more deeply than most of his colleagues, he was not seriously worried about whether Uppingham would be treated in the same way as the nine. In 1865, when he was examined by the Taunton Commissioners, he was well disposed towards the government, for Thring's impression from the interview, as noted in his diary, was that the Commissioners were going to urge the other Endowed Schools to imitate Uppingham, rather than to interfere with Uppingham itself:

> The Commission are going to recommend to Parliament my plan (they don't call it mine) of a few schools for the University, preparatory schools with exhibitions . . . and Uppingham apparently is to be the example which is to prove the practicality of this. . . . A perpetual feeling of a new world rolling into sight for schools, and of our work here being sanctified and blessed beyond my dreams . . . my old dream being embued with vitality, and likely to become law all over England (Parkin, I, 150–151).

By March of 1868, when the report was issued, he was not so sanguine: " 'Put not your faith in princes,' " he wrote, "especially in parliamentary princes" (Parkin, I, 160). In fact, he found the report deeply distressing; it did not embody any of his ideas (though it did agree with his concept of a hierarchy of schools) and, to his mind, it defined a good school by reference to the successful nine. Many were content with this definition, but Thring had spent his life trying to move away from it. After looking closely at the report, he wrote that it was "the most disastrous, as it is the most unexpected reverse, that the cause of true work has received or can receive" (Parkin, I, 172). Favorable to the Commissioners when he believed that they were devoted to carrying out his ideas, he now turned against them and described them, quite inaccurately, as "a lot of squires and a stray lord or two [appointed] to gather promiscuous evidence on an intricate professional question, and sum up, and pronounce infallible judgment on it" (Parkin, I, 169).

Thring had hoped that the Taunton Commissioners' Report would reinforce "skilled workmen" such as himself, but their plan of inspection, examination, and certification of teachers, and their claim to being able to reshape endowments drastically, made him regard the Commissioners as unprincipled amateurs dependent on outside inspectors, *not* headmasters but mere mechanics incapable of understanding the true life of any particular school. He knew that endowments could be very restricting and he approved of changes in that "dead hand." But he felt there was less to fear from tradition than from the interference of an inspector or any other government organization, central or local, which would examine and judge according to a given pattern. "Minds," he wrote, "cannot be inspected." [19]

From Thring's point of view, the fearsome aspects of the report, and the bill as first presented to Parliament, were not passed into law. The "blind, clever, ignorant" men would not be watching and inspecting. But the power of the Commissioners to draw up schemes aroused Thring's anger. Once the Act had made the threat formal, Thring could not rest until he had experienced the worst. With a determination almost obsessive, he wanted the Commissioners to show him how they would desecrate his school.[20]

III

Adding to the difficulty of the situation were the conflicting points of view of Thring and Lyttelton. Thring's principles were never concretely defined: to him they were a matter of feeling, not of logic, and he was intolerant of anyone—whether masters in his own school or outsiders—who would not agree with him. He wished to maintain his independence. The Headmasters' Conference was a necessary defensive arrangement; besides, he dominated it. The Commission could be of use if it gave him a scheme which would free him from his own governors.

In 1870 he and Lyttelton opened correspondence. Lyttelton assured him that the Commissioners were not his natural enemies. In reply Thring attempted to acquaint Lyttelton with the inner life of the school and the great danger of government officials who were not actual "workers." He wrote, "I found, in fact, *my life*, with the best part of it gone, absolutely at the mercy of Parliament and this bill. . . . For neither the Commission nor Parliament has as yet entered in the great trade question, of how the trade of schoolkeeping can be carried on so as to give to *each boy* in every school a fair chance" (Parkin, I, 179).

There were three principal areas of disagreement. Lyttelton favored state action and support; Thring opposed free education. Lyttelton, although profoundly religious, believed that headmasters need not be clergymen; Thring, himself a clergyman, disagreed. Lyttelton believed that all talented young men should have the opportunity to go as far as their talents would take them; Thring believed the consideration of talent carried less weight than that of character.

In December 1872, the Commissioners sent Thring a scheme for Uppingham which he found impossible, principally because it gave too much power to the governors of the school. Threatening to resign, he persuaded his masters to support his protest. He was aware that he was giving the Commissioners the impression that he was a man who would brook no argument, even in areas which were their proper concern.[21] The Commissioners, who were trying to be logical and sensible, had some right to be annoyed with Thring's recalcitrance. It is likely, however, that they did not appreciate as highly as did Thring himself the successful educational work he was doing. Thring glowed when he was told that "the stupidest boy who went out of Uppingham knew and felt he had a mission in life" (Parkin, I, 238).

On 7 May 1873, he presented his case to the Commissioners in London (Parkin, I, 192). The first half-hour was stormy, and consisted of an argument between Thring and Lyttelton. Lyttelton saw no reason why Thring should not accept the Commission's ruling in regard to Uppingham's Board of Governors. But Thring objected to the governors' having any power of decision concerning studies in the school; he felt he could continue his work only if he were an autocrat. Lyttelton accused Thring of running his head against a wall and Thring said he would do so if necessary. Lyttelton finally left in a rage against this self-righteous, stubborn man; Robinson and H. J. Roby (who had succeeded Hobhouse as a Commissioner) continued the discussion for two hours. Ultimately, Thring had his wishes granted. He received for the school the sort of scheme he wanted, despite Lyttelton's assertion that his demands violated the logic of the Commissioners' work.

Thring characterized the discussion with the noble lord as "slightly gladiatorial." In the confrontation of these two men, passionately concerned with the nature of secondary education in England, neither man was able to communicate with the other, and the important philosophical differences between them were left unresolved. Lyttelton could not discuss his "elitist" concept with Thring; Thring could not present his concept of "education for character." Thring had won what he wanted from the Commission. Even so, it was difficult to prevent Uppingham from becoming yet another Public School. Gradually, his secondary innovations—the music lessons, the aesthetically pleasing classrooms—became paramount. Presumably he had succeeded in his aims, but, as a recent biographer has remarked, "He knew that he was being praised for the wrong achievements and imitated for false reasons. People were praising him because he had raised an insignificant little country grammar school to the status of a great Public School . . . and he knew that this mattered less than nothing." [22] Soon after Thring's death, the numbers in the school rose to 500, and the Houses had more than thirty boys each. Uppingham sank back to being merely a "great" Public School.

The example of a successful Uppingham led to increased activity on the part of numerous secondary private schools. For those that were endowed, Lyttelton, as Chief Endowed Schools Commissioner, provided the means of breaking free from the confines of their restrictive foundations. As a single illustration among many, one might cite the case of Repton, where the ties of the foundation to the local town—the right of any male resident to a free education—held back the school in its attempt to rise. Dr. S. A. Pears, the headmaster, was eager to put Repton in a class with the older Public Schools, and such was the course he urged upon the Taunton Commissioners: "For sometime past the school has been claiming, and has virtually attained, the position of a public school; that is, we have boys of the same rank as the public schools, our system is the same; they are doing as well at the universities. . . . The constitution of the board of governors would probably settle whether it was to take the place of a public school or to be a village school." [23] Under Pears' guidance, Repton had become a *de facto* Public School, but its strength depended upon a strong headmaster. Because of its unrevised constitution, it could easily decline. The Endowed Schools Commissioners could stabilize Repton's position and ensure its remaining in the first rank. But not until they gave Repton its scheme in 1874 could it consider itself a *de jure* Public School. Thus Lyttelton supervised the creation of schools which were outside a comprehensive system, and were dedicated to a social rather than an intellectual elite.

In 1874 Parliament decided to transfer the functions of the Endowed Schools Commission to an enlarged Charity Commission. By the transfer, a newly elected Tory House wished to express its censure of a Liberal Commission headed by Gladstone's brother-in-law, one which had, in fact, stirred up considerable controversy. The Commission's most enduring work had been in the area of the best endowed schools. There, it had acted to regularize administration, to liberalize, or to discard altogether, outmoded trusts, and to allow schools to use their scholarships for the more talented members of the middle class. The Commissioners were attacked for meddling, but their object was to aid those schools which were obviously in difficulty, and to make sure that those which were in a good state of health should remain so.

Once the schools had been stabilized by the Commissioners' schemes, they were free to cater, without the restraints of central inspection and examination urged by the Taunton Report, to a middle class willing to make economic sacrifices to secure their sons a decided social advantage. These "new" Public Schools were not the creators of the class distinctions that marked the late nineteenth century, but they unquestionably sustained them. The result might not have surprised either Lyttelton or Thring, but it certainly would not have pleased them. In both careers, there were elements of disappointment and anticlimax, of tragedy and failure. Lyttelton, in what Gladstone called his "manful effort to fulfil the law of duty," [24] drove himself to melancholia and suicide. Thring, with his belief that material success was the antithesis of "true life," left a legacy that was little more than a "new" Public School.

The nature of party has been one of the most persistent problems for historians of any period of British history: William O. Aydelotte was concerned to discover something of its nature in the 1840s; and if there is one thing that historians are sure of—if little else—it is that change takes place, and that party towards the end of the century was different from what it was earlier. For actual developments in party in the earlier period the most important study is Norman Gash, Politics in the Age of Peel *(London, 1953), and for the later period H. J. Hanham,* Elections and Party Management: Politics in the Time of Disraeli and Gladstone *(London, 1959).*

The present article discusses the role of the most important Liberal party organizer and gives a sense of how a political party coped with new electoral forces. In the case of the Liberal party, the article also discusses how the party survived the internal split caused when the leader of a new sort of politics, Joseph Chamberlain, left the Liberals in 1886 over the question of Irish Home Rule. Barry McGill teaches British history at Oberlin College. The article is reprinted from The Journal of Modern History *xxxiv (1962), 19–39, by permission of the author and publisher, the University of Chicago Press. Copyright © 1962 by the University of Chicago.*

Francis Schnadhorst and
Liberal Party Organization

WHEN LORD RANDOLPH CHURCHILL contested John Bright's seat at Birmingham in 1885, he spoke of "the dark and evil deeds of Mr. Schnadhorst." [1] Even after his retirement Schnadhorst was remembered as the nightmare of Tory nurseries. [2] Omitted from the *Dictionary of National Biography*, he has remained a mysterious, faintly sinister figure. And an error in *Who Was Who, 1897–1916*, makes it difficult to trace his obituary in *The Times*. [3]

F. H. Herrick has shown that Ostrogorski erred in ascribing the growth of the National Liberal Federation to the operation of the minority clause in the Reform Act of 1867. It remains true that among the Liberal associations reorganized in the 1860s the Birmingham Liberal Association was distinguished for its genuinely popular and representative character. [4] And if it was William Harris who put forward the scheme for organizing Birmingham Liberals so as to circumvent the minority clause, it was Schnadhorst who built durable political machinery upon the foundations of the initial success.

Francis Schnadhorst was born on August 24, 1840, in Birmingham, where his father was the proprietor of a drapery and hosiery shop in Bull Street. After education at King Edward VI's Grammar School he went into the family business. A staunch Nonconformist, he was active enough in the Birmingham Mutual Improvement Society to become its secretary, and he was a founder and onetime president of the Central Literary Association.

He began the career of political organizer, which was to lead him to national prominence, as vice-chairman and joint secretary of the newly organized Liberal committee in his ward in 1867. His effectiveness at the ward level prompted the leaders of the Central Nonconformist Committee to seek him out in 1870.[5] While acting as part-time secretary to this committee, Schnadhorst was defeated as the Liberal candidate from St. Mary's ward in the Council election of 1872.[6] But in 1873 he succeeded William Harris as secretary of the Birmingham Liberal Association.

In his new post Schnadhorst showed his mettle as an organizer in the school board election of 1873, which returned a Nonconformist majority with Joseph Chamberlain as chairman and in the subsequent Council election, which resulted in Chamberlain's election as mayor. The close, if not intimate, association of the two Nonconformist Birmingham Liberals, cemented by a series of local and parliamentary elections, continued until the disruption of the Liberal party in 1886.[7]

The general election of 1874 tested the strength of the Birmingham Liberal Association, for the Conservatives had greatly improved their electoral machinery since 1868. Despite the Conservatives' success nationally, in Birmingham the Liberals won all three seats again, and Schnadhorst and his system attracted the attention of Liberals who had been less successful in their own constituencies. From 1874 to 1877 Schnadhorst spent much of his time expounding the Birmingham system in other urban constituencies. In April 1877 Chamberlain presented him with an honorarium of £1,000 on behalf of the Birmingham Liberals. By that time the Executive Committee of the Nonconformist National Education League had determined to dissolve its organization and to form in its place what became the National Liberal Federation.[8] Again it was William Harris who suggested a federation of Liberal constituency associations, and again it was Schnadhorst who made the idea a reality.

The delegates who met at Birmingham on May 31, 1877, to found the National Liberal Federation represented ninety-five Liberal associations, but only forty-six of the ninety-five were actually constituency associations.[9] Even the total number was a disappointment to the moving spirits of the National Education League.[10] If the new Federation were to be a success, permanent organizers of the caliber of the Birmingham Liberal Association's secretary had to be found. Schnadhorst, while continuing as full-time secretary to the Birmingham Association, now accepted the post of part-time secretary to the National Liberal Federation (NLF), which paid him £250 a year at first.[11]

From the beginning the Federation was most effective in the midlands and the north where the "forward Liberalism" or radicalism of the Chamberlain type was strongest. A London office for the Federation was suggested and rejected in 1879.[12] But the predominance of midland radicalism in its leadership did not mean that the NLF was committed to a specific program or that it undertook to draw up a program based on Birmingham radicalism. Instead, it encouraged co-operation among those Liberal associations sharing a genuinely popular and representative character. Schnadhorst's missionary work had established connections between Birmingham and other constituencies, and the habit of co-operation had begun to form in the years from 1874 to 1877. This co-operation involved concerted agitation as issues arose in Parliament.[13] The formal statement of policy issued in 1880 simply confirmed previous practice: the NLF was based "upon a principle of organization," not upon a political platform.[14]

But the issues with respect to which the NLF helped to organize public opinion were not necessarily formulated by the Marquis of Hartington, then the leader of the party in the House of Commons. And for Schnadhorst there was no question that the NLF should serve to democratize the process of selecting Liberal candidates at the constituency level. He believed that this could be done by urging Liberals to model their local associations after

Birmingham's. His object inevitably required the diminution of the local influence of Whig magnates. Hartington and the Whigs were therefore rightly suspicious of the NLF and hostile to Schnadhorst.[15] By 1879 the *Edinburgh Review* was reassuring Whigs by predicting a short life for the NLF on the ground that "political associations of a permanent character have never taken root in this country." [16]

To what extent the NLF should be given credit for the Liberal victory in the general election of 1880 is an important question, but not one to which any precise answer is possible. Schnadhorst claimed that "in nearly all the constituencies where it had been established the Liberal candidates were elected." [17] The second annual report of the NLF, given at Darlington, February 3, 1880, listed ninety-seven affiliated associations. Of these only sixty were representative of places which were actually parliamentary constituencies.[18] Among these sixty the Liberals actually lost seats in Greenwich (1), Hastings (1), Leominster (1), Maidstone (2), and Sheffield (1). The Liberals made no gains from Conservative incumbents at Birkenhead, Cirencester, Guildford, Portsmouth, Mid-Surrey, Thirsk, or Wenlock, although all of these had affiliated associations. In twenty-seven of the remaining constituencies the Liberals held seats which had been won in 1874.

Schnadhorst made the particular claim for the NLF that it had helped to unite Liberals in constituencies where sixteen seats had been lost in 1874 despite a total Liberal vote in each which outnumbered the total Conservative vote.[19] The problem of superfluous candidates, who let in a Conservative by dividing the Liberal poll, was not new. In 1868 when the Liberals had won a great victory there had been forty constituencies where more Liberal candidates had stood than there were seats to be won. In 1874 there had been twenty-one such constituencies among the English boroughs alone, and seven seats, of the sixteen Schnadhorst mentioned, were lost as a result. In 1880 there were too many Liberal candidates in only nine of the English borough constituencies, and in only one of the nine, the Tower Hamlets, was a seat lost as a consequence.[20] Certainly the NLF was strongest among the English borough constituencies, and the Tower Hamlets was not listed among the affiliated constituencies of the NLF in the second annual report (1880). But three of the nine constituencies where there were superfluous Liberal candidates in 1880 had Liberal associations affiliated with the NLF: Darlington, Hartlepool, and Middlesborough.[21]

Schnadhorst exaggerated by claiming success "in nearly all the constituencies" where the NLF had affiliates. Yet the relative success in solving the problem of superfluous candidates must be attributed to improved local organization, and this in constituencies where the Liberal associations were affiliated with the NLF. And Schnadhorst could have pointed to the fact that in the sixty constituencies where there were such affiliates, the Liberals won twenty-eight seats from Conservative incumbents.

If these twenty-eight could be attributed simply to the new model organization, the NLF's role in the Liberal victory of 1880 would have to be accepted as substantial, though not so great as Chamberlain's claim for it.[22] But there are difficulties in the way of such an attribution. In the first place, allowing that good organization made the Liberal vote most effective by uniting Liberals behind an agreed slate of candidates, the Liberal vote itself remains to be explained. In twenty-seven of the sixty seats referred to above, Liberal candidates had been successful prior to the election of 1880. It is arguable that where the Liberals had been successful in 1874, when the Conservatives had won their first majority in the House of Commons since 1841, the Liberals might have succeeded again in 1880 without benefit of new organization. Second, Gladstone's crusade, renewed for the general election, cannot be ignored as an influence on the total Liberal poll, especially in the north and midlands where the NLF was also strongest.

The third difficulty is the Irish vote in Great Britain. F. H.

O'Donnell, who was vice-president and secretary of the Home Rule Confederation of Great Britain in 1876, stated that there were then 150 branches of the Confederation, most of them where the major parties were fairly evenly matched and where the Irish vote could therefore determine the result. O'Donnell's figures are not trustworthy: in his *History* he alternately claims fifty and sixty branches among the boroughs of Great Britain.[23] But he does list eleven constituencies by name where branches of the Home Rule Confederation were established, and eight of these had Liberal associations affiliated with the NLF by 1880.[24] If an organized Irish vote was cast *en bloc* for the Liberals in 1880, its delivery in these eight constituencies would have to be considered, apart from the existence of the NLF, as a reason for the success of local Liberals.

It cannot be shown here either that the Irish vote in Great Britain was highly organized in 1880, or that, being organized, it was delivered *en bloc* to the Liberals. Unfortunately Conor Cruise O'Brien's admirable study of Parnell's party casts no light on the matter.[25] And although it is known that large numbers of immigrant Irish workers lived in and around Glasgow, Liverpool, and London, it is also known that many Irish workers were transients who could not be kept on the registers. But to whatever extent the Irish vote in Britain was effectively organized in 1880, it is likely that it was cast for Liberal candidates because Beaconsfield went out of his way to attack Home Rule.[26]

Clearly Schnadhorst exaggerated the part played by the NLF in the election of 1880. He omitted reference to the seats lost by Liberals where associations affiliated with the NLF were established. He ignored the effect of Gladstone's oratorical campaign. He took no account of the Irish vote in those constituencies where the Home Rule Confederation and the NLF overlapped.

After the election of 1880 Schnadhorst concentrated upon organizing the county constituencies. Their size presented difficulties unfamiliar to the urban party workers who now formed the hard core of "NLF Liberalism." In a paper read at Cardiff in October 1880 Schnadhorst pointed out that it was not only the size, and therefore the cost of contesting county divisions, which impeded the formation of democratically organized Liberal associations in the counties. While pointing out that no county divisions had been completely organized in this way in time for the election of 1880, Schnadhorst showed that opposition from Whig magnates threatened the tentative beginnings of democratic organization in the county towns and in the populous areas outside but adjoining the parliamentary boroughs.[27]

In 1868 there had been no Liberal candidates for sixty-six seats in Great Britain, fifty-three of them county seats; in 1874 there had been no Liberal candidates for 142 seats, 117 of them county seats; in 1880 there had been no Liberal candidates for ninety-one seats, seventy-three of them county seats. Schnadhorst stated that of the county seats actually won by Liberals in 1874 only twenty-six had been in England proper, and in thirteen of these success had been due to an arrangement with the Conservatives. Only six of the twenty-six had been won by a majority of votes cast in a contested election. While the problem in urban constituencies had been to eliminate superabundant Liberal candidates, the problem in the counties was to break down the preserves of Whig magnates whose apathy or preference for a compromise with Conservatives stood in the way of any contests at all. For Schnadhorst one object of the NLF was to ensure the maximum number of contests by Liberal candidates who had been adopted by representative associations.

The imminence of franchise reform made improved county organization urgent for the NLF. In "The next Reform Bill," which he read at Newcastle-on-Tyne in November 1881, Schnadhorst sketched what he hoped would be achieved. A single, uniform household franchise for counties and boroughs, coupled with "a simple and effective lodger franchise" was his goal. Although this was not accomplished by the act of 1884, his suggested pattern for redistribution of seats was an accurate forecast. He proposed that the boroughs too small to continue as parliamentary boroughs should lose their seats but retain an identity by giving their names to new county divisions to be carved out of the huge existing county constituencies. And he condemned the two-member constituencies. "With the Liberal party this principle [of two-member constituencies] introduces compromise into the selection of candidates, one of whom must be moderate and the other advanced. I believe this is bad for the electorate, and that it is well in the political as in the religious life for each man to be compelled to choose definitely on which side he will serve." [28]

Besides planning the extensive reorganization of liberalism in the counties, Schnadhorst actively assisted those participating in demonstrations designed to help the Liberal parliamentary party, especially in its efforts to pass the new franchise bill. When the House of Lords rejected the bill in July 1884, a great demonstration in London occurred, followed by protest meetings in Leicester and Manchester. They all owed something to Schnadhorst. The Aston riots in October were more serious. They were the result of the determination by Birmingham Conservatives to challenge the NLF in its heartland. Sir Stafford Northcote and Lord Randolph Churchill were invited to address a rally at Aston Manor, outside Birmingham. Despite restriction of tickets to known Conservatives, numbers of hecklers stormed the enclosure and attacked the distinguished guests. Northcote and Churchill escaped disheveled, but some people were injured and the fireworks display depicting Northcote was set off upside down.

In defending himself in the House of Commons against Churchill's accusation of complicity in the riot, Chamberlain relied upon affidavits supplied to him, according to Garvin, by Schnadhorst. These affidavits, or some of them, were subsequently proved false. Garvin concludes, "His [Schnadhorst's] relations with his chief, though politically active had never been personally intimate; and they were henceforth carried on with a certain chill." [29] But two letters from Chamberlain, quoted below, which happened to be transcribed in the Officers' Committee minutes of the NLF, show that the chill had worn off by the summer of 1885.

Schnadhorst's division of labor between the Birmingham Liberal Association and the NLF changed in 1881 when he began to give more time to the NLF. In January 1884 he resigned as secretary of the Birmingham Association and became full-time secretary of the national organization at £800 a year. In October 1884, the month of the Aston riots, the NLF presented him with £1,000 in recognition of his special services in organizing demonstrations and in raising a special fund for agitation in favor of the franchise bill.[30]

Meanwhile, Sir Charles Dilke and Chamberlain, who had served on the Executive Committee of the Liberal Central Association since 1877, pressed Gladstone for concessions to the Radical wing of the party. One of the points at issue had been their dissatisfaction with the personnel and methods of the Liberal Central Association (LCA), where the chief whip, Lord Richard Grosvenor (later first Baron Stalbridge), belonged to the Whig faction of the party. The resignation of the government in June 1885 did not lessen their determination to reform the LCA, for Gladstone's retirement was confidently predicted and a general election was known to be imminent.[31]

In these circumstances Chamberlain wrote to Schnadhorst, informing him that Dilke and he had made their complaint of the excessively Whig character of the LCA to Gladstone. When asked to suggest a remedy they had urged (1) the addition of Radical M.P.s to the executive committee, (2) the appointment of a Radical whip, and (3) "above and beyond all these what I consider of infinitely greater importance, the nomination of yourself as joint paid secretary with Mr. Wyley [*sic*], the present secretary." [32]

Chamberlain added that if this proposal were rejected at first, he would continue to urge it, and he pointed out that Schnadhorst would not have to give up his secretaryship of the NLF in order to accept this new post at party headquarters. The next day Chamberlain wrote again, saying:

> The only objection offered was that you are regarded by many persons as so terrible and dangerous that the subscriptions which are now received chiefly from Liberal peers, would be stopped if you were publicly advertised as Secretary of the Association. I protested against this view, and honestly believe it to be exaggerated, but at the same time the wealthy members of our party are such fools that it is quite possible that any evidence of closer union between the Caucus and the Central Association would prove alarming to them.

The alternatives proposed were (1) that Schnadhorst should name a representative to give his views to the LCA or (2) that Schnadhorst should accept the post of joint secretary without his name being published as holding the post. If Schnadhorst chose the second course, he was to see the chief whip, Lord Richard Grosvenor, about his salary.

In fact Schnadhorst reported to the Officers' Committee of the NLF that he had seen Grosvenor and had found him hostile to the appointment of an additional secretary to the LCA. Instead Schnadhorst accepted a seat on the Standing Committee of the LCA, which was to meet daily until the forthcoming general election was over.[33] In this way began the liaison between the party headquarters, or LCA, and the extraparliamentary organization, the NLF, with Schnadhorst's own service providing the link until until his retirement in 1894.

The chief whip continued to control the party funds and the policy of the LCA, to which some constituencies still looked for candidates. Now, through Schnadhorst, the NLF had gained a footing within the LCA. Surveying the condition of Liberal organization in constituencies throughout the country, as Schnadhorst undertook to do in his capacity as secretary to the NLF, was a good way of asserting the special role of the NLF.[34] The division of labor between the two organizations was not spelled out formally in 1885. But at least the NLF, which had grown up outside the official party organization, was now brought into close co-operation with it and was conceded a role as the eyes and ears of the party in the constituencies.

Schnadhorst's forecast was that there would be 366 Liberal seats, plus twenty-six "possibles," in the new house of 670 M.P.s.[35] No doubt it was Schnadhorst's new dual capacity that made Chamberlain confident of the accuracy of this prediction. It foretold a minimal majority of sixty-two over Conservatives and Home Rulers combined. In fact, in the election of 1885 the Liberals won 335 seats, a total exactly equaled by the combination of 249 Conservatives and eighty-six Home Rulers.[36] Chamberlain felt that the Irish vote in Britain, which Parnell had delivered to the Conservatives, largely explained the discrepancy.[37] But it is possible that Schnadhorst had allowed for the Irish vote in his forecast, which he made in October 1885.

In an election speech on October 17 at Birmingham, where he had the refusal of the Liberal nomination for either of two seats, Schnadhorst denounced "the price which was being paid for the Irish vote" by the Conservatives.[38] Although Parnell did not publicly pronounce in favor of the Conservatives until November 21, Schnadhorst had clearly anticipated his pronouncement. Indeed, Schnadhorst's speech suggests that he hoped to profit in 1885 from a reaction by English voters against a Conservative alliance with Parnell, such as actually occurred against Gladstonian Liberals in the election of 1886. But he overlooked the disbelief of the electorate in a Conservative-Irish alliance, a disbelief which Gladstone's calculated silence in the autumn of 1885 did nothing to dispel.

Admittedly, no election predictions in this period were very good. And the new extension of the franchise and redistribution of seats made it especially unlikely that anyone could forecast the results of the election of 1885 precisely. It remains worthwhile to consider Schnadhorst's prediction because Chamberlain took it seriously enough to act upon it and because an understanding of Schnadhorst's calculations in 1885 sheds light on his subsequent predictions, upon which Gladstone and others were to act.

As has been shown, Schnadhorst ignored the Irish vote in Britain, probably mistakenly, in his explanation of the results of the election of 1880. Now in 1885 he led Chamberlain to believe that the Irish vote accounted for the failure of his prediction to come true. But on both occasions he overestimated the effectiveness of the NLF. That is the consistent thread in all his calculations.

Sorting out the relative effects of Gordon and the Soudan, and of the Irish vote, in the English boroughs in 1885 is probably impossible. But there can be no doubt that the results among the English borough seats threw off Schnadhorst's calculations, though they had been the core of "NLF Liberalism" from its inception. There was a very close vote in some of the Birmingham divisions, and Liberals lost ground in the midlands and in the metropolitan area. Since 1880 the Conservatives had greatly improved their organization, owing partly to the efforts of Captain R. W. E. Middleton, their new chief agent.[39] But Schnadhorst could not admit that the NLF was less effective in 1885 than he had claimed it to have been in 1880. Therefore, he blamed the Irish vote.

The polling in the election of 1885 was not completed until December. By December 18 Herbert Gladstone had flown "the Hawarden kite." Parliament met in January 1886 and Salisbury resigned on January 28. Schnadhorst had his last "confidential talk" with Chamberlain on February 7, and he wrote on February 13 deploring Chamberlain's decision to resign from Gladstone's government on the Home Rule issue; the resignation actually occurred on March 26.[40] In April Chamberlain complained to J. T. Bunce, editor of the *Birmingham Post*, that Schnadhorst was working to produce a decision in favor of Home Rule by the Birmingham Liberal Association, whose secretaryship he had resigned only two years earlier.

Schnadhorst was not able to postpone a vote against Home Rule by the Birmingham "2,000" on April 21, but at the more critical meeting of the executive of the NLF in London on May 5 a majority voted for Gladstone and Home Rule. A subsequent meeting of the General Committee on June 2 accepted the resignations of William Harris, who had been chairman of the General Committee, J. T. Bunce, Richard Chamberlain, Dr. Crosskey, William Kenrick, and J. Powell Williams: the whole Birmingham contingent save for Schnadhorst himself.[41]

But Birmingham sent a new set of representatives led by Dr. B. W. Foster (created Baron Ilkeston in 1910), who was elected the new chairman of the General Committee, and this group included William Allard who had succeeded Schnadhorst as secretary of the Birmingham Liberal Association in 1884 and who continued in that position after the election of 1886. The vote against Home Rule by the Birmingham Association did not cut off the permanent personnel of that Association from the NLF even in the critical months of 1886.[42] Schnadhorst may well have foreseen the permeation of the Birmingham Association by Gladstonians which was to happen in 1888.[43]

Although Garvin implies that he was, it is unlikely that Schnadhorst was confident of a Liberal victory in 1886.[44] Gladstone was clear that a dissolution was the necessary consequence of his defeat in the House of Commons on the Home Rule bill.[45] Whatever encouragement Schnadhorst held out to the cabinet which decided on dissolution (June 8, 1886), he knew of the compact by which the Conservatives were leaving uncontested the seats of Liberals who voted against Home Rule.[46] And no one could have been more aware than he of the difficulty of putting up an approved Gladstonian Liberal candidate in opposition to an incumbent who had the support of his local Liberal association in opposing Home Rule. In fact sixty-two of the Liberals who had voted against Home Rule held their seats in the election of 1886, twenty-five of them unopposed.[47] Chamberlain had not only "trimmed his vessel and touched his rudder" so that he could adapt his record to any conceivable outcome of the election, as Gladstone put it; he had made certain of his own reelection.

Even if Schnadhorst had supposed that the vote of the Irish in Britain would counterbalance the vote drawn off by the followers of Hartington and Chamberlain, he understood the difficulty of finding new Liberal candidates to contest the seats of incumbent Unionist Liberals. Arnold Morley, who had succeeded Lord Richard Grosvenor as chief whip, told Gladstone early in July, "Our greatest difficulty has been in getting good candidates." Later in the month he added, "Schnadhorst thinks we shall win more seats from the Tories than they will from us, but the results as between ourselves and the 'Unionists' he thinks are doubtful." [48]

Not very sanguine about the prospects of a Liberal majority, Schnadhorst certainly miscalculated the dimensions of the defeat which now overwhelmed the Liberals. In the event, the Conservatives won 316 seats and the Liberal Unionists seventy-eight, leaving 191 to the Liberals and eighty-five to the Home Rulers.[49] In Great Britain the Liberals polled 1,338,718 votes, while the combined Conservative and Unionist poll was 1,416,718.[50] The discrepancy between the narrow margin of the popular vote and the vast difference in numbers of M.P.s elected cannot be explained entirely by the absence of contests for lack of Gladstonian Liberal candidates. Where there were contests the poll fell below the level of the previous general election. And among the exceptionally large number of closely contested seats the Conservatives and Unionists had the advantage of winning about thirty-five seats more than the Liberals.[51] The popular vote, taken by itself, explains why Schnadhorst and others anticipated a closer result in terms of seats won.

But Schnadhorst may have been too complacent about the county divisions. Chamberlain's henchman Jesse Collings, who had addressed himself particularly to the aspirations of the agricultural laborers, had followed Chamberlain in the party schism. The laborers were uninterested in the Irish problem, save for their dislike of migrant Irish labor. And the Conservatives exploited their opportunity for regaining ground among the county divisions which had supplied the Liberal majority in 1885.

Moreover, as in 1885, Schnadhorst was too ready to take the paper strength of the NLF as a guarantee of effectiveness. It was true, as Robert Spence Watson later put it, that seventy M.P.s not previously members and fifty Liberal associations not previously affiliated now joined the NLF. It was true, too, that no associations formally withdrew in 1886, and that the Liberal agents "almost without exception" were loyal.[52] But, without withdrawing, several associations, like Birmingham's, indorsed Unionist candidates. More of them, without indorsing Unionism, were too weakened by the split in the party at the constituency level to be reliable engines for a Liberal campaign.

Possibly Schnadhorst would have been more effective than Wyllie as secretary of the Liberal Central Association from the beginning of 1886. It was July, and polling had already begun when Arnold Morley told Gladstone he wanted Schnadhorst to replace Wyllie.[53] As it happened, Schnadhorst achieved the promotion Chamberlain had sought for him in July of 1885 only after Chamberlain had broken with the party.

While Morley arranged to install Schnadhorst as secretary of the LCA, the NLF considered moving its headquarters from Birmingham to London. The move was accomplished in October 1886, and it meant that Schnadhorst could serve as liaison between the two bodies more conveniently than he could have done had the NLF remained in Birmingham. Schnadhorst, who had always stressed the role of the NLF as the voice of the provinces, had some doubts about this removal to the metropolis, and John Morley opposed the move on the same grounds.[54] But the NLF went to Parliament Street, next door to the LCA, in the double house numbered 41–42.[55]

In his new capacity as secretary of the LCA Schnadhorst addressed himself to questions beyond the scope of the secretary of the NLF. In the years from 1886 to 1892 he dealt not only with the organizational blueprint of the party, but with finances, and with the selection of candidates. He was particularly concerned with the policy respecting labor candidatures.

Organization was the immediate problem in 1886. The election had been a disaster even if the Home Rule schism had not broken the façade of unity in the NLF. Schnadhorst reorganized the metropolitan area where the Liberals had begun to do badly even in 1885. The London Liberal and Radical Union (later the London Liberal Federation), with branches in all the metropolitan constituencies, was itself affiliated with the NLF.[56] At the same time a new division of the NLF for the Home Counties was established, superseding the old London and Counties Union.[57] The Scottish whip, Edward Majoribanks (later Lord Tweedmouth), reported that he was trying to affiliate the Glasgow Liberal Federation with the Scottish Liberal Federation.[58] By 1887 the NLF was truly national in that there was no longer any considerable area in England without Liberal associations affiliated with the NLF, although there were still some local Liberal associations which remained unaffiliated. The Welsh National Liberal Council was affiliated; the Scottish Liberal Federation was autonomous but co-operated with the NLF.

Robert Hudson was appointed assistant secretary of the NLF in June 1886, and in October 1888 William Woodings became special secretary in charge of a new department wholly concerned with voters' registration.[59] Beginning in 1887 the by-elections ran strongly against Salisbury's government, and Arnold Morley told Gladstone that Schnadhorst had "revolutionized" the conduct of elections at the LCA.[60] In February 1888 Richard Chamberlain conceded that very few Liberal associations remained in the hands of Liberal Unionists.[61] And in May 1888 Joseph Chamberlain had to withdraw from the Birmingham Liberal Association to found his own Unionist Association.[62] William Harris and Dr. Crosskey, who had resigned from the General Committee of the NLF in 1886, now returned to it, and R. W. Dale, who had also been temporarily estranged, was serving on it in 1888.[63]

Schnadhorst's labors in the reorganization which had begun to bear such fruit in 1888 were fully appreciated within the party. He was presented with £10,000 in 1887 at a banquet at which Gladstone spoke. In the same year the Liberal Publications Department was established at Parliament Street under the auspices of both the LCA and the NLF. A. H. D. Acland and James Bryce were the first co-chairmen of the new department, which was joined by J. A. Spender in 1891.[64]

The secession of the Liberal Unionists had removed from the party a great number of the wealthy men whose subscriptions had been mentioned as a reason for not appointing Schnadhorst to the LCA in the summer of 1885. Gladstone may have been exaggerating when he wrote to Carnegie in 1887, "while we have $\frac{9}{10}$ or indeed $\frac{10}{10}$ of the operations to carry on, all our wealth, except perhaps $\frac{1}{10}$, has absconded." [65] But though Carnegie responded with $25,000, finances continued to be a difficulty.

Perhaps the Liberal party ought to have attempted at this juncture to democratize its finances by seeking small contributions on a national scale. This approach was strongly urged in 1902, and it was finally adopted in 1925 at the time of the Liberal Million Fund.[66] In 1880 Schnadhorst had argued that individuals should accept the same responsibility for financing the party of their choice as they were accustomed to accept for their church or their school.[67] But even the NLF with an annual operating budget of a few thousand pounds had found a few rich contributors indispensable to the special funds it raised from time to time.[68] The far greater needs of the LCA, which collected and dispensed the election funds, dictated a continuing reliance upon the rich contributor.

As secretary of the LCA, Schnadhorst was directly concerned with raising money. He addressed a party meeting on the subject on June 28, 1887, which led Gladstone to contribute from his own pocket as well as to write the letter to Carnegie quoted above.[69] In 1891 it was Schnadhorst who arranged for the contributions from James Williamson and Sydney Stern, who were rewarded with peerages in 1895.[70]

The idea of recommending for honors those whose political services had included substantial donations to party funds was not new in 1891. Prior to 1885 Sir Stafford Northcote had been ready to promise a baronetcy and to consider the promise of a peerage to Conservatives offering to contest seats in the next general election.[71] A promise of honors to those who contested or won certain seats, without regard to any more considerable political services, is distinct from a promise of honors in return for a sum of money. Yet the guarantee of some contests was as good as a donation from the point of view of the party organizers, who collected funds to pay the costs of contests. Thus, Northcote's practice prior to 1885 may serve to put Schnadhorst's negotiations with Stern and Williamson in their proper historical perspective.

The ennoblement of Stern and Williamson brought indignant protests from within the Liberal party in 1896 when Rosebery's honors list had appeared.[72] And though the other evidence of Schnadhorst's activity in fund-raising came to light only in 1901, after his death, it proved even more startling because it showed that he had received and disposed of £5,000 without the knowledge of Arnold Morley, his superior at the LCA.

The story of this negotiation appeared in correspondence between Cecil Rhodes and Schnadhorst, published by *The Spectator* in 1901. The letters showed that Rhodes had sent £5,000 to Schnadhorst for the Liberal party in 1891. Schnadhorst had accepted Rhodes's original conditions: that only Gladstone know of the contribution, and that it be returned if the Liberals pressed for Home Rule without the Irish M.P.s at Westminster. Schnadhorst had reassured Rhodes subsequently when a speech by John Morley had suggested that the Liberals might evacuate Egypt.[73]

From the viewpoint of Herbert Gladstone, who was chief whip in 1901, and of Robert Hudson, who was Schnadhorst's successor as secretary of both the LCA and the NLF, the noteworthy aspect of the correspondence was not that Schnadhorst should have undertaken to speak for Liberal policy in advance of the general election of 1892 and to guarantee that Rosebery would be the next Liberal foreign secretary. What shocked them was that Arnold Morley had been ignorant of the whole transaction and that the use of the money had gone unrecorded at party headquarters.[74]

Campbell-Bannerman began to question whether a public discussion of the LCA and the NLF and their respective funds was now necessary. In fact, Campbell-Bannerman's and Sir William Harcourt's public denial that they had been influenced by Rhodes's contribution to the party when they served on the South African Committee was considered sufficient, and the Liberal organization refused to answer subsequent comment in *The Spectator*.[75]

Hudson's failure to find any record of the money led Herbert Gladstone to write, ". . . it is hardly conceivable that he [Schnadhorst] 'trousered' it." [76] An entry in the minutes of the General Purposes Committee, NLF, of September 3, 1890, suggests a solution to the mystery of the money. Heading the list of subscribers to the NLF fund for propaganda and registration work in the constituencies is "A Friend per Mr. Schnadhorst £5,000." Because the money was given to the NLF rather than to the LCA, Arnold Morley could not have known of it from the LCA accounts, which he kept entirely in his own hands.[77] The correspondence between Herbert Gladstone and Campbell-Bannerman shows that Hudson was likely to have missed the entry in the minutes of September 1890, quoted above, because he was looking for something subsequent to Rhodes's letter of February 1891. The 1890 date is not too early for Schnadhorst to have indicated a pledge from Rhodes, though it precedes the letter enclosing payment by five months. Schnadhorst had spent the winter of 1889–1890 in South Africa, where he met Rhodes, and pledges, distinguished from actual payments, were customarily entered in the NLF minutes in the manner of the entry of September 1890. There is no reason to doubt that, on receipt of the cash, Schnadhorst paid it into the NLF fund.

Whether or not Schnadhorst ought to have kept his chief at the LCA informed of Rhodes's gift, his failure to do so and his readiness to decide that the money so given to the party should go to the NLF rather than to the whip's fund illustrates an ambiguity in the party organization. Prospective donors might be ignorant of the different roles of the LCA and the NLF. While Schnadhorst was secretary of both, they might understandably suppose that he was as appropriate an agent of the party as the chief whip himself. But if the whip were to be bypassed by the donors he could not effectively control the LCA funds, however closely he guarded their amount and disposition from the secretary of the LCA who was also secretary of the NLF.

Though there is no evidence that Schnadhorst's successor, Hudson, attempted to play a lone hand with contributions, the problem was not wholly peculiar to Schnadhorst's tenure of office. For example, in 1903 Herbert Gladstone was furious on discovering that Lewis Harcourt, having received £10,000 from the South African millionaire Joseph B. Robinson, refused to turn the money over to the whip. Harcourt made his own allocation of it among the Home Counties Liberal Federation, the Free Trade Union, and the National Reform Union.[78]

Since its foundation in the 1870s the LCA had had a committee in charge of candidatures. Until the closer co-operation of the LCA and the NLF in 1886, the LCA had not relied upon the NLF for its constituency reports. Undoubtedly Schnadhorst had made the results of the NLF survey of the constituencies available to the committee of the LCA to which he had been appointed in the summer of 1885. But it was only after the election of 1886, when he became secretary of the LCA, that complete surveys of the constituency associations by the NLF became a regular feature of the NLF's co-operation with the LCA.

In February 1890 William Woodings, in charge of registration of voters, was instructed by the NLF to supply a list of the English and Welsh constituencies which had adopted candidates. Officers of the NLF were then to confer with Arnold Morley, the chief whip, on ways and means of filling vacancies.[79] In July 1890 the NLF undertook its second survey of the constituency associations. This required a temporary organization of district agents, usually recruited from among the regular constituency agents, who were paid by the NLF for the period of the survey. For the purposes of the 1890 survey, Wales and Monmouth, London, and the Home Counties were omitted, and the rest of England was divided into eleven districts with an agent in charge of each. The object was to investigate the quality of each constituency association in time to correct deficiencies before the general election. Like its Conservative counterpart, the National Union of Conservative and Constitutional Associations, the NLF had constantly to guard against deterioration at the constituency level where the vital work of registration and canvassing was done. By February 1891 the General Purposes Committee was considering the reports of the district agents, and Schnadhorst followed these up with an informal report, unfortunately unrecorded, on the parliamentary candidates.[80]

In July 1889 the NLF had approved Schnadhorst's own candidature at Newcastle-under-Lyme. There was some opposition to this from within the party, although the chief whip approved it. Schnadhorst relinquished this opportunity to enter the House of Commons, but his failing health, rather than any adverse opinion within the party, was the reason.[81] Without ever having stood as a candidate himself, he sat on the committee of the LCA in charge of candidatures, and he was therefore in a position to influence the choice of candidates where the local associations were open to suggestions. For example, he strongly urged his friend Henry Broadhurst to consider standing for Cirencester after Broadhurst's defeat in the general election of 1892. When Broadhurst eventually settled himself at Leicester, Schnadhorst made no secret of his antipathy for the other Liberal M.P. there, Walter Hazell. He wrote to Broadhurst: "I should not have weeped if Hazell had been beaten—if by about five I should have been glad. I have my knife into that gentleman; why, I will tell you when I see you." [82]

The business of placing candidates was at the heart of the Liberal party's relations with labor candidates. And the number of labor candidates began to be significant at the same time that Schnadhorst became secretary of the LCA.[83] After the disastrous election of 1886 the Liberals might have been expected to recruit more vigorously from the left. Their failure to do so is not entirely explained by Gladstone's preoccupation with Ireland or by the hostility of such Liberal M.P.s as Sir Joseph Pease, Alfred Illingworth, and James Kitson (president of the NLF from 1886 to 1890, and later created Baron Airedale).

The constitutions of Liberal associations affiliated with the NLF required the associations to be open to all professed Liberals and to be representative of the local membership. On the face of it there was nothing to prevent the working classes from making their numbers tell. They had only to join and to vote as a bloc and they could capture control of the local associations where they were a majority. In fact, George Lansbury was secretary of the Bow and Bromley Liberal and Radical Association, and both Arthur Henderson and Ramsay MacDonald were Liberal agents. But the mass of working-class voters did not identify themselves with the Liberal party to the extent of joining the constituency associations.[84]

Admittedly the warm welcome to the newly enfranchised workingmen, which Schnadhorst had urged upon the Liberal associations, had not been generally extended. It is also true that the great majority of nonunion workers did not produce their own local political leadership after the manner of the middle and lower middle classes, who had made the NLF an effective force for liberalism from 1877 to 1885. And where the workers were unionized, union membership cut across constituency boundaries. Except for a handful of miners' constituencies, there were no seats controlled by an indisputable majority of workers belonging to trade unions.

These were the circumstances when in 1886 the TUC established the Labour Electoral Committee in order to increase the number of labor candidatures. H. H. Champion was secretary of the metropolitan branch of what he called the National Labour party, which was affiliated with the Labour Electoral Association, and he tried to increase the number of labor candidatures by supporting men who were independent of local Liberal associations, like John Burns at Battersea, while at the same time pressing the Liberal chief whip to use his influence to secure the adoption of labor candidates by local Liberal associations.[85]

Besides Champion there was James Tims of the Metropolitan Radical Federation who asked the NLF to arrange the retirement of fifty Liberal candidates in 1890 so that the seats might be contested by the direct representatives of the trade unions.[86] Meanwhile, in 1888, Keir Hardie had contested Mid-Lanark independently of the Liberal association there, which had not only refused to adopt him but had refused to test the opinion of all Liberals in the constituency respecting his candidature. Schnadhorst had tried to conciliate Hardie by offering to find him a seat elsewhere for the next general election and to pay £300 a year toward his maintenance if he were elected. Hardie rejected Schnadhorst's offer, but, as Pelling points out, his quarrel was with the local Liberal association, not with the leaders of the Liberal organization.[87]

What were the leaders of the Liberal organization doing to assist the Labour Electoral Association? As Arnold Morley had told Champion in 1888 and as Schnadhorst had told Tims in 1891, neither the LCA nor the NLF could dictate to the local associations. Yet a number of constituencies sought the advice of the LCA concerning candidates, and where the LCA was footing the bill its advice concerning candidates would be accepted. A letter from Arnold Morley to Gladstone shows the direction of Morley's and Schnadhorst's thought on the matter in December 1891. Morley wrote:

> I send you a statement giving lists of Labour candidates already settled and others not yet settled but who are more or less suitable. Also a list of candidates who are wholly impecunious, but who are suitable for this purpose. I have also stated in each case of the candidates fixed the estimate, which Mr. Schnadhorst and I, after careful consideration, have thought necessary. I hope Mr. Carnegie will be attracted by the proposal. Should he be willing to take charge of the Labour candidates, I hope he will do it through us. Any promise to contribute towards the expenses of every Labour candidate would be dangerous as if it became known it might lead to some of them starting without the approval of the Association, and possibly against a Liberal. The total estimate for the candidates fixed is £12,400.[88]

Evidently Carnegie was not attracted by this modest proposal.

Even without the list of names and estimates originally inclosed with it, Morley's letter reveals the attitude of the chief Liberal organizers toward labor candidatures. Supposing that Carnegie supplied the money, financial aid would be given in amounts determined by the Liberal Central Association to those labor candidates who were approved by the Liberal Central Association.

If we assume that the total estimate which Carnegie was to be asked to supply was for election, not maintenance, expenses, then the number of candidates contemplated can be deduced from the sum of money. H. J. Hanham estimates that after 1885 the usual subsidy to candidates was about £300.[89] If £300 per candidate was the average sum estimated by Morley and Schnadhorst, it follows that about forty candidates were to be considered "settled" or "fixed" when the £12,000 was collected. And Morley's letter refers to others "not yet settled" and to an additional list of men "suitable for this purpose." Altogether more than forty—perhaps the fifty James Tims had demanded—may have been considered.

But Carnegie was not forthcoming and in the general election of 1892 there were only twenty-one labor candidates who could have had the assistance of the Liberal Central Association. Nine of these were "Lib-Labs" who had won seats in 1885, and all of them except Broadhurst won again in 1892.[90] Likewise successful were three others: Maddison, who was adopted by the Liberal Association of Hull, and Sam Woods, of the Lancashire Miners, both new recruits; W. P. Byles, whose partnership in William Byles and Son and proprietorship of the *Bradford Observer* put him on a different footing from these workingmen candidates, and who at least called himself a labor candidate and had no local Liberal opposition. In addition there were nine unsuccessful labor candidates who stood without Liberal opposition and who probably had the support of the LCA.[91]

This list of twenty-one candidates excludes the three successful labor candidates: Burns, Hardie, and J. H. Wilson, who stood without the assistance of the LCA, as well as sixteen other labor candidates who were unsuccessful in opposition to Liberals.[92]

The victory of J. H. Wilson, an executive of the Labour Electoral Association (LEA), over both a Liberal and a Liberal Unionist at Middlesborough revealed how uneasy the alliance of the LEA and the LCA actually was. It showed, too, that just as the tactics of the Liberals at Mid-Lanark had alienated Hardie in 1888, so the tactics used by Wilson and his followers antagonized the regular members of the Middlesborough Liberal Association.

Without much of a following within the Association, Wilson hastily enrolled some eight hundred adherents after the Liberal favored by the local committee of selection had agreed to abide by the decision of the whole Association concerning its candidate. Wilson's object was not to secure his own adoption by the Liberal Association but to prevent any orderly meeting of the Association in the hope that the Liberals would indefinitely defer formal adoption of a candidate and leave him a clear field against the Liberal Unionist.[93]

While the workers refused to join the local Liberal associations, and the associations remained reluctant to adopt labor candidates, the only way to increase the "Lib-Lab" contingent was by an arrangement for labor candidatures made at the top—an anticipation of the compact between Herbert Gladstone and Ramsay MacDonald in 1903.[94] It was beside the point to emphasize, as Threlfall did, that the Liberal Newcastle program included nine of the fourteen points demanded by the Labour Electoral Association.[95] It was equally true and beside the point to say, as Spence Watson did, that being a worker was not the sole, or the chief, requirement for a candidate.[96] With the example of the Irish Home Rulers before them, the working-class leaders were convinced that only a sizable contingent of working-class M.P.s would compel attention to working-class grievances.

Without the assistance of Carnegie, the best the LCA had been able to do for the Labour Electoral Association in 1892 was twenty-one candidatures, of which eleven had been successful. Three labor M.P.s had been elected without Liberal support, and a fourth, Ben Tillett, had come close to winning a seat. The founding of the Independent Labour Party (ILP) in 1893 was therefore not surprising. But far more formidable than the ILP was the shadow it cast before it: the adumbration of a parliamentary campaign by the trade unions, this time independent of any Liberal co-operation, which occurred in 1900.

At more than one point in time the gradual transformation of the Liberal party into a Liberal–Labour party seemed possible. Certainly most of the trade-union leaders in 1892 rejected Keir Hardie's dialectic to the effect that the Liberal party had served its historic mission. Their disappointment with the results of co-operation with the Liberals in 1892 must be counted a significant reason for the divergence between liberalism and labor. The failure of the Liberal Central Association to do more for labor candidatures, even without Carnegie's financial assistance, must be traced to the policy administered by Arnold Morley and Francis Schnadhorst.

As the chief Liberal whip, Arnold Morley was ultimately responsible for the allocation of party funds and the placing of candidates where the LCA could place them in 1892. But Schnadhorst was his principal source of information, his authorized agent in dealing with Hardie in 1888, and, in preparing the estimate of labor candidates' expenses, his collaborator. Schnadhorst's correspondence with Gladstone shows him irritated by Sidney Webb's pretensions in the Holborn Liberal and Radical Association, confident that there was no consensus of Liberal opinion in favor of payment of M.P.s (in 1888) as there was among labor leaders, and fearful of "independent labour candidates whom we cannot adopt as they are being started against long tried Liberals like Illingworth." On the other hand, in discussing the danger of a Liberal schism over labor questions, he said "the blame is not entirely on the side of the workers." [97]

The crusader's zeal which had animated Schnadhorst's challenge to the Hartington Whigs in the early 1880s had vanished along with the Whigs by 1892. Schnadhorst's brand of liberalism triumphed with the passing of the third franchise reform. He had remained loyal to Gladstone on the Home Rule question, although by 1887 he was doubtful whether that issue was as clear to the voters as it might have been. His comment on the agenda which became the Newcastle program in 1891 was that of a master tactician, not that of a true believer. By then he had occupied for five years that citadel of the Liberal party organization which, with Chamberlain's aid, he had been storming in 1885. And in his turn he had to confront a left wing as impatient of administrative considerations as he had been in the days before the liaison between NLF and LCA. His own friendship was with the older generation of trade unionists like Henry Broadhurst, and if Schnadhorst was not automatically hostile to new labor candidatures like Hardie's, neither was he really enthusiastic about them.

Understandably the loyal Liberals had closed ranks in 1886. Without Schnadhorst realizing it, the NLF had become more conservative. It was not only George Lansbury who felt that its resolutions were "cut and dried" before the annual conference.[98] After the disastrous election of 1895, the complaints about the subservience of the NLF to the LCA boiled over.

A group of Radical and Labour M.P.s acting together demanded then that the NLF be separated altogether from the LCA. Besides Dilke and Labouchere, this faction within the party included Hazell, whom Schnadhorst thoroughly disliked, and Sir Wilfred Lawson, who criticized the peerages for Stern and Williamson.[99] In November 1895 James Annand urged the divorce of the NLF and the LCA so that the NLF could debate issues freely without fear of embarrassing the leadership.[100] The next month the General Purposes Committee of the NLF agreed to consider a resolution sent to it by the General Committee raising the question of the representative and democratic quality of the NLF machinery.[101]

Some of the criticism may be explained by the invariable practice within both parties of blaming the organization for defeat in a general election. But the narrow interpretation of its proper role insisted upon by the NLF, which consistently refused any co-operation with Fabians or with branches of the LEA, had, while certainly preserving it from permeation, destroyed its claim to be the true voice of radicalism in the era of new unionism.[102]

The general election of 1892 was the last in which Schnadhorst played a part. Like Gladstone, who had hoped for a majority of eighty and had got one of forty, Schnadhorst was bitterly disappointed. After the election he wrote to Broadhurst: "There is not the slightest intention of recognizing my work in any way and that being so I have no burning zeal to continue a work which will be more difficult in the future than even the last six years. It is quite possible, unless the leaders shew a different spirit, that two years or less may see a smash up of the Liberal party from which it won't recover for a generation. This is my deliberate opinion." [103]

It was hardly fair to say that his work had gone unrecognized: the party had given him £10,000 in 1887 and was to give him £5,000 in November 1892.[104] In fact, broken health explains his outburst. When the Radical and labor criticism of the liaison between the LCA and the NLF appeared, "the Carnot of the Liberal party" had left his post.

Schnadhorst's health had deteriorated for years before his final retirement. He had spent the winter of 1882–1883 in Australia. By the winter of 1886–1887 he seemed prematurely old and very deaf to his colleagues. He fell ill in the summer of 1889 and spent the following winter in South Africa. Herbert Gladstone thought that he was never the same after this illness, and he was obliged to go abroad again in the winter of 1893. On his return from Australia in the spring of 1893 he resigned the secretaryship of the NLF, accepting instead the post of chairman of the General Committee. According to the minutes, he last attended on September 5, 1894, when he gave a statement on finances. In November 1894 his retirement from both the NLF and the LCA was accepted. Schnadhorst died a little over five years later on January 2, 1900, in his sixtieth year, at the Priory, a private lunatic asylum at Roehampton.[105]

In this article James Cornford deals with the changes in the Conservative party and he pays particular attention to what was happening in the constituency itself. Party organization, as discussed in the previous article, has not received as much attention as more familiar political history. Now more and more historians are also turning to consider the electors in their constituencies. Elements of this problem are also discussed in the suggestive study by John Vincent, The Formation of the Liberal Party, 1857–1868 *(London, 1966), and the book he edited and introduced,* Pollbooks: How Victorians Voted *(Cambridge, 1967). Henry Pelling, best known for his study of the early years of the Labour party, has also worked in this area in his* Social Geography of British Elections 1885–1910 *(London, 1967) and* Popular Politics and Society in Late Victorian Britain *(London, 1968).*

James Cornford is professor of government at Edinburgh University. The present article is reprinted from Victorian Studies VII *(1963), 35–66, by permission of that journal.*

JAMES CORNFORD

The Transformation of Conservatism in the Late Nineteenth Century

THE GROWTH OF modern party organization in Britain has been treated until recently as if it occurred in a social vacuum. Concern for delineating the development of formal structure (the apparatus of power) and for unraveling political intrigue (the struggle for power) has predominated over concern for discovering where parties found their support (the sources of power). The aim of this essay is to show how the development of formal organization within the Conservative party was related to a change in the basis of its support and to suggest how this change was related to wider social developments. Such an attempt requires a change of perspective from what one might call the traditional political history of the period, with its emphasis on the parliamentary struggle and the impact on party fortunes of the great questions of the day, especially of course the Irish question. If one is primarily interested in the doings of Cabinet and Commons, then it is possible to concentrate on the immediate issues and problems of policy that most obviously affect their day-to-day behavior. The danger lies in attributing to these factors the behavior not only of the politicians but of the electorate as well. The break-up of the Liberal party over the question of Irish Home Rule, particularly the secession of Chamberlain and the ending of his crusade to bring "gas and water socialism" to Westminster, had important consequences for British politics. But this is not to say that any major realignment of political loyalties took place in the electorate as a consequence of Home Rule. A voter may temporarily desert his party, where a politician must commit himself for good.

Because the results of elections are extremely important, that is to say they decide which party is going to exercise power, historians have tended to ignore the continuity of political allegiance and to concentrate their attention on and attach great significance to the issues on which elections were fought, particularly where it is a question of power changing hands. But because the result of an election is important, it does not mean that the issues are important in the sense that they are determining factors in the allegiance of any great number of voters. In fact it can be shown that a very small proportion of the electorate has to change its vote or even simply to abstain from voting in order to alter the balance of power. In the general elections of 1885 and 1886, for instance, seventy-three single-member constituencies in Britain which were contested on both occasions passed from the Liberals to the Conservatives. The Liberal vote in 1886 was down by 56,606, the Conservative up by 20,130. If we assume that the Conservative gain was made entirely from former Liberal voters, then seventy-three seats, or 146 on a division in the House of Commons, changed hands because 3.7 per cent of the 1885 voters changed allegiance, and a further 6.8 per cent abstained. Even in this case of two elections fought within a year of each other and on the same register, we cannot tell how much of the abstention was voluntary, and how much due to migration and death. When it comes to elections fought five years and more apart, the difficulties of interpretation increase with the greater likelihood that political changes may be due to changes in the size and composition of the electorate. Such factors must add to our caution in assessing the political changes so much exaggerated by the vagaries of the simple majority system.

Thus it is necessary to make a distinction between the role of specific issues at elections and the continuing social bases of po-

litical support, because the importance of Home Rule in accounting for Conservative success, both by the conversion of Liberals,
and, as I shall argue, by the effect of dissension on the Liberal election performance, has rather absolved historians from asking other
questions about the nature of Conservative support. These questions should be asked because it seems that the paradox of Conservative hegemony in the early years of the mass electorate has
obscured the fundamental development of late nineteenth-century
politics—that, with the extension of the suffrage, class was becoming the most important single factor in deciding political allegiance.

I

Recently, Frank Bealey and Henry Pelling have pointed to the
"sectionalism" of British politics in these years, stressing religious
and regional differences as against class and regarding London as
something of an exception,[1] whereas the emphasis in this account
is upon the emergence of class as a national factor with London
as an exemplar of this trend.[2] This difference of approach may in
part arise from their wish to distinguish the period from the
greater homogeneity of contemporary Britain and mine to distinguish it from the greater heterogeneity that went before. It
may arise in part also because they are concerned to point out
the difficulties in the way of independent working-class representation—an extreme form of political class-consciousness—while
the intention here is to show the importance of class in relation
to the existing parties, whose political dialogue was not couched
in the language of the class struggle.

There are two problems which such a question raises—the
definition of class and the manner of demonstrating its importance. Briefly, I would accept three separate criteria to define
class position, the first two covering roughly what Marx meant

by class,[3] and the third added by Weber: [4] the economic or "market situation," meaning source and size of income, degree of security of employment, and opportunities for promotion; the "work situation," meaning the social relationships in which the individual is involved by the kind of work he does; and the "status situation," meaning the place of the individual in the hierarchy of prestige of the society at large. The first two refer to the conditions of production, the third to that of consumption or "style of life." These conditions may be regarded as interdependent, but not necessarily synchronized—status distinctions may outlast the economic conditions that give rise to them, thus accounting for the awkward fact that "classes coexisting at any given time bear the marks of different centuries on their brow." [5] These distinctions help also to account for the fact that common economic conditions have not always, or even often, led to a common class-consciousness, an identification of interests, between groups with different work and status situations, notably white collar and manual workers.[6] Again, "work situation" may be seen as an important factor in the different development of political class-consciousness between groups with the same economic and status situation. As Weber pointed out, class and community are not the same thing (*From Max Weber*, p. 184). Class is only a potential basis for action, and the social relations of "work situation" or actual community may be such as to discourage the development of the attitudes relevant to political class-consciousness. Thus varieties of "work situation" may account for the different attitudes and traditions within each of the myriad occupations, both among manual workers, who are generally referred to as the "working classes," and among the nonmanual workers or "middle classes." This broad dichotomy we accept both as convenient shorthand for the complex realities of class and as in general the most important actual social division in England at this time.

Unfortunately, in trying to demonstrate the importance of class, one is forced by the nature of the available evidence to represent these distinctions by a number of rather crude indices, and the further caution should be added that these indices describe the characteristics of the constituencies as units but not necessarily those of the people whose political behavior we are trying to explain. To show that the more prosperous a constituency the more Conservative it was is not to prove that the more prosperous people were the ones that voted Conservative.[7] This is a limitation that only a survey could overcome and nobody, alas, can poll the dead. It is, however, of some value if the findings do not contradict the hypothesis.

The analysis presented here, partial and elementary though it is, would not have been practicable without the use of a high-speed computer. Although the great bulk of historical material is not susceptible to statistical treatment, there are fields, of which electoral behavior is one, that almost require it if the mass of evidence is to be analyzed at all and any attempt made to verify the explanations advanced by historians.[8] It is doubtful, however, that methods requiring a regular series of statistics could profitably be applied before the election of 1885. The differences of county and borough franchise, open voting, the prevalence of two-member constituencies, the large numbers of uncontested elections, the extensive corruption, and the small number of elections fought under the same conditions (1868, 1874, 1880) make this approach more hazardous than rewarding, and to go back before 1868 would multiply the hazards.[9] But these methods are not, in any case, offered as a substitute for the detailed local knowledge that marks the best studies of political history. Nor are they offered as a substitute for the imagination and intuitive feel which the historian, and for that matter the social scientist, should bring to his subject. Their results will be as interesting or as trivial as the insights which prompted their use: statistical significance is, of itself, meaningless. But what they can do, where the evidence is suitable, is to test the ideas generated by the study of a particular case against a large number of cases—not simply to test whether a hypothesis is "right or wrong," but to specify to what extent, under what conditions, and in what kind of places it does or does not apply. The arguments accepted by historian and social scientist do not differ in kind,[10] and yet instead of mutual comprehension and profit, there is more often suspicion and hostility. As Daniel Bell has put it: "Many social scientists, trained largely in technique, scorn ideas—and history—as vague and imprecise, while the humanist mocks the jargon and often the minute conclusions of the social scientist. Both are talking past each other. No one can quarrel with language or procedures, however technical, that aim for precision rather than obfuscation. But even at best such procedures, by the modes of abstraction employed, narrow the range of one's vision." [11] It would, however, be wrong to assume from this that historians have a monopoly of insight. To the ecological and statistical techniques which historians of elections should find invaluable,[12] one must also add the ideas that political scientists and sociologists have advanced about electoral behavior. Two quotations may serve to indicate my own debt in this respect. The first is the argument, put forward by A. L. Lowell more than sixty years ago, for examining not one election at a time but a number of elections over time: "The results of any particular election can, no doubt, be explained by reference to the circumstances under which it took place, to the nature of the issues presented, to the reputation of the candidates and to the state of prosperity or depression of industry at the moment; and yet if the phenomenon is repeated with great regularity for a considerable length of time we should be justified in concluding that it is due to some enduring cause, and that the form in which the issues are presented is itself a result of that cause." [13] The second is a view of the social significance of the individual voting decision offered by the high priest of modern social theory, Talcott Parsons, which is also relevant to the distinction made earlier between the role of issues at elections and the continuing social bases of party support. "Since the intellectual problems involved in a rational solution are not practically soluble," Parsons writes, "my thesis is that the mechanisms [of reaching a voting decision] are typically non-rational. They involve stabilization of political attitudes in terms of association with other members of the principal solidary groups in which the voter is involved . . . it may be said that the question is not so much . . . *for what* he is voting as it is *with whom* he is associating himself in voting." [14]

II

In 1868 the Conservative party was still predominantly the country party, whose strength lay in the county constituencies and the small agricultural boroughs. It was still a party set in a convention of politics which thought in terms not of classes but of communities. It was the country party because it was held to represent the interests of the agricultural community as a whole, on the assumption that the interest of the laborer, the tenant farmer, and the landlord was one. The method of conducting politics closely reflected this assumption. There was little formal political organization. The landlords, the "men of influence," controlled the political allegiance of their social inferiors and settled among themselves by bargain, treaty, and alliance the representation of the counties; and such was their influence that in the words of the Liberal agent, Joseph Parkes, "the pollbook is almost a topography of the estates." [15] At the center they met as a loose confederation united by ties of interest and attitude under a leader of their own order. Central organization was sketchy. The Carlton provided a meeting place, a convenient social setting for the very personal business of party management. The Whips were the agents of the leader in this business, and the party's election machinery, so far as it existed, was in the hands of his solicitors, who attempted at election time to coordinate the activities of the motley array of Constitutional Clubs, registration societies, and Workingmen's

Conservative Associations unevenly distributed about the country. Party management had still much of the style and ethos of estate management.

From 1846 the party had been in a minority in the Commons, owing its brief spells of office to the skill of its leaders and the quarrels of its less socially homogeneous opponents. Outside the agricultural constituencies, it had the support of a few towns, and elsewhere of certain distinct and faithful minorities which it attempted to augment either by bribery or by its willingness to take up the cause of the industrial working classes against their Liberal employers.

In 1885, by contrast, the Conservative party owed half its strength in the Commons to urban constituencies. It had a central organization with a full-time paid agent and several secretaries, and a national organization of Conservative associations designed to bring in supporters by the latest propaganda methods without relying on traditional social influences or earlier electioneering devices. The party was to hold power, with one short break, for the next twenty years. The transformation is striking enough, but how was it accomplished and what did it mean?

After a genuflection towards the genius of British Conservatism, the usual account makes Disraeli the hero and initiator of this change, as the man who saw a future for Conservatism in the age of democracy. He has traditionally been credited by his admirers with a consistent and constructive policy towards the working classes, and to this theme of sympathetic and imaginative policy has been added by recent studies [16] the theme of a nascent party organization with which the fruits of this policy might be reaped in the conditions of a mass electorate, created by himself. But curiously, the strongest impression one gets from these studies is that of the extreme reluctance of the party management to change its way and of the eventual frustration and resignation of party agents who tried to implement a policy of progressive organization. It is not necessary to deny Disraeli's popular sympathies nor his belief that the working classes could be converted to Conservatism in order to doubt their influence on his practical politics. He had won his way to leadership in an aristocratic party whose members were by modern standards free of party control; his experience had been gained in twenty years of coaxing a cantankerous minority in the Commons. Even when he was at last Prime Minister, his difficulties in managing the party were not at an end,[17] so that it is not surprising that Salisbury should have found that Disraeli's "only fixed political principle was that the party must on no account be broken up," and that popular opinion had completely mistaken his party in foreign policy, where he had always followed the advice either of the minister concerned or of the Queen, sometimes without even going through the procedure of consulting the Cabinet.[18]

The proof that Disraeli set out to win working-class support is based chiefly on his Reform Act of 1867 and on the housing, sanitary, and Trades Union legislation of his government of 1874–1880. Though he also had other good reasons for putting through Reform himself, particularly keeping control of the redistribution, it has recently been suggested that he was very reluctant to adopt Reform at all, and that it was Derby who pressed it upon him. It was certainly Derby who drafted the original bill.[19] On the second count, the evidence of R. A. Cross, the Home Secretary responsible for the legislation, is interesting. When the Cabinet met for the first time in 1874, Cross confessed himself "disappointed by the want of originality shown by the Prime Minister. From all his speeches I had quite expected his mind was full of legislative schemes, but such did not prove to be the case; on the contrary, he had entirely to rely on the various suggestions of his colleagues." [20]

It may also be that his part in the creation of the new party organization has been exaggerated. Disraeli was never free from the assumptions and concerns of the old conventions of politics. If he encouraged the growth of central organization before the election of 1874, he was equally responsible for its decline and failure in 1880, when, as he told Salisbury, "the Committee with their wonderful organisation, and vast resources, and great preparation and experience, appear to be quite demoralised, and have scarcely sent me a telegram, tho' they promised to do so every half hour." [21] The agent he had himself appointed, J. E. Gorst, who did his best to foster new sources of support for the party, found it impossible to overcome the social prejudices of his colleagues in the party management. After the unexpected successes in the borough elections of 1874, he wrote to Disraeli to complain that no effort was being made to strengthen their borough supporters through the exercise of the patronage that they now commanded: "your colleagues (who are none of them Borough Members themselves) either fail to see the necessity for such a policy or despair of maintaining permanently our position in the Boroughs." [22] And earlier he had written to the Chief Whip to protest the snubs which cabinet members offered to provincial Conservatives: "looking back over the 9 months we have been in office, I cannot but perceive that all our patronage has been divided between the personal friends of the ministers and our political opponents." [23] As no heed was paid to his warnings, Gorst finally resigned from his position; and having found it impossible to reform the party from within, he joined hands with the provincial borough leaders in an assault from without. They started to use the annual meetings of the National Union of Conservative Associations as a platform from which they could attack the party management. [24]

The crux of the matter was the neglect of their borough supporters by the Conservative leaders. It was a neglect that reflected the social assumptions of a party of country gentlemen, not in the least eager to welcome the support of outsiders and certainly unwilling to share the rewards of office with them. The bitterness of Gorst's tone is explained by his feeling that he himself had been inadequately rewarded for his work, but the neglect he described was real enough. A supporter wrote to Cross:

> "Blessed is he who expecteth nothing from the Conservative party if he works in South East Lancashire" may fairly be said. What have the Liberals done? Made Baronets of Sir Benjamin Hayward, Thomas Bazely, William Fairbairn, Joseph Whitworth, offered one to R. N. Philips; Knights of Thomas Potter, James Watts, John Potter, Joseph Heron, Sir Thomas Baker, Henry Roscoe, Joseph Lee cum aliis.
>
> *Tory Honours*
> It is true that Callender had a baronetcy offered. . . . What did not John Hicks do for this party? And what has not W. Cunliffe Brooks done? Either of them, without sons, and of unbounded wealth deserve recognition and South East Lancs would not feel quite so much in the cold.
>
> As a Lancashire man think of our teeming population and do remove the stigma of neglect.[25]

In fact the existence of men, whose Liberal equivalents were both accepted and honored, was barely acknowledged by the Conservative leaders, and it is my contention that the drive to complete the organization of the party came not from the leaders and party managers, but from just these urban provincial supporters who felt themselves neglected. And further, that besides its ostensible purpose of improving the methods of gaining mass support, the new organization had the secondary function of integrating these local leaders, whose social backgrounds and traditions were different from those of the old backbone of the party, by providing a common ground upon which they could meet the Tory gentlemen as colleagues, without it being necessary for them to penetrate *en masse* the inner circle of the country houses.

Because the final struggle for reorganization was conducted under the flamboyant leadership of Lord Randolph Churchill, both the source of initiative for reform and its integrative function have tended to be obscured in the excitement of his tilt at the party leaders. Furthermore the quite correct deflation by Ostrogorski, Lowell, and others of Churchill's spirited talk of "democracy" has led to a misconception of the aims of the reformers and to an underestimation of the extent of their achievement. To appreciate these, it is necessary to understand the notions of organization entertained by the old guard of the party managers whom they were attacking, and to realize that this attack, having been mounted in the late seventies before Churchill had been heard of, was prior to and independent of Churchill's campaign against the Parliamentary leadership. Indeed the plan of reorganization adopted in 1886 closely resembled the proposals made by the provincial leaders before Churchill appeared on the scene.

III

After the great victory of 1874, the impetus at the center to reform died away. Disraeli, old, tired, and much preoccupied with foreign affairs, seemed to have lost interest; while Gorst, disappointed in his hopes of preferment and antipathetic to his aristocratic colleagues, for two years struggled in vain to instill some sense of urgency into the party management. In this time he had, as he told Disraeli in his letter of resignation, "the misfortune to witness the whole system, to establish which so much trouble was taken, gradually fall into decay." The chief cause of the decay, Gorst went on to say, was the removal of the conduct of elections from the central office into the hands of the Chief Whip. Despite his knowledge of local conditions, the agent had only rarely been consulted, with the result that "the established principle of noninterference with local leaders has in many instances been neglected; and those leaders have been constantly offended and alienated in the distribution of patronage and other matters." [26] There were in fact two conflicting principles of noninterference. It had been Gorst's policy to encourage local leaders to form associations and then to turn over to them the business of choosing candidates and running elections. What he objected to was the Whips' habit of supporting candidates without first consulting the local associations and their tendency to aid and abet corrupt practices in the conduct of elections, which acted to discourage respectable supporters from political activity. The principle of noninterference on the part of the old guard consisted in a reluctance to stimulate local activity for fear that it might upset the traditional patterns of political behavior. This is well exemplified in a case reported to Salisbury by Edward Stanhope after the disastrous defeat in the general election of 1880. Stanhope had been put in charge of an enquiry into the organization in the counties, during which "we have found one county without any attempt at any organization whatever, namely Dorsetshire. In consequence of this I spoke to Edward Digby, who told me that he had discussed the matter with his colleague Mr. Floyer and they had deliberately come to the conclusion that it was better to have none, for fear of raising the activity of the Liberal party. . . . We have felt it very difficult to know what step to take, and it has occurred to us that your connection with the county might make you disposed to say a word to Lord Digby on the subject or any other Dorsetshire men of influence who would be likely to take the matter up. . . . Of course we are ready here to render any assistance, if asked. But we can do nothing unless asked." [27] So strongly did Stanhope respect the prerogatives of the landed gentry that, not only did he regard it as impossible that the central agencies of the party should take any initiative in promoting local organization, but in asking for help, he approached Salisbury not as leader of the party but as a Dorsetshire landowner.

It was such attitudes that Gorst and the borough leaders attacked at the annual meetings of the National Union. Their demands may be briefly summarized as follows: that every constituency ought to have an association to provide a regular and permanent organization for the purpose of registering voters, making propaganda, choosing candidates, and conducting elections; that these local associations should be linked in provincial unions in order to make the best use of regional resources; that the provincial unions should be represented on the council of the National Union, then a largely co-optative body, so that, in the words of a speaker at the Annual Conference in 1878, when "each gentleman on the Council felt that he represented an important district of the country, they would be enabled to inaugurate measures which would be of the greatest benefit to the organisation of the party; in which, at the present time, the Council did not feel they could wisely take initiative in starting." [28]

Discussion of the National Union controversy in the eighties has been confused by the assumption that the attempt to alter its constitution was an attempt to make it into a policy-dictating convention in the American style. But the National Union, unlike the National Liberal Federation, had never been concerned to promote a particular program—nor were its critics. What they wanted was that certain methods of organization, considered by them essential to survival in the new conditions of an enlarged and growing electorate, should be adopted throughout the country by the Conservative party, and that this should be done through the agency of associations affiliated to the National Union.

Churchill certainly gave cause for the suspicions that he wanted to start a caucus of his own in imitation of Chamberlain.[29] He had talked both in public and in private about the value of the caucus, and it is perfectly possible that he thought he was going to promote one. But when he came to grips with the task, certain problems immediately confronted him. The caucus was essentially an organization independent of official party management, growing from the provinces, and designed to push a particular program. The National Union was an adjunct of the party management, promoted from the center for propaganda purposes. Neither Churchill nor his supporters had any program. The debate in the National Union had never been about measures, but about methods of organization. At the height of the National Union crisis, when Churchill resigned from the council in May 1884, the Memorandum sent by his provincial supporters demanding his return to the council specifically stated that: "We recognise as fundamental principles in any Conservative organisation:—Non-interference on the part of political associations with the direction of matters incident to the duties and policy of our member in Parliament . . . [and] that every political Association responsible for the interests of the party in the various parliamentary districts ought to enjoy full independence in the management of its local political matters." [30]

There were to be no fiats on policy from the localities to the center, and none on organization from the center to the localities. The two features of caucus politics most offensive to the conservative-minded of both parties, and essential to the power of a caucus boss, were repudiated by Churchill's supporters. Churchill's personality and ambitions have, in fact, tended to obscure the issues at stake. The real question was whether the party was to continue to rely on the methods of social influence and bribery, which had once been adequate but which were becoming increasingly irrelevant with every major political development: Disraeli's Reform Bill, the Ballot Act of 1872, the Corrupt Practices Act of 1883, and the enfranchisement of the county householders in 1884. The clash between the party management and the National Union was not a question of pro- or antidemocratic attitudes, but of attitudes arising from quite different social situations.

The informal influence of property and social status through personal knowledge and contact, which had been and was still a plausible basis for county and small town politics, simply did not exist in the cities. All the obvious means of mobilizing support were in the hands of their opponents. As W. H. Smith lamented: "The Radicals have the Trade Unions, the Dissenting Chapels and every society for the abolition of property and morality working for them. Our supporters only want to be left alone to enjoy what they have: and they think they are so secure that they will make no sacrifice of time or of pleasure to prepare against attack or to resist it." [31]

When Churchill joined the attack on the party management in 1883, practically nothing had come of the attempts to remedy this situation. The famous Central Committee had been appointed in 1880 to look into the state of the organization, and Gorst had been recalled as party agent to placate the borough leaders who were furious at the debacle in the general election and were beginning to make a nuisance of themselves on the council of the National Union.[32] But Gorst once again fell foul of the Whips, in trying to prevent their encouragement of corrupt practices,[33] and after a brief spell of activity,[34] resigned. Gorst's resignation was partly prompted by the personal bitterness which existed between himself and what he called "the old identity," and by the fact that he was acting in the Commons in calculated defiance of the leaders with whom he was supposed to cooperate as agent. But there was more to it than this. For his successor, G. C. T. Bartley, who was also anxious to promote local organization,[35] found that the position accorded to the agent was quite inadequate for the efficient performance of his duties. In a letter of resignation in November 1884, he said that he did not feel he had the confidence of the leaders of the party, that he had not been asked to be present at any discussion of party policy, and that he had to rely for information on the newspaper reports. His own opinion was never asked, and no use was made of the knowledge of constituency opinion which he had presumed it was his duty to obtain. He pointed out that many of the local agents were apathetic, that the Conservative press was miserable, that there were few good candidates coming forward, and that those who did come forward neglected their constituencies, and finally that the party had no policy to meet the franchise and redistribution question on which the whole political future depended. The work needed to deal with this situation required an agent who was more than a clerical secretary and who would enjoy "the full confidence of the party leaders and receive from them their constant direction, support and assistance. I see no indication yet of being treated in this manner and I therefore prefer to retire." [36] Add to this lamentable picture the fact that the National Union, the only national Conservative organization, was still a voluntary body to which many borough and most county associations were not affiliated, and that these were only in spasmodic and informal contact with the party management through the central committee, and you have a situation not much different in essentials from that which obtained ten years earlier.

By the time Churchill resigned at the end of 1886, the demands of the provincial leaders put forward at every conference of the National Union since 1876 had been met by a scheme whose "object," in the words of the report, "has been to establish a connection, by a regular succession of representative grades, between the smallest associations and the individual elector, through the district Associations and the Central Associations of each constituency, up to the Councils of the Provincial Unions: and from these again to the council and conference of the National Union." [37] And this scheme was given the official blessing of the new party agent, who was to be in the future the intimate link between the leader of the party and this new national and inclusive organization.

This is the essential step in the transformation. It can partly be attributed to Churchill's audacious leadership which, though it may have been self-interested and ill-informed, had this merit— that by attacking the leaders directly, he made them aware of the strength of a movement which they had formerly been content to ignore. It may also be attributed in part to Salisbury's growing appreciation that there was a desire for reform among provincial Conservatives who were not supporters of Churchill,[38] and in part to the effect of a somewhat neglected factor which greatly enhanced both the actual importance and the awareness of the importance of urban Conservatism—the settlement of the redistribution accompanying the extension of the county franchise in 1884.

The main lines of the redistribution scheme were settled by private treaty between the party leaders after prolonged negotiations through the late summer and autumn of 1884, in which Gladstone's determined moderation overcame not only the divisions between the Whigs and the Radicals in his own cabinet, but also the reluctance of an equally divided Conservative party to negotiate at all. The scheme, though a compromise between the conservatism of the Whigs and the unexpected radicalism of a section of the Conservatives led by Churchill and Hicks Beach, was still an extensive one.[39] It radically altered the balance of representation in the counties in favor of population and the industrial North, virtually destroyed the small borough, introduced widely the single-member constituency, and recognized fully the great cities. But it did not go far enough for the advanced Conservatives.[40]

The motives of the other participants in the struggle are clear enough. The Whigs wanted to escape extinction, the Radicals to extinguish them. Though few of them can have hoped to put it off forever, and still fewer dared oppose it openly, the "old identity" of the Conservative party wanted to put off for as long as possible the awful prospect of giving the vote to the county householder; and at the least they hoped to make some short-term profit from the embarrassments of the Liberals. Like the Whigs, they wished to preserve as far as possible the pattern of deferential community politics, which was already subject to increasing strain and which Chamberlain was threatening to disrupt altogether by his appeals to the class interests of the agricultural laborer. The attitude of the advanced Conservatives on certain points is also straightforward. In criticizing the failure to separate urban and rural population and to obtain grouping, they were criticizing the failure to achieve familiar aims of Conservative policy. The advantages of raising the limit of population were also obvious: far more Liberal than Conservative seats would be extinguished. What requires more explanation is why they should have expected the Conservative party to do any better in a political structure dominated by the great urban centers and the single-member constituency. And the explanation lies in their confidence in the strength of that new support, which Salisbury himself aptly dubbed when he told Northcote: "I believe there is a great deal of Villa Toryism which requires organization." [41] Both by agreeing to negotiate redistribution at all [42] and by the radical settlement he then extracted from the Government, Salisbury committed himself to that organization.

IV

The general election of 1885 was the first in which the cities came into their own and the last before Home Rule broke up the Liberal party. This is not to say that the Irish Question was not already influential, but at least it was not the explicit issue of the election. Gladstone had not yet made his decision in favor of Home Rule,[43] and the future Liberal Unionists were still in the Cabinet. The results of the election produced three novelties—the Irish party, eighty strong; a Liberal majority in the English counties; and a Conservative majority in the English boroughs, where they won 114 of 226 seats.

The distribution of these seats is set out in Table I. To summarize the results as briefly as possible: the Conservative strength in 1885 lay in London, Lancashire, and the nonindustrial counties,

TABLE I

CONSERVATIVE SEATS IN THE ENGLISH BOROUGHS IN THE
GENERAL ELECTION OF 1885

BY AREA

	Total No. of Seats	No. Conservative
The Metropolitan Boroughs	62	37
Yorkshire and the North [1]	40	13
Lancashire and Cheshire	39	29
North Midlands [2]	35	3
West, East, and South Midlands [3]	25	13
South-East and West [4]	25	19
TOTAL	226	114

BY SIZE OF POPULATION IN 1881

	Total No. of Seats	No. Conservative
The Metropolitan Boroughs	62	37
Boroughs over 250,000	36	20
Boroughs of 100–250,000	33	12
Boroughs of 50–100,000	41	14
Boroughs of 35–50,000	25	13
Boroughs under 35,000	29	18
TOTAL	226	114

[1] Northumberland, Cumberland, and Durham.

[2] Warwicks, Staffs, Derby, Nottingham, Lincoln, Leicester, and Northampton.

[3] Salop, Hereford, Worcester, Monmouth, Berks, Wilts, Oxford, Gloucester, Norfolk, Cambridge, Suffolk, and extra-metropolitan Essex.

[4] Sussex, Hants, extra-metropolitan Kent, Somerset, Devon, and Cornwall.

and in the largest and smallest of the boroughs. This pattern, established before Home Rule, generally held in the next five elections. That is to say that in the elections that went in their favor, those of 1886, 1895, and 1900, the Conservatives increased their

TABLE 11

RELATION BETWEEN CONSERVATIVE VOTE AND THE SIZE OF POLL
IN THE ENGLISH BOROUGH CONSTITUENCIES 1885–1906

BY AREA

	No. of Constituencies with correlations of:			
	Less than −.20	Total less than −.50	Total more than −.50	More than −.80
The Metropolitan Boroughs	4	10	49	33
Yorkshire and the North	15	28	8	4
Lancashire and Cheshire	5	13	21	6
North Midlands	12	18	12	6
West, East, and South Midlands	3	8	12	5
South-East and West	4	8	9	4

BY SIZE OF POPULATION IN 1881

	No. of Constituencies with correlations of:			
	Less than −.20	Total less than −.50	Total more than −.50	More than −.80
The Metropolitan Boroughs	4	10	49	33
Boroughs over 250,000	4	11	24	13
Boroughs of 100–250,000	8	15	8	3
Boroughs of 50–100,000	13	21	8	—
Boroughs of 35–50,000	8	14	10	2
Boroughs under 35,000	7	14	12	6

The discrepancies between these figures and the numbers of seats given in Table I are accounted for by the two-member constituencies for which only one set of figures is given, and by the few constituencies not contested more than twice, for which no correlation can be calculated.

support most where they had been most successful in 1885, and that in the elections which went against them they maintained support best there also. There are two important exceptions to this statement: Birmingham's complete change of allegiance after 1886 and the landslide in Lancashire in 1906, upon which I shall reserve comment for the moment. With these exceptions, though the number of seats won might rise by fifty in 1900, or drop by fifty in 1906, the distribution of Conservative support remained much what it had been in 1885; what one would have judged to be safe Conservative seats by their vote in 1885 remained faithful in 1906. As far as one can tell merely by looking at the figures, there are two general trends over these six elections which help to explain Conservative successes. The first is that the elections in which Conservatives were most successful were also those with most uncontested seats.[44] The second is that the Conservative percentage of the poll varied in inverse proportion to the size of the poll; in fact the smaller the poll the larger the Conservative share of it, and this was most true in the constituencies where the Conservatives were most successful.[45] These points together suggest that the chief factor in Conservative success was lack of enthusiasm among the Liberals, on the assumption that a low poll reflects Liberal abstentions; this assumption seems fair, since in the great majority of constituencies, while the Conservative vote increased steadily from election to election whatever the result, the Liberal vote fluctuated sometimes by as much as 10 per cent.[46] Whatever the causes, whether dissension over Home Rule in 1886 or the difficulty of opposing a patriotic cry in 1900, the effect was not that the Conservatives were able to persuade erstwhile Liberals to join their camp, but that the Liberals failed to put forward candidates or to get out their vote.[47] Equally in the election of 1906, it does not appear that thousands of former Conservatives voted Liberal, since in the majority of constituencies which changed hands the Conservative vote was very little if at all smaller than in 1900 and in some it was larger; but a much higher poll, in what was in some cases a much larger electorate, swamped what had previously been comfortable majorities.[48] From this it appears that potential support for the Conservatives was at once smaller and more reliable than that for the Liberals.

TABLE III

THE GENERAL ELECTION OF DECEMBER 1910 COMPARED WITH THE GENERAL ELECTIONS FROM 1885 TO JANUARY 1910.

Election	Number of Seats Contested in Common	Turnout	Unionist %
1885	355	83.0	47.9
Dec. 1910		83.1	49.9
1886	310	74.6	52.3
Dec. 1910		83.1	48.4
1892	354	80.7	50.3
Dec. 1910		83.1	49.1
1895	299	80.2	52.4
Dec. 1910		83.4	48.2
1900	281	77.1	52.5
Dec. 1910		83.2	47.9
1906	329	84.5	45.1
Dec. 1910		83.3	50.0
Jan. 1910	349	88.3	49.2
Dec. 1910		83.1	49.6

If this was the pattern after 1885, how did it compare with what went before? The most sophisticated attempt to analyze voting strength in the three elections, 1868, 1874, and 1880, which took place in the same constituencies,[49] shows the Conservatives more successful than the Liberals only in the counties and the small boroughs, while falling well behind the Liberals in the large English boroughs. In 1880 the Conservatives won only twenty-four out of the 114 seats in Hanham's largest category, seats in

towns with populations over 50,000 in 1871 in the United Kingdom (*Elections*, p. 92, n. 2). Perhaps, then, the great conversion
to Conservatism took place between 1880 and 1885, as Sir Robert
Ensor has argued, again as a result of an accumulating disgust with
Gladstone's Irish policy? [50] If however the analysis is confined to
the sixty-two largest seats of all, that is, constituencies with elec-
torates of more than 17,500 in 1880 which were contested in both
1868 and 1880, a distinct trend towards Conservatism can be established. The Conservatives gained only two seats, nineteen in 1880
to seventeen in 1868, but their percentage of the vote rose from
37.5 to 44.3; and as a contemporary pointed out in 1881, "the excess of Liberals by no means indicated a corresponding excess of
Liberal feeling among the constituencies, but was due only to the
defective working of our present system of representation." [51]
What happened between 1880 and 1885 was not a mass conversion, but the Redistribution Act, with its reallocation of seats and
its single-member constituencies. Where Conservative supporters
had formerly been swamped in huge constituencies, they were
now high and dry on islands of their own. [52]

V

In the debates on the Redistribution Bill, G. J. Goschen had ut-
tered a prophetic warning: "Let us beware that the single member
constituencies do not develop into one class constituencies, whose
members will come here feeling themselves responsible, not to the
whole people of the country, but to the particular class living in
the district by which they are returned." [53] After the election of
1885, at least one Liberal had an explanation for the Conservative
majority in the boroughs. *The Times* reported that "Mr. Trevelyan . . . affects to deplore the secession from the Liberal ranks
of persons belonging to the upper classes or swayed by the miserable desire to imitate them," while *The Times* itself concluded

that "the more closely the figures are examined . . . the more striking becomes the evidence of a general revolt of the English boroughs against the doctrines lately forced upon them under the name of Liberalism" (30 November 1885, p. 9).

How far in fact can this "general revolt" be put down, as Goschen feared and Trevelyan averred, to the class composition of the constituencies? In an attempt to answer this question, I applied a number of tests to the Metropolitan constituencies and found the following: (1) that there was a high correlation (+0.74) between the Conservative percentage of the poll and the prosperity of the constituency, using rateable value per head of population as a measure of prosperity; [54] (2) that where two constituencies had the same rateable value per head the outer and less congested district tended to be more Conservative; (3) that where there was a high proportion of nonresident voters—the City, Westminster, Holborn, Marylebone—the constituencies were strongly Conservative. To this one might add that the outer suburbs, in the county divisions of Middlesex, Surrey, Kent, and Essex, which were still the exclusive preserve of middle-class commuters,[55] had been solidly Conservative in 1880 (Hanham, *Elections*, p. 226), and going that way since 1868 when Lord George Hamilton, then a young sprig of a Guards Officer standing for the first time, was returned at the head of the poll for Middlesex: "My electoral success," he modestly relates, "was due to the strange chance of my being selected for a constituency which, unknown to the wire-pullers, had during the past ten years been converted from Radicalism to Conservatism. The rapid extension of suburban railroads and the outpouring of professional men, tradesmen, and clerical employees into the rural outskirts of London had steadily changed the tone and politics of the constituency." [56]

This pattern was reproduced in Bristol, where the Western Division, dominated by the prosperous residential district of Clifton, returned Hicks Beach for the next twenty years, with a large majority composed, according to an opponent, of "the two classes of the luxurious rich and the dependent and obsequious poor." [57] In Leeds the North Division comprising the suburb of Headingley, and the Central Division comprising the business district, became safe Conservative seats, and Herbert Gladstone, on the advice of the local Liberal leader, chose the working-class Western Division, which he won every time in the six general elections.[58]

In Sheffield, the sitting Liberal, A. J. Mundella, and his prospective colleague, Bernard Coleridge, both said that they would rather leave Sheffield than stand for either of the residential divisions, Eccleshall and Hallam, or the Central Division, and insisted on being adopted for Brightside and Attercliffe, the two overwhelmingly working-class divisions.[59] This proved a sensible attitude, since the Conservatives won Brightside only once, Attercliffe not at all, but the Central, Eccleshall, and Hallam Divisions at every election.

These, of course, are the easy cases, the ones that support the argument. Even in London, where the initial tests of the 1885 results supported the class division so strongly, there were important exceptions, which further tests [60] only made the more obvious. In general it may be said that the syndrome of characteristics favorable to Conservative success in a Metropolitan borough over the six elections was as follows: a high rateable value per head; a large number of nonresident electors; a low population density; a large proportion of workers in service industries, particularly domestic servants, in its working population; a large proportion of professional men among its occupied males; a low degree of poverty; and a low infant mortality rate. And yet there were in the East End central, densely populated, poor, overcrowded, highly industrialized constituencies which returned Conservatives more often than not. Of course even the poorest constituency had a middle-class element,[61] seen in Booth's maps as a thin red line down either side of the main streets; and although this was much smaller than elsewhere, in relation to the size of the electorate and particularly considering that the poll sometimes fell below 60 per cent, it was not a negligible factor. Booth, describing the political life of the East End, reported that "the Conservative clubs . . . belong mainly to the upper or lower middle class; only one of them, with 200 members, is *called* a working man's club." Nevertheless, this can hardly explain the frequency of Conservative victories before 1906, which must be accounted the idiosyncrasy of East End politics. Of the thirty-two political clubs that Booth found at the end of the eighties, twenty-two were Liberal and Radical, six were Conservative, three were socialist, and one Irish Home Rule. "Judging by the clubs," Booth commented, "there would seem to be no doubt of the political complexion of East London; and the weekly papers mostly taken—*Reynold's* and the *Dispatch*—tell the same story. But the tone is not so much Liberal or even Radical, as Republican, outside of the lines, authorized or unauthorized, of English party politics, and thus very uncertain at the ballot box." [62] In 1906 the Conservatives won only two out of twenty-odd East End seats, and four of them went to Labour (three Labour Representation Committee candidates and one Lib-Lab). Though there was clearly working-class Conservatism in East London, it was not the reliable enduring kind found in the middle-class constituencies.

The same thing might be said of working-class Conservatism where it manifested itself most strongly, that is in Lancashire. In the election of 1906, five seats which the Conservatives had won in all the other elections, and five more that they had won more often than not, went Labour.[63] The Irish Question was so important in Lancashire politics that again it can be made to explain too much. The Irish vote clearly played an important part in at least two of the Manchester constituencies,[64] and in Liverpool where the Scotland Division returned T. P. O'Connor, the only Irish nationalist M.P. to sit for an English constituency. Again the anti-Irish vote is clearly important, especially in Liverpool, where racial and religious hostilities are still alive today. But there was also in Lancashire's Conservatism a tradition of working-class hostility to the doctrines of the Manchester School and militant middle-class Nonconformity, which went back to the clashes of the Chartists with the Anti-Corn Law League [65] and the activities of Tory Radical critics of the factory system. As late as 1885 eight out of nine officers of the Manchester Liberal Association were in the cotton trade (Hanham, *Elections,* p. 127), and class antagonism was directed against the Liberals. At the turn of the century, an Independent Labour Party lecturer in Clitheroe "went so far as to illustrate the attitude of the Liberal Party to social reform with a lantern slide of Sir William Harcourt drinking champagne at a public dinner while a half-clothed little girl was to be seen selling matches in the street outside" (Bealey and Pelling, p. 106).

The immediate social effect of the Industrial Revolution was not to make cities more, but less, alike.[66] It is this that accounts for the characteristic differences between the politics of Manchester and those of the last major exception to the electoral pattern we traced earlier, Birmingham. The peculiar class hostility in Lancashire arose in part from the structure of the cotton industry. Cobden himself attributed the healthier political tradition in Birmingham to "the fact that the industry of the hardware district is carried on by small manufacturers, employing a few men and boys each, sometimes only an apprentice or two; whilst the great capitalists in Manchester form an aristocracy, individual members of which wield an influence over sometimes two thousand persons. The former state of society is more natural and healthy in a moral and political sense. There is freer intercourse between all classes than in the Lancashire town, where a great and impassable gulf separates the workman from his employer." [67] Now the striking thing about the politics of Birmingham at the end of the century is not so much that the Home Rule crisis should have disturbed its course as that the course should have been changed with such unanimity. Although in the words of a local historian the city was "practically divided up into separate constituencies of rich and poor, artisan and manufacturer," [68] the Caucus won every seat in 1885; and afterwards while two middle-class constituencies were left to the Conservatives, it held the other five for the Liberal Unionists.

In part this may be attributed to the effectiveness of the Caucus and the disruption of the Liberals; but the willingness of the Caucus itself to follow Chamberlain's lead must also be explained, and here the continuity of independent small-scale production [69] and the strength of the traditional philosophy of class cooperation may have played their part. There is no doubt that the middle-class Radicals of the Birmingham tradition regarded themselves not as the representatives of their class but of their community, and continued to stress this idea from the agitation for the Great Reform Bill to the Radical Programme of 1885. Thus Thomas Attwood claimed that "the interests of masters and men are, in fact, one," [70] Cobden and Bright hammered away at landlord government and privilege, Bright's brother-in-law described the Reform question in 1859 as "whether the industry of England shall attain its due share in the government of England," [71] and Chamberlain later dressed up social reform in the guise of municipal improvement. They all invoked for their policies the common interests of the industrial classes, whether by inveighing against a common enemy or by appealing to a common civic pride.[72] This was not necessarily cant. As a Manchester man observed in 1912, Cobden "would never have understood the modern tendency to group employers of labour in the same category as landowners, and as forming a class apart from what is now called 'Labour.' " [73] Nor was this attitude held only by middle-class politicians. When Mundella was brought to Sheffield by the Trades Unions to run against Roebuck in 1868, a working man refused to vote for him, though "out of humour with Roebuck," on the grounds that "it would be to prefer class representation rather than the representation of the several interests of the entire body of electors." [74]

In the decline of this philosophy lay the roots of urban Conservatism. As the Radicals went further in their appeals to working-class interests, so they lost the adherence of a growing number of the middle-classes, and even in the late fifties the boroughs began to be contested against them not by old-fashioned Tories, but by "Liberal Conservatives" (for instance, Thomas Dyke Ackland at Birmingham in 1854) or even by old-fashioned Radicals (for instance, Roebuck at Sheffield).[75]

VI

It is beyond the scope of this essay to do more than suggest some of the long-term social developments which seem the most important conditions hastening the decline of the view that votes should be cast in favor of "the several interests of the entire body of electors":

(1) The development of independent working-class organizations which gave both political experience and increased political influence, and which, though often of great respectability and without much political initiative, certainly frightened the middle classes.

(2) Changes in the structure of industry: the introduction of factory methods into a wide variety of existing manufactures and the introduction of new heavy industry. The effect of growth in the size of industrial undertakings is manifold; but briefly it may diminish the independence of the worker, change the way he is paid, alter the methods of dealing with unemployment, prevent any contact with his employer, introduce a class of managerial employees, alter the avenues for upward social mobility, and create even wider distinctions of wealth between the employer and the employed.

(3) Changes in the occupational structure resulting from industrial change, in particular the disproportionate increase after 1850 of white-collar workers: clerks, schoolteachers, shopkeepers, the professions, and other managerial employees. Though the economic position of many in these groups is precarious and little better than that of the artisan, they are socially distinct and may entertain aspirations well above their economic position. Many of them have minimal contact with the working classes but a great deal with their social superiors. They provide at least a potential rank and file for a non-working-class party.

(4) Changes in the physical environment: the growth of the Metropolis and the great towns, destroying any sense of community, separating population by class particularly in the third quarter of the century, when the middle classes were enabled to leave the towns for peripheral suburbs but the working classes could not afford the fares. Not only was class separated from class, but in large enough groups to make separate constituencies.

In relating these general developments to political change, there are clearly further "intervening" factors which may have modified or altered their impact on particular places or groups of people. There are the questions of incidence and timing—when and where each development became important. There are local traditions, religious and ethnic differences which may have delayed, transformed, or prevented their expected effect. It is not difficult to think of exceptions to the pattern drawn here, but until the absence of certain conditions and the presence of others have been examined in each case, it is not necessary to reject it. But not until this has been done can the following be offered as more than tentative conclusions:

(1) That the transformation of Conservatism was not the result of conscious adaptation by the old Tory party to the condi-

tions of a mass electorate, but a struggle on the part of a new body of supporters to force the party to face the consequences of social change.

(2) That this struggle was not between pro- and antidemocratic factions, nor merely due to an individual's bid for power, but about the methods of political organization relevant to different social contexts.

(3) That the decisive factor in committing the party to the transformation was the redistribution settlement of 1884, with its recognition of the city and industrial primacy, and the premium thus placed on urban support for Conservatism.

(4) That the social basis of this support was middle-class; that it had been growing steadily from at least 1868 and was not the product only of the political crises of the eighties; and that working-class Conservatism was either deferent, indifferent, or based on traditional hostility to Liberalism and the Irish; and that though important in explaining Conservative success between 1885 and 1906, it was not in the long run reliable, being vulnerable to the appeal of a working-class party.

(5) That the ultimate effect of this new support, springing as it did from the disintegration of the urban community, was to shift the emphasis in politics from the interests which all classes in a particular community had in common to the interests which particular classes had in common with similar classes in other communities. So the transformation of Conservatism was more than a matter of techniques of organization—it was the transformation from a recognizably eighteenth-century party with its hierarchical social assumptions to a recognizably twentieth-century party with its role of representing the interests of particular classes.

In this concluding essay John Roach deals with the problem of the role of the state and the changing ideas of Liberal intellectuals, the modifications of the hopefulness they had felt earlier in the century. Had Victorian society and its government been able successfully to handle its problems?

John Roach is the author of Public Examinations in England 1850–1900 *(Cambridge, 1971) and is professor of education at the University of Sheffield. The present article was originally published in the* Cambridge Historical Journal xii *(1957), 58–81, and is reprinted by permission of its publisher, Cambridge University Press.*

JOHN ROACH

Liberalism and the Victorian Intelligentsia[1]

ENRY SIDGWICK WAS one of the most prominent university reformers in later Victorian Cambridge. His resignation of his Trinity fellowship in 1869 helped to precipitate the final abolition of religious tests in 1871, and, in the following decades, he was the leader of those who wished to develop research and to open up new branches of study. In national politics he was, as might have been expected, a Liberal, yet, when the Home Rule crisis of 1885–1886 came to a head, his allegiance veered over sharply. In 1885 he voted Liberal "after some hesitation"; the next year he voted for the Tory candidate for the borough of Cambridge who was elected by an increased majority. That summer he wrote: "Unionists gaining slowly but steadily. Dined in Hall, and was surprised to find the great preponderance of Unionist sentiment among the Trinity fellows—a body always, since I have known Trinity, preponderantly Liberal." [2] In the history of Victorian politics more attention might be given to the change which converted a large part of the educated classes from the Liberal side to the Conservative. J. F. Stephen, writing in 1880 to the first Earl of Lytton, said of the Conservative leaders that they were "all of them people whose political creed was chosen when the Conservative party was emphatically the stupid party, and when to be a Conservative meant to be opposed to pretty well all the main intellectual movements of the time." [3] The phrase, "the stupid party," comes from J. S. Mill,[4] whose books had been the chief intellectual influence in triumphant mid-Victorian Liberalism. By the end of his life Mill himself was becoming skeptical of the results achieved by democracy. In *Representative Government* (1861) he had pointed out that a popular assembly was not fitted to conduct administration or to frame laws, and that one of the great problems of democratic government is to combine popular rule with the skilled administration of the modern state.[5] The need for increased efficiency in a more competitive age was worrying many Englishmen by 1870, and, although their criticisms cut across party and sectional boundaries, they were hostile to much in conventional Liberalism. One answer was the "social engineering" of the Fabians; another approach was Matthew Arnold's assault on our educational system and on the Philistinism of our semieducated middle classes. The only remedy for the anarchic individualism of English life lay, he thought, in the positive activity of the state, which should purify and deepen the national culture and give it direction and purpose.

By the 1860s many Liberal intellectuals like Arnold were becoming highly critical of their creed. Their chief political representative was Robert Lowe, the great adversary of the Reform Bills of 1866 and 1867. He had many connections with the Philosophic Radicals, and he remained a believer in the great Liberal principles of administrative reform and efficient, economical government. But, partly as a result of his residence in Australia (1842–1850), he was deeply suspicious of political democracy. He believed that universal suffrage would produce corrupt and ineffective government, and would lead, in the end, to the overthrow of the institutions and the property built up by centuries of toil and self-denial. He had claimed, in a speech of 1865, that he had been a Liberal all his life, and that he had full confidence in the further progress of society, but, he went on, "because I am a Liberal and know that by pure and clear intelligence alone can the cause of true progress be promoted, I regard as one of the greatest dangers with which this country can be threatened a proposal to subvert the existing order of things, and to transfer power from the hands of property and intelligence [to] the hands of men whose daily life is necessarily occupied in daily struggle for existence." [6]

That statement is very characteristic of many of the "old Liberals." The final cleavage in the Liberal party was, of course, produced by the Home Rule Bill of 1886, but the more deep-rooted causes which, for a quarter of a century, had been building up towards such a break have been little examined, and are of great interest and importance. In the middle of the nineteenth century it must have appeared that Liberalism was the creed of the future and that Conservativism was merely a relic of the past. In fact Conservativism proved itself to be the more vigorous of the two, since Liberalism, however powerful the front which, in Gladstone's heyday, it presented to the world, was fatally weakened by its own internal divisions. Most of the intelligentsia in mid-Victorian England had been Liberal; some of them were politicians who were actively concerned with practical affairs, others were scholars and men of letters whose interest was more indirect. Among both groups, which naturally shade into one another, were many who, like Robert Lowe, had accepted Liberal principles as those of reform and of efficient government. They had believed deeply in the triumph of their ideals, but, as those ideals came gradually to be realized, their faith was shaken. Exalted political principles seemed to them to be employed to justify self-interested conclusions. The Liberalism, which, in their eyes, was the servant of great political causes, appeared to result in the triumph of petty and confined political objectives. The rising tide of democracy seemed to threaten the dominance of a harsh popular despotism which would be fatal to individual achievement or to anything which rose above the general level of mediocrity. What was the use of reforming institutions at home if the decline of any true sense of social discipline made it impossible for them to work effectively? What was to be the future of the country if national interests abroad were to be sacrificed to a purely parochial view of British policy which neglected the future in exchange for some immediate gratification or for the ease and comfort of the individual voter? To Liberals who felt like this a crisis of conviction was gradually developing; on the other side the Radicals felt them to be a drag on the further reforms which they wished to carry out. The exposure and unraveling of these divisions within Liberalism is a major exercise both in political history and in the history of ideas, toward which this article attempts to make a small contribution.

One clue to the problem lies in the ideas of two prominent "old Liberal" writers and thinkers, J. F. Stephen (1829–1894) and H. S. Maine (1822–1888). The *St James's Gazette* wrote of Maine that in later life he became a strong anti-Radical, having at first favored "that moderate, cautious constitutional Liberalism which in the past has done so much for liberty, for progress, and for ordered reform." [7] Stephen's sentiments were expressed in some of his letters written during the 1880s to the wife of the Liberal politician, M. E. Grant Duff. "The old maxims of government, the old Liberalism in which your husband and I used to believe, and in which I fancy he still believes, have been and are being utterly given up, and in their place is being erected a tyrannical democracy, which will change the whole face of society and destroy all that I love or respect in our institutions." This was, he wrote, "the story of the Paradise Lost of Liberalism." [8] Stephen's criticism of Mill in *Liberty, Equality, Fraternity*, and Maine's criticism of democracy in *Popular Government* are among the many chapters of that story. It brings in the influence of Indian examples on English affairs, and helps to remind us that the traffic of ideas with our greatest dominion was not all one way. It is connected with the fear of Socialism and of the breakdown of ordered government, which was very common among intellectuals in the last decades of the century. Maine and Stephen became friends at Cambridge. Maine, who had been Senior Classic in 1844, became Regius Professor of

Civil Law in 1847, the same year as Stephen went up to Trinity. They had met two years earlier through a close friend of the Stephen family, who, like Maine, was a member of "the Apostles." Maine brought Stephen into "the Apostles" in his first term; [9] he later introduced him to J. D. Cook of the *Morning Chronicle* and the *Saturday Review*, and gave him his chance as a journalist; [10] he was his predecessor as Legal Member of Council in India. They remained closely connected until Maine's death; he was the scholar and thinker, Stephen rather the man of affairs and the publicist, but their qualities complemented one another very well, and their points of view can be treated in combination.

At Cambridge Stephen's great rival, both at "the Apostles" and at the Union, was W. V. Harcourt, whom he later came to regard as a typical exemplar of the popular Liberalism which he so deeply distrusted. In his Union speeches Stephen generally took the conservative line. Characteristic of later dislike of Liberal Utopianism is an amendment which he successfully carried to a motion extolling the glorious future destinies of the country: "That this House, while it acknowledges the many dangers to which the country is exposed, trusts that through the help of God we may survive them." [11] The same point of view repeated itself when he started to write for the *Saturday Review* and later for the *Pall Mall Gazette*. By the 1850s journalism had ceased to be mere hackwork, and had become, as M. M. Bevington says, "the chosen means of expression, partly vocation and partly avocation, of brilliant young men who wished to influence public opinion." [12] The *Saturday*, started in 1855, collected a remarkable group of contributors. It aimed to interest cultured opinion; its tone was destructive and it was highly critical of the vulgarity and sentimentality of the middle classes. Of such a point of view Stephen was the perfect representative, and he figured prominently in the paper's columns. Ten years later (1865) came the foundation of the *Pall Mall Gazette*, which carried the same tone into daily journalism. In its early years Stephen was its dominant personality—in 1868 he wrote 226 leading articles—and it gave him the opportunity to write about politics.[13] Like J. D. Cook, the editor of the *Pall Mall*, Frederick Greenwood, was a man of first rate ability. John Morley, who succeeded him when he left the paper in 1880, said of him that "he soon began to do his best to encourage a vigorous all-round reaction against the Liberalism associated with Mill in one field and Gladstone in another. Hitherto he had taken it on trust as other people took it, but as things went on, as the incidental drawbacks of the creed came into view, a Tory instinct . . . revolted . . . against theories of liberty, equality and fraternity." [14]

Stephen himself was a Utilitarian and a Liberal, though, already in the 1850s and 1860s, he was a Liberal critical of Liberal assumptions. He had reviewed Mill's *Liberty* when it came out in 1859, and had expressed his general agreement with its conclusions, praising the book for its rebuke to current "complacent optimism." [15] In 1865 he stood unsuccessfully as Liberal candidate for Harwich, and he stood again for Dundee in 1873, in the hope that, if elected, he might became Solicitor-General.[16] He was still thinking of standing in the General Election of 1874,[17] and, even though he had by that time really moved right away from Gladstonian Liberalism, he complained a couple of years later: "I am too thorough a Tory at heart ever to get into Parliament honestly as a Liberal and I have been too much mixed up with Liberals all my life and especially when I stood for Dundee, three years since that I cannot honourably turn Tory now that the Tories are in power." [18] In the early days of the *Pall Mall* R. H. Hutton of the *Spectator* had written to him and complained of his attacks on Gladstone in that paper; though Hutton considered him to be "the only link between the Pall Mall and any hearty Liberalism," he was using his powers to depreciate the only great man in the Liberal party.[19] The general sentiments of the *Pall Mall* at that time can be traced in the political articles, probably written by Stephen himself.[20] The death of Palmerston, the paper said, marked the change from the freedom and shrewdness of the older political school to a new school of "narrower doctrine, more scrupulous conscience, more anxious temperament," the replacement of "the politicians of the *salon*" by "the politicians of a creed." [21] When the Reform Bill of 1867 was passed, the *Pall Mall* preached rather uneasily that the educated classes must make the best of it and must train themselves to act as natural leaders of the people.[22] The law must certainly be brought into accord with the existing democratic condition of society, and majorities must rule; [23] yet party wranglers mean the postponement of necessary reforms,[24] and, when political democracy has come in, it remains to be seen whether it will sink into a condition of easy indifference or petty narrow-mindedness. Meantime the politicians of the day lack foresight and spend too much time retailing commonplaces to the electorate.[25]

Stephen's objections to Liberalism went far deeper than dislike of isolated acts of policy. He thought that it was hypnotized by material achievement and success, that it valued comfort at the expense of more important things, and that it produced a petty, trivial view of life, "a quiet ignoble littleness of character and spirit." [26] He believed that it ignored the fact that human life was rough and difficult and that pain was one of the great constituents and checks of nature.[27] Since it concentrated on putting right minor political and social grievances, it forgot that human nature is basically good, and that human communities are held together not ultimately by law or force, but by the social elements within them. "Society" he wrote, "is the work of law in some proportion, but in a much greater proportion it is the work of very different agents—love of companionship, curiosity, the desire of all sorts of advantages which are to be derived from mutual assistance founded on mutual good will." [28] It is natural therefore that he should have been interested both in Burke and in de Maistre, and that he should have been for many years on terms of personal friendship with Carlyle.[29] Liberalism seemed to him too, not only to produce a poor and thin view of humanity, but also to reduce politics to the level of petty rivalries and interests. His suspicions grew more intense as the years passed. In 1873 he gave two lectures at Edinburgh on parliamentary government.[30] He acknowledged that British institutions had solved many problems and that Parliament must continue to decide major problems of political power, but he thought it quite unsuited to settle the details of legislation or to control the administration. Important legislation was often held up by the accidents of the party struggle, by the short terms of ministerial office, and by the lack of any real coherence in the executive. In the departments themselves there was great need for more expert knowledge and for giving the permanent heads higher standing and greater independence. In saying this Stephen was echoing the commonly felt sentiment, which has already been mentioned, that England was doing less than many other countries to achieve a more efficient organization of the national life.

From 1869 to 1872 Stephen was in India, and his experiences there confirmed the conclusions to which he had already been coming at home.[31] In India great results were achieved through the discipline which Englishmen were rejecting in the metropolis. If only they would submit to similar restrictions there, they might emulate the startling achievement which enabled a handful of their countrymen to rule 150,000,000 people. India was, he wrote to his friend Lytton, who was then Viceroy (1876–1880), "the best corrective in existence to the fundamental fallacies of Liberalism," "the only government under English control still worth caring about." [32] "There," he wrote in 1882, "you see real government; here you see disorganized anarchy which is quickly throwing off the mask." [33] India provided the efficiency in administration and the purpose in government in which dominant English Liberalism was so lacking. It was his Indian experience which inspired the criticism of Mill in *Liberty, Equality, Fraternity;* indeed, he called his book "little more than the turning of an Indian lantern on European problems." [34] The influence of India on British politics in this, the heyday of British rule, should not be ignored; one obvious example, which will recur later, is the development of British Imperialism; another lies in the reform of the Civil Service. Maine too was deeply influenced in his study of early societies by Indian examples. He wrote after the publication of *Popular Government:* "If there were an ideal Toryism I should probably be a Tory; but I should not find it easy to say which party I should wish to win now. The truth is, India and the India Office make one judge public men by standards which have little to do with public opinion." [35]

Mill and Stephen had been quite friendly in the 1860s, and had many ideas in common. Writing to Mill from India, Stephen said that he was writing a commentary on the Indian law of evidence, which was to be based on Mill's logic; in describing Indian life, he added "I hope some day to set forth certain qualifications to your essay on Liberty, which it has led me to believe in." [36] These qualifications took shape on the voyage home in 1872, and appeared first as articles in the *Pall Mall Gazette* before they were published as a book in the spring of 1873. Mill had argued, in *Liberty*, that, although the people might choose their own rulers, this does not remove the danger of governmental and social tyranny. This can be averted only by the adoption of a simple principle "that the sole end for which mankind are warranted, individually or collectively, in interfering with the liberty of action of any of their number is self-protection." [37] So far as man's conduct concerns himself alone, he must be perfectly free. Stephen accepted the phrase, "Liberty, Equality, Fraternity," as a summary of the creed which he wished to attack, and took the three subjects in that order. Dealing first with liberty, he argued that it was impossible, as Mill had done, to distinguish between acts which affect the individual alone and those which affect others as well, because all our acts are at the same time both individual and social. His real point was that Mill's distinctions are so finely spun that they do not apply to the real world at all, and are therefore quite insufficient to bear the weight of the arguments which Mill has based upon them.[38] He was writing as if society and the individuals who compose it were static, as if the great changes which ushered in the modern world had done their work, and the operation of history has ceased. Serene upon the high tableland of Liberal principle, Man has little to do but to take at his will from the stores so abundantly placed before him. This, to Stephen, was an utterly false view, for the processes of history could never stop, though it was certainly true that its modes of operation could be transformed.

First of all, life was a never ceasing struggle.[39] Always and everywhere men and nations covet the same things, and the success of the one must mean the defeat of the other. Hence the crucial importance in human history of war,[40] for he who fights the hardest imposes his solution upon the rest of his fellows.[41] Indeed, it is the fact that life is a struggle, and often a hard and bitter one, which canalizes human energies and gives them depth and direction. Without these restraining forces man's powers might all too often run to waste.[42] This state of affairs, Stephen argued, was as true of civilized modern communities as of any primitive tribe. India had shown him the real complexity of the work of government in its relation to the organization of society. The American Civil War had illustrated the power which rested in the hands of the modern state and these lessons had been confirmed by the recent history of Bismarckian Germany. As he wrote some years later about a magazine article of Goldwin Smith's,

It is to me very strange that a man who since he reached years of discretion and industry has seen the Americans and the Italians and the Germans of the North and the Germans of the South, both as against each other and as against the French, decide by the strong hand and by the fiercest wars of history where their boundaries are to run, should think that the decision of such questions by war is obsolete anachronism. . . .[43]

Nineteenth-century English Liberalism had grown out of a special situation which did, to a very large extent, allow the solution of political problems by argument, but it was an oversimplification, if no worse, to write, as Mill did in *Utilitarianism*, that "no one whose opinion deserves a moment's consideration can doubt that most of the great positive evils of the world are in themselves removable, and will, if human affairs continue to improve, be in the end reduced within narrow limits." [44] Stephen was one of the very few English thinkers of his day who saw the weaknesses of this type of statement. The existence of lasting conflicts between men and nations was something which English Liberals practically denied, or to which they at least closed their eyes. In 1873, when *Liberty, Equality, Fraternity* came out and Mill died, Europe was entering on the forty years of political and economic struggles which rocked the balance of world power and led up to the great wars of the twentieth century. During the same period Liberal democracy was eclipsed, over much of the continent of Europe, first by a militarist state of the type of the Second German Reich and later by totalitarian states like the Third. Stephen's indictment of the Liberals of his day, that they underestimated the role of force in human affairs, has certainly been amply justified.

Both he and Mill had begun from the ethical and logical postulates of Utilitarianism, but they had developed them in very different directions. The latter had drawn out of them a political theory in which Liberty appeared as something good in itself apart from its Utilitarian justifications. Stephen felt himself to be a follower of the older and more orthodox Utilitarian school, though he seemed to be combining two arguments which were not necessarily consistent. The first is the Utilitarian; the second is a more nebulous and never very clearly defined belief in the life of human society in itself, quite apart from the standards of utility. All through his book there is an undertone of thought struggling with the Utilitarianism which is the official basis, so to speak, of Stephen's ideas. An interesting expansion and confirmation of this statement is contained in a slightly later magazine article.[45] Caesar, Stephen says, can make anything law and set up any standard of justice or injustice he pleases, but, if he were to do so, he would in fact be working against the interests of the human race and would achieve the most terrible results. "It cannot be too strongly asserted that the end at which laws should aim, and by their attaining which they must be judged, is their conformity with the permanent principles of human nature and society; principles which are antecedent to and independent of all laws whatever, whatever may have been their origin." [46]

Stephen would probably have urged that this meant no more than that the utility of laws and institutions is ultimately related to their conformity to such a standard as this. It is not difficult to see how his Utilitarian principles started him on this road, but it is difficult to see how his empiricism could carry him to his final destination. Quite apart from their empirical justification, the "permanent principles of human nature and society" are now coming to mean something in themselves, just as "liberty" does to Mill.

The most serious criticism of Stephen's argument is that, in correcting some of Mill's extravagances, he has almost explained liberty away altogether. It is one thing to argue that the problems of morals and legislation have no short and simple answer. It is another to say that the question whether liberty is a good or a bad thing is unanswerable because it is entirely a matter of circumstances.[47] Admit, if you will, that Mill went too far, admit that the answers of nineteenth-century Liberalism were intolerably facile, there still remains something which cannot be explained away, a residuum which is an indispensable part of the autonomy of human personality. If liberty is merely a term of negation,[48] then in what sense is man man at all? In what sense can he claim to be the living acting being which Stephen, as much as Mill, claimed him to be? Moreover, if society is built up by the love of comradeship, by curiosity, by the desire for the advantages of mutual assistance, as he had suggested, that requires a power of human effort and activity which is hardly consistent with the view that the sphere of liberty is simply that area which may at any time be left free from constraint. In his own way Stephen had a deep sense of the value of individual effort, and the view of social man, which he at least in part developed, could only rest upon a richer conception of individuality than he allowed. There was in his thought little room for the ordinary man, little prospect held out to him for the development of such faculties as he possessed. It is clear from Stephen's correspondence that the advance of democracy merely filled him with disgust. He did not see in it any prospect of growth or of an enriched experience for mankind in general, which must, in growing, make its blunders and mistakes.

Much the same criticisms apply to his discussion on equality. There could, on Utilitarian principles, be no other defense of equality than that it was expedient, whereas Mill appeared to be arguing on the presumption that it was just in itself.[49] The question of equality must be strictly related to fact and experience, which show us that there are many inequalities, such as those of age and sex, which are in fact irremovable. Once again Stephen is arguing that force is a permanent factor which does not disappear, but merely changes its form.[50] He also feared that the tendencies of the age towards greater equality would make true government, as he had seen it in India, impossible. Once again he had made a valuable analysis, and had exposed some of the current cant of equality. In political life the party boss is no very rich exchange for the despot. But, accepting as he did, that the clock cannot be put back, is there no more to be said than this? He had said nothing about the possibility of educating public opinion, or of the growth in political maturity of a popular electorate. Although there may be fundamental inequalities between men, there are, as he would have agreed himself, many more which already have been, and are still being removed.

The most positive part of his book lies in his treatment of Fraternity. Mill had claimed that, as mankind progresses, men will more and more treat one another as brothers and work for the common good.[51] In fact, there can never be agreement among men as to the standards of happiness which are desirable, and the legislator and the moralist have the task of imposing their own.[52] A vague, generalized love of the human race can afford no basis for religion; indeed, apart from the commands of religion, there can be no basis for such love.[53] It is one question whether God made all men and ordered them to love one another ". . . how it is proposed to get people to love one another without such a belief I do not understand." [54] The "Religion of Humanity," centering on the future and the collective power of the human race, is a myth, an artificial creation which cannot stir the hearts and wills of living men.[55] Whatever the truth about religion—and of that Stephen was himself uncertain—it cannot be unimportant.[56] Ultimately our views on moral subjects depend on our view of human personality and its relation to a future life.[57] If there is a God, morality depends on his law, and there is a direct connection between the belief in God and the sanction of morality.[58] The second would not survive the decay of the first.[59] The problems of man's relations with man could not, Stephen thought, be settled in terms of his petty immediate interests, but only in relation to the general moral and religious order.[60] We have now tracked his thought very near to its source. The chatter about liberty, equality, fraternity was bad because it assumed that there were ready answers to the problems of political obligation. In fact these problems were essentially "religious" in that they were ultimately related, as Conservative political philosophy had always said, to moral and spiritual issues. Stephen can be treated as a Conservative only in a restricted sense. His own religious position was complex, and he would have urged no more than that religion, if true, is important, though the whole tendency of his mind was to go much further. His position was very similar to that of his friend Carlyle. He was a grandson of one of the members of the Clapham Sect, and he had grown up in the Evangelical tradition.[61] Like Carlyle he was a Puritan who saw political problems in absolutes, the forces of the living God arrayed against the powers of darkness. Both sat loose to their creed, but neither had lost the sense of the power and majesty of God, the duty of His creatures to do Him service, and the awfulness of the punishment awaiting those who failed. In comparison with such a belief, the platitudes of contemporary English Liberalism seemed hollow shams. Both believed that only through discipline were great achievements possible. Stephen had criticized Mill for saying that Calvinism, with its theory of submission to God, numbs the will. In fact, he thought, self-control, which subordinates the faculties and desires to a higher purpose, enriches and strengthens the personality. In history Calvinism had been the creed of the most vigorous nations of the world, for "willing obedience enforced on oneself at all risks, and in the face of any amount of dislike, is the greatest of all agents in ennobling and developing the character, whether it is rendered to a principle or to a person; for it implies action, and action of the most unremitting and various kinds." [62] Both Carlyle and Stephen feared sentimentality and stressed the demands of justice to the last farthing. Both saw the reality of power and its essential place in political ideas and political history.

Stephen praised Carlyle for his resolute support of every form of virtue,[63] and other critics have emphasized his conviction that justice will prevail.[64] How was this to be harmonized with his praise of Frederick the Great? Stephen's answer was that, since systems do succeed and do produce general happiness, they must contain some degree of truth, and their success is proportioned to the degree of truth which they contain, though he admitted that there were complicating factors which Carlyle had not worked out with sufficient clarity.[65] The bare statement that "might is right" is, according to this approach, an expansion of the saying that "By their fruits ye shall know them," and is an affirmation, not of harsh and brutal tyranny, but of the fundamental identity of truth and utility. We must not measure the events and happenings of the world by standards of theory, but by the relevance of facts as we find them. Since man is a social being and since the institutions of human society are fundamentally good, whatever suits the life of society has its own goodness. Both Stephen and Carlyle would have said, not so much that might is right, but that right is might and prevails by its own strength.[66]

There were, of course, differences between them. Carlyle was not a logical thinker at all; his vision was prophetic, intuitive, or to use a word of Stephen's own, transcendental. Stephen was an empiricist, a man devoted to fact and evidence and determined to advance no further than they led him. By the time that he wrote *Liberty, Equality, Fraternity* he had found weaknesses enough for himself in the English parliamentary system without needing to rely exclusively on Carlyle for his ammunition. His book came out in the very heyday of Liberalism, Gladstone's first ministry. The clouds which he perceived had hardly risen above the horizon of most Englishmen, and, as might have been expected, the book exerted little influence. It went into a second edition in 1874, and has never been reprinted. It was not likely to assist his own political ambitions, and he noted that the publication of extracts during the Dundee election in a local newspaper would not help his cause. His successful rival there belonged to what he would have called the sentimental Liberal school, and it pleased him that both of them had fought the struggle under their true colors.[67] As the years passed, the *Saturday Review* "old Liberalism," of which *Liberty, Equality, Fraternity* was one of the products, grew more and more out of sympathy with Gladstone. Stephen's correspondence with Lytton in India shows this breach growing steadily wider. What is Liberalism? Stephen asked in a letter of 1879.[68] It ought to connote an enlarged and educated attitude of mind, superior to vulgar passions and appreciative of great institutions and great enterprises. Yet in fact it had come to mean a petty-minded attitude to public life and national concerns—what Stephen described as "the small dissenter way of looking at all national and international affairs." In another letter he wrote that the Liberals were falling away to Radicalism on one side and Conservatism on the other. So far as the Radicals were concerned, it would not be "very difficult to show that they are the very reverse of Liberal, insofar as that word connotes either special cultivation of intellect taste and feeling or a cheerful hopeful view of life as a whole." [69] All parties, the two friends agreed, suffered from the need to kowtow to the demands of an immense popular electorate; "there is no field in England," Lytton wrote, "for practical statesmanship in the only matters I understand or care about. I do not appreciate the charm of being the official drudge and humble servant of a public I thoroughly despise." [70] A year later the Viceroy was contemplating life in an Italian villa, away from "an England full of Morleys Chamberlains et id genus omne, . . . free at least from puritanical atheists and political prigs." [71] To Stephen his old rival Harcourt, "Sir Bogus Blubber Harcourt," as Lytton christened him,[72] seemed to embody the type of the successful modern politician. Should Beaconsfield go, he might perhaps take his place, "for he has many of the qualities which enable a man alternately to bully and to wriggle." [73] "His superiority to his fellows," Stephen wrote, "appears to me to consist in the fact that he knows what a humbug and impostor, and mere noisy mouthpiece of ignorant popular views he is, whereas most of them do not. I do not think he feels degraded by it any more than he would by holding a bad hand at whist. He recognizes the condition of his whole career as being that he should understand, if possible anticipate, and at all events carry out the wishes of King Mob." Gladstone was even more dangerous because disinterested, a man of convictions and of good faith, but "the mouthpiece of blind and furious passions." [74] On another occasion he was described as "positively revolutionary . . . on the high road towards a destruction of nearly everything which I for one, and I suppose many thousand others chiefly like and value in English life and society." [75]

Gladstone's two great preoccupations of this time, the campaign against the Bulgarian atrocities and the Midlothian Campaign, both disgusted the two friends. Stephen deplored the "beginnings of an outbreak of pseudo-Christian John Bullism about the Bulgarians." [76] He liked atrocities no better than his neighbors, but he despised those who clamored against things of which they really knew nothing, and about which they had neither the intention nor the ability to do anything.[77] A few months before the Congress of Berlin he considered that the country, what with atrocity agitations, jingoism, and the behavior of all the politicians, had, during the previous two years, behaved contemptibly.[78] He did not share Gladstone's belief in the universal sovereignty of principles of abstract justice, a theory which appeared to him to involve the comparison of conditions which were really not comparable. He held to the view of power expounded in *Liberty, Equality, Fraternity*. Nations, though they certainly had many interests in common, did not form members of a community, they were of their nature rivals for the good things of the world, and each man's duty was therefore "to do his best for his own side." [79] Both he and Lytton believed that Liberalism stood for a neglect of British interests, which might ultimately be fatal to the existence of the Empire. "I quite agree," Stephen wrote to his friend some years later, "in your feeling of disgust at our modern practical scepticism about England and English affairs. It is intolerable. England seems to me to have become a huge Glad-

stone with a conscience like the liver of a Strasburg goose." [80]
The Midlothian Campaign was as hateful as foreign affairs. "What
a tornado of chatter the people's William seems to be now spouting over the North!" wrote Lytton.[81] "I entirely agree," his cor-
respondent answered, "in all you say about Gladstone's spouting.
. . . It makes me sad to see Gladstone mad in white satin, and
Harcourt shamming mad in white linen, and Grant Duff dancing
before the ark in a way which unites solemnity with respectability
(as a particular style of funeral was once advertised to do)." [82]
The Liberal victory of 1880 meant the victory of the numerical
majority over the "respectable and wealthy part of English society." It would lead to the government of the country by the
standards of the industrious workman earning his 30 or 40 shillings a week, "a prospect," Stephen wrote, "which does not please
me a bit." [83]

As the years of Gladstone's second government passed, a large
part of the "respectable and wealthy" classes became more and
more unhappy. The Third Reform Bill, Egypt, Ireland, all seemed
to bring new disasters and dangers. The last item in the reckon-
ing was, of course, the Home Rule Bill of 1886, but it was only
the last entry in a catalogue of grievances which had been mounting up long before 1880. When the final debates were going on,
Stephen wrote to Lady Grant Duff in India that he would not
bother her with politics, but that some of her friends' sayings
about Gladstone might amuse her.

> Bowen remarks "He combines the piety of David with the
> inaccuracy of Ananias." Labouchere is credited with saying "I
> should not like to play cards with him. He would always have
> aces up his sleeve and be fully convinced that God had put them
> there." Morris the Irish judge observes "Old Parliamentary
> hand! he ought to have said leg." All these I think ingenious,
> but they give a very false idea of the feelings with which what
> he beautifully describes as "the classes" regard him.[84]

It was from them, "the educated and driving part of the country," [85] Stephen thought, that real leadership ought to come, but to any such concept Liberalism was fatal because it had "taught the public that there is no such thing anywhere as legitimate authority." [86] The discipline and sense of obedience necessary to any healthy social organism had gone by the board. The greatest peril lay in Ireland, for Liberal policy there contained two great dangers: that of disrupting the unity of the empire and of promoting social revolution at home.[87]

With his interest in India and his almost mystical belief in the future of the British–Indian despotism, Stephen was naturally highly sensitive to anything which appeared to endanger our imperial destinies. Once again a triumphant democracy seemed to lack any sense of national greatness or any determination to preserve it.[88] Yet the swing towards the Imperialism of the nineties was already on the way, and Stephen, as a publicist, had his hand in it. It was India which filled men with the fullest sense of Britain's imperial mission. Lytton had proclaimed the Queen as Empress of India, and in his speech at the great Durbar had made considerable use of a draft sent out by Stephen.[89] Stephen had defended the Viceroy's Afghan policy in *The Times;*[90] he had written in the same place against the Ilbert Bill of 1883,[91] and then against Irish Home Rule; in all his letters he had proclaimed Britain's imperial destiny and her power over subject races. The fear of imperial disaster, caused by a breach with Ireland, naturally led those who opposed it in the imperialist direction.

Irish affairs had other implications nearer home. Irish land reform meant interference with the rights of property, which might begin the deluge in England.[92] If a social revolution were to begin in Ireland and the English poor were to make common cause with it, what would become of the upper classes? [93] The danger seemed to lie in the advent of a "dominant intolerant Socialism in which we the haves will be very roughly handled by the have nots." [94] There were more idealistic motives, too. Henry Sidgwick, a much more definite Liberal than Stephen had ever been, wrote that he had always been in sympathy with the Irish political movement. "But to abandon the landowners of Ireland to the tender mercies of the people who have for eleven years carried on an unscrupulous private war against their rights of property—rights which those of us who supported the Land Bill of 1881 morally pledged ourselves to secure to them—this is a national crime and deep moral disgrace in which I can have no part." [95]

The most powerful literary expression of the "old Liberal" point of view during the eighties was Maine's *Popular Government*, published in 1885. Stephen had written five years before that the main fault of modern Liberal doctrines was to "sin by an insufficient sympathy with the historical way of looking at things." [96] Maine had been the chief representative of the historical point of view in England, and through his studies of early institutions, he has deeply influenced the way in which Englishmen view their law and government. *Popular Government* itself was a successful book—it had, by 1909, gone into six editions—but to read now it is a rather disappointing one. It lacks the vigor and sweep of *Liberty, Equality, Fraternity;* its arguments are facile rather than profound, and, despite its author's prose of philosophic detachment, it seems sometimes to be inspired more by querulous dislike of his opponents than by any other sentiment. One very interesting feature, which the book shares with Stephen's later letters, is an undertone of fear for the future. Ever since 1867, Maine wrote, the democratic flood has been rising higher and higher; the parliamentary struggles over the Reform Bill of 1884 offer the gloomiest of auguries for the future of the country. "We are drifting towards a type of government associated with terrible events—a single Assembly armed with full powers over the Constitution, which it may exercise at pleasure . . . a theoretically all-powerful Convention, governed by a practically all-powerful secret Committee of Public Safety. . . ." [97] The fundamental danger lay in the exaltation of democracy as

something good in itself, quite apart from its practical consequences. In fact, popular government is fragile, difficult to work,
and has no necessary connection with human improvement, which
has always been the work of minorities. Contrary to the democratic belief, the natural condition of man is hostile to change, and
there is no security that the multitude will be able to choose its
own best interests. The only safeguard against the capricious
power of an unchecked majority would lie in a strong constitution, like that of the United States, which has successfully controlled and channeled the forces of an immense and expanding
democracy. In England, without any such control, the mighty
power of democracy will "spread destruction far and near." [98]

Maine put much more emphasis on constitutional checks and
balances, while Stephen had been primarily interested in the moral
background of Liberal doctrines, but naturally the two men used
many of the same arguments. There is the same sense that the
business of government is badly managed, and the responsibilities
of the executive and the legislative branches of government badly
defined.[99] There is the same distrust of platitude and loose generalization in politics, and of the enfeebling effect which they
have on the public mind.[100] There is the same appreciation that,
if political power be cut up into tiny morsels, it will all be swept
together into the hands of the wire-puller and the party caucus.[101]
Maine's feelings on the point must have been further strengthened
by the growth of the Liberal caucus in Birmingham. He also says
explicitly, what Stephen had only hinted, that Englishmen had
been able to devote themselves without fear to political wrangles
because of very particular circumstances. "We are singularly little
sensible, as a nation, of the extraordinary good luck which has be-
fallen us since the beginning of the century. . . . The fact is that,
since the century began, we have been victorious and prosperous
beyond all example." [102]

The deepest note touched in *Popular Government* is not heard
in *Liberty, Equality, Fraternity*, and the difference is the result of

the decade which separates the two books. This is the fear that triumphant democracy will overthrow individual property, first property in land and later property of every sort.[103] If the needy become the depositories of political power, it is only reasonable to suppose that they will use that power in what they conceive to be their own interests, which will mean the redressal of all economic inequalities. If that be done, it will strike at the very root of individual enterprise and individual desire for self-better- ment, which must, of their very nature, at the same time as they produce a greater aggregate of wealth, produce also inequalities of condition between men. Yet if these desires be thwarted of their fulfilment, wealth may dwindle or even disappear.[104] Hith- erto democracy has been made to work only by party manage- ment and its handmaid, corruption. In England severe measures have been taken against the last, but it may return under another form for "there are two kinds of bribery. It can be carried on by promising or giving to expectant partisans places out of the taxes, or it may consist in the directer process of legislating away the property of one class and transferring it to another. It is this last which is likely to be the corruption of these latter days." [105]

Maine saw *Popular Government* as an extension of his lifelong study of the history of early institutions, and the ideas which it contains need to be referred back to the theories developed in his four earlier books, *Ancient Law* (1861), *Village Communities in the East and West* (1871), *The Early History of Institutions* (1875), and *Dissertations on Early Law and Custom* (1883). Al- though some of his beliefs have been disproved, his work still stands as that of a great pioneer in the study of the institutions of early man, and it was through this long list of historical studies, rather than through his views on contemporary politics, that he influenced the outlook of his generation. His master concept was that, in Aryan societies, men lived originally in close-knit kinship communities under patriarchal power. Gradually, as these com- munities broke up, the institutions of the state developed, individual property replaced joint ownership, and men won their place in society through their own efforts, instead of accepting the place into which they had been born in their own clan or family group. This change had been fully accomplished only in a few very advanced societies, while in many others, especially in the East, it had never really taken place. The whole process, summed up in a famous phrase, was the movement from Status to Contract.[106] The gradual unfolding of ancient legal systems provided Maine with abundant material. He began with the early history of Roman law; he used the history of feudal and of Teutonic customs, the Brehon laws of Ireland, the customs of the South Slavs, and, above all, the Indian village community and the Hindu joint-family, which still displayed, in the middle of the nineteenth century, the ancient power of kin connection and the weakness, in many societies, of the ideas of individual enterprise and initiative.

The lessons which Maine drew from these early societies were similar to those which Stephen had drawn from his critique of Liberalism. Maine had found, when he began, that the way towards a true understanding of early societies was barred by the hypothesis of a state of nature, an *a priori* construction quite unrelated to the facts. In later years he was to derive the theory of popular government from the same hypothesis.[107] The idea of the law of nature was, of course, Roman. Its function was to remedy the defects of the existing law, and it was looked at through the medium of that law. Largely through the agency of Rousseau and the French Revolutionaries, the idea of a law of nature, concerned with what is, had been transformed into the idea of a state of nature, concerned with what ought to be. Its purpose, instead of being remedial and conservative, had become anarchical and revolutionary.[108] Similarly the idea of human equality had been Roman in origin, and had contained merely a statement about the position of men under the Roman legal system. It had later been extended to imply that men ought to be equal; the word equality was beginning to "express the sense of a great standing wrong suffered by mankind." [109] In modern society, just as in ancient Rome, the rule of equality—expressed, in Benthamite terms, as the greatest happiness of the greatest number—was a useful practical rule in legislation. Where Bentham had erred had been to extend that working rule into an explanation of moral phenomena.[110] The danger lay, as Stephen had already urged, in the explanation of politics on *a priori* principles, and the canonization of those principles whether they worked or not.

Like Stephen, too, Maine had an acute sense of the importance of power in the development of society. He had certainly criticized the Austinian theory of sovereignty as applying not to all societies but only to the modern western state with a strong and active legislature, and he had pointed out that the history of institutions showed that sovereignty was composed of many elements other than pure force,[111] but it is clear that he gave power a very large place in his theories. The patriarchal theory itself rested upon the dominant authority of the paterfamilias. Out of the power of the head of the household grew the power of the chief and, much later, the power of the state.[112] "It is a special form of Power, that called by jurists Sovereignty, which has created the modern kinship known as Nationality, which enables us to speak of Englishmen, Frenchmen, Australians, Americans." [113] Like Stephen he pointed out that, in civilized communities, the force which is the motive power of law retreated into the background, but that it is nonetheless real for that.[114] In the growth of civilization the vital creative power has always been that of minorities. The natural condition of man, as we have seen, was to be unprogressive and to scorn all change. But progress though limited had been real, and its instrument had always been a minority which had brought about innovations which the multitude would have rejected.[115]

Where such progress had taken place, one of its chief accompaniments had been the wider diffusion of the concept of private property. Among the South Slav communities, for instance, it had been the more adventurous and successful who wished to turn their share of the communal goods into several properties at their own exclusive disposal. The process had gone further in Austria-Hungary than in Turkey because it was a natural result of greater riches and more stable government.[116] One special form of the same process had been the gradual emancipation of women and their property from the despotism of the family group which exhibited "the substitution of individual human beings for compact groups of human beings as the units of society." [117] When in medieval Europe the tribal organization was replaced by the feudal the change was, in many respects, a gain. The authority which the lord acquired over the waste and his partial exemption from customary rules meant that he could undertake the clearance of the great wastes with which Europe was then covered in a way which village-communities could never have done. Feudal forms of property were more tolerant of agricultural novelties than communal, the deficiencies of which had been clear in the English common fields which had survived into the nineteenth century. Moreover, the serf classes may have had better treatment from a lord than from a peasant community, from which they would have been excluded.[118] Then, with the break-up of feudal society, came, on the one side, the modern idea of state sovereignty, and, on the other, "the conception of land as an exchangeable commodity." [119] In England landed property had changed hands by purchase and sale much more frequently than elsewhere. As a result the feeling was widespread that property rights rested on original agreements, which formed a great safeguard for their security, and increased the respect in which they were held as part of the established institutions of society.[120] In England the principle of "several and absolute property in land" had been carried to its farthest point, and it was to that, Maine thought, that "we are indebted . . . for such an achievement as the cultivation of the soil of North America." [121] The process of turning joint-ownership into absolute property may be highly complex and difficult,[122] but there was no doubt in Maine's mind that the whole progress of civilization was closely bound up with it. "Nobody is at liberty to attack several property and to say at the same time that he values civilization. The history of the two cannot be disentangled." [123]

When he published his first major work, *Ancient Law*, in 1861, Maine wrote that in civilized societies law was tending to withdraw more and more into the background and to leave individuals to settle their lives according to freely accepted contractual rules.[124] The supremacy of contract was part of the background of a mature civilization. By the time that he published *Popular Government* in 1885 he was dominated by the fear that democratic rule would result in an attack on individual property. The change is an interesting commentary on a quarter of a century of English politics as it appeared to a man of his point of view. The fear of Socialism was strong among men of his class and training. In the history of ideas his forebodings look forward to those of Lecky and Mallock. In practical affairs he expressed the dread— widespread at the time—of a harsh popular despotism, dominated by a small group of "Irreconcilables" who wanted to bring in the millennium at once.[125] Neither Maine nor Stephen were practical politicians, but there were many, in the 1880s, among that class, who shared their views. In general they had remained loyal to the Liberal party; even Lowe had held high office in the Gladstone ministry of 1868–1874. They still hoped to restrain their party from the Radical excesses of Chamberlain or Morley and to prevent the succession to Gladstone from falling into Radical hands; they were held back, especially in the case of the Whig aristocrats, by long-held loyalties; they saw little hope of carrying out Liberal principles, as they understood them, on the Conservative side. Yet their position gradually became more and more impossible. They disliked, for instance, the Irish land legislation of the Gladstone government of 1880. The Land Bill of 1881 appeared to go back on the long-established Liberal tradition of liberating land-owner-ship from all fetters on free contractual dealings and to exalt over landowners and tenants alike the power of a state official.[126] As the Duke of Argyll, who left the government over this issue, said in the Lords, "the scheme of the Government will tend to paralyse the ownership of land in Ireland by placing it, for all time to come, under new fetters and limitations under which it is not placed in any other civilized country in the world." [127] Another aristocrat, Lord Dufferin, wrote that the extreme Liberals were trying to buy the support of the masses by distributing among them the property of their political opponents; "it is towards a social rather than a po-litical revolution that we are tending—at least, if what is taking place in Ireland is any indication of the future." [128] The speeches of Joseph Chamberlain, especially "the unauthorized programme" of 1885—a graduated income tax, taxation of unoccupied land and ground rents, the reestablishment of small proprietors on the land by state authority—seemed to lead in the same direction. This was the "ransom" which the rich were to pay to the poor for the en-joyment of their privileges.[129]

The most prominent politician among the Liberals of the Right was the Marquis of Hartington, but the chief representative of the intellectual Liberalism, with which this paper has been chiefly concerned, was G. J. Goschen. Of German descent, he belonged to a family with large interests in the City, and he had made his name as an authority on finance and banking. In 1877 he had spoken against further parliamentary reform, his only sup-porter being the veteran Lowe, and had attacked the way in which contemporary Radicalism expected government to inter-fere in financial affairs and to readjust the relations between capital and labor.[130] He held no office in the second Gladstone adminis-tration, but he was a leading spokesman of the "Moderate Liberals" [131] who wanted firm government in Ireland and who disliked Chamberlain's socialistic policies. He voted against the government over the Irish Land Bill of 1881. He did not oppose the extension of the franchise in 1884, but he wanted to include safeguards for minorities and for the classes which would be swamped by a large democratic vote. He spoke out, at the same time, against the tendency of politicians to glide along with the democratic stream, saying "my party seem to breathe an atmosphere of Utopia, and to feel a confidence I cannot share. . . ." [132] The parallel between the views of the Goschen-Hartington group in Parliament and the views of Maine and Stephen is very close, though the practicing politicians naturally had less liberty to criticize than the independent critics.

The Home Rule Bill provided the great catalyst which separated men out according to their real beliefs. To the old Liberals the shock was great. Gladstone and his followers seemed to be appealing to the passions of the mob by representing the struggle as one between the general interest and the special interests of limited classes.[133] The unity of the Empire was to be broken up, and Ireland abandoned to men whom Englishmen regarded as blood-stained terrorists and put under the authority of new laws relating, in Hartington's words, "to property, liberty, and security of life." [134] The abyss seemed to open before men's feet. The real conflict between the revolution and the English constitution was at hand, wrote Lord Selborne, who had been Lord Chancellor (1872–1874, 1880–1885). Gladstone's measures tended towards the unsettlement of the whole constitution "which is the real secret of their acceptance by the revolutionists [Maine had called them Irreconcilables] . . . who are the only people, except the Irish, who heartily go with them." [135] In December 1885 Goschen had been discussing Home Rule with some Dublin merchants, and had told them "that nothing was more important than to convince the English public that the question is not one of land-owning merely, that there are menaces, not only to unpopular landlords, but to property of every kind. . . ." [136] To have gone into an alliance with Parnell, wrote Stephen's old friend, Grant Duff, "would have meant for me the renunciation of all the sentiments and most of the opinions on which my political life had been founded." [137]

This sense of disillusionment was felt as keenly among intellectual circles as in the old aristocracy. The intellectual and literary society of London and the universities had been mainly Liberal; it now became mainly Unionist.[138] At Oxford Stephen's cousin, A. V. Dicey, who had been a Liberal, became, for a generation, a leading speaker and writer against Home Rule. The head of his college, Warden Anson of All Souls', took the same path, and became Unionist member for the University in 1899.[139] At Cambridge, Henry Sidgwick did not stand alone in his opinions,[140] which were shared by many of the leading men of the day. In 1887 steps were taken among Cambridge Liberal Unionists to organize an address to Lord Hartington; among those who supported the idea or who spoke at the public meeting at which the proposal was adopted were the Master of Trinity, H. M. Butler, the orientalist Robertson Smith, the theologian Hort, the classical scholars Kennedy and Jebb, and many others but little less eminent.[141] The motion was moved by the historian Seeley, who contrasted the new Liberalism, "the violent usurpation of government by an unscrupulous minority," with the Liberalism which he and his hearers had practiced all their lives. "In our Liberalism," he said, "it was always a commonplace that liberty is wholly different from licence, and that anarchy is as great an evil as tyranny, but the new system seems to know nothing of such a distinction." In Seeley's words lies much of the division between the two Liberalisms, new and old. Old Liberalism had finally taken shape as Liberal Unionism, and Unionism, as has been shown in Stephen's case, was closely linked with Imperialism. What Unionists feared can be seen from a remark of H. M. Butler's in 1887 that Liberal policy might well in a few years lead to "the relinquishment of Gibraltar, the abandonment of India, the repudiation of the colonies, and the resignation of our duties as a great fighting power in Europe." [142] Seeley himself had published *The Expansion of Europe* in 1883, a book which was to be one of the major influences in developing the imperialist idea.[143] Half of the book deals with India, and the parallel with Stephen's arguments is very close. There is the same sense of the magnitude of the British task and of the stupendous experiment involved in introducing one way of life into the midst of another. There is the same belief that British civilization is the superior, that Britain cannot abandon her task without disaster ensuing, and that the connection may persist and grow stronger rather than the reverse. With the Queen's jubilee of 1887 the tide of imperialism was beginning to rise high; there were strong old Liberal currents among the floodwater.

Notes

The Nineteenth-Century Revolution in Government: A Reappraisal

[1] G. R. Elton, *The Tudor Revolution in Government* (Cambridge, 1953).

[2] L. B. Namier, *The Structure of Politics at the Accession of George III* (1929), I, p. 164.

[3] Cf. "Society is not made by men, though social laws are nothing but laws of human behaviour. Because it is true that society is nothing except men and their habits and laws, and that all social institutions are the product of human activities, it does not follow that men make societies. For to make is to contrive for a purpose, and implies a conscious end and a knowledge of means. It is only because we use words that suggest purposes to describe nearly all the consequences of human activities that it comes natural to us to describe social and political institutions as if they were made by men. . . . Men are always trying to adapt their institutions to their desires, and to some extent they succeed. But all this makes it no less true that these institutions are not the realizations of human purposes, and that they affect these purposes just as much (and perhaps much more) than they are affected by them" (J. Plamenatz, *The English Utilitarians* [Oxford, 1949], p. 151).

[4] A. S. Foord's "The Waning of the Influence of the Crown," *English Historical Review* LXII, 484–507, is, of course, the sort of work referred to here. But the point may apply equally to "administrative" historians, who, quite legitimately, confine their attention to a single concrete event or series of events, e.g. E. Hughes, "Sir Charles Trevelyan and Civil Service Reform, part i," *ibid.*, LXIV, 53–67.

[5] R. Prouty, *The Transformation of the Board of Trade 1830–55* (1957), published since this article was written, throws some interesting light upon the growth of the Board of Trade's activities, especially in the regulation of merchant shipping.

[6] A. V. Dicey, *Lectures upon the relation between Law and Public Opinion in England during the Nineteenth Century* (1905).

[7] S. E. Finer, *The Life and Times of Sir Edwin Chadwick* (1952).

[8] R. L. Lewis, *Edwin Chadwick and the Public Health Movement 1832–54* (1952).

[9] There is a very brief but interesting mention of the question in H. R. G. Greaves's *The Civil Service in the Changing State* (1949). Mr. Greaves distinguishes three stages of development, the "oligarchic maladministration and interfering paternalism" of the eighteenth century, "the regulatory state" of the nineteenth, and "the social service democracy of the twentieth century"; and argues that the last was born before the first was dead, and that the second never existed except in men's minds. It is certainly true and pertinent to observe that on occasions "eighteenth-century" forms of government merged imperceptibly into "twentieth-century." But it seems misleading to draw a fundamental distinction between the eighteenth- and nineteenth-century concepts of the State, except insofar as notions of efficiency in, and methods of, conducting State business are concerned. However, Mr. Greaves does not define his categories or elaborate his thesis in any detail.

[10] Whether or not Dicey himself intended it, his work has commonly been taken to offer such an explanation. The preface to the first edition says, rather vaguely, "It has been written with the object . . . of drawing from some of the best known facts of political, social, and legal history certain conclusions which, though many of them are obvious enough, are often overlooked, and are not without importance" (Dicey, *Law and Public Opinion*, pp. viii–ix).

[11] Public Record Office, C.O. 384/30, unmarked memorandum, Stephen to T. F. Elliot, 31 July 1832.

[12] Cf. J. Willis, *The Parliamentary Powers of English Government Departments* (Cambridge, Mass., 1933), pp. 13–15. Willis observes

that the appointment of preventive officers was "fundamentally at variance with the general principles of the Common Law, which like the nineteenth-century God waits for you to commit the sin and then pounces." However, he also makes the assumption that the "new era" did not set in until 1906.

[13] For a detailed working out of this type of process in a particular field, see O. MacDonagh, "The Regulation of Emigrant Traffic from the United Kingdom, 1842–55," *Irish Historical Studies* ix, 162–189; "Emigration and the State, 1833–55: An essay in Administrative History," *Transactions of the Royal Historical Society*, fifth series, 5, (1955), 133–159; and section v and vi of "Irish Emigration to the United States of America and the British Colonies during the Famine," *The Great Famine*, a symposium (Dublin, 1956), pp. 359–376.

[14] W. L. Burn, "Free Trade in Land: An Aspect of the Irish Question," *Trans. Royal Hist. Soc.* fourth series, xxxi, 68. See also R. D. C. Black, "The Classical Economists and the Irish Problem," *Oxford Economic Papers*, new series, v, 26–40.

[15] Dicey, *Law and Public Opinion* (2nd ed., 1914), p. 44.

[16] Cf. "The most significant thing about this discovery of a note in Gladstone's own hand of the cabinet voting, on 24 January 1854, on the proposal to abolish patronage is the fact that the Whig leaders were solidly opposed to reform while the Peelites, and the one time radical, supported it" (Hughes, "Trevelyan," p. 62).

[17] J. Morley, *The Life of William Ewart Gladstone* (1903), p. 511.

[18] On this point, Professor A. Briggs appears to cite and use a quotation wrongly (one cannot speak certainly since Professor Briggs gives no references in his work) when he writes, "In an age when the shadow of democracy was already looming on the horizon, men like Vaughan, Jowett and Trevelyan realized the need for a plentiful supply of informed gentlemen. 'Our people are few compared with the Multitudes likely to be arrayed against us,' Trevelyan had written to Delane, 'and we must prepare for the trial by cultivating to the utmost the superior morality and intelligence which constitute our real strength,'" *Victorian People* (1954), p. 171. In fact, the sentence

quoted occurs in Trevelyan's *Thoughts on Patronage*, and it is preceded immediately by a sentence which runs as follows. "We are
apparently on the threshold of a new era pregnant with great events,
and England has to maintain in concert with her allies the cause of
right and liberty and truth in every quarter of the world" (Hughes,
"Trevelyan," p. 70). Thus, "Our people" would seem to refer, not to
the "gentlemanly" classes, but to the English people as a whole; while
"the Multitudes" would seem to refer, not to the working classes,
but to foreign powers.

[19] The commission to Trevelyan and Northcote in 1853; the appointment of the select committee of 1860; the Order in Council of
4 June 1870; and the appointment of the Ridley and Playfair commissions of 1874 and 1886. The Order in Council of 21 May 1855
(when, incidentally, Gladstone was out of office) represented, in the
circumstances, a retrograde rather than a progressive step. Its "actual
effects . . . were (*a*) to limit the Commissioners' certificate to the
junior situations in the civil establishments; (*b*) to make competition
a permissive but not a compulsory method of selection for such
certificates; and (*c*) to leave the power of appointment in all cases
where it had previously rested—with the political heads of the departments" (*Royal Commission on the Civil Service: Fourth report*, Parl.
Papers, 1914, xvi [Cd. 7338], pp. 5–6).

[20] For the practical consequences of Fitzjames Stephen's Bentham-
ism (a "Benthamee Lycurgus," he described himself), see J. Roach,
"James Fitzjames Stephen (1829–94)," *Journal of the Royal Asiatic
Society* (April 1956).

[21] P.R.O. C.O. 384/81, 1694 Emigration, 30 August 1848; 384/84,
4584 Emigration, 22 May 1849; R. J. Purcell, "The New York commissioners of emigration, 1847–60," *Studies*, xxxvii, 28–42; *Twentieth
Report New York Commissioners of Emigration* (New York, 1866).
F. H. Hitchens's *The Colonial Land and Emigration Commission*
(Philadelphia, 1931), pp. 148–50, is misleading on this point, as he
confuses the project for a central station at Liverpool with the depots
for Australian emigrants, which had been in existence for some time.

[22] M. Oakeshott, *Political Education* (Cambridge, 1951), p. 10.

The Nineteenth-Century Revolution
in Government: A Reappraisal Reappraised

[1] O. MacDonagh, "The Nineteenth-century Revolution in Government: A Reappraisal," *Historical Journal* I (1958), 52–67 (referred to hereafter as MacDonagh, *H.J.*) [Chap. 1 in this volume—ED.].

[2] F. M. G. Wilson, "Ministers and Boards: Some Aspects of Administrative Development since 1832," *Public Administration* XXXIII (1955), 43.

[3] MacDonagh, *H.J.*, p. 67.

[4] *Ibid.*, p. 55. Dicey himself used the short title *Law and Opinion* for his book, and it has been generally used ever since. Cf. *Memorials of A. V. Dicey*, ed. R. S. Rait (1925), p. 189, etc. Why Dr. MacDonagh prefers the form *Law and Public Opinion* is not clear.

[5] K. B. Smellie, *100 Years of English Government* (2nd ed., 1950), p. 331.

[6] Article on Dicey in *Chambers's Encyclopaedia* (new ed., 1955).

[7] M. Ginsberg, ed., *Law and Opinion in England in the 20th Century*. The quotation is from p. vii.

[8] W. I. Jennings, *Law and the Constitution* (1933).

[9] MacDonagh, *H.J.*, p. 56; A. V. Dicey, *Lectures on the Relation between Law and Public Opinion During the 19th Century* (2nd ed., 1914) (referred to hereafter as Dicey).

[10] W. I. Jennings, "In Praise of Dicey," *Public Administration* XIII (1935), 128.

[11] Dicey, p. 134 and n. My italics.

[12] *Ibid.*, pp. 44, 174–175; cf. *ibid.*, pp. 39, 125, 145, and 146 n.

[13] *Ibid.*, p. xxx n.

[14] *Ibid.*, p. 146 n.

[15] Dicey, pp. 303–305.

[16] *Ibid.*, pp. 306–307.

[17] *Ibid.*, p. 308 n.

[18] *Ibid.*, pp. 309–310.

[19] *Ibid.*, p. 146.

[20] *Ibid.*, p. 147.

[21] *Ibid.*, p. 237.

[22] *Ibid.*, pp. 232, 64–65.

[23] *Ibid.*, p. 224.

[24] *Ibid.*, pp. 234–235, 221–223.

[25] *Ibid.*, pp. 277, 279.

[26] *Ibid.*, p. 46.

[27] Dicey, p. 411 n.

[28] J. Corlett, *Financial Aspects of Elementary Education* (1929), p. 47.

[29] Dicey, p. 277.

[30] *Ibid.*, p. 203.

[31] *Ibid.*, p. 188.

[32] *Ibid.*, pp. 306–307.

[33] *Ibid.*, p. 39 n.

[34] *Ibid.*, p. 180 n.

[35] *Ibid.*, pp. 62–64.

[36] *Ibid.*, pp. 21–22.

[37] *Ibid.*, p. 68.

[38] *Ibid.*, p. 300.

[39] *Ibid.*, p. 64.

[40] *Ibid.*, p. 66.

[41] *Ibid.*, p. 201.

[42] *Ibid.*, pp. 33–34.

[43] *Ibid.*, pp. 291, 284–285.

[44] *Ibid.*, p. 240.

[45] *Ibid.*, pp. 217.

[46] *Ibid.*, pp. 276–277, 279.

[47] Cf. Jennings, *Law and The Constitution*, esp. pp. 210ff., and C. T. Carr, *Concerning English Administrative Law* (1941), pp. 21ff.

[48] Dicey, pp. xxiii, 465.

[49] *Ibid.*, pp. xxiv–xxvi.

[50] *Ibid.*, p. viii.

[51] *Ibid.*, p. xxiv.

[52] *Memorials of A. V. Dicey*, p. 1; cf. *ibid.*, p. 6, where Dicey claims to have had "memories . . . of English political life for about ten years earlier" than 1848, i.e. from the age of 3; it is not surprising that he adds that these memories were "indistinct and often childish."

[53] E. Halévy, *Growth of Philosophic Radicalism* (English ed., 1928), p. 514.

[54] T. K. Djang, *Factory Inspection in Great Britain* (1942), p. 34.

[55] MacDonagh, *H.J.*, pp. 58–61, for the model, p. 65 for the quotation.

[56] O. MacDonagh, "The Regulation of the Emigrant Traffic from the United Kingdom, 1842–55," *Irish Historical Studies* ix (1954–55), 163.

[57] O. MacDonagh, "Emigration and the State, 1833–55: An Essay in Administrative History," *Transactions of the Royal Historical Society*, fifth series, 5 (1955), 133 (referred to hereafter as Mac-Donagh, *T.R.H.S.*).

[58] O. MacDonagh, "Delegated Legislation and Administrative Discretions in the 1850's: A Particular Study," *Victorian Studies* ii (1958–59), 43 (referred to hereafter as MacDonagh, *V.S.*).

[59] E. Stokes, *The English Utilitarians and India* (1959).

[60] MacDonagh, *H.J.*, p. 66.

[61] E.g. in the crucial case of the three individuals who suggested the appointment of emigration officers in the period 1831–33 (Mac-Donagh, *T.R.H.S.*, p. 135).

[62] *Ibid.*, pp. 133–134.

[63] MacDonagh, *H.J.*, pp. 65–66. My italics.

[64] It is all the more strange that Dr. MacDonagh should be blind to the unconscious influence of ideas in administrative history, since he expressly warns his readers against the danger of letting themselves be influenced unconsciously by intellectual concepts in their own study of history (*ibid.*, p. 52).

[65] *Ibid.*, p. 61. My italics.

[66] *Ibid.*

[67] *Ibid.*, pp. 57–58.

[68] *Ibid.*, p. 58.

[69] *Ibid.*, p. 59.

[70] *Ibid.*

[71] MacDonagh, *T.R.H.S.*, pp. 134, 158.

[72] *Ibid.*, p. 134.

[73] The most recent and fullest account of the background to the setting-up of the Metropolitan Police is to be found in L. Radzinowicz, *History of English Criminal Law* (1948–), esp. vol. III, *Reform of the Police*, where the contributions of Bentham, Colquhoun, Chadwick, and Peel are indicated.

[74] MacDonagh, *H.J.*, p. 58.

[75] *Ibid.*

[76] E. Halévy, *Triumph of Reform* (1950 ed.), pp. 114–116; M. W. Thomas, *Early Factory Legislation* (1948), p. 55.

[77] MacDonagh, *H.J.*, p. 66.

[78] E. Halévy, *Triumph of Reform*, pp. 123–124, 286; *Liberal Awakening*, p. 40.

[79] S. and B. Webb, *English Prisons under Local Government* (1922), pp. 110–111.

[80] *Ibid.*, p. 110.

[81] MacDonagh, *H.J.*, p. 61.

[82] *Ibid.*, p. 59.

[83] *Ibid.*

[84] F. Smith, *Life and Work of Sir James Kay-Shuttleworth* (1923), esp. pp. 94ff.

85 MacDonagh, *T.R.H.S.*, p. 133.

86 E. Halévy, *Growth of Philosophic Radicalism* (1928). The theme is fundamental to the book; for characteristic expressions of it, see pp. 490, 514.

87 C. T. Carr, *Concerning English Administrative Law* (1941), pp. 8–9.

88 R. Prouty, *Transformation of the Board of Trade, 1830–55* (1957), p. 1.

89 MacDonagh, *V.S.*, pp. 31 and 44.

90 J. B. Brebner, "Laissez Faire and State Intervention in 19th Century Britain," *Journal of Economic History*, Supplement VIII (1948), 59–73; the quotations are to be found at pp. 59–61.

91 L. Robbins, *The Theory of Economic Policy in English Classical Political Economy* (1952), esp. pp. 14–15, 30–31, 40–41, 57–59, 191.

92 R. A. Lewis, *Edwin Chadwick and the Public Health Movement* (1952), p. 188.

93 M. Bowley, *Nassau Senior and Classical Economics* (1937), p. 265, quoting from an unpublished lecture delivered between 1847 and 1852.

94 Lewis, *Edwin Chadwick*, p. 130.

95 For a parallel study in another field, see my unpublished Ph.D. thesis, "Regulation of Railways by the Government in Great Britain: the Work of the Board of Trade and the Railway Commissioners, 1840–1867" (Leicester, 1959).

"Statesmen in Disguise":
Reflexions on the History of the Neutrality of the Civil Service

1 See Establishment Circular 26/53 (14 August 1953); Cmd. 8783 on *Political Activities of Civil Servants* (March 1953); Cmd. 7718, *Report of the Committee on the Political Activities of Civil Servants* (presented to Parliament June 1949, reprinted 1958). See also, *Public Administration* (Journal of the Royal Institute of Public Administration), XXXI, 163; XXXII, 324, and K. C. Wheare, *Government by Com-*

mittee: An Essay on the British Constitution (Oxford, 1955), pp. 24–28.

[2] W. H. Robson, *The Civil Service in Britain and France* (1956), chap. 2, "Civil Servants, Ministers, Parliament and the Public," by the Earl Attlee; Herbert Morrison, *Government and Parliament. A Survey from the Inside* (Oxford, 1954), pp. xiv, 311–336.

[3] Attlee, "Civil Servants," p. 16.

[4] Sir James Graham, House of Commons, 19 April 1853, Hansard, 3rd series, cxxvi, p. 112.

[5] On the Patent Office, which interested Dickens, see Victor G. Alexander, "A Nineteenth Century Scandal," *Public Administration* xxviii, 295–304.

[6] The Northcote–Trevelyan Report. See *Parliamentary Papers* xxvii (1854), 367–387; also *Public Administration* xxxii (1954), 1–51, with an important article by Prof. E. Hughes.

[7] *Parl. Papers* (1854–55), xx, 71–80. See also K. C. Wheare, *The Civil Service in the Constitution* (1954).

[8] S. E. Finer, "The Individual Responsibility of Ministers," *Journal of Public Administration* xxxiv, 377–396, 380.

[9] Sir Stafford Northcote, H. of C. 21 July 1859; Hansard, 3rd series, clv, 255; Gladstone to Northcote, 25 July 1859; Andrew Lang, *Life, Letters and Diaries of Sir Stanford Northcote* (Edinburgh, 1890), i, 160, cit. A. Lawrence Lowell, *[The] Government of England* (New York, 1918), i, pp. 191–192.

[10] Earl Gray, *Parliamentary Government Considered with Reference to Reform* (1864), p. 300.

[11] *Ibid.,* p. 331.

[12] *Ibid.,* pp. 295–314.

[13] *Ibid.,* pp. 42–43.

[14] H. Taylor, *The Statesman* (Cambridge, 1957) (first published 1836), chap. xii, pp. 75ff.

[15] Taylor, *The Statesman*, pp. 82–83.

[16] Charles Buller, "Responsible Government for Colonies" (1840).

Notes

The most easily available editions is in E. M. Wrong, *Charles Buller and Responsible Government* (Oxford, 1926).

[17] E. Hughes, "Sir James Stephen and the Anonymity of the Civil Servant," *Public Administration* xxxvi, 29–33.

[18] Debate in H. of C. 8 April 1806. *The Trial by Impeachment of Henry Lord Viscount Melville* (1806), p. xliv.

[19] L. B. Namier, *Structure of Politics at the Accession of George III* (1929 ed.), i, 47–53; M. A. Thomson, *The Secretaries of State 1681–1782* (Oxford, 1932), pp. 128–142. See also for the old system and the transitional period S. E. Finer, "Patronage and the Public Service," *Public Administration* xxx, 329.

[20] On this see J. E. D. Binney, *British Finance and Administration 1774–9* (Oxford, 1958).

[21] See Sir Thomas L. Heath, *The Treasury* (Whitehall Series, 1927), p. 12.

[22] See E. Jones Parry, "Under-Secretaries of State for Foreign Affairs, 1782–1855," *English Historical Review*, xlix, 308–320. I owe this reference to Mr. Hinsley of St John's College, Cambridge.

[23] *Correspondence and Diaries of J. W. Croker*, ed. Louis Jennings (1884), ii, 74, Croker to Graham 20 November 1830; *ibid.*, i, p. 81.

[24] *The Diaries and Correspondence of the Right Hon. George Rose*, ed. Rev. Leveson Vernon Harcourt (1860), i, 24. I owe this quotation to Mr. I. R. Christie, indeed I owe much in this paragraph to the help of Mr. I. R. Christie and Professor E. Hughes. I wish I could have included all that they told me. I need not say how important for the understanding of this period and these problems are Mr. Christie's *The End of North's Ministry* (1958) and Professor Hughes's various articles and his *Studies in Administration and Finance 1558–1825* (Manchester, 1934).

[25] Sir William Blackstone, *Commentary on the Laws of England*, Bk. i, chap. 8 (last para. but three) (16th ed. 1825, i, 335); W. S. Holdsworth, *A History of English Law*, x (1938), p. 514.

[26] Hampden Gordon, *The War Office* (Whitehall Series, 1935), pp. 32–33.

[27] Oliver MacDonagh, "Emigration and State 1833–55: an Essay in Administrative History," *Transactions of the Royal Historical Society*, fifth series, 5 (1955), 133–159; M. W. Thomas, *The Early Factory Legislation* (Leigh-on-sea, 1948), pp. 254ff.

[28] Oliver MacDonagh, "The Nineteenth Century Revolution in Government. A Reappraisal," *The Historical Journal* i (1958), 52–67.

[29] Roger Prouty, *The Transformation of the Board of Trade 1830–55* (1957).

[30] E. T. Cook, *The Life of Florence Nightingale* (1913), i, pp. 401–407.

[31] Walter Bagehot, *The English Constitution*, part of no. vi on "Changes of Ministry" (1920 ed.), pp. 183–190.

[32] See 13 and 14 Vic. cap. 94 (1850). Mr. G. F. A. Best of Trinity Hall is at present engaged in a history of the Ecclesiastical Commissioners.

[33] F. M. G. Willson, "Ministries and Boards," *Public Administration* xxxiii, 43ff.; Lowell, *Government of England*, i, pp. 83–85.

[34] See Hansard, 3rd series, clxxv, 371–382, Sir John Pakington's speech.

[35] From the papers of Sir James Graham in the possession of Sir Fergus Graham, published with the kind permission of Sir Fergus Graham. Charles Trevelyan to Sir James Graham, 14 October 1843 (two letters). Graham to Trevelyan, 14 October. Sir Robert Peel to Graham, 15 October (bundle 66 [b]). The letters in the *Morning Chronicle* appear on 14 October and 15 October. They are referred to in the leading article of 17 October. I owe the references in the *Morning Chronicle* to the kindness of Mrs. Woodham Smith who is investigating the whole matter for her forthcoming book on the famine in Ireland. See also Miss Lucy Brown, *The Board of Trade and the Free-Trade Movement* (Oxford, 1958), p. 33, quoting Peel papers (B.M. Add. mss. 40, 449, fos. 84–85, Graham to Peel, 14 October 1843).

[36] Sir George Otto Trevelyan, *Life and Letters of Lord Macaulay* (2nd ed., 1877), ii, pp. 378–380.

[37] Alexander Bain, *Autobiography* (1904), p. 201, mentioned in S. E. Finer, *The Life and Times of Sir Edwin Chadwick* (1952), p. 317.

[38] E.g. Blomfield, bishop of London in 1834. Finer, *Chadwick*, p. 163.

[39] E.g. Christie in the Andover Enquiry, *ibid.*, p. 260.

[40] *Ibid.*, pp. 279–280.

[41] *Ibid.*, p. 407.

[42] *Ibid.*, pp. 238–240.

[43] *Ibid.*, p. 321.

[44] G. Birkbeck Hill, *Life of Sir Rowland Hill K.C.B. etc. and History of Penny Postage* (2 vols., 1880). His interview with Cobden, II, pp. 73–75; his approaches to M.P.s to get Maberley removed, II, p. 198; to get particular returns, pp. 149 and 185; his relations with *The Times*, II, p. 116.

[45] Peel to Graham, 14 October 1843 (Graham papers, *loc. cit.*). For the attitude of Porter and Macgregor and in particular for their relation to the Committee on Import Duties see Miss Lucy Brown, "The Board of Trade and the Tariff Problem 1840-9" (*E.H.R.* LXVIII, 394–421), and her *Board of Trade and Free-Trade*, esp. chaps. 2 and 12. For their connection with the Anti-Corn Law leaders see E. I. Barrington, *The Servant of All. Pages from the Family, Social and Political Life of my father James Wilson* (2 vols., 1927), e.g. I, 6, 26, 66. Dr. McCord informs me that there is further evidence of the intimacy of Porter with the Anti-Corn Law League in the papers of George Wilson now in the Reference Library at Manchester.

[46] See Sir Lewis Namier, "Monarchy and the Party System" (Romanes lecture, 1952), *Personalities and Powers*, particularly pp. 21–25; note especially the quotation on p. 24 from J. C. Herries. J. C. Herries to Sir Wm. Knighton, 27 February 1827, in *Letters of King George IV*, ed. A. Aspinall, III, p. 200.

[47] For a discussion of the law touching the subject see E. Jones Parry, *E.H.R.* XLIX, pp. 309–313.

[48] The most convenient edition for Trollope's *Autobiography* and

his *Three Clerks* is in the World's Classics series. For Yates see *Edmund Yates, His Recollections and Experiences* (1885).

[49] There is probably an analogy here with the advantages and troubles that derived from the recruitment into the education office of Sir Michael Sadler and Sir Robert Morant, each with another career behind him, at the end of the century. On Sir Robert Morant in particular there is now a reasonably large literature.

[50] Mr. R. J. Lambert of Sidney Sussex is now working on Sir John Simon's activities. I believe that what he may produce may be of the greatest importance [published in 1963—ED.]. Simon's own work, *English Sanitary Institutions* (1890) is, however, extremely revealing.

[51] See debate on 12 April 1864. Hansard (3rd series), CLXXIV, pp. 897–912.

[52] E.g. see Brown, *Board of Trade and Free-Trade*, p. 209.

Parties and Issues in Early Victorian England

[1] This paper deals more fully with a question that was first opened up for discussion in an earlier article: W. O. Aydelotte, "Voting Patterns in the British House of Commons in the 1840s," *Comparative Studies in Society and History* V (1963), 134–163. The reader is referred to this article for a fuller account of the technical research which is taken as the basis of the present discussion. The author is indebted to the editor of *Comparative Studies in Society and History* for permission to reprint some of the figures in Table II and to republish several phrases which had to be repeated.

[2] The term "ideology" is used in this article only in the restricted sense of the set of objectives pursued by each party in the House of Commons, as revealed by the votes of party members in the division lists. No attempt will be made to describe a party "program" in the sense of an amalgam of the pledges and promises made by various candidates in the general election of 1841, which might, as Betty Kemp has pointed out, be a rather complicated affair. Betty Kemp,

"The General Election of 1841," *History*, new series, xxxvii (1952), 146–157. Still less will any attempt be made to describe, for either party, an "ideology" in the sense of a general rationale or theory of politics designed to govern political decisions or to justify them. These notes deal only with the causes each party supported or opposed in Parliament.

3 Robert Trelford McKenzie, *British Political Parties* (New York, 1955), p. 1.

4 Norman Gash, "Peel and the Party System, 1830–50," *Transactions of the Royal Historical Society*, fifth series, 1 (1951), 62.

5 Robert K. Webb, *Harriet Martineau: A Radical Victorian* (London, 1960), p. 363.

6 A. J. Balfour, Introduction, in Walter Bagehot, *The English Constitution* (London, 1928), p. xxiv.

7 Harold J. Laski, *Parliamentary Government in England* (New York, 1938), pp. 64, 69–73, 83, 86.

8 Robert Trelford McKenzie, "Laski and the Social Bases of the Constitution," *British Journal of Sociology* iii (1952), 260–263.

9 Sir Ivor Jennings, *Party Politics*, ii, *The Growth of Parties* (Cambridge, 1961), p. 332; iii, *The Stuff of Politics* (Cambridge, 1962), p. 466.

10 Richard Hofstadter, *The American Political Tradition* (new ed., New York, 1954), p. x.

11 John Higham, "The Cult of the 'American Consensus': Homogenizing Our History," *Commentary* xxvii (1959), 94, 95, 99.

12 C. Vann Woodward, "Our Past Isn't What It Used to Be," *New York Times Book Review*, July 28, 1963. It should be added that not all students of American politics subscribe to these views. Higham, in the article referred to in note 11, expresses reservations about the "massive grading operation" which he describes. Seymour Martin Lipset, though keenly aware of the circumstances that work for political consensus, nevertheless holds that parties do on the whole represent the interests of different classes, as can be shown from an analysis of their appeals and their support. Seymour M. Lipset,

Political Man: The Social Bases of Politics (Garden City, N.Y., 1960), pp. 220–223, 290–294, 306–309. David B. Truman writes, in regard to the American Congress: "Ample evidence already exists to support the proposition that, at least in the act of voting, the party label is consistently the most reliable predictor of a legislator's actions." David B. Truman, *The Congressional Party: A Case Study* (New York, 1959), pp. vi–vii. Some other studies which express reservations about an undue emphasis on consensus in American politics are: Talcott Parsons, " 'Voting' and the Equilibrium of the American Political System," in *American Voting Behavior,* ed. Eugene Burdick and Arthur J. Brodbeck (Glencoe, Ill., 1959), pp. 80–120; Herbert McClosky, Paul J. Hoffman, and Rosemary O'Hara, "Issue Conflict and Consensus Among Party Leaders and Followers," *American Political Science Review* LIV (1960), 406–427; and J. W. Prothro and Charles M. Grigg, "Fundamental Principles of Democracy: Bases of Agreement and Disagreement," *Journal of Politics* XXII (1960), 276–294.

[13] Anthony Trollope, *Phineas Redux* (London, 1873), chap. xxxiii.

[14] Bagehot, *The English Constitution,* pp. 126–128.

[15] William Ewart Gladstone, "The Declining Efficiency of Parliament," *Quarterly Review* XCIX (1856), 529–530.

[16] Charles C. F. Greville, *The Greville Memoirs (Second Part): A Journal of the Reign of Queen Victoria from 1837 to 1852* (London, 1885), II, p. 291.

[17] Arthur Aspinall, ed., *Three Early Nineteenth-Century Diaries* (London, 1952), p. xxvi.

[18] A. Lawrence Lowell, *The Government of England* (new ed., New York, 1924), I, p. 452.

[19] V. O. Key, Jr., *Politics, Parties and Pressure Groups* (4th ed., New York, 1958), p. 244.

[20] Archibald S. Foord, *His Majesty's Opposition, 1714–1830* (Oxford, 1964), p. 8.

[21] D. W. Brogan, Foreword, in Maurice Duverger, *Political Parties: Their Organization and Activity in the Modern State,* trans.

Barbara and Robert North (London, 1954), pp. v, viii. For a different version of de Jouvenel's epigram, see *ibid.*, pp. 201–202.

[22] Lewis B. Namier, *England in the Age of the American Revolution* (London, 1930), p. 207.

[23] Lowell, *The Government of England*, I, p. 452.

[24] "As a first step toward the introduction of concreteness into the idea of consensus, let us turn our back on the ethereal notion of 'basic' or 'fundamental' consensus and examine opinions on specific issues" (V. O. Key, Jr., *Public Opinion and American Democracy* [New York, 1961], p. 28).

[25] Gash, "Peel and the Party System," *Transactions of the Royal Historical Society*, fifth series 1 (1951), 57–58.

[26] *Ibid.*, pp. 62–63.

[27] Lewis B. Namier, *Monarchy and the Party System* (The Romanes Lecture) (Oxford, 1952), p. 26.

[28] Derek Beales, review of Sir Ivor Jennings, *Party Politics*, in *Historical Journal* v (1962), 194.

[29] Richard Pares in *King George III and the Politicians* (Oxford, 1953), p. 192, states: "between 1807 and 1841, the man without a party label almost disappeared from the House of Commons." For the Parliament of 1841 this statement is confirmed by the present investigation.

[30] This includes a man who died before Parliament met, another who succeeded to a peerage before Parliament met, and a third who was elected later to fill one of the two seats which Daniel O'Connell secured in the general election. This disposition follows the principles Namier laid down in *England in the Age of the American Revolution*, pp. 248–249.

[31] For examples of the first usage, see *Times*, July 2, 3, 5, and 6, 1841; for examples of the second, see *Times*, July 15, 16, 17, and 19, 1841.

[32] "To use the term 'Whig' simply to denote political opinions is to forfeit half the flavour and force of the word" (Donald Southgate, *The Passing of the Whigs, 1832–1886* [London, 1962], p. 76).

[33] A good account of the method can be found in the articles contributed by Louis Guttman to *Measurement and Prediction*, ed. Samuel A. Stouffer *et al.* (Princeton, 1950), which is the fourth volume of *Studies in Social Psychology in World War II*. However, much more has been written on this subject, by Guttman and others, since this volume appeared, and the literature on scalogram analysis is now considerable.

[34] For a more extended discussion of this point, see Aydelotte, "Voting Patterns," *Comparative Studies in Society and History* v, 151.

[35] The eighteen items in Table III were selected merely for illustration. It should not be inferred that the numbers of divisions in each of the three groups here described were the same. Actually, of the 111 divisions examined, 80 proved to fit this scale, though not all were wholly regular. Of the 80, 37 items devided the Liberals, 20 were straight party votes, and 23 divided the Conservatives. Even these figures, however, should not be taken to indicate the general incidence of intraparty cleavages: the divisions studied were selected simply because of their interest for various purposes, and no formal sampling procedure was employed. Nevertheless, this finding—that only one fourth of the items in this scale were straight party votes, while other items not in the scale were not party votes at all—fits quite well with the results obtained by A. Lawrence Lowell in his important study, over half a century ago, of party cohesion in the House of Commons in the period 1836–99. Lowell computed, for several dates about a decade apart, the proportion of divisions that were straight party votes in the sense that the two parties voted on opposite sides, each with a dissidence of less than 10 per cent. He gave no figures for the 1840s, but he found the proportion of straight party votes to be 23 per cent in 1836 and 16 per cent in 1850. By contrast, party cohesion was, according to his figures, much greater and rapidly increasing in the last three decades of the century, after the Reform Act of 1867. A. Lawrence Lowell, "The Influence of Party Upon Legislation in England and America," *Annual Report of the American Historical Association for the Year 1901* (Washington, 1902), I, 321–542. The present investigation is, of course, addressed to a different question from that considered by Lowell: it attempts to show that,

even in a situation where straight party voting was infrequent, parties could still be related to attitudes on issues in a different and more complex way.

[36] Halévy notes a similar difficulty in distinguishing in terms of votes between the groups on the Left in 1835. His text does not, however, make it clear how thorough or extensive his analysis was. Elie Halévy, *A History of the English People in the Nineteenth Century,* trans. E. I. Watkin (New York, 1951), iii, p. 180, n. 1.

[37] G. Kitson Clark, "The Repeal of the Corn Laws and the Politics of the Forties," *Economic History Review,* second series, iv (1951), 7–8.

[38] Norman Gash, *Politics in the Age of Peel: A Study in the Technique of Parliamentary Representation, 1830–1850* (London, 1953), pp. 3–11.

The Corn Laws and High Farming

[1] Betty Kemp has focused on this distinction in her important article, "Reflections on the Repeal of the Corn Laws," *Victorian Studies* v, 3 (1962), 189–204.

[2] *Corn and Currency* (new ed., London, 1828), p. 77.

[3] *The Farmers' Magazine* iv (January 1836), 12.

[4] (London, 1836), esp. p. 10.

[5] For a discussion of the committee's behavior see 3 Hansard, xxxv (21 July 1836), pp. 381–397.

[6] On the remarkable increase in the yields of wheat per acre which occurred around about 1840 see M. J. R. Healy and E. L. Jones, "Wheat Yields in England, 1815–59," *Journal of the Royal Statistical Society,* ser. A, cxxv, pt. 4 (1962), 574–579. However, in attributing these increased yields to "the huge increase in agricultural inputs with the rise in farm product prices after 1837" (p. 577), they scarcely do justice to the new techniques which guided investment and to the new willingness to invest. On the question of remunerative prices see the controversy over Earl Ducie's claim that by putting his main

emphasis upon pastoral farming, and by using some fifteen pounds of capital per acre, he could grow wheat at a profit even if it were to sell down to twenty-eight shillings the quarter ton (*The Farmers' Magazine*, 2nd ser. x [August 1844], 113–126).

[7] See, for example, the reply to Lefevre's pamphlet by E. S. Cayley, *A Letter to Henry Handley, Esq., M.P.* (London, 1836).

[8] *The Farmers' Magazine* VIII (June 1838), 441.

[9] 3 Hansard, LX (9 February 1842), 202.

[10] *John Bull*, 12 October 1842.

[11] *The Farmers' Magazine* II (January 1835), 60.

[12] *Ibid.*, 2nd ser. XI (January 1845), 23–25.

[13] *Ibid.*, 2nd ser. XI (March 1845), 251.

[14] *Ibid.*, 2nd ser. VII (May 1843), 375.

[15] "Science and Agriculture," LI (June 1842), 739. Attributions of authorship of articles cited in *Blackwood's Edinburgh Magazine* were kindly furnished by Prof. Walter Houghton, editor of the Wellesley *Bibliography of Victorian Periodicals*.

[16] Report from the select committee on agricultural customs, 1847–48, VII, Q. 56.

[17] Arthur Underhill, "Changes in the English Law of Real Property during the Nineteenth Century," *Select Essays in Anglo-American Legal History* (Boston, 1909), III, pp. 673ff.

[18] *Profitable Investment of Capital, or Eleven Years Practical Experience in Farming: A Letter From Lord Kinnaird to His Tenantry* (2nd ed., Edinburgh, 1849), pp. 5–6.

[19] *English Agriculture in 1850–51* (London, 1852), p. 477.

[20] "British Agriculture and Foreign Competition," LXVII (January 1850), 96–97.

[21] See his testimony, Sessional Papers, 1845, XII, QQ. 56ff., that of the secretary of the Company, Thomas May, QQ. 420ff., that of John Thompson, who was erecting various tileries in Surrey for Parkes, QQ. 173ff., and that of Earl Ducie, whom Parkes had advised on the drainage of his estates, QQ. 1410ff.

[22] QQ. 423–424.

[23] Q. 148.

[24] *Ibid.*, 111.

[25] LXVII (January 1850), 95.

[26] Sessional Papers, 1845, XII, 114.

[27] 3Hansard, LXXXIII (27 January 1846), 276.

[28] 3 Hansard, LXXXIII (27 January 1846), 255.

[29] *Ibid.*

[30] *Ibid.*, p. 256.

[31] *Ibid.*, pp. 264–266.

[32] *Ibid.*, pp. 266–268.

[33] *Ibid.*, pp. 268–270.

[34] In an article published in 1840, "Some Introductory Remarks on the Present State of Agriculture as a Science in England," *Journal of the Royal Agricultural Society* I (1840), 3, Philip Pusey gave figures as high as eight or ten pounds per acre. In 1845 several witnesses before the Richmond Committee reported successful drainage at a quarter of the earlier cost. See QQ. 57 and 1415.

[35] Sessional Papers, 1845, XII, 113.

[36] 3 Hansard, LXXXIII (27 January 1846), 269–270.

[37] *Ibid.*, p. 270.

[38] *Ibid.*

[39] *Ibid.*, p. 268.

[40] *Bell's Weekly Messenger*, 25 May 1846.

[41] *The English Landed Estate in the Nineteenth Century* (Baltimore, 1963), p. 149.

[42] *Ibid.*, p. 150.

[43] Lord Ernle, *English Farming Past and Present* (6th ed., London, 1961), p. cxiii.

[44] A return of the number of applications under the Act of last session, c. 101, in England, Ireland, and Scotland, and the total sum

applied for in each country, 1847, xxxiv, 301, indicates that through the end of January, 1847, there had been 168 applications from Scotland amounting to approximately £800,000, and 48 applications from England, amounting to approximately £200,000.

[45] Henry Charles Mules, before the Select Committee of the House of Lords appointed to consider whether it would not be desirable that the powers now vested in the companies for the improvement of land should be made subject of general regulation, 1854–55, vii, Q. 31.

[46] Q. 58.

[47] Q. 322.

[48] Q. 347.

[49] Arthur Underhill, "Property," *Law Quarterly Review* li (1935), 225.

[50] The editor of the 8th edition of Sir Bernard Burke, *History of the Landed Gentry of Great Britain and Ireland* (London, 1894), explained that some families had been cast into oblivion who had made use of the Settled Land Act and "who [had] severed their connection with their ancestral homes. . . ." By 1921, however, the sins of which these men were guilty had come to provide their own norm. As the editor of the 13th edition explained, ". . . The history of a family is retained after its head has ceased to be a landowner."

[51] 3 Hansard, xc (23 February 1847), 405.

[52] 1854–55, vii, Q. 4.

[53] 1847–48, vii, QQ pp. 145, 704–715.

[54] See 3 Hansard, lxxiv (26 April 1844), p. 280; xc (22 February 1847), pp. 383–385; xci (26 March 1847), pp. 541–543; xcii (12 May 1847), pp. 719–721; and cx (1 May 1850), pp. 1061–1066.

[55] *The Anti-Corn Law League* (London, 1958), pp. 203–204.

[56] *Ibid.*, p. 201.

[57] *Ibid.*

[58] *Ibid.*, p. 204.

Notes

Tory Paternalism and Social Reform
in Early Victorian England

[1] T. C. Hansard, *Parliamentary Debates of Great Britain*, 3d ser. (hereafter cited as Hansard) 1833, xv, p. 1160; xvi, p. 642, 1002; xvii, pp. 79–114; xx, pp. 449, 527, 576, 583. G. Kitson Clark, in *Peel and the Conservative Party* (London, 1929) notes the heterogeneous nature of the ten hour men in the Commons and the failure of the Conservative leaders to support the bill (p. 141).

[2] John Drinkwater, *Letter to Michael Sadler* (London, 1833), p. 4; London *Times*, February 29, 1844.

[3] *Leeds Mercury*, July 28, August 12, 1837; *Stamford Mercury*, July 28, 1837; *Fraser's Magazine*, April, 1841; *Leeds Intelligencer*, April, 1841; Hansard, 1842, LXIII, p. 447.

[4] *Manchester Guardian*, May 17, 1834.

[5] Hansard, 1834, XXIV, pp. 346–351, 1061.

[6] *Ibid.*, xxv, pp. 912–915; 1253–1257. To check the political affiliations of those voting in key divisions, I have used C. R. P. Dod, *Parliamentary Companion*, for 1832, 1837, 1841, and 1847.

[7] Hansard, 1841, LVII, pp. 792, 794, 797–804; 1842, LXIII, p. 447.

[8] Henry Dunn, *National Education, The Question of Questions* (London, 1838), p. 7.

[9] Coleridge, *Complete Works* (London, 1853), VI, pp. 55, 59, 67, 68.

[10] Hansard, 1839, XLVIII, pp. 268, 603, 622.

[11] *Parliamentary Papers of Great Britain* (hereafter cited as *Parliamentary Papers*), 1838, VII, Committee on Education, pp. 1–42 and 180–197.

[12] Hansard, 1839, XLVIII, pp. 580–681.

[13] W. Cooke Taylor, *Life and Times of Sir Robert Peel* (London, 1851), II, pp. 406–417.

[14] Monypenny and Buckle, *Disraeli* (London, 1912), II, p. 231.

[15] John Morely, *Life of Gladstone* (London, 1903), I, p. 238.

[16] *Parliamentary Papers*, p. 1842, xv, Labor in Coal Mines, pp. 255–

257; Hansard, 1842, LXII, pp. 1320–1366; LXIV, pp. 783, 936; LXV, p. 1100.

[17] Edwin Hodder, *The Life and Work of the Seventh Earl of Shaftesbury* (London, 1880), I, pp. 426–429; II, p. 110.

[18] Hansard, 1844, LXXIII, pp. 1241–1266, 1371–1462.

[19] *The Economist*, April 24, 1844, pp. 722–723.

[20] William O. Aydelotte, "The House of Commons in the 1840's," *History* XXXIX (October 1954), 258–260.

[21] Hodder, *Shaftesbury*, I, 300. Lord Ashley added that there was in the Duke of Wellington nothing tender or soft: "He was a hard man." Hansard, 1840, LV, pp. 434–438.

[22] Hodder, *The Life of Samuel Morley* (London, 1887), p. 79.

[23] John Francis, *History of English Railways, 1820–1845* (London, 1851), II, pp. 39, 129–150; *The Economist*, July 6, 1844, p. 962.

[24] Hansard, 1884, LXXII, p. 250; 1847, CXI, p. 639.

[25] Hansard, 1847, XCI, p. 639; 1848, XCVIII, p. 1178; *Standard*, May 9, 1848; *Morning Advertiser*, May 4, 1848; *John Bull*, May 13, 1848.

[26] Anon., *Liberals and Conservatives, and Their Policy toward the Working Classes* (London, 1855), p. 12 (copy in the Chadwick MSS, University College, London); Hansard, 1854, CXXXIV, 1296. Palmerston has been much maligned by those who believe that the Whigs were careless of the people's well-being while the Tories were more solicitous. A recent reviewer in the *Times Literary Supplement* (February 3, 1956), in defending Carlyle, has described Palmerston as one of "the ignorant and jaunty aristocrats . . . uninterested in the condition of the people." Nothing could be farther from the truth.

[27] Hansard, 1850, CXIII, 759, 1071; 1851, CXVI, 501. In 1851 Lord Stanley, a year later prime minister in a Troy ministry, urged the repeal of the Merchant Marine Act because of its interference in the shipping business.

[28] Somervell, *Disraeli and Gladstone* (London, 1926), p. 76.

[29] Coleridge, "A Lay Sermon," *Works*, VI, p. 225.

[30] *John Bull*, May 13, 1848.

[31] Hansard, 1839, XLVIII, p. 578; L, p. 357; 1848, XCVI, p. 1022, XCVII, p. 798.

[32] *The Times,* May 14, 1838, November 2, 1843.

[33] Chadwick MSS, letter on Newcastle, September 28, 1853, unaddressed.

[34] J. T. Smith, *Government by Commission, Illegal and Pernicious* (London, 1849), pp. 15–19; *Centralization or Representation* (London, 1848).

[35] Charles Dickens, *Our Mutual Friend* (London, 1953), p. 132.

[36] Hansard, 1839, XLV, p. 1323; L, p. 357; Chadwick MSS, sketch of his life; *Stamford Mercury,* August 1, 1839.

[37] *Parliamentary Papers,* 1835, XXVII, Select Committee on Prisons; 1838, XXVI, Select Committee on Education; 1838, XXIX, Select Committee on Highways; 1839, XXIX, Royal Commission on Police; 1844, XXVI, Report of the Lunacy Commissioners; 1845, XXVI, Health of Towns Report; J. P. Fearon, *The Endowed Charities* (London, 1856).

[38] Chadwick MSS, letter on Newcastle, September 28, 1853.

[39] Hansard, 1847, XCIII, pp. 1094 and 1115. The fifty-nine who opposed the act in 1847 were mostly Protectionist Tories, men like C. N. Newdegate, R. Spooner, and Young Englanders like Lord John Manners.

[40] Elie Halévy, *The Growth of Philosophical Radicalism* (Boston, 1955), p. 230; Edmund Burke, "Thoughts and Details on Scarcity," *Complete Works* (Boston, 1894), V, p. 131ff.

[41] Aydelotte, "The House of Commons in the 1840's," p. 258.

[42] Hansard, 1850, CXII, pp. 1242–1243; CXIII, p. 4.

[43] See note 37; *Parliamentary Papers,* 1854, XXVIII, Report on Gateshead, p. 155.

The Transition to Democracy
in Victorian England

[1] Alexis de Tocqueville, *Democracy in America,* edited with an introduction by Henry Steele Commager (New York, 1947), p. 216.

[2] R. A. J. Walling, ed., *The Diaries of John Bright* (New York, 1931), p. 297.

[3] G. D. H. Cole and A. W. Filson, *British Working Class Movements: Select Documents 1789–1875* (London, 1951), p. 381.

[4] *Manchester Guardian*, September 3, 1866. Cited hereafter as *M.G.*

[5] *Ibid.*, January 7, 1859.

[6] *Ibid.*, May 8, 1850.

[7] S. Maccoby, *English Radicalism 1853–1886* (London, 1938), p. 82, quoting *The National Review*, April 1863. For a satiric description of the middle-class conception of its philanthropic role see the excerpt from *Porcupine* in Margaret B. Simey, *Charitable Effort in Liverpool in the Nineteenth Century* (Liverpool, 1951), p. 56.

[8] *M.G.*, October 14, 1858.

[9] J. M. Ludlow and Lloyd Jones, *Progress of the Working Class 1832–1867* (London, 1867), p. 294.

[10] *M.G.*, January 7, 1859. Samuel Smiles, sensitive to every nuance of mid-Victorian culture, also called for a greater sympathy between classes: "Thus only can the breath of society be sweetened and purified" (Asa Briggs, *Victorian People* [London, 1954], pp. 142–143).

[11] See D. Simon, "Master and Servant," in J. Saville, ed., *Democracy and the Labour Movement* (London, 1954).

[12] See R. Y. Hedges and A. Winterbottom, *Legal History of Trade Unionism* (London, 1930), chap. 5.

[13] G. M. Young and W. D. Handcock, eds., *English Historical Documents 1833–1874*, p. 390, quoting the Census Report of 1851–53 on Religious Worship.

[14] *M.G.*, January 7, 1859.

[15] See E. J. Hobsbawm, "The Labour Aristocracy in 19th Century Britain," in Saville, ed., *Democracy and the Labour Movement*.

[16] See Richard D. Altick, *The English Common Reader* (Chicago, 1957); B. Simon, *Studies in the History of Education, 1780–1870* (London, 1960); F. Smith, *A History of English Elementary Education, 1760–1902* (London, 1931); H. F. Mathews, *Methodism and the Education of the People, 1791–1851* (London, 1949); S. E. Maltby,

Manchester and the Movement for National Elementary Education, 1800–1870 (Manchester, 1918); M. Tylecote, *The Mechanics' Institutes of Lancashire and Yorkshire before 1851* (Manchester, 1957); M. Arnold, *Reports on Elementary Schools, 1852–1882* (London. 1910); for excellent descriptions of the educational situation in two different industrial areas, see Education Commission, *Reports of the Assistant Commissioners Appointed to Inquire into the State of Popular Education in England, 1861* (London, 1961), II, 175–242, on Rochdale and Bradford, and 245–301, on the Potteries and the Black Country.

[17] E. R. Jones, *The Life and Speeches of Joseph Cowen, M.P.* (London, n.d.), p. 96.

[18] *M.G.*, March 24, 1866.

[19] *Ibid.*, January 15, 1859.

[20] *Ibid.*, January 1, 1859.

[21] *Ibid.*, May 1, 1850. For an account of the mutual improvement societies and working-men's clubs see Ludlow and Jones, *Progress of the Working Class*, pp. 174–180.

[22] See J. M. Baernreither, *English Associations of Working Men* (London, 1891); Ludlow and Jones, *Progress of the Working Class*, chap. 2; G. D. H. Cole, *A Short History of the British Working Class Movement* (London, 1948), pp. 152–168.

[23] *M.G.*, September 3, 1866.

[24] Ludlow and Jones, *Progress of the Working Class*, pp. 291–292.

[25] Jones, *Joseph Cowen*, pp. 96–97.

[26] See S. and B. Webb, *The History of Trade Unionism* (London, 1920), pp. 180–232; Cole, *British Working Class Movement*, pp. 169–185; Briggs, *Victorian People*, chap. 7, *The Age of Improvement* (London, 1959), pp. 408–410; G. D. H. Cole has described the wide variation within the mid-Victorian trade union movement in "Some Notes on British Trade Unionism in the Third Quarter of the Nineteenth Century," *International Review for Social History* II (1937).

[27] *M.G.*, September 7, 1866.

[28] Briggs, *Victorian People*, p. 178.

[29] See E. R. Wickham, *Church and People in an Industrial City* (London, 1957). Chapter 4 not only describes the religious situation in Sheffield between 1850 and 1900, but also notes the presence of similar patterns in other cities. See also K. S. Inglis, "Churches and Working Classes in Nineteenth Century England," *Historical Studies: Australia and New Zealand*, VIII, No. 29 (1957).

[30] *M.G.*, January 5, 1859.

[31] *Ibid.*, April 27, 1850.

[32] Wickham, *Church and People*, p. 159. For examples of the relationship between the working classes and religious institutions in Liverpool, Bradford, and Manchester see the evidence presented to the Select Committee of the House of Lords on Deficiency of Means of Spiritual Instruction, *Parliamentary Papers*, 1857–58, IX, 382f., 416f., 448f.

[33] *M.G.*, May 1, 1850.

[34] Wickham, *Church and People*, p. 141.

[35] Young and Handcock, *English Historical Documents*, p. 315.

[36] *M.G.*, May 3, 1848; London *Times*, May 1, 1848.

[37] *M.G.*, May 3, 6, 17, 1848; London *Times*, June 1, 8, 21, 1848; *Illustrated London News*, June 10, 24, 1848.

[38] London *Times*, June 8, 1848.

[39] *Journal of the House of Commons*, 1847–48, pp. 636–638.

[40] See Frances E. Gillespie, *Labor and Politics in England* (Durham, 1927); S. Maccoby, *English Radicalism, 1832–1852* (London, 1935), and *English Radicalism, 1853–1886* (London, 1938).

[41] Gillespie, *Labor and Politics*, pp. 85–110; Maccoby, *English Radicalism*, pp. 314–315; *Illustrated London News*, January 12, 1850.

[42] *M.G.*, December 6, 1851.

[43] *Illustrated London News*, March 6, 1852; *M.G.*, March 6, 1852.

[44] *M.G.*, January 1, 1859.

[45] See *M.G.*, January 1859, *passim*; Gillespie, *Labor and Politics*, pp. 178ff., describes Radical activity in the Midlands and the North.

[46] *M.G.*, February 2, 1859; Gillespie, *Labor and Politics*, p. 154.

[47] Gillespie, *Labor and Politics*, pp. 238–286; Maccoby, *Radicalism 1853–1886*, pp. 84–99; Cole and Filson, *British Working Class Movements*, pp. 529–532; *M.G.*, April 20, 1864, May 16, 17, 1865, November 20, 1866, February 20, 1867.

[48] T. W. Reid, *Life of the Right Honourable William Edward Forster* (London, 1888), I, p. 367.

[49] *Saturday Review*, August 4, 1866.

[50] J. E. T. Rogers, ed., *Speeches on Questions of Public Policy by John Bright, M.P.* (London, 1869), II, pp. 100–101.

[51] *M.G.*, December 6, 1851.

[52] *Ibid.*, February 2, 1859.

[53] John Saville, *Ernest Jones: Chartist* (London, 1952), pp. 62–76.

[54] *M.G.*, January 12, 1859.

[55] W. L. Guttsman, "The 1859 Election in Seven Yorkshire Cities," *International Review of Social History* II (1957), Pt. 2.

[56] *Ibid.*, p. 253.

[57] Cole and Filson, *British Working Class Movements*, p. 529.

[58] *M.G.*, April 1, 1864.

[59] *Ibid.*, September 24, 1866.

[60] *Ibid.*, September 25, 1866.

[61] Reid, *Life of Forster*, I, pp. 392–396.

[62] On Tyneside a group of middle-class Radicals, led by Joseph Cowen, refused to stop short of manhood suffrage. In Birmingham the household suffrage position won a more complete triumph among both the middle and working classes, whereas another Midland town, Leicester, approximated the Lancashire and Yorkshire pattern, in that a substantial segment of the middle class held aloof from the Radicals. Such diversity, while of considerable importance, should not be permitted to obscure the unity of middle-class Radicalism in the industrial towns. See Jones, *Joseph Cowen;* R. A. McKinley, ed., *A History of the County of Leicester*, IV (London, 1958), pp. 216–224; and my article, "The Origins of the Birmingham Caucus," *Historical Journal*, II, No. 2 (1959).

[63] Reid, *Life of Forster*, I, p. 399.

[64] *M.G.*, November 20, 1866.

[65] Cole and Filson, *British Working Class Movements*, p. 535.

[66] H. J. Hanham, *Elections and Party Management: Politics in the Time of Disraeli and Gladstone* (London, 1959), pp. 68–90.

[67] *Ibid.*, p. 81.

[68] Royden Harrison, "The British Working Class and the General Election of 1868," *International Review of Social History*, v (1960), part 3, and vi (1961), part 1. Harrison has shown the importance of Liberal money in inducing Howell to enter into these Lib-Lab arrangements, which did not spring spontaneously from the Liberal inclinations of the working-class leadership. On the other hand, the deal with Howell would not have worked had not the vast majority of the artisan class been very favorably disposed to the Liberal party.

[69] G. D. H. Cole, *British Working Class Politics 1832–1914* (London, 1941), pp. 52–76; Hanham, *Elections and Party Management*, chaps. 7 and 15; H. Pelling, *The Origins of the Labour Party 1880–1900* (London, 1954), pp. 3–8.

[70] Pelling, *Origins of the Labour Party*, p. 218.

[71] *Ibid.*, pp. 235–238.

Educational Policy and Social Control
in Early Victorian England

[1] Form of Report for Her Majesty's Inspectors of Schools, *Minutes of the Committee of Council on Education*, 1840–41, p. 13. This important source, published annually by the Department, is cited below as *Minutes*.

[2] *Minutes*, 1845, i, 266.

[3] E.g. First Report, *Parl. Papers*, 1836, xxxv, 83ff.

[4] E.g. Horner, "Report of 18 January, 1837," *Parl. Papers*, 1837, xxxi, 98–99.

[5] The Commission on the Hand-loom Weavers is a good example.

[6] R. K. Webb, *The British Working Class Reader 1780–1848* (London, 1955).

[7] *Minutes*, 1845, i, 266, n. 2.

[8] *Minutes*, 1840–41, 31–32.

[9] For the significance of this common analogy see p. 219.

[10] See, for example, J. M. Goldstrom, "The Changing Social Content of Elementary Education as reflected in School books in use in England 1808–1870" (unpub. Ph.D. thesis, University of Birmingham, 1968).

[11] See especially, Sidney Pollard, "Factory Discipline in the Industrial Revolution," *Economic History Review*, 2nd ser., xvi (1963–64); M. Sanderson, "Education and the Factory in Industrial Lancashire, 1780–1840," *ibid.*, xx (1967).

[12] J. P. Kay, *The Moral and Physical Condition of the Working Classes Employed in the Cotton Manufacture in Manchester* (London, 1832). There are two editions which differ significantly. In what follows the first edition is used unless otherwise stated, and is cited as *Manchester*.

[13] *Manchester*, p. 49.

[14] *Ibid.*, pp. 50–51 and 72.

[15] *Ibid.*, p. 47.

[16] *Ibid.*, p. 51.

[17] *Ibid.*, pp. 61–63.

[18] *Ibid.*, 2nd ed., Introductory Letter, p. 5.

[19] *Ibid.*, p. 60.

[20] B. C. Bloomfield, ed., "The Autobiography of Sir James Kay-Shuttleworth," *Education Libraries Bulletin*, Suppl. 7, p. 4.

[21] *Manchester*, p. 61, n. 1. For a full presentation of Chalmers's very influential ideas see his *The Christian and Civic Economy of Large Towns*, 3 vols. (Glasgow, 1821–25).

[22] *Manchester*, 2nd ed. Introductory Letter, pp. 8–11.

[23] *Manchester*, p. 69.

[24] *Minutes*, 1845, i, 265.

[25] *Ibid.*, pp. i, 266–267.

[26] *Ibid.*, pp. 265 and 271.

[27] Public Record Office, M.H. 32/49, Kay to Lewis, n.d.

[28] *Minutes*, 1840–41, 168.

[29] *Ibid.*

[30] *Minutes*, 1844, ii. 107.

[31] E.g. *Minutes*, 1845, i, 140.

[32] *Minutes*, 1844, ii, 522.

[33] *Minutes*, 1840–41, 452–453.

[34] *Ibid.*

[35] *Ibid.*, p. 437.

[36] *Ibid.*, p. 430.

[37] *Minutes*, 1844, ii, 509. Startling for his own political naïveté!

[38] *Ibid.*, p. 257.

[39] *Ibid.*, p. 215.

[40] *Minutes*, 1846, 311.

[41] *Manchester*, 2nd ed., pp. 9–10.

[42] See N. J. Smelser, *Social Change in the Industrial Revolution: An Application of Theory to the Lancashire Cotton Industry, 1770–1840* (London, 1959).

[43] E.g. *Minutes*, 1840–41, 201–202.

[44] *Minutes*, 1844, ii, 267.

[45] *Ibid.*, 1844, ii, 157.

[46] *Ibid.*, 1850–51, p. 119.

[47] *Ibid.*, 1844, ii, 261.

[48] *Minutes*, 1844, ii, 214–215.

[49] *Minutes*, 1845, i, 155.

[50] *Minutes*, 1844, ii, 276.

[51] Sir James Kay-Shuttleworth, *Four Periods of Public Education* (London, 1862), pp. 490–491.

[52] *Minutes*, 1845, i, 258.

[53] *Minutes*, 1840–41, 188ff.

[54] *Ibid.*, p. 145.

[55] *Ibid.*, pp. 45–51.

[56] For a clear expression of these themes see "Report on the Training of Pauper Children," *Poor Law Commission, Fourth Annual Report, Parl. Papers* 1838, xxviii, esp. 393–394.

[57] "Training of Pauper Children," 286ff.

[58] E.g. *Minutes*, 1844, ii, 289–291.

[59] "Training of Pauper Children," 282ff.

[60] *Minutes*, 1839–40, 75.

[61] "First Report on Battersea," *Four Periods*, pp. 313–314.

[62] E.g. Vehrli's address quoted in *Four Periods*, pp. 305–306.

[63] Cf. the treatment in Hugh Pollard, *Pioneers of Popular Education 1760–1850* (London, 1956), pp. 214ff.

[64] *Minutes*, 1845, i, 271.

[65] *Minutes*, 1844, ii, 507.

[66] *Minutes*, 1846, ii, 47.

[67] *Ibid.*, p. 49.

[68] E.g. *Minutes*, 1845, 118 and 168.

[69] E.g. *Minutes*, 1844, ii, 288–289.

[70] *Minutes*, 1840–41, 163–164.

[71] *Ibid.*, 1840–41, 192–193.

[72] *Ibid.*, p. 163.

[73] *Minutes*, 1845, i, 370.

[74] *Minutes*, 1844, ii, 11.

[75] *Ibid.*, p. 90.

[76] *Minutes*, 1846, i, 27ff.

[77] *Minutes*, 1857–58, 478.

[78] See, for example, Frank Smith's judgment, "the Minutes went to the roots of the schools' weakness" (*The Life and Work of Sir James Kay-Shuttleworth* [London, 1923], p. 173).

[79] For an elaboration of these points see J. R. B. Johnson, "The Education Department 1839–1864: A study in Social Policy and The Growth of Government" (unpub. Cambridge Ph.D. thesis, 1968), pp. 416–501.

[80] The analysis that follows is based on the text of the *Minutes* themselves, elaboration of particular points being drawn from actual departmental practice in the years immediately following their passage. For a much fuller discussion see *ibid.*, pp. 286–308.

Lyttelton and Thring: A Study in Nineteenth-Century Education

[1] T[homas] S[eecombe], "Lord Lyttelton," *Dictionary of National Biography* (London, 1885–1900), XII, p. 374.

[2] John Bailey, ed., *The Diary of Lady Frederick Cavendish* (London, 1927), I, p. xix.

[3] "Address on Education," *Transactions of the National Association for the Promotion of Social Science, 1868* (London, 1869), p. 64.

[4] It was also called the Endowed School Commission (since its recommendations were limited to endowed schools) and the Schools Enquiry Commission. Lyttelton's most interesting fellow members were Dean Hook, a high churchman who had become famous for his work at Leeds; Frederick Temple, at the time Headmaster of Rugby and later Archbishop of Canterbury; Edward Baines, the leader of the Nonconformist interest in Leeds; W. E. Forster, who carried the Endowed Schools and Elementary Education Acts; and Peter Erle, the Chief Charity Commissioner. The Assistant Commissioners who did the field work included Matthew Arnold, James Bryce, and T. H. Green.

[5] *Endowed Schools Commission's Report*, I, 110; 1867–68 (3966) XXVIII.

[6] *Report of the Select Committee on the Operation of the Endowed Schools Act*, Q.1261; 1873 (254) VIII.

[7] *Report on the Operation of the Endowed Schools Act*, p. 24; 1872 (524) XXIV.

[8] See, for instance, Christopher Cookson, "The Scholarship Question," *Thirteen Essays on Education* (London, 1891), p. 114.

[9] 32 and 33 Victoria c. 56. Sections 9 and 10.

[10] Hansard, *Parliamentary Debates*, 3rd Ser., CCXXI (3 August 1874), p. 1136.

[11] Hansard, 3rd Ser., CCV (24 April 1871), pp. 1564–1565.

[12] See Sir Arthur Hobhouse, *The Dead Hand* (London, 1880).

[13] J. L. Hammond and L. T. Hobhouse, *Lord Hobhouse* (London, 1898), II, p. 118.

[14] 15 June 1869, British Museum, Add. MS 44240, f. 97.

[15] See L. V. Lester-Garland, *A Memoir of Hugo Daniel Harper D.D.* (London, 1896), pp. 70–76.

[16] Edward Thring, *Theory and Practice of Teaching* (Cambridge, 1883), pp. 122–124.

[17] *Education and School* (London, 1867), p. 158.

[18] G. R. Parkin, *Edward Thring, Life, Diary & Letters* (London, 1898), II, 118.

[19] Quoted in J. H. Skrine, *A Memory of Edward Thring* (London, 1890), p. 247.

[20] *Select Committee Report*, H. G. Robinson, Q.2188; 1873 (254) VIII: "We have dealt with Uppingham, which is an admirable school which we cannot improve, because Mr. Thring gave us no rest until we took the case in hand."

[21] Parkin, *Edward Thring*, I, 219. "I am quite baffled how to act about the Commissioners. . . . My convictions are so intensely against all their principles (as far as they have any), and I fear I shall only appear to them as a cantankerous, self-asserting bigot."

[22] Geoffrey Hoyland, *The Man Who Made a School* (London, 1946), p. 93.

[23] *Endowed Schools Commission's Report*, IV, Q.4419.

[24] W. E. Gladstone, in *Brief Memorials of Lord Lyttelton* (London, 1876), p. 45.

Francis Schnadhorst and Liberal Party Organization

[1] W. S. Churchill, *Lord Randolph Churchill* (London, 1906), I, p., 286.

[2] J. Annand, "The Reorganization of Liberalism," *The New Review* XIII (November 1895), 496.

[3] He died on January 2, 1900, not June 2, as in *Who was Who*.

[4] F. H. Herrick, "The Origins of the National Liberal Federation," *Journal of Modern History* XVII (1945), 116–119; and see Asa Briggs, *History of Birmingham* (Oxford, 1952), II, pp. 166–172. Trygve R. Tholfsen describes the background in "The Origins of the Birmingham Caucus," *History Journal* II (1959), 161–184.

[5] R. W. Dale (Congregationalist) and H. W. Crosskey (Unitarian) were the leading Nonconformist clergymen on the Committee. R. A. Armstrong, *Henry William Crosskey* (Birmingham, 1895), p. 267.

[6] Briggs, *History of Birmingham*, II, 194.

[7] J. L. Garvin, *Life of Joseph Chamberlain* (London, 1932), I, 478, n. 1, emphasizes that Schnadhorst was never Chamberlain's intimate friend.

[8] Herrick, "Origins of the National Liberal Federation," pp. 125–127.

[9] I.e., the Liberal associations of Bilston and Burslem, which were not parliamentary constituencies, were not on a footing with those of Hereford and Leominster, which were parliamentary boroughs.

[10] Herrick, "Origins of the National Liberal Federation," pp. 125–26.

[11] General Committee Minutes, NLF, July 2, December 11, 1877. I am grateful to the Executive of the Liberal Party Organization for permission to quote from these minutes of the NLF.

[12] General Committee Minutes, October 28, 1879.

[13] Schnadhorst gave as examples Sandon's education bill, the Plimsoll agitation, and the uproar over the slavery circulars (F. Schnadhorst, "The Caucus and its Critics," NLF pamphlet [n.d.], pp. 18–19). I am indebted to G. E. V. Awdry, Librarian, the National Liberal Club, for help in finding such pamphlets.

[14] Cf. Herrick, "Origins of the National Liberal Federation," p. 129.

[15] B. Holland, *Life of Spencer Compton Cavendish, 8th Duke of Devonshire* (London, 1913), I, pp. 245–246.

[16] "The Government and the Opposition," *Edinburgh Review* CXLIX (1879), 265.

[17] Schnadhorst, "The Caucus and its Critics," p. 20.

[18] *Ibid.*, pp. 21–26. Three were Scottish and two Welsh; the remainder were English and almost all of them boroughs.

[19] *Ibid.*, p. 20.

[20] Schnadhorst listed Glasgow, Leeds, Chelsea, Marylebone, Stoke-on-Trent, Nottingham, Scarborough, and Southwark as places where "the new organization" achieved Liberal unity and saved seats lost in 1874; of these, only Leeds, Stoke-on-Trent, and Southwark appear in the second annual report, but the others may have affiliated in the weeks between its preparation and the general election in April 1880.

[21] The assumption is made throughout that the actual Liberal vote could have been polled without the superfluous candidate.

[22] In a letter published by *The Times*, April 13, 1880, Chamberlain claimed that the caucus was well established in 67 boroughs and 10 county divisions, and that the Liberals had won or kept 60 seats in the former and all seats in the latter.

[23] F. H. O'Donnell, *History of the Irish Parliamentary Party* (London, 1910), I, pp. 162–163, 433.

[24] Dundee, Birmingham, Liverpool, Leeds, Manchester, and New-castle-on-Tyne appear in the second annual report; Schnadhorst referred to Glasgow and Chelsea (above, n. 20) as affiliated although they were not listed in the report. O'Donnell refers to London generally, specifying only Chelsea.

[25] C. C. O'Brien, *Parnell and His Party, 1880–1890* (Oxford, 1957), pp. 124–125.

[26] W. F. Monypenny and G. E. Buckle, *Life of Disraeli* (London, 1920), vi, pp. 514–516.

[27] Schnadhorst, "County organization," NLF pamphlet (1880), 4, 7.

[28] Schnadhorst, "The Next Reform Bill," NLF pamphlet (1881), 10.

[29] Garvin, *Chamberlain*, i, pp. 478 and 479, n. 1.

[30] Officers' Committee Minutes, NLF, June 17, 1881, January 7, and October 13, 1884.

[31] The Liberal Central Association, founded in the 1870s, replaced the Liberal Registration Association, founded in 1860, as the national party headquarters. See H. J. Hanham, "British Party Finance, 1868–1880," *Bulletin of the Institute of Historical Research* xxvii (1954), 81. Dilke had become chairman of the elections committee of the LCA in 1876. Trevelyan, John Morley, and Shaw-Lefevre joined Dilke and Chamberlain for regular discussions of policy and organization beginning July 4, 1885. See S. Gwynn and G. M. Tuckwell, *Life of Dilke* (London, 1917), ii, 149.

[32] Chamberlain's letter, dated July 16, 1885, is transcribed in the Officers' Committee Minutes, NLF, of July 20. Arnold Morley referred to "Wyley" as Wyllie in 1886.

[33] Chamberlain's letter dated July 17, 1885 is transcribed, with Schnadhorst's report to the Committee, in the Officers' Committee Minutes, July 27, 1885.

[34] The reference to this 1885 survey appears in the General Purposes Committee Minutes, NLF, July 16, 1890, when a similar survey was contemplated.

[35] Gwynn and Tuckwell, *Dilke*, ii, pp. 193–194.

Notes

36 If the usually accepted figures are used. Cf. R. C. K. Ensor, *England, 1870–1914* (Oxford, 1936), p. 94.

37 Garvin, *Chamberlain*, II, p. 189.

38 According to *The Times* obituary, January 5, 1900, Schnadhorst refused the Liberal nomination for both South and East Birmingham. His speech was reported in *The Birmingham Post*, October 19, 1885.

39 Middleton was serving on the Executive Committee of the National Union of Conservative and Constitutional Associations in April, and on its Council by May 1885, according to the annual report of the NUCCA, 1885.

40 Garvin, *Chamberlain*, II, pp. 214–215.

41 General Committee Minutes, NLF, June 2, 1886.

42 *Ibid.*, June 2 and September 10, 1886.

43 Garvin, *Chamberlain*, II, pp. 318, 354.

44 *Ibid.*, pp. 251–252.

45 John Morley, *Life of Gladstone* (London, 1903), III, pp. 341–342.

46 *The Times*, May 17, 1886.

47 *Ibid.*, July 19, 1886.

48 Morley to Gladstone, July 1 and July 25, 1886, W. E. Gladstone papers, British Museum, London, Add. MSS, 44253.

49 Using the figures given in Ensor, *England*, p. 99.

50 The figures given by R. S. Watson, *The National Liberal Federation* (London, 1907), p. 143; John Morley claimed slightly different ones (*Gladstone*, III, 346).

51 About 131 seats in Great Britain might have been reckoned marginal on the basis of the poll in 1886: 70 were won by Conservatives, 13 by Liberal Unionists, and only 48 by Gladstonians.

52 Watson, *National Liberal Federation*, p. 57.

53 Morley to Gladstone, July 12, 1886, Add. MSS, 44253.

54 Annand, "Reorganization of Liberalism," p. 499; M. Ostrogorski, *Democracy and the Organization of Political Parties* (London, 1902), I, pp. 300–301.

[55] The LCA remained at No. 41 until 1911, when it moved to 21 Abingdon Street.

[56] Morley to Gladstone, November 2, 1886, Add. MSS, 44253. The Labour Electoral Committee had its Metropolitan Radical Federation, with branches in the working-class constituencies, which was represented at the annual NLF conferences. See H. M. Pelling, *The Origins of the Labour Party, 1880–1900* (London, 1954), pp. 61, 62, 77.

[57] William Allard was secretary of the Home Counties division until he left to become secretary of the Liberal League in 1901.

[58] Marjoribanks to Gladstone, December 11, 1886, Add. MSS, 44342.

[59] Hudson, who was knighted in 1906, succeeded Schnadhorst in both the LCA and NLF on Schnadhorst's retirement. Woodings, who had sided with Chamberlain in 1886 (*The Times*, July 3, 1886), later became secretary of the Midland Liberal Federation until 1897.

[60] Morley to Gladstone, September 2, 1887, Add. MSS, 44253.

[61] *The Liberal Unionist*, February 1, 1888.

[62] Garvin, *Chamberlain*, II, p. 354. Chamberlain's new organization was first called the National Radical Union, then the National Liberal Union (see J. Powell Williams, *The Liberal Unionist*, October 1, 1889) and was independent of Hartington's Liberal Unionist Association in London.

[63] General Committee Minutes, NLF, November 25, 1886, April 11, 1888.

[64] J. A. Spender, *Sir Robert Hudson: A Memoir* (London, 1930), p. 45.

[65] Quoted by F. Bealey and H. Pelling, *Labour and Politics, 1900–1906* (London, 1958), p. 42; see B. J. Hendrick, *Life of Andrew Carnegie* (New York, 1932), I, 320. Asa Briggs has pointed out that in Birmingham the rich Liberals divided about equally in 1886, only half becoming Liberal Unionists (*History of Birmingham*, II, p. 185).

[66] In 1902 promoters of the National Liberal Election Fund deplored dependence "upon the goodwill and pleasure of a few rich men" (draft circular appended to Executive Committee Minutes,

NLF, October 1, 1902). But Dr. Massie, chairman of the Finance Committee, retorted that the promoters would find themselves similarly dependent (Finance Committee report, Executive Committee Minutes, December 3, 1902).

[67] Schnadhorst, "County Organization," pp. 8–9.

[68] One of the NLF special funds had collected £4,065 in 1881, £2,000 of it from two individuals (General Committee Minutes, NLF, November 8, 1881).

[69] Gladstone to A. Morley, June 29, 1887, Add. MSS, 44253.

[70] They became Lord Ashton of Ashton and Lord Wandsworth, having been, respectively, M.P. for Lancashire North, 1886–1895, and M.P. for the Stowmarket division of Suffolk, 1891–1895. Rosebery insisted on a letter from Gladstone confirming the bargain of 1891, and Arnold Morley wrote to Gladstone (March 2, 1895, Add. MSS. 44254) reminding him of Schnadhorst's suggestions which Morley had adopted. Lord Tweedmouth had already written more explicitly "with regard to the cases of Stern and Williamson, who during our period of opposition prior to 1892 received assurances that their desires to enter the House of Lords would . . . be gratified" (February 28, 1895, Add. MSS, 44342). Tweedmouth urged that a "quid pro quo" be given to the donors.

[71] The Northcote (Iddesleigh) Diary, consulted at the Public Record Office, London, has been transferred to the British Museum, where its manuscript number is not known. The page references to the typescript are: p. 349 (February 18, 1882), and p. 396 (December 15, 1883). Cf. H. J. Hanham, "The Sale of Honours in Late Victorian England," *Victorian Studies* III (1960), 281–285 and n. 15.

[72] *Manchester Guardian*, March 27, 1896; and see Sir Wilfrid Lawson's letter in *The Times*, March 31, 1896.

[73] *The Spectator*, August 17 and 24, 1901; the actual correspondence appeared in the issue of October 12, 1901, showing Rhodes's letter of February 23, 1891, his subsequent letter of April 25, 1892, and Schnadhorst's reply of June 4, 1892.

[74] Arnold Morley to Campbell-Bannerman, October 15, 1901, and Herbert Gladstone to Campbell-Bannerman (2 letters), October 22,

1901, Campbell-Bannerman papers, British Museum, Additional MSS, 41216.

[75] Campbell-Bannerman asked H. Gladstone, "Are we to explain (as we should be compelled to do in the end) the difference between the Whip's 'party fund' and the N.L.F.'s Exchequer—and thus do our family washing in public?" (October 19, 1901, Add. MSS, 41216).

[76] H. Gladstone to Campbell-Bannerman, October 22, 1901 (first letter), *ibid.* Gladstone pointed out that the NLF had never financed contests.

[77] A. Morley to Campbell-Bannerman, October 15, 1901, *ibid.* Morley stressed that the LCA accounts were secret from Schnadhorst.

[78] H. Gladstone to Campbell-Bannerman, July 24, 1903, *ibid.*

[79] General Purposes Committee Minutes, NLF, February 12, 1890.

[80] July 16, 1890, February 4, 1891, *ibid.*

[81] The General Purposes Committee approved the candidature July 18, 1889; cf. Herrick, "Origins of the National Liberal Federation," p. 124, n. 3. In September 1890 Arnold Morley told Gladstone that Schnadhorst was abandoning his candidacy. Sir William Harcourt and John Morley evidently disapproved of Schnadhorst's standing (A. Morley to Gladstone, September 29, 1890, Add. MSS, 44254).

[82] Schnadhorst to Broadhurst, September 13, 1892, and (respecting Hazell) August 31, 1894, Henry Broadhurst papers, vol. IV: I am indebted to the Librarian for access to materials at the British Library of Political and Economic Science.

[83] Two workingmen had been elected in 1874; three in 1880; 11 in 1885; and 9 in 1886. All of them had accepted the Liberal whip in the house of commons.

[84] Briggs, *History of Birmingham*, II, 192–193, points out some workers' organizations in Birmingham refused to be merged in the Liberal Association, and Birmingham was exceptional for its highly organized political life.

[85] Champion's letterhead survives in Champion to Broadhurst, June 20, 1888, Broadhurst papers, III. Pelling, *Origins of the Labour Party*, pp. 62–63, describes Champion's efforts.

[86] General Committee Minutes, NLF, March 18, 1891. Tim's letter was dated November 17, 1890; Schnadhorst's reply, for publication, March 6, 1891.

[87] *Origins of the Labour Party*, p. 68.

[88] Morley to Gladstone, December 21, 1891, Add. MSS, 44254. Although Carnegie contributed anonymously to John Burns's election expenses (Hendrick, *Carnegie*, I, p. 259), he seems to have rejected this proposal (Morley to Gladstone, April 20, 1892, Add. MSS, 44254).

[89] *Elections and Party Management* (London, 1959), p. 379.

[90] Besides Broadhurst they were Abraham, Arch, Burt, Cremer, Fenwick, Leicester, Pickard, and John Wilson.

[91] They were Aspinwall, Bloor, W. J. Davis, W. Johnson, Ben Jones, Steadman, Threlfall Ward, and.Wattridge.

[92] Burns preferred to stand independently, though he had no Liberal opponent; Hardie had no Liberal opponent by accident; Wilson was the only independent to win a three-cornered contest. Not all of the 16 were supported by the LEA: e.g., Hargrove, who opposed Fenwick at Houghton-le-Spring; but none of the 16 was aided by the LCA.

[93] W. S. Robson was the Liberal and his side of the story is given by G. W. Keeton, *A liberal Attorney General* (London, 1949), pp. 70–76.

[94] See P. P. Poirier, *The Advent of the Labour Party* (London, 1958), chaps. 10 and 15.

[95] T. R. Threlfall, secretary of the LEA and defeated "Lib-Lab" candidate for the Kirkdale division of Liverpool in 1892, "The Political Future of Labour," *Nineteenth Century* XXXV (February 1894), 212.

[96] *The National Liberal Federation*, p. 126.

[97] For his comment on Webb, Schnadhorst to Gladstone, September, 10, 1888; for payment of M.P.s, Schnadhorst to Gladstone, October 27, 1888; for the independent candidates, September 21, 1891; for the danger of schism, September 25, 1891, Add. MSS, 44295.

[98] Lansbury transmitted the resolution of the Bow and Bromley Liberal and Radical Association to send no more delegates to the annual NLF conferences "to vote on cut and dried resolutions" (General Purposes Committee Minutes, NLF, January 9, 1891).

[99] *The Times*, March 4, 11, and 13, 1896.

[100] "The Reorganization of Liberalism," pp. 500–501.

[101] General Purposes Committee Minutes, NLF, December 4 and 18, 1895.

[102] *Ibid.*, Nov. 5, 1890, for the Fabians; and June 3, 1896, for the LEA.

[103] Schnadhorst to Broadhurst, August 30, 1892, Broadhurst papers, vol. IV.

[104] General Purposes Committee Minutes, NLF, November 2, and December 7, 1892.

[105] Schnadhorst suggested a reduction of his salary, from £1,050 to £800, when he resigned the secretaryship; and the NLF and LCA voted him a pension of £500 p.a. on his retirement (General Purposes Committee Minutes, NLF, September 6, 1893, and November 7, 1894).

The Transformation of Conservatism in the Late Nineteenth Century

[1] *Labour and Politics 1900–1906: A History of the Labour Representation Committee* (London, 1958), pp. 1–23; esp. Tables 1 and 2 on pp. 4–5.

[2] Without denying the great political importance of religious differences, one can question the value of denomination as an independent factor, once differential social recruitment is taken into account. The fact which Bealey and Pelling point out (p. 3), that the areas more Nonconformist than Anglican in 1851 add up to "little more than a simple list of counties principally affected by industrialisation," cannot be wholly accounted for by "initial failure of the Church of England to adapt itself to the population movements and

other problems occasioned by the emergence of an industrial society." The social role of the Established Church, where it was effective, has also to be considered, and thus the possibility that the success of Nonconformity may also have rested on attitudes of social independence quite as relevant to politics as to religion. Consider, for instance, Miss M. K. Ashby's comments, in her *Joseph Ashby of Tysoe. 1859-1919. A Study of English Village Life* (Cambridge, 1961), on her father's conversion to Primitive Methodism, that "he could not give himself within a church whose leaders in and round his village hated his older friends' crusade for the Union. His mother sympathised here: she agreed that clergymen had no business to take sides with landlords and farmers; she too hated the demand for servile manners . . . [and that after Joseph Arch's visit to Tysoe] young Joseph Ashby had his first inkling of the relation of religious sects to the simpler, the economic aspects of life: the labourers who could and dared make claims for themselves and their children were Primitive Methodists" (pp. 76–77, 79–80). For a similar conclusion see Ieuan Gwnedd Jones, "The Election of 1868 in Merthyr Tydvil: A Study in the Politics of an Industrial Borough in the Mid-Nineteenth Century," *Journal of Modern History* xxxiii (1961), 285–286.

[3] See Reinhard Bendix and S. M. Lipset, "Karl Marx's Theory of Social Classes," in *Class, Status, and Power*, ed. Bendix and Lipset (Glencoe, Ill., 1953), pp. 27–35.

[4] See "Class, Status, Party," in *From Max Weber: Essays in Sociology*, ed. H. H. Gerth and C. Wright Mills (New York, 1958), pp. 180–195.

[5] Joseph A. Schumpeter, *Imperialism and Social Classes* (New York, 1951), p. 145.

[6] There is an excellent treatment of this problem in David Lockwood, *The Blackcoated Worker. A Study in Class Consciousness* (London, 1958), to which I am much indebted.

[7] See W. S. Robinson, "Ecological Correlations and the Behavior of Individuals," *American Sociological Review* xv (1950), 351–357.

[8] There is an interesting critique of a conventional historical account of an election in Lee Benson, "Research Problems in Ameri-

can Political Historiography," in *Common Frontiers of the Social Sciences*, ed. Mirra Komarovsky (Glencoe, Ill., 1957), pp. 113–183.

[9] D. C. Moore, in "The Other Face of Reform," *Victorian Studies* v (1961), 7–34, has, however, shown that the counting of heads from the poll books can reveal interesting patterns of electoral behavior even before 1832.

[10] See Morris Ginsberg, "Social Change," *British Journal of Sociology* IX (1958), 205–229.

[11] *The End of Ideology* (New York, 1961), p. 15.

[12] For good examples of the application of these techniques with a historical bias, see Duncan MacRae, Jr., and James A. Meldrum, "Critical Elections in Illinois, 1888–1958," *American Political Science Review* LIV (1960), 669–683, and Rudolph Heberle, "The Ecology of Political Parties, A Study of Elections in Rural Communities in Schleswig-Holstein, 1918–1932," *American Sociological Review* IX (1944), 401–414. For the most thorough attempt to apply the method of multivariate analysis to a historical problem, see Lee Benson, *The Concept of Jacksonian Democracy: New York as a Test Case* (Princeton, 1961).

[13] "Oscillations in Politics," *The Annals* (July 1898), quoted in Robert T. Bower, "Opinion Research and Historical Interpretation of Elections," *Public Opinion Quarterly* XII (1948), 459.

[14] "Voting and the Equilibrium of the American Political System," in *American Voting Behavior*, ed. Eugene Burdick and A. J. Brodbeck (Glencoe, Ill., 1959), pp. 92, 96. For similar speculation on the role of occupational "stereotypes" in forming the allegiance of party members, see A. H. Birch, *Small-Town Politics. A Study of Political Life in Glossop* (Oxford, 1959), p. 94.

[15] Quoted in Norman Gash, *Politics in the Age of Peel* (London, 1953), p. 178.

[16] See H. J. Hanham, *Elections and Party Management. Politics in the Time of Disraeli and Gladstone* (London, 1959), and E. J. Feuchtwanger, "J. E. Gorst and the Central Organisation of the Conservative Party, 1870–1882," *Bulletin of the Institute of Historical Research* XXXII (1959), 192–208.

¹⁷ E. J. Feuchtwanger, in "The Conservative Party under the Impact of the Second Reform Act," *Victorian Studies* II (1959), 289–304, shows how difficult Disraeli's position was as leader after Lord Derby's death, particularly in managing the Lords.

¹⁸ Memorandum by Balfour of a conversation with Salisbury on the foreign policy of Disraeli's cabinet, 8 May 1880, Balfour Papers, British Museum Add. MS 49688/24.

¹⁹ See W. D. Jones, *Lord Derby and Victorian Conservatism* (Oxford, 1956), pp. 296–304. It may be that Derby's local knowledge prompted him, since Lancashire was the one industrial area where an organized Conservative working class was strongly in evidence. He had been much impressed with the behavior of the operatives during the cotton famine.

²⁰ R. A. Cross, *A Political History* (privately printed, 1903), p. 25. Indeed it has been suggested that the development of sanitary legislation was largely independent of party politics. See G. Kitson Clark, *The Making of Victorian England* (London, 1962): "This policy was pressed forward continuously whatever party was in power, and the claim of Disraeli and the Conservative party to special initiative in the matter does not appear to be substantial" (p. 110).

²¹ Beaconsfield to Salisbury, 2 April 1880, Salisbury Papers (Beaconsfield).

²² Gorst to Disraeli, 2 December 1874, Disraeli Papers, quoted in Hanham, *Elections and Party Management*, p. 390.

²³ Gorst to Dyke, 19 November 1874, Disraeli Papers, quoted in H. J. Hanham, "Political Patronage at the Treasury, 1870–1912," *Historical Journal* III (1958), 78–79.

²⁴ See the MS Minutes of the Annual Conferences of the National Union of Conservative Associations for 1876 through 1879.

²⁵ J. W. Maclure to Cross, 14 January 1886, Salisbury Papers (Cross).

²⁶ Gorst to Disraeli, 3 March 1877, Disraeli Papers, Box A.

²⁷ Stanhope to Salisbury, 12 May 1880, Salisbury Papers (Stanhope). This point has been very well made in D. C. Moore's unpubl.

diss., "The Politics of Deference. A Study of the Political Structure, Leadership, and Organisation of English County Constituencies in the Nineteenth Century," (Columbia, 1959)—a work to which I am greatly indebted for an understanding of the social background of county politics and the assumptions and attitudes of the traditional party management.

[28] Minutes of the National Union Conference for 1878.

[29] Edward Percy to Salisbury, 13 December 1883, Salisbury Papers (Northumberland).

[30] 16 May 1884, Report to the National Union Conference for 1884.

[31] Smith to Salisbury, 14 August 1883, Salisbury Papers (Smith).

[32] Gorst to Salisbury, 20 September 1880, Salisbury Papers (Gorst); Edward Percy, Chairman of the National Union, to Salisbury, 6 and 29 October 1880, Salisbury Papers (Northumberland).

[33] Gorst to Smith, Chairman of the Central Committee, 8 September 1880 and 20 April 1881, Hambleden Papers, Series I.A.

[34] Gorst to Smith, 10 August 1881, Hambleden Papers, Series I.A.

[35] See his report on "The Condition of the Conservative Party in the Midland Counties" presented to the National Union Conference in 1883.

[36] Bartley to Sir Stafford Northcote, 8 November 1884, Salisbury Papers (Bartley).

[37] Report of the National Union Conference for 1886.

[38] See a letter to *The Times*, 29 May 1884, from Henry Howorth of Eccles, in which he declares that the National Union is "a nondescript body, not in any way representing or professing to represent the constituencies of this area" and that Churchill's Fourth Party— "when they indulge in the fantastic eccentricities which they have practised lately, are not dancing to the music of any responsible body of opinion outside, but to their own shrill trumpets only." But he also says that "We all wish to see a properly representative body with proper consultative functions and the sooner it is created the better,

either by converting the present Union (which is a mere sham institution packed with cooptative members) into a reality, or by ignoring it altogether and starting de novo." Salisbury apparently had already been thinking along these lines, for in a Memorandum dated 12 May 1884, Balfour had sketched out a plan for a national organization, bypassing the National Union, but remarkably similar in its details to the eventual settlement (Balfour Papers, British Museum Add. MS 49838/183–202).

[39] The main features of the original Liberal proposals, drawn up by Hartington and Dilke, included: (1) Lancashire and Yorkshire urban throughout, with single-member constituencies; (2) remaining rural counties, two-member constituencies; (3) boroughs of less than 10,000 population merged in counties; (4) boroughs of 10–40,000 population to lose one member if they had two before; (5) the Metropolis to have 55 members instead of 22; (6) 12 additional members for Scotland (Dilke to Gladstone, 18 September 1884, Gladstone Papers, British Museum Add. MS 44149/232). The original Conservative proposals, made by Hicks Beach, were briefly as follows: (1) boroughs of less than 25,000 population to be disfranchised; 80,000 to be the minimum for retaining two members; (2) complete separation of urban and rural districts; all towns with populations of more than 10,000 to be grouped into constituencies of not less than 25,000 population; (3) the revision of borough boundaries by a commission; (4) single members throughout boroughs and counties, particularly the latter; (5) the representation of Ireland to be reduced failing adequate provision for the representation of the loyal minority (Hartington, "Notes of Conversation with Sir Michael Hicks Beach," 29 October 1884, Gladstone Papers, British Museum Add MS 44147/158–164). In the final settlement, the population limits were compromised at 15,000 for disfranchisement and 50,000 for keeping two seats; grouping and changes in the Irish representation were not accepted by the Government, but the widespread adoption of single-member constituencies and an independent boundary commission were.

[40] In fact Churchill considered rebellion against Salisbury and Northcote, but thought better of it (Churchill to Hicks Beach, 29 November 1884, St. Aldwyn Papers, P.C.C./20).

[41] 25 June 1882, Iddesleigh Papers, British Museum Add. MS 50020/32.

[42] As late as October, Rowland Winn, the Chief Whip, was planning to force a dissolution on the Government, and Salisbury approved of his tactics (Northcote to Salisbury, 7 October 1884, Salisbury Papers [Northcote], and Salisbury to Northcote, 9 October 1884, Iddesleigh Papers, British Museum Add. MS 50020/87).

[43] He still hoped that the problem might not be treated as a party issue but settled by the Conservatives with his assistance. He attempted to approach Salisbury on the subject in December 1885; see B. E. C. Dugdale, *Arthur James Balfour* (London, 1936), I, 93.

[44]

Year:	1885	1886	1892	1895	1900	1906
Number of seats won by Conservatives:	114	165	132	175	177	62
Uncontested seats:	3	31	17	34	59	3

[45] Because there were systematic differences in the turnout between constituencies, which probably reflect other factors than political participation, the relation between Unionist vote and turnout has been calculated in two different ways. For the overall picture multiple regressions of changes in turnout and Unionist vote have been calculated for all constituencies contested at each pair of elections, as follows:

1885/1886	−0.361
1886/1892	−0.086
1892/1895	−0.033
1895/1900	−0.083
1900/1906	−0.223

These correlations are clearly too small to support the argument, but the overall figures conceal wide individual variations, and for the particular group of seats which we are considering, the English boroughs, the correlations calculated for each constituency over the six elections (set out in Table II) show more than half over −0.5 and more than a quarter over −0.8.

[46] This conclusion must, however, be treated with some caution, as there are other factors influencing turnout, the most important of

which might be called involuntary abstention: the actual electorate being diminished by death and migration, though the official figures remained the same throughout the year. It is difficult to know how to allow for this factor. Comparisons between overall turnout at different elections are vitiated by the changing numbers of seats contested. However, if we assume constant rates of death and migration throughout the period, it is possible to compare the turnout at the election of 1910 (when maximum depletion of the actual electorate should have taken place) with the previous elections which all took place earlier in the year, using the figures for turnout and Unionist vote for those seats only that were contested at both elections (see Table III). As far as this comparison goes, it does suggest that turnout fell below the level caused by involuntary abstention and that this low turnout was favorable to the Conservatives. It is also possible that involuntary abstention through migration favored the Conservatives too. In London at least the arguments for and against reforming the registration system were conducted on party lines. The Liberals wished to make the Metropolis a single parliamentary borough, in order to avoid disfranchisement caused by moving across borough boundaries, which was held by them to be particularly unfair to the working classes. The Conservatives wished to maintain the system, in order to preserve the plural voting qualifications of their middle-class supporters. It was Liberal and Labour members who tried repeatedly to reduce the residence requirement for getting on the register; see H. L. Morris, *Parliamentary Franchise Reform in England and Wales from 1885 to 1918* (New York, 1921), pp. 14–19, 24–25, 87.

[47] If voluntary abstentions are really an important factor, one might suggest that the reason the Liberals did so badly in 1886 and 1900 was that the elections were fought specifically on issues which had nothing to do with the social cleavages underlying party support but on which public opinion generally favored the patriotic or Conservative point of view. For the acute problems of the Liberals in fighting the election of 1900, see Philip P. Poirier, *The Advent of the British Labour Party* (New York, 1958), pp. 122–123.

[48] Of the single-member constituencies contested at both the elec-

tions of 1900 and 1906, 109 changed hands from Conservatives to Liberals. The Conservatives lost 15,703 votes, or 1.8 per cent of the total vote in 1900; the Liberals gained 214,991 or 25.0 per cent of the 1900 total. In fact there were just under 200,000 Liberal voters in 1906 who either had not or could not have voted in 1900. It is possible, of course, that in 1906 all former Conservatives voted Liberal and vice versa; this argument rests on the assumption that the minimum changes of party allegiance necessary to explain the results took place.

[49] Hanham, *Elections and Party Management*, pp. 191–200, esp. Table VIII.

[50] "Some Political and Economic Interactions in Later Victorian England," *Transactions of the Royal Historical Society* XXXI (1949), 17–28.

[51] Alfred Frisby, "Has Conservatism Increased in England since the Last Reform Bill?" *Fortnightly Review* XXX (1881), 728.

[52] That this would be the case was known to the Conservatives before the settlement was made. E. Ashmead Bartlett told Balfour, 29 November 1884 (Salisbury Papers [Balfour]), that "Sheffield, Bradford, Bristol, Hull ought certainly to be divided into single member wards. If so we shall win:

	Total	Conservative
Sheffield	4	3
Bradford	3	? 2 ?
Bristol	3	2
Hull	2	1"

[53] Quoted in Charles Seymour, *Electoral Reform in England and Wales* (New Haven, 1915), p. 505.

[54] The source for rateable values is the *Census of England and Wales, 1881*, Supplementary Metropolitan Tables, Table D, pp. 33–35; *Parliamentary Papers*, House of Commons (hereafter *PP*), 1883, C. 3567, lxxix.

[55] See H. J. Dyos's unpubl. diss., "The Suburban Development of London South of the Thames, 1836–1914" (London, 1952); and Michael Robbins, *A New Survey of England: Middlesex* (London, 1953), pp. 79–80, 194.

[56] Lord George Hamilton, *Parliamentary Reminiscences and Reflections, 1868 to 1885* (London, 1917), p. 11.

[57] *Western Daily Press,* 1886, cutting in St. Aldwyn Papers, Misc. P.P. 11/2.

[58] Letters of James Kitson to Herbert Gladstone in the Viscount Gladstone Papers, British Museum Add. MS 46027/123–133. I am indebted to Dr. D. C. Moore for drawing my attention to this correspondence.

[59] Mundella to R. E. Leader, 31 March 1885, in Leader, "MSS on the Political History of Sheffield," IV (1873–1894), f. 512, and Coleridge to Leader, 19 April 1885, f. 510.

[60] Based on Charles Booth's unique set of maps on London poverty compiled from the reports of the London School Board visitors in 1889, in Booth, *Life and Labour of the People in London,* II, *London Street by Street* (London, 1892); on P. G. Hall's unpubl. diss. "The Location of Industry in London. 1851–1939" (Cambridge, 1959); and on various indices of social characteristics—i.e., number of female domestic servants per 100 families, the infant mortality rate—calculated from Census of 1901.

[61] See *Life and Labour of the People in London,* I, *East London* (London, 1889), Tables VII–XV.

[62] *East London,* p. 99. This isolation from the main current of national politics is still apparent, as Angus Buchanan has shown in an interesting article on "East End Politics" in *Socialist Commentary* (March 1961), pp. 13–15.

[63] In the first group were Birkenhead, one of the Blackburn seats, Manchester North East, Preston, and St. Helens; in the second, Barrow-in-Furness, one of the Bolton seats, Manchester South West, Salford North, and one of the Stockport seats. Of these seats Birkenhead and Salford North were won by Lib-Labs, the remainder by L.R.C. candidates; see Bealey and Pelling, Appendix A and chap. ix.

[64] Manchester North and South West were two of the eight seats which were won by the Conservatives in 1885 and lost in 1886, presumably by the change in the Irish vote under orders from Parnell and the Bishops; see C. H. D. Howard, "The Parnell Manifesto of

21 November 1885 and the Schools Question," *English Historical Review* LXII (1947), 42–51.

⁶⁵ For anti-Liberal activities see Arthur Redford, *The History of Local Government in Manchester* (London, 1940), II, 17, 114; and Norman McCord, *The Anti-Corn Law League, 1838–46* (London, 1958), p. 100. For the Conservatism of the United Textile Factory Workers Association and its electoral importance, see Bealey and Pelling, pp. 16–18.

⁶⁶ See Asa Briggs, rev. L. S. Marshall, *The Development of Public Opinion in Manchester 1780–1820*, in BJS II (1951), 173: "The most important point in the local-national history of the early nineteenth century was not that Birmingham and Sheffield were like Manchester, but that they were different. Their social structure and their politics were so different that they were able to provide alternative philosophies and panaceas both before and after the Great Reform Bill. . . . The first effect of the 'industrial revolution' was not to generalize conditions throughout England, but to differentiate local social structures."

⁶⁷ Cobden to Joseph Parkes, 9 August 1857, quoted in John Morley, *The Life of Richard Cobden* (London, 1881), II, 199. T. R. Tholfsen, "The Origins of the Birmingham Caucus," *Historical Journal* II (1959), 161–184, gives a good picture of the social ethos resulting from this industrial structure, in which the popular radicalism of Birmingham flourished.

⁶⁸ R. K. Dent, *The Making of Birmingham* (Birmingham, 1894), p. 517. In 1885, with all the seats contested, the Liberals took 59 per cent of an 80 per cent poll for the whole borough, with percentages ranging from 54 to 67 in the individual constituencies. In the six seats contested in 1892, they won only 28 per cent of a 70 per cent poll, with individual percentages ranging from 29 to 34.

⁶⁹ For this see in particular the evidence of the representatives of the Birmingham Chamber of Commerce in the *2nd Report of the Royal Commission on Trade and Industry*, Minutes of Evidence and Appendix, Pt. 1, Qq. 1591, 1595; *PP*, 1886, C. 4715, xxi; and E. J. Hobsbawm, "The Labour Aristocracy in Nineteenth Century Britain," in

Democracy and the Labour Movement, ed. John Saville (London, 1954), p. 208.

⁷⁰ Report of the Proceedings of the Town Meeting in Support of Parliamentary Reform, 13 December 1830, quoted in Asa Briggs, "Thomas Attwood and the Economic Background of the Birmingham Political Union," *Cambridge Historical Journal* IX (1948), 191.

⁷¹ E. A. Leatham at Huddersfield, quoted in W. L. Guttsman, "The General Election of 1859 in the Cities of Yorkshire," *International Review of Social History* II (1957), 245.

⁷² See T. R. Tholfsen, "The Transition to Democracy in Victorian England," *IRSH* VI (1961), 226–248.

⁷³ G. B. Hertz, *The Manchester Politician, 1750–1912* (London, 1912), p. 53.

⁷⁴ Letter in the *Sheffield Daily Telegraph,* July 1868.

⁷⁵ Roebuck's gradual conversion to Conservatism did not seem as eccentric in Sheffield as it did at Westminster. Many of the prominent figures on his election committee in 1868, including William Fisher, Mark Firth, John Brown, and Thomas Gainsford, became Conservatives in the seventies and were among those who took the initiative in welcoming a Conservative candidate to replace Roebuck, and formed the backbone of the Conservative group on the town council. See *Sheffield Daily Telegraph, Sheffield and Rotherham Independent, Sheffield and Rotherham Red Book,* "MSS for the Political History of Sheffield," IV, f. 481, and J. M. Furness, *Record of Municipal Affairs in Sheffield* (Sheffield, 1893), pp. 37–74.

Liberalism and the Victorian Intelligentsia

¹ I have to thank Professor W. L. Burn, who read the article at an early stage and greatly improved it by his criticisms. Dr. G. Kitson Clark has also helped me with advice and suggestions.

² A. S(idgwick) and E. M. S(idgwick), *Henry Sidgwick,* [*A Memoir*] (London, 1906), pp. 430, 449, 450.

³ J. F. Stephen to Lord Lytton, 2 April 1880. All Stephen's corre-

spondence is in the Cambridge University Library. Most of his letters exist only in the form of copies made by his wife. I have also used her copies of Lytton's letters to Stephen.

4 *Autobiography* (London, 1873), p. 289.

5 *Representative Government*, chaps. v, vi.

6 A. Patchett Martin, *Life and Letters of Viscount Sherbrooke*, ii (London, 1893), pp. 263–264.

7 M. E. Grant Duff, *Sir Henry Maine*, [*a brief Memoir . . . with some of his Indian Speeches and Minutes . . .*] (London, 1892), p. 75.

8 Stephen to Lady Grant Duff, 30 April 1886, 18 May 1883.

9 L. Stephen, *Life of [Sir] J[ames] F[itzjames] Stephen* (2nd ed. (London, 1893), pp. 263–264.

10 M. M. Bevington, *The Saturday Review 1855–1868, Representative Educated Opinion in Victorian England* (New York, 1941), p. 13.

11 Minute Book of the Cambridge Union Society, 16 May 1848; see also the description of another debate in L. Stephen, *Sketches from Cambridge by a Don* (London and Cambridge, 1865), pp. 67–68; and *Life of J. F. Stephen*, pp. 98–99.

12 Bevington, *Saturday Review*, pp. 1–2.

13 Stephen, *Life of J. F. Stephen*, p. 213, n. 2; J. W. Robertson Scott, *The Story of the Pall Mall Gazette* (London, 1950), p. 148.

14 *Recollections*, i (London, 1917), pp. 168–169.

15 "Mr. Mill on Political Liberty," *Saturday Review*, vii, 187, 12 February 1859; for the attribution, see Stephen, *Life of J. F. Stephen*, p. 314.

16 Stephen to his wife, 23 July 1873.

17 Stephen to Emily Cunningham, 30 January 1874.

18 Stephen to Lytton, 6 September 1876.

19 R. H. Hutton to Stephen, 27 November 1868.

20 It has not been possible to trace any list of contributions to the

Pall Mall Gazette. The only guide to what J. F. Stephen wrote in it is the list of the total number of his articles, each year from 1865 to 1878, which is given in Stephen, *Life of J. F. Stephen*, pp. 213–214, note. I have taken a single year (1867), and worked through the leading articles, attempting to decide, from internal evidence, which of them were written by Stephen.

[21] "Lord Palmerston," 19 October 1865. The style and ideas suggest that Stephen was the author, and there seems to be an echo of them in "The Premier's Lesson to his Enemies," 3 March 1868, which J. W. Robertson Scott (*Pall Mall Gazette*, p. 160, n. 1) attributes to Stephen.

[22] "Cumulative Voting," 15 March 1867; "Mr. Carlyle on the Falls of Niagara," 10 August 1867; "The Liberalism of the Future," 11 October 1867.

[23] "Discussions on Democracy," 10 January 1867; "Cumulative Voting Considered," 6 March 1867; "The Triumph of Pure Reason," 15 August 1867.

[24] "The Possibilities of the Session," 22 January 1867.

[25] "The Abyssinian Debate," 27 November 1867; "Mr. Gladstone at Oldham," 19 November 1867.

[26] "Liberalism," *Cornhill Magazine*, v, 81, January 1862; for the attribution see Stephen, *Life of J. F. Stephen*, p. 484.

[27] "Pain," *Essays by a Barrister* (London, 1862), esp. pp. 147–148.

[28] "Sovereignty," *Horae Sabbaticae* ii, (London, 1892), 69.

[29] For Stephen's interest in Burke and de Maistre, see his essays on those writers in *Horae Sabbaticae;* for Carlyle see Note 66.

[30] Reprinted in *Contemporary Review*, December 1873, January 1874.

[31] See my article, "James Fitzjames Stephen (1829–94)," *Journal of the Royal Asiatic Society*, Parts 1 and 2 (1956).

[32] Stephen to Lytton, 15 March 1878, 10 May 1876.

[33] Stephen to Lady Grand Duff, 13 July 1882.

[34] Stephen to Lytton, 2 May 1876.

[35] Grant Duff, *Sir Henry Maine*, pp. 74–75.

[36] Stephen to Mill, 3 August 1871.

[37] *On Liberty*, in *Utilitarianism, Liberty, Representative Government* (Everyman ed., London, 1944), pp. 72–73.

[38] L[*iberty*], E[*quality*], F[*raternity*] (2d ed., London 1874), x, 24, and n. Page references are to the second edition. I have dealt with this book so fully because it has not been reprinted since 1874 and is not easy to come by. [It is now available, ed. R. J. White (Cambridge, 1967)—ED.]

[39] *Ibid.* p. 96.

[40] *Ibid.* pp. 182–184.

[41] *Ibid.* p. 21.

[42] *Ibid.* pp. 46–47.

[43] Stephen to Lytton, 18 September 1877. Goldwin Smith (1823–1910) had been Regius Professor of Modern History at Oxford 1858–1866. The article was "The Policy of Aggrandizement," *Fortnightly Review*, September 1877.

[44] *Utilitarianism*, p. 14.

[45] "Caesarism and Ultramontanism," *Contemporary Review*, XXIII (May 1874), esp. 1011–1012.

[46] *Ibid.* p. 1017.

[47] L[*iberty*], E[*quality*], F[*raternity*], pp. 53–54, 200.

[48] *Ibid.*, p. 197.

[49] *Ibid.*, pp. 215, 217.

[50] *Ibid.*, pp. 243–245.

[51] *Ibid.*, p. 280.

[52] *Ibid.*, p. 283.

[53] *Ibid.*, pp. 291–292.

[54] *Ibid.*, p. 304.

[55] *Ibid.*, pp. xxxiv–xxxv.

[56] *Ibid.*, pp. 309–310.

[57] *Ibid.*, pp. 320–321.

[58] *Ibid.*, pp. 77–78.

[59] *Ibid.*, p. 326.

[60] *Ibid.*, pp. 62–63.

[61] Stephen, *Life of J. F. Stephen*, chaps. i, ii.

[62] From the second article on *Liberty, Saturday Reivew,* vii, 214, 19 February 1859.

[63] "Mr. Carlyle," *Fraser's Magazine,* December 1865; for the attribution see Stephen, *Life of J. F. Stephen,* p. 202.

[64] J. MacCunn, *Six Radical Thinkers* (London, 1910), pp. 175–176.

[65] *Fraser's Magazine,* lxxii, 789.

[66] L. Stephen, "Carlyle's Ethics," *Hours in a Library* (London, 1892), iii, pp. 286–294; R. H. Murray, *Studies in the English Social and Political Thinkers of the Nineteenth Century* (Cambridge, 1929), i, p. 339.

[67] Stephen to his wife, 4, 6 August 1873.

[68] Stephen to Lytton, 23 October 1879.

[69] Stephen to Lytton, 2 August 1878.

[70] Lytton to Stephen, 17 July 1877.

[71] Lytton to Stephen, 26 May 1878.

[72] Lytton to Stephen, 2 January 1891.

[73] Stephen to Lytton, 28 September 1876.

[74] Stephen to Lytton, 1 October 1879.

[75] Stephen to Lytton, 25 December 1879.

[76] Stephen to Lytton, 20 July 1876.

[77] Stephen to Lytton, 6 September 1876.

[78] Stephen to Lytton, 15 March 1878.

[79] Stephen to Lytton, 30 August 1877.

[80] Stephen to Lytton, 23 February 1885.

[81] Lytton to Stephen, 18/25 December 1879.

[82] Stephen to Lytton, (3) February 1880.

[83] Stephen to Lytton, 14 April 1880.

[84] Stephen to Lady Grant Duff, 4 June 1886.

[85] Stephen to Lytton, 29 June 1877.

[86] Stephen to Lytton, 8 July 1879.

[87] See Stephen's letters in *The Times*, 4, 5, 21 January, 29 April, 1 May 1886.

[88] Stephen to Emily Cunningham (Lady Egerton), 10/11 April 1887.

[89] Stephen to Lytton, 26 October, 24, 30 November 1876, 6 January 1877.

[90] See Stephen's letters to *The Times*, 16, 22, 28 October, 12, 15, 20 November 1878. This question involved him in controversy with Lord Lawrence (*ibid.* 22 October, 19 November 1878), with Lord Northbrook (*ibid.* 12 November 1878), and with Vernon Harcourt (18 November 1878).

[91] 1, 2 March 1883. Two letters of November 2 and 9 were reprinted as *Letters on the Ilbert Bill* (London, 1883); for letters on Ireland, see n. 87 above.

[92] Stephen to Lady Grant Duff, 15 December 1881.

[93] Stephen to Lady Grant Duff, 9 June 1886.

[94] Stephen to Lytton, 5 October 1889.

[95] A. S. and E. M. S., *Henry Sidgwick*, p. 524.

[96] Stephen to Lytton, 6 May 1880.

[97] *Popular Government* (6th ed., London, 1909), p. 126.

[98] *Ibid.*, p. 111.

[99] *Ibid.*, pp. 236–239.

[100] *Ibid.*, pp. 106–108.

[101] *Ibid.*, pp. 29–34, 93–94.

[102] *Ibid.*, p. 150.

[103] *Ibid.*, p. 228.

104 *Ibid.*, pp. 44–50.

105 *Ibid.*, p. 106.

106 *Ancient Law* [with Introduction and Notes by Sir Frederick Pollock] (new ed., London, 1930), pp. 180–182.

107 *Popular Government*, p. vii; [*Dissertations on*] *Early Law and Custom* (London, 1883), pp. 192–193.

108 *Ancient Law*, pp. 97ff.

109 *Ibid.*, pp. 102–103.

110 [*Lectures on the*] *Early History of Institutions* (London, 1875), pp. 399–400.

111 *Ibid.*, lectures xii, xiii.

112 *Early Law and Custom*, p. 242.

113 *Ibid.*, pp. 215–216.

114 *Ibid.*, pp. 388–389.

115 *Popular Government*, pp. 42–43, 97–98.

116 *Early Law and Custom*, pp. 253ff.

117 *Early History of Institutions*, p. 327.

118 *Village Communities* [*in the East and West*] (3rd ed., London, 1876), pp. 161–166.

119 *Early History of Institutions*, pp. 86–87.

120 *Early Law and Custom*, p. 325.

121 *Early History of Institutions*, p. 126.

122 *Ibid.*, pp. 207–208.

123 "The Effects of Observation of India on Modern European Thought," *Village Communities*, p. 230.

124 *Ancient Law*, p. 332.

125 *Popular Government*, p. 26.

126 Arthur D. Elliot, *Life of Lord Goschen* (London, 1911), I, pp. 251–252.

127 (8th) Duke of Argyll, *Autobiography and Memoirs* (London, 1906), II, p. 377.

[128] *Ibid.*, II, p. 380.

[129] Elliot, *Lord Goschen*, I, pp. 306–307; Bernard Holland, *Life of the Eighth Duke of Devonshire* (London, 1911), II, p. 72; Lord Morley, *Recollections*, I, pp. 201–202.

[130] Elliot, *Lord Goschen*, I, pp. 162–164.

[131] *Ibid.*, I, p. 254.

[132] *Ibid.*, I, pp. 282–284.

[133] *Ibid.*, II, pp. 67–68; Holland, II, 155; A. G. Gardiner, *Life of Sir William Harcourt* (London, 1923), I, p. 581.

[134] Holland, *Duke of Devonshire*, II, p. 154.

[135] Earl of Selborne, *Memorials*, Part II, *Personal and Political, 1865–95* (London, 1898), II, p. 227.

[136] Duke of Argyll, *Autobiography*, II, p. 417.

[137] M. E. Grant Duff, *Out of the Past* (London, 1903), I, pp. 217–218.

[138] G. M. Trevelyan, *Sir George Otto Trevelyan, A Memoir* (London, 1932), p. 124.

[139] R. S. Rait, ed., *Memorials of A. V. Dicey* (London, 1925), pp. 95ff.; *D.N.B. 1912–21*, "Anson, Sir William Reynell."

[140] See p. 323.

[141] *Cambridge Review*, 8 June 1887; *Cambridge Chronicle*, 17 June 1887 (from which the extracts from Seeley's speech are taken).

[142] J. R. M. Butler, *Henry Montagu Butler, A Memoir* (London, 1925), p. 98.

[143] R. C. K. Ensor, *England 1870–1914* (Oxford, 1936), p. 163.

Brief Bibliographical Note

THIS NOTE WILL be brief for several reasons. In some cases, titles of relevant studies have been indicated in connection with the particular articles reprinted, and the footnotes in the articles themselves provide guidance for earlier literature. Second, the reader has available a recent and short bibliography of the period in Josef L. Altholz, *Victorian England 1837–1901* (Cambridge, 1970). It is a good working bibliography, which can be supplemented by those published in the *American Historical Review* and, most important, the annual bibliography in the July issue of *Victorian Studies*. Those two periodicals, as well as, among others, *Economic History Review, English Historical Review, Historical Journal, History, International Review of Social History, Journal of British Studies, Journal of Interdisciplinary History, Journal of Modern History,* and *Past and Present,* are invaluable for articles and, in most cases, book reviews. Lionel Madden, *How To Find Out about the Victorian Period* (Oxford, 1970), is useful.

The standard accounts of nineteenth-century Britain, despite their considerable age, are still of great value, most notably Elie Halévy's classic work in several volumes, *A History of the English People in the 19th Century,* left unfinished at his death in 1937: *England in 1815* (New York, 1949), *The Liberal Awakening 1815–1830* (New York, 1949), *The Triumph of Reform 1830–1841* (New York, 1950), *Imperialism and the Rise of Labour 1895–1905* (New York, 1951), and *The Rule of Democracy 1905–1914,* 2 volumes (New York, 1952). After his death his rough manuscript and notes were published as *The Victorian Years 1841–1895* (New York, 1951).

Two other standard older works are those in the Oxford History of England: E. L. Woodward, *The Age of Reform 1814–1870* (Oxford, 1938), and R. C. K. Ensor, *England 1870–1914* (Oxford, 1936). More recent general accounts of great value are Derek Beales, *From Castlereagh to Gladstone* (New York, 1969); Asa Briggs, *The Age of Improvement 1783–1867* (New York, 1959); W. L. Burn, *The Age of Equipoise* (New York, 1964); G. Kitson Clark, *The Making of Victorian England* (London, 1962); H. J. Hanham, *The Nineteenth Century Constitution* (Cambridge, 1969), a collection of documents and commentary; the relevant parts with excellent bibliographical footnotes of R. K. Webb, *Modern England* (New York, 1968); and G. M. Young, *Portrait of an Age* (New York, 1953), perhaps the greatest essay ever written on the period and, in a shorter form, part of G. M. Young, ed., *Early Victorian England 1830–1865*, 2 volumes (Oxford, 1934). Also the collection Young edited with W. D. Hancock should be mentioned: *English Historical Documents, 1832–1874* (London, 1956).

Clearly, even within the strict definition of the Victorian Age and within the focus of the relationship of government and society in that period, a vast number of books and articles could be listed and the interested reader would be wise to purchase Altholz's bibliography. I will limit myself here to giving the titles of a very few more recent books which may be of particular interest to the readers of this collection: Olive Anderson, *Liberal State at War: English Politics and Economics During the Crimean War* (London, 1967); Philip Appleman, William A. Madden, and Michael Wolff, *1859: Entering an Age of Crisis* (Bloomington, Ind., 1959); Geoffrey Best, *Mid-Victorian Britain 1851–75* (London, 1971); Robert Blake, *Disraeli* (London, 1966); Asa Briggs, *Victorian Cities* (London, 1963); Asa Briggs, *Victorian People* (Chicago, 1955); Lucy M. Brown, *The Board of Trade and the Free Trade Movement* (Oxford, 1958); J. B. Conacher, *The Aberdeen Coalition 1852–1855* (Cambridge, 1968); Maurice Cowling, *1867: Disraeli, Gladstone and Revolution* (Cambridge, 1967); S. E. Finer, *Sir Edwin Chadwick* (London, 1952); J. L. Hammond and M. R. D. Foot, *Gladstone and Liberalism* (London, 1952); Brian Harrison, *Drink and the Victorians* (Pittsburgh, 1971); J. F. C. Harrison, *The Early Victorians 1832–1851*

(New York, 1971); Gertrude Himmelfarb, *Victorian Essays* (New York, 1968); E. J. Hobsbawm, *Industry and Empire* (London, 1968); E. J. Hobsbawm, *Labouring Men* (New York, 1967); Walter Houghton, *The Victorian Frame of Mind 1830–1870* (New Haven, 1957); Royston J. Lambert, *Sir John Simon and English Social Administration* (London, 1963); Norman McCord, *The Anti-Corn Law League* (London, 1958); Philip Magnus, *Gladstone* (London, 1954); David Newsome, *Godliness and Good Learning* (London, 1961); David Owen, *English Philanthropy 1660–1940* (Cambridge, Mass., 1964); Harold Perkin, *The Origins of Modern English Society 1780–1880* (London, 1969); Roger Prouty, *The Transformation of the Board of Trade* (London, 1959); Melvin Richter, *The Politics of Conscience: T. H. Green and His Age* (London, 1964); R. T. Shannon, *Gladstone and the Bulgarian Agitation 1876* (London, 1963); F. B. Smith, *The Making of the Second Reform Bill* (London, 1966); Paul Smith, *Disraelian Conservatism and Social Reform* (Toronto, 1967); F. M. L. Thompson, *English Landed Society in the Nineteenth Century* (Toronto, 1963); and Paul Thompson, *Socialists, Liberals and Labour: The Struggle for London, 1885–1914* (Toronto, 1967).

About The Author

Peter Stansky was born in New York City. He was educated at Yale College, King's College, Cambridge and received his Ph.D. from Harvard University. He is the author of *Ambitions and Strategies: The Struggle for the Leadership of the Liberal Party* (as well as articles and reviews), and he has edited *The Left and War: The British Labour Party and World War I* and *Nineteenth-Century Essays* by John Morley. With William Abrahams, he has written *Journey to the Frontier: Two Roads to the Spanish Civil War* and *The Unknown Orwell.* He is associate professor of history at Stanford University.